The International Monetary Fund in the Global Economy

The explosive growth and increasing complexity of global financial markets are defining characteristics of the contemporary world economy. Unfortunately, financial globalization has been accompanied by a marked increase in the frequency and severity of financial crises. The International Monetary Fund (IMF) has taken a central role in managing these crises through its loans to developing countries. Despite extensive analysis and criticism of the IMF in recent years, key questions remain unanswered. Why does the Fund treat some countries more generously than others? To what extent is IMF lending driven by political factors rather than economic concerns? In whose interests does the IMF act? In this book, Mark Copelovitch offers novel answers to these questions. Combining statistical analysis with detailed case studies, he demonstrates how the politics and policies of the IMF have evolved over the last three decades in response to fundamental changes in the composition of international capital flows.

MARK S. COPELOVITCH is Assistant Professor in the Department of Political Science and the Robert M. La Follette School of Public Affairs at the University of Wisconsin–Madison.

The International Monetary Fund in the Global Economy

Banks, Bonds, and Bailouts

MARK S. COPELOVITCH
University of Wisconsin–Madison

CAMBRIDGE UNIVERSITY PRESS
Cambridge, New York, Melbourne, Madrid, Cape Town, Singapore,
São Paulo, Delhi, Dubai, Tokyo

Cambridge University Press
The Edinburgh Building, Cambridge CB2 8RU, UK

Published in the United States of America by Cambridge University Press, New York

www.cambridge.org
Information on this title: www.cambridge.org/9780521143585

First published 2010

Printed in the United Kingdom at the University Press, Cambridge

A catalogue record for this publication is available from the British Library

Library of Congress Cataloguing in Publication data
Copelovitch, Mark S., 1975–
The International Monetary Fund in the global economy : banks, bonds, and bailouts / Mark S. Copelovitch.
p. cm.
Includes bibliographical references.
ISBN 978-0-521-19433-4 – ISBN 978-0-521-14358-5 (pbk.)
1. International Monetary Fund. 2. International economic relations. 3. Globalization. 4. Policy sciences. I. Title.
HG3881.5.I58C66 2010
332.1′52–dc22 2010000057

ISBN 978-0-521-19433-4 Hardback
ISBN 978-0-521-14358-5 Paperback

To Beth

Contents

Figures

Tables

Preface

This book was written in the relative calm between two global financial storms. I began the research for this project in 2001, in the wake of the Asian financial crisis and shortly before Argentina's default on its $155 billion in external debt. As I finish writing, in the autumn of 2009, the world economy is beginning a slow recovery from the most severe financial crisis since the Great Depression. As the financial turmoil has deepened and spread across the globe over the last two years, the IMF, once again, has assumed a central role in efforts to restore and maintain international financial stability. As of November 2009 the Fund has provided more than $85 billion in credit to eighteen countries hit hardest by the crisis, including Belarus, Iceland, Hungary, Latvia, Pakistan, Romania, and Ukraine. In addition, the IMF has also committed an additional $80 billion to three countries (Colombia, Mexico, and Poland) under the terms of its new crisis prevention lending arrangement, the Flexible Credit Line.

This resurgence in IMF lending represents a sharp reversal from the start of the decade, when few emerging market countries borrowed from the Fund and many observers questioned the continued relevance of – and need for – the IMF in an apparently stable global economy awash in private international capital flows. In contrast, the focus today has shifted toward the urgent need to strengthen the Fund, in order to ensure that it has sufficient resources to meet its members' needs during the current crisis. In February 2009 the Japanese government committed an additional $100 billion to bolster the Fund's $250 billion in lendable resources. Soon afterwards Dominique Strauss-Kahn, the IMF's managing director, announced plans to seek a doubling of the Fund's coffers to $500 billion – a plan subsequently endorsed by the new US Treasury secretary, Timothy Geithner. In March the European Union (EU) responded with its own commitment to provide $100 billion in resources to the Fund. At the Group of Twenty summit in London in April, these pledges were reinforced by a formal commitment on the part of G-20 governments to triple the Fund's resources to $750 billion, through a mix of $500 billion in loans and a one-time issuance of $250 billion in special drawing rights (SDRs), the IMF's notional currency.[1] In addition to these commitments to increase the IMF's lending capacity, the issues of reforming both the governance of the Fund and the tasks it performs have once again been placed on the international agenda. Indeed, IMF reform is once again a central topic of discussion among economic policymakers in both the developed and developing worlds.[2]

Thus, to paraphrase Mark Twain, reports of the IMF's death have been greatly exaggerated. Rather than becoming obsolete, the Fund remains a central force in the global economy, and understanding how it operates is critical if we are to make informed decisions about whether (and how) to reform the institutions and rules of global financial governance. In emphasizing the highly political nature of IMF lending, as well as the ways in which financial globalization has altered the Fund's policies over time, this book may therefore benefit policymakers as they seek to identify and implement effective and feasible policy responses to the current global financial crisis. At the same time, the arguments and findings in this book contribute to ongoing scholarly research in political science and economics. Analytically, the book clarifies our understanding of the complex connections between international economics and international politics. In addition, by explaining the policies and behavior of one of the most prominent multilateral institutions, it sheds light on the determinants of international cooperation more generally. In short, both economic policymakers and scholars of international political economy will, I hope, find much of interest in the pages that follow.

This book is the culmination of nearly eight years of research that began during my graduate study in the Department of Government at Harvard University. In truth, however, its roots go back even further. Indeed, I owe a great debt to my professors in the Directed Studies program and the Political Science and Economics Departments at

[1] Mark Landler and David E. Sanger, "G-20 pact has new rules and $1.1 trillion in loan pledges" (www.nytimes.com/2009/04/03/world/europe/03summit.html?_r=1&hp).

[2] See, for example, Edwin M. Truman, "IMF reform: an unfinished agenda" (www.petersoninstitute.org/publications/opeds/oped.cfm?ResearchID=1106).

Yale University, who first piqued my interest in the study of political economy and international relations as an undergraduate and who – though I did not realize it at the time – set me on the path toward an academic career. I owe particular thanks to Xavier Sala-i-Martin, who introduced me to the challenges and puzzles of macroeconomics, and to David Cameron and Yitzhak Brudny, whose courses and advice opened my eyes to the possibility of graduate study in political science.

As a graduate student in the Department of Government at Harvard University, I was privileged to have an exceptional group of faculty advisors and teachers. Jeff Frieden, my dissertation committee chair, offered tough criticism, strong encouragement, and sage advice at each stage of my studies, and he always managed to strike the right balance between the three. I owe my greatest intellectual and pedagogical debts to Jeff: he taught me most of what I know about international monetary and financial relations, emphasized the importance of clarity and rigor in my thinking, writing, and analysis, and instilled in me an appreciation of the fundamental and inextricable link between politics and economics. It is extremely rare in academia for a single individual to be a pre-eminent scholar, an engaging and talented teacher, and a true mentor. Jeff is all these things, and I am deeply indebted to him for the support and advice he has given me over the years. I have also come to overlook his one true fault – a misguided yet unwavering devotion to the New York Yankees – in light of these many redeeming qualities.

I am also extremely grateful to my other advisors at Harvard. Andy Moravcsik took me under his wing upon my arrival in Cambridge and offered me crucial guidance, helped me to secure much-needed funding, and gave me the opportunity to gain valuable research and teaching experience. He also provided incisive criticism throughout my dissertation research and always challenged me to think about the "big picture" in my work. Lisa Martin was always available to read and discuss my work, and her comments and suggestions invariably pushed me to clarify my thinking and focus my argument and analysis. Having benefited from Lisa's advice as her student, I am now extremely fortunate to call her a colleague at the University of Wisconsin. Unfortunately for Lisa, this allows me to lapse periodically into my former role and show up at her door seeking advice. Thus, I also owe Lisa particular thanks for reading and commenting on the final version of this book manuscript. Finally, Michael Hiscox helped me to think through the connections between international trade and finance, and he offered critical advice as I was navigating the academic job market. I have been extremely fortunate to train with and learn from such talented individuals, and I owe them my thanks and appreciation.

I also have many friends and colleagues to thank for their help in completing this project. In particular, I owe special thanks to David Singer for his feedback and support. Over the years David has preceded me at each stage of graduate school, the academic job market, and the publishing process by a year or so; consequently, he has borne the unfortunate burden of my frequent pleas for advice along the way. Because he is a true mensch and friend, David has never complained about this harassment, and I'm enormously grateful for his help. I also owe many thanks to Jon Pevehouse, Nadav Shelef, and Hillel Soifer, each of whom read the entire manuscript and provided extremely detailed comments and suggestions. This book is undoubtedly better as a result. Any remaining errors and weaknesses remain my fault alone and are likely due to the fact that I – either foolishly or inadvertently – ignored their wise recommendations.

At Harvard, I was fortunate to find an unusually close and talented group of friends. My classmates and colleagues, including Fiona Barker, Tammy Frisby, Casey Klofstad, Shannon O'Neil, Sonal Pandya, Nathan Paxton, Will Phelan, David Singer, Hillel Soifer, and Annie Stilz, were – and continue to be – a welcome source of advice, intellectual engagement, and camaraderie. I also thank the many participants in the Research Workshop on Political Economy and the Weatherhead Center for International Affairs graduate workshop for their helpful comments and suggestions at early stages of this project. Finally, my friends outside academia, whether by politely listening to me discuss my research, or simply by forcing me to forget about it periodically, also deserve my deepest thanks.

This book was completed at the University of Wisconsin–Madison, where I have been on faculty since 2006. It is difficult to imagine a better environment in which to launch one's academic career. My colleagues in the Department of Political Science and the La Follette School of Public Affairs have been congenial and supportive, and I am deeply privileged to work with them. I owe particular thanks to my fellow assistant professors in political science – Helen Kinsella,

Jimmy Klausen, Nils Ringe, and Nadav Shelef – for their comments and suggestions during our writing group meetings over the last year. In addition, I offer my thanks to Scott Gehlbach, Melanie Manion, and Scott Straus for their guidance at various stages of the writing and publishing process. Last, but certainly not least, I gratefully acknowledge the excellent research assistance provided by Andria Hayes-Bircher and Tom Hinds.

Many institutions have provided me with financial and research support for this project, and I am in their debt as well. At Wisconsin, I have received generous support from the Center for International Business Education and Research (CIBER), the Center for World Affairs and the Global Economy (WAGE), the Department of Political Science, the Graduate School, the International Institute, the Robert M. La Follette School of Public Affairs, and the Wisconsin Alumni Research Foundation (WARF). The Center for Globalization and Governance at Princeton University provided a wonderful environment in which to begin the book phase of this project, and I thank Helen Milner for the opportunity to spend the 2005/6 academic year in residence as a postdoctoral fellow. At Harvard, the Center for European Studies and the Weatherhead Center for International Affairs both provided me with office space, travel and research support, and intellectually rich environments in which to work. The Government Department, the Krupp Foundation, the Mellon Foundation, the Graduate Society, the Graduate Student Council, and the Graduate School of Arts and Sciences at Harvard all provided generous financial support that enabled me to complete the research and writing of my dissertation. My wife and I also had the privilege of living and working with the Harvard undergraduates and our fellow resident tutors at John Winthrop House for two years, from 2003 to 2005. One could not ask for a warmer and more interesting community of scholars and friends, let alone such wonderful babysitters!

The research and analysis in this book draw heavily on internal documents from the IMF archives in Washington, DC. I am especially grateful to Premela Isaac, Jean Marcoyeux, and the rest of the staff at the archives for arranging my initial visit, assisting me patiently as I conducted my research, and responding to my repeated e-mail requests for further information. Premela, in particular, deserves thanks for saving me several additional trips to Washington over the last three years as new documents of interest became available.

I also owe thanks to administrators and officials at the Bank for International Settlements, the European Central Bank, the Bank of England, and the UK Financial Services Authority, for facilitating visits during the course of my research that deeply enhanced my knowledge and understanding of economic policymaking and global financial governance.

It was a pleasure to work with John Haslam at Cambridge University Press. I thank John for his enthusiasm about the project and his efficiency in managing the review process. I also thank Carrie Cheek and Jo Breeze for their help in shepherding this book through the publication and editing process. Many thanks also go to the anonymous reviewers of the manuscript, whose comments were enormously helpful in improving the argument and quality of the book.

My greatest thanks and final acknowledgments go to my family. My elder sister, Natalie, was my first teacher and role model, and she has always been my biggest supporter, even from afar. My parents, Bernard and Temah Copelovitch, instilled in me a love for books and learning and encouraged me to take full advantage of the educational opportunities presented to me (though perhaps they did not expect me to take the lesson to heart for quite so long!). More importantly, they taught me the importance of family, determination, and hard work, and I am forever in their debt for the innumerable sacrifices they have made on my behalf. For years my father has sent me *New York Times* articles on international finance and the world economy, sometimes to solicit my opinion on the topic, but more frequently to ask whether I might find a job in the various New-York- or Washington-based institutions mentioned in the articles. I've always thought this was due to his worries that his son wasn't keeping busy (or getting paid) tucked away in the confines of academia. Hopefully, once he reads this, he'll agree that this wasn't the case. Either way, I hope the articles and questions keep coming.

I also owe thanks to my in-laws, Ken and Sue Cohn, for welcoming me into their family and home – and, most of all, for graciously not asking the question of how I was going to support their daughter (or grandchild) during my years in graduate school. I enjoyed my frequent conversations and visits with my "grandfather-in-law," Robert Rodman, who was fascinated by my research and eagerly awaited this book's arrival. Unfortunately, he passed away last year, but I am certain that he would have fervently read this book in the hopes of finding both the solution to the global financial crisis and advice on his investment portfolio.

Finally, I could not have completed this project without Beth, my wife and partner. This book is dedicated to her, since – like most everything in my life – it simply would not have happened without her by my side. Any words to describe how important she is to me, or how critical her support and love have been as I have worked to complete this project, will invariably fall short. I owe her, as well as our children, Micah and Dafna, my love and thanks for being there – and for waiting.

Mark S. Copelovitch
Madison, Wisconsin
December 2009

1 *The International Monetary Fund in the global economy*

Introduction

This is a book about the impact of globalization on international politics. To be more specific, it is a book about the connection between changes in the composition of international capital flows and changes in the politics and policymaking of the International Monetary Fund (IMF, or Fund), the central institution of global financial governance. Financial globalization – the explosive growth in the size, depth, and complexity of international markets – is the defining characteristic of the contemporary world economy. Indeed, international financial integration today has reached (and in many ways surpassed) levels not seen since the "first globalization," in the era prior to World War I (WWI).[1] Over the last three decades private international capital flows to developing countries have grown exponentially, from nearly zero in 1970 to $491 billion in 2005.[2] Daily foreign exchange trading has increased from $850 billion in 1986 to $3.2 trillion in 2007.[3] In the first quarter of 2007 commercial banks reported $25 trillion in total foreign claims, up from $17 trillion in 2005.[4] At the same time, international investors held over $20 trillion in sovereign and private bonds, with net issuance increasing at a rate of 18 percent per year.[5]

Unfortunately, as starkly illustrated by both the current global crisis and the major upheavals of the 1980s and 1990s, this resurgence of financial globalization has been accompanied by a corresponding increase in the frequency and severity of financial crises.[6]

[1] Frieden (2005); James (2001); Frankel (2000).

[2] World Bank (2006).

[3] BIS [Bank for International Settlements] (2007a).

[4] BIS (2007b).

[5] Ibid. By comparison, worldwide annual trade (exports) totaled $12.4 trillion in 2006 (http://stat.wto.org).

[6] Bordo *et al.* define financial crises as "episodes of financial-market volatility marked by significant problems of illiquidity and insolvency among

The macroeconomic impact of these crises has been dramatic and severe: cross-country estimates suggest that the output losses resulting from recent crises have, on average, equaled over 10 percent of GDP, while the fiscal costs of resolving banking crises in developing countries exceeded $1 trillion in the 1980s and 1990s.[7] The damage caused by financial crises also has real and costly implications for individuals. Crises nearly always result in severe inflation and rising unemployment, both of which undermine living standards and contribute to rising levels of poverty in crisis-stricken countries. Furthermore, government bailouts of failed banks can result in dramatic reductions in social spending, and bank failures can eliminate the savings of millions of citizens. For example, many of these adverse effects were starkly apparent during the height of Argentina's financial crisis in 2001–2002, when unemployment rates approached 25 percent, poverty rates surpassed 50 percent, and the collapse of several major financial institutions wiped out the savings of many middle-class Argentines.[8] Closer to home, the fallout from the subprime mortgage crisis has had substantial real effects on the US economy: unemployment and home foreclosures are on the rise, economic growth has ground to a halt, and millions of individuals have seen their retirement savings washed away as financial markets have collapsed.

More broadly, financial distress in one country can have severe consequences for broader regional and global financial stability. This risk of cross-border financial "contagion" has increased dramatically in recent years, as a result of the surge in global financial integration and capital mobility. Indeed, sharp reversals in the direction and magnitude of international bank lending and bond financing now frequently transmit financial instability from one market to the next with nearly unprecedented speed. For example, the collapse of cross-border

financial-market participants and/or by official intervention to contain such consequences" (2001: 55). Financial crises encompass both banking crises, in which financial distress erodes the capital reserves of the banking system and results in the failure of major banks in a country, and currency crises, in which governments face speculative attacks on their exchange rates. In most major financial crises, both elements (banking distress, currency crashes) are evident.

7 Barth, Caprio, and Levine, (2005); Caprio and Klingebiel (2003); Hoggarth, Reidhill, and Sinclair (2003).

8 Mishkin (2006).

interbank lending in 2007/8, as a result of the subprime mortgage crisis in the United States, led directly to the failure of Northern Rock (the eighth largest bank in the United Kingdom) and the dramatic collapse of Iceland's economy. Similarly, Thailand's financial and currency crisis in mid-1997 rapidly escalated into a global problem, as international investors pulled their money out of South Korea, Indonesia, and other east Asian markets and instability spread to a number of eastern European and Latin American countries.

In short, cross-border financial crises have become a defining feature of the international financial system over the last three decades. In this environment, the IMF has occupied center stage in efforts to manage these crises and restore global financial stability.[9] Above all, the Fund's key role has been that of de facto international lender of last resort (LOLR): it has served as a source of emergency financing to countries facing financial and currency crises or an inability to repay their international debt.[10] Since the onset of the Latin American debt crisis in 1982, the IMF has provided over $400 billion in such loans to developing countries. Most recently, the Fund has lent more than $85 billion in credit to eighteen countries (including Belarus, Hungary, Iceland, Latvia, Pakistan, Romania, and Ukraine) hit hardest by the global credit crunch.[11] In exchange for this assistance, the Fund has gained substantial control over economic policymaking in its borrower countries through its use of conditionality – the policy reforms it requires in return for credit.

The IMF's role as lead crisis lender in the global economy has transformed it into one of the world's most powerful multilateral institutions. At the same time, however, the Fund's central role in global financial governance has subjected it to a firestorm of criticism in developing countries and the industrialized world alike. The IMF's critics have assailed it for a variety of shortcomings, including failing to maintain global financial stability, misdiagnosing the causes of (and solutions to) financial crises, exacerbating poverty in the developing world, and catering

[9] On the sources and mechanisms of contagion, see Claessens and Forbes (2001) and Eichengreen, Rose, and Wyplosz (1996).

[10] Strictly speaking, the IMF is not a true lender of last resort, as it cannot issue its own currency and its loans do not meet Walter Bagehot's (2006 [1873]) classic criteria. Nonetheless, the IMF is the closest substitute to a LOLR in the current world economy (Kenen 2001).

[11] See www.imf.org/external/np/fin/tad/extarr1.aspx.

to the demands of Wall Street bankers and rich-country governments.[12] These critiques intensified in the aftermath of the major financial crises of the mid to late 1990s, as numerous academics and policymakers advocated the radical curtailment of the IMF and its lending policies.[13] Indeed, even those deeply involved in shaping global policy responses to these crises, such as former US Treasury secretary Robert Rubin, called for substantial reform of the "international financial architecture," in order to avoid the need for future large-scale IMF loans and to enhance global financial stability in the coming decades.[14] In short, virtually no one in today's global economy is happy with the IMF, and almost everyone has a proposal for how it should be reformed.[15]

The policy debate about the IMF's role in governing the global financial system is important, but it has developed in the absence of a full and clear understanding of how the Fund operates and makes policy decisions. In fact, analytical studies of the IMF and its policies are surprisingly limited given the amount of ink devoted to more normative critiques of the Fund.[16] This gap in the political economy literature is problematic, in view of the substantial variation in the IMF's lending policies over the last two decades. During this period many of the IMF's loans have far exceeded the standard amount of financing these borrowers were eligible to receive under the Fund's quota-based credit system; others, however, were substantially smaller in size.[17] Similarly, the Fund's use of conditionality has varied greatly over the last twenty years, with some loans containing only a handful of conditions, while others require the borrower country to implement a wide variety of economic policy reforms in exchange for IMF credit.[18]

[12] See, for example, Stiglitz (2002). [13] Calomiris (1998); Meltzer (2000).

[14] Rubin (1998).

[15] Eichengreen (1999), Kenen (2001), and Truman (2006) provide comprehensive surveys of these proposals.

[16] See Stone and Steinwand (2008) and Joyce (2004) for surveys of the existing empirical literature on IMF lending.

[17] The IMF operates similarly to a credit union: each member state provides a portion of the Fund's lendable "quota" resources and is eligible to borrow in proportion to these contributions. Country quotas are determined largely by country size: a country's gross domestic product (GDP) and its quota are almost perfectly correlated (0.92). See www.imf.org/external/np/exr/facts/quotas.htm.

[18] Appendix 1 illustrates the substantial variation in IMF lending from 1984 to 2003. I discuss this variation in both loan size and conditionality in further detail below.

Until very recently, explaining this variation in IMF lending was a topic of interest only to academic economists, central bankers, and economic policymakers. By and large, the economics and policy literatures treat the Fund as an apolitical institution whose policies are set by its staff of macroeconomic experts, based on a combination of country-specific and global macroeconomic factors.[19] Variation in IMF lending, in this view, is simply the result of cross-national differences in borrower countries' financial needs and economic characteristics, as well as changes over time in global financial conditions such as world interest rates and levels of financial stability. This "technocratic" view of IMF lending contrasts starkly with popular perceptions of the Fund, however. The conventional wisdom among the media, politicians, and the general public is that the IMF is an overtly *political* institution. Nevertheless, there is considerable disagreement about the nature of politics within the IMF. Some observers accuse the Fund of being a "pawn" or "lapdog" of the government of the United States.[20] In this view, the IMF provides "bailouts" (i.e. large loans on lenient terms) to countries deemed important by the US Treasury or national security officials, whether or not such policies are warranted by economic conditions. In contrast, others attack the Fund for being a "runaway" bureaucracy, neither accountable to its member states nor responsive to the needs of its borrowers.[21] Former US Senator Lauch Faircloth (Republican – North Carolina) articulated this view most colorfully during the Asian financial crisis, when he attacked the Fund as "a set of 'silk-suited dilettantes' given to a diet of 'champagne and caviar at the expense of the American taxpayer.'"[22] From this perspective, the IMF is yet another example of the threat posed by globalization to national sovereignty and governments' economic policy autonomy.

While recent studies in international political economy provide some empirical support for each of these political views of the IMF, scholars continue to disagree about the key economic and political determinants of Fund lending behavior. Indeed, despite the recent

[19] Knight and Santaella (1997); Bird and Rowlands (2003); Joyce (2004).

[20] David E. Sanger, "A Fund of trouble: as economies fail, the IMF is rife with recriminations." *New York Times*, October 2, 1998.

[21] Ibid.

[22] David Rogers, "IMF funds approved by Senate." *Wall Street Journal*, March 27, 1998.

surge in scholarly work on the IMF, many critical questions about the Fund and its policies remain unanswered.[23] What explains the substantial variation in the size and terms of IMF loans? To what extent is IMF lending driven by political factors rather than economic concerns? Why does the Fund treat some countries more generously than others, and why does this vary over time, even for individual borrowers? In whose interests does the IMF act? More broadly, what do the politics and policies of the IMF tell us about the dynamics of policymaking within international organizations in general? This book offers answers to these empirical and conceptual puzzles.

The argument in brief

My central argument in this book is that the IMF's lending policies have varied systematically over the last two decades in response to changes in patterns of financial globalization. Variation in the composition of private international capital flows, I argue, has shaped the preferences of both the Fund's largest shareholder countries and its professional staff economists over IMF lending decisions. In turn, changes in these actors' preferences explain variation in the size and terms of Fund loans over time and between cases. Thus, IMF lending is not a technocratic process; rather, the Fund is a highly political institution whose policies depend on the interests of not only its largest shareholders but also its bureaucrats, both of whom exercise partial but incomplete control over IMF policymaking. In order to explain the politics of IMF lending, it is therefore necessary to understand how the composition of international capital flows has changed over time, as well as how these changes affect the preferences of the key actors involved in Fund decision-making.

In contemporary global finance, countries borrow in different ways from a number of different lenders. Some governments rely on bank lending from a handful of large commercial banks located in the advanced industrialized countries, while others issue sovereign bonds to investors around the world. In some countries governments are the

[23] Recent studies include those by Dreher and Jensen (2007), Broz and Hawes (2006), Gould (2006), Vreeland (2005), Copelovitch (2005), Oatley and Yackee (2004), Stone (2008, 2004, 2002), Dreher and Vaubel (2004a), and Thacker (1999).

primary international borrowers, while in others private firms have joined in the search for foreign capital. Finally, some countries borrow funds primarily from one or two of the world's largest economies – such as the United States or the United Kingdom – while others have a more heterogeneous portfolio of country creditors. This variation in the composition of international capital flows shapes the politics of IMF lending in two ways. First, it determines the preferences of the Fund's largest shareholder countries, the "G-5" governments (the United States, Japan, Germany, the United Kingdom, and France), over the size and terms of IMF loans. These countries exercise de facto control over the IMF executive board and act collectively as the Fund's political principal. At the same time, they are also home to the largest private creditors in global markets, including the world's largest commercial banks. As a result, the financial exposure of G-5 commercial banks heavily influences G-5 governments' preferences over IMF lending policies. Consequently, IMF loan size and conditionality vary widely based on the *intensity* and *heterogeneity* of G-5 governments' domestic financial ties to a particular borrower country. When private lenders throughout the G-5 countries are highly exposed to a Fund borrower, G-5 governments collectively have intense preferences and are more likely to approve larger IMF loans with relatively limited conditionality. In contrast, when G-5 private creditors' exposure to a country is smaller or more unevenly distributed, G-5 governments' interests are weaker and less cohesive, and the Fund approves smaller loans with more extensive conditionality.

Second, variation in the composition of private international debt also shapes the IMF staff's own preferences over the characteristics of Fund loans. While G-5 governments exercise ultimate control over the IMF's lending decisions, the Fund's professional staff enjoys substantial autonomy over its day-to-day operations. The IMF staff acts as the member states' agent in negotiating lending arrangements with borrowers, and it enjoys agenda-setting power over the executive board: the board cannot approve a loan without first receiving a staff proposal. Moreover, while the executive board formally has the authority to amend staff proposals, it rarely does so in practice.[24] These delegated responsibilities give the staff significant influence over IMF lending. As with G-5 governments, IMF staff

[24] Martin (2006); Gould (2006); Southard (1979).

preferences over Fund loan characteristics vary systematically based on patterns of financial globalization. Unlike G-5 governments, however, the IMF staff is focused more broadly on the Fund's key policy objectives: assisting borrower countries in resolving their balance of payments problems and facilitating their return to private international capital markets.[25] IMF programs, therefore, are not intended to be a long-term substitute for private capital flows; rather, a Fund loan is intended to signal to private international creditors that "a country's economic policies are on the right track, it reassures investors and the official community and helps generate additional financing. Thus, IMF financing can act as a *catalyst* for attracting funds from other sources."[26]

Triggering this "catalytic effect" on private capital inflows has been a key policy goal of the IMF since the Latin American debt crisis of the 1980s. Two changes in the composition of international capital flows have made achieving this goal more difficult for the Fund, however. On the one hand, the composition of *international creditors* has changed, as bondholders have increasingly replaced commercial banks in global financial markets. On the other hand, the composition of *international borrowers* has also evolved, as private firms have joined sovereign governments in search of foreign capital. Together, these changes in international debt composition have significantly complicated the IMF staff's central policy goal of "catalyzing" private capital flows. The shift from bank lending to bond financing, as well as the shift from sovereign borrowing to "private–private" flows, has increased collective action problems among private international creditors and made it less likely that they will respond to an IMF loan with new lending of their own. At the same time, the shift from sovereign borrowing to "private–private" debt has also reduced the efficacy of IMF conditionality. In sovereign borrowing cases, the logic of conditionality remains intact: the Fund can provide a loan covering part of a government's payments deficit, while requiring it to undertake policy reforms aimed at closing the rest of the financing gap. In cases in which non-sovereign debt predominates, however, standard

[25] My claim is not that G-5 governments are uninterested in these goals. Rather, I argue that such concerns are often subordinated to their domestic financial interests, whereas they are the primary concern of Fund bureaucrats.

[26] See www.imf.org/external/pubs/fr/exsp/what.htm.

IMF macroeconomic conditionality is less effective: even if the government undertakes policy reforms, these reforms will not necessarily solve the country's balance of payments problems, which are driven primarily by private borrowers' behavior.

In response to these changes in the composition of international capital flows, I argue, the IMF staff has altered the characteristics of the lending programs it designs and proposes to the executive board for approval. All else equal, the Fund staff has proposed larger loans with more extensive conditionality to countries whose external debt consists of larger shares of bond financing and non-sovereign borrowing. In these cases, more IMF financing and more extensive policy adjustment are necessary, since stronger signals are required in order to generate "catalytic financing" from a disaggregated, heterogeneous group of private international lenders. In contrast, when international capital flows consist primarily of sovereign bank lending, IMF loans typically are more modest in size and contain somewhat fewer policy conditions.

In sum, the IMF's lending policies have varied substantially over the last two decades in response to variation in the composition of international capital flows. Changes in the patterns of financial globalization shape the preferences of both key actors involved in IMF decision-making: G-5 governments and the Fund's professional staff. In turn, IMF lending behavior varies over time and between cases in accordance with shifts in the composition of private international lending to the Fund's borrower countries.

The IMF and international relations

Given the IMF's central role in governing global financial markets, understanding and explaining what it does is a critical issue not only for economists and those interested in international finance but also for international relations scholars studying both international political economy and international cooperation. Indeed, by focusing on the politics of IMF lending, this book engages one of the core puzzles in international political economy: what is the relationship between markets and politics? Ultimately, it offers two answers to this critical question. First, it argues that global markets shape international politics by influencing the domestic preferences of the largest countries in the world economy – countries that are both the major creditors in the international financial system and the dominant political actors within the IMF. Second, the book argues that the structure of global financial markets also shapes the preferences of supranational bureaucrats within the international financial institutions. In particular, changes in the composition of international capital flows shape the IMF staff's own expectations about market actors' responses to the Fund's lending policies. Thus, this study provides important insights into the complex and dynamic patterns of interaction between states, international organizations, and markets in the contemporary global economy.

More broadly, understanding the IMF and its policies has important implications for theories of international cooperation and international institutions. In particular, it enhances our understanding of the internal politics and policymaking processes within international organizations. By focusing directly on the dynamics of policymaking within one of the largest and most important multilateral institutions, this book sheds light on an important yet under-researched question: what exactly do international organizations do, and what factors most affect their behavior? Surprisingly, international relations scholars have paid relatively little attention to this question about the policies, or "outputs," of international institutions. Rather, most work in the field has sought to develop and test theories of various "outcomes" of international cooperation. For many years scholars of international institutions sought primarily to explain states' initial decisions to engage in cooperation and create international institutions.[27] More recently, the literature has shifted toward explaining other types of "outcomes," including choices about the design of international institutions,[28] as well as the sources of and variation in compliance with the rules they produce.[29] This extensive literature on outcomes has significantly enhanced our understanding of both the "beginning" (cooperation/institutional design) and "end"

[27] Keohane (1984); Snidal (1985); Martin (1992); Martin and Simmons (1998).

[28] Raustiala (2006); Koremenos (2005); Koremenos, Lipson, and Snidal (2001); Abbott and Snidal (2000).

[29] Von Stein (2005); Simmons and Hopkins (2005); Simmons (2000); Downs, Rocke, and Barsoom (1996); Chayes and Chayes (1993). The literature on international cooperation and institutions is too extensive to summarize here fully and adequately. See Martin and Simmons (1998) and Simmons and Martin (2002) for comprehensive overviews.

(compliance/institutional effects) stages of international cooperation. By comparison, however, we still know relatively little about the intermediate stage of the process – that is, about the politics of decision-making within specific international organizations and the sources of the policies these organizations produce. By casting light on the political economy of decision-making within the IMF, this book seeks to enhance our understanding of how global governance and international-level policymaking actually occur within existing multilateral institutions.

Finally, explaining the lending behavior of the IMF addresses a key question for both rationalist and constructivist scholars of international institutions: what is the relative influence of states and bureaucrats within international organizations? Rationalists have addressed this issue largely from a state-centric standpoint by focusing on principal–agent problems and the logic of delegation.[30] In contrast, constructivists have focused more extensively on the independent influence of supranational bureaucrats, arguing that they are "authorities in their own right, and that authority gives them autonomy vis-à-vis states, individuals, and other international actors."[31] This book's findings strongly suggest that these approaches are complementary, and that we cannot explain international organizations' behavior without considering the interests and influence of both sets of actors. Moreover, the book provides concrete, testable hypotheses about the sources of these actors' preferences, as well as an explanation as to how and why these preferences change over time in response to developments in the global economy.

IMF lending: an overview

In contrast to domestic markets, the international financial system lacks clear "rules of the game" for dealing with financial instability.[32] There is neither a clearly defined international lender of last resort nor an institutionalized sovereign bankruptcy procedure to ensure that financial crises are managed and resolved in an orderly fashion.[33]

[30] See, for example, Hawkins *et al.* (2006).

[31] Barnett and Finnemore (2004, 5). [32] IMF (2000).

[33] At the domestic level, the central bank is traditionally the provider of LOLR financing to financial institutions in distress and/or directly to the market itself, through the purchase of domestic assets. On the issues of whether an

In the absence of these institutions for maintaining financial stability, responsibility for managing financial crises in global markets has fallen largely to the IMF. To achieve this goal, the Fund's primary policy tool is the *conditional loan* to countries experiencing balance of payments problems. These loans are designed to enable a borrower country to continue servicing its external debt while simultaneously undertaking policy adjustments designed to ensure longer-term debt sustainability and to generate economic growth. IMF programs are intended to be a short-term substitute for private capital flows: Fund borrowers are expected to repay their IMF loans in due course and eventually resume borrowing on global financial markets. Although all the Fund's member states are eligible for IMF financing, the primary borrowers since the 1970s have been middle-income developing countries ("emerging markets") such as Argentina, Mexico, and Turkey.

The IMF's main lending instruments, often called "facilities" or programs, are the stand-by arrangement (SBA) and arrangements under the Extended Fund Facility (EFF). SBAs are designed to assist countries facing short-term (one- to two-year) balance of payments problems, while extended arrangements are designed to assist countries facing slightly longer-term difficulties (usually three years) requiring more extensive structural economic reforms. In response to the Asian financial crisis, the IMF established an additional short-term lending instrument, the Supplemental Reserve Facility (SRF).[34] SRF loans, which supplemented stand-by or extended arrangements, were designed for countries facing "severe balance of payments difficulties arising from a sudden loss of market confidence accompanied by capital flight and a sharp drain in international reserves"; the loans were made for one year and carried an additional penalty rate over and above the market rate for stand-by and extended

international LOLR is feasible and desirable, see Fischer (1999) and Giannini (1999). On recent proposals to develop a sovereign bankruptcy procedure, see Krueger (2001) and Rogoff and Zettelmeyer (2002).

[34] In 1999 the Fund also established the Contingent Credit Line (CCL) facility, to assist countries that had strong fundamentals but that might be vulnerable to contagion. Between 1999 and 2003, however, no member borrowed from the Fund under this new lending facility, as a result of concerns that such borrowing would trigger (rather than stem) private capital outflows by signaling a country's potential debt problems. The IMF abolished the CCL facility in late 2003.

arrangements.[35] In October 2008 the IMF established another new lending instrument, the Short-term Liquidity Facility (SLF), which further enhanced its ability to provide immediate financial assistance to countries facing severe liquidity crises as a result of the global credit crunch.[36] Subsequently, the Fund replaced the SLF (as well as the SRF) in March 2009 with an additional new facility, the Flexible Credit Line (FCL), which is designed to provide pre-emptive financial assistance for the purposes of crisis prevention.[37]

In addition to providing short- to medium-term balance of payments financing, the IMF began providing long-term (five- to ten-year) loans to very low-income countries in the mid-1980s under two additional lending instruments: the Structural Adjustment Facility (SAF) and the Enhanced Structural Adjustment Facility (ESAF). In 1999 the Poverty Reduction and Growth Facility (PRGF) replaced both the SAF and ESAF. These long-term lending instruments serve a very different purpose and a very different group of countries from the Fund's non-concessional loans: whereas middle-income countries approach the Fund for short-term, temporary balance of payments assistance when they face difficulty servicing their private external debts, low-income borrowers depend almost entirely on the Fund and other official international creditors for long-term access to external financing.[38] Moreover, the sources of financing for the two varieties of IMF lending are completely separate. PRGF loans are fully financed from a separate dedicated trust fund, rather than from the IMF's main quota resources; the PRGF trust borrows directly

[35] www.imf.org/external/np/exr/facts/howlend.htm, and appendix 2 for further details. The Fund eliminated the SRF in 2009, once it had established the new Flexible Credit Line.

[36] See www.imf.org/external/pubs/ft/survey/so/2008/POL102908A.htm.

[37] See www.imf.org/external/np/pdr/fac/2009/032409.htm. Mexico and Poland became the first countries to take advantage of the FCL, in April 2009.

[38] In 2001 the seventy-seven PRGF-eligible countries owed, on average, 91.3 percent of their outstanding external debt to official creditors, as compared to 44.5 percent for the average non-PRGF country (World Bank 2003). Similarly, the average non-PRGF country owed outstanding private external debt of $18.1 billion in 2001, while the average PRGF-eligible country owed only $465.4 million; twelve of the PRGF-eligible states did not borrow at all on private international markets, and an additional twenty-five owed less than $50 million to private international creditors (World Bank 2003). Examples of PRGF-eligible countries include Burkina Faso, Bangladesh, and Liberia.

from national governments and multilateral institutions and lends on a "pass-through" basis to eligible countries.[39] Finally, PRGF loans are extended at a below-market ("concessional") interest rate of 0.5 percent and are based on a "poverty reduction strategy" jointly prepared by the country and the IMF staff, in consultation with the World Bank. These arrangements closely resemble the long-term development financing provided by the World Bank and other multilateral development banks (MDBs), and they are available only to very poor countries falling below the World Bank's GDP per capita ceiling for concessional financing.[40] Although roughly one-third of all Fund lending arrangements over the last decade have been concessional loans, these loans represent only a very small portion (approximately 7 percent) of the total amount of current IMF lending.[41] Since the purposes and sources of concessional IMF financing are different from those of non-concessional Fund lending, the factors influencing IMF decision-making over PRGF loans are likely to be substantially different from those affecting Fund decisions about the provision of short-term balance of payments financing. In analyzing the IMF's role in governing global finance, I therefore set concessional lending aside and focus exclusively on the Fund's role as a non-concessional lender to those middle-income developing countries that normally borrow on private international markets.

The empirical puzzle: variation in IMF lending

The substantial variation in the IMF's non-concessional loans over the last two decades constitutes a key empirical puzzle in the contemporary world economy. IMF lending programs consist of two elements: a certain amount of financing and a set of economic policy adjustments, or "conditionality," that the borrower country must implement in order to receive IMF credit. Along each of these dimensions, non-concessional Fund loans have varied widely over the last

[39] IMF (2004). Thus, PRGF financing is more akin to bilateral foreign aid than multilateral crisis lending.

[40] Currently, the ceiling is $1,025 per capita in 2005 dollars; as of August 2007 seventy-eight countries were eligible for PRGF financing (www.imf.org/external/np/exr/facts/prgf.htm).

[41] 108 of 316 loans from 1989 to 2001 were PRGF arrangements (or their predecessors).

two decades. Indeed, despite the claims of some critics that the IMF imposes an identical set of conditionality in all cases, the Fund's lending policies exhibit substantial variation over time and across cases. Between 1984 and 2003 the IMF provided 197 non-concessional loans to forty-seven middle-income developing countries, totaling SDR 253.8 billion.[42] While the mean loan amount was SDR 1.21 billion, these loans have ranged widely in size, from SDR 7.1 million (Belize 1984) to SDR 22.8 billion (Brazil 2002). This variation is not simply a function of a country's size, or the size of its external debt. Clearly, these factors matter to some extent: absolute loan size is strongly correlated with country size and somewhat correlated with country indebtedness.[43] When controlling for country size by measuring loans in relation to a country's IMF quota, however, one sees substantial puzzling variation. Turkey, with only the eighteenth largest quota among developing countries, has received three of the ten largest loans over the last twenty years; Uruguay, with the thirty-third largest quota, received the fifth largest loan ever (SDR 2.13 billion, equivalent to 694 percent of its quota) in 2002; and Thailand, with the twenty-second largest quota, received a loan of SDR 2.9 billion (505 percent of quota) in 1997.[44] On the other hand, many large countries of substantial economic and political importance in international relations have received relatively modest loans (e.g. Russia 1999: 56 percent of quota; Brazil 1992: 69 percent; Argentina 1996: 46 percent). Furthermore, individual countries have received very different loans at different times from the IMF. Argentina and Mexico are two prominent examples: Argentina's ten IMF loans during the 1984–2003 period ranged in size from 47 percent of its quota to 527 percent, while Mexico's five loans over the same period ranged in size from 120 percent of quota to 688 percent.

[42] The SDR, or special drawing right, is the Fund's unit of account. Its value is derived from a basket of major international currencies. Currently (as of December 17, 2009) one SDR equals $1.57085 (www.imf.org).

[43] The correlation between absolute loan size (log) and country GDP (log) is 0.86. Pairwise correlations between absolute loan size and three key measures of indebtedness (external debt/GDP, debt service/exports, short-term debt/reserves) are −0.06, 0.40, and 0.20, respectively.

[44] Rankings exclude the Organization for Economic Co-operation and Development (OECD) countries.

This variation in loan size is particularly puzzling given the Fund's explicit limits on the amount that countries may borrow. Formally, access to non-concessional IMF credit is restricted to 100 percent of quota annually and 300 percent of quota cumulatively, except in "exceptional circumstances."[45] It is clear that the Fund has defined "exceptional circumstances" quite broadly in recent years: fifty of its 197 non-concessional loans between 1984 and 2003 exceeded the 100 percent quota limit, and twenty-four loans were equivalent to at least 200 percent of a country's quota. The economic and political reasons for this behavior are less clear, however. For example, there is ample evidence that countries of similar size and macroeconomic characteristics have received widely different treatment from the IMF over the last two decades. Moreover, it does not appear that IMF lending is linked simply to the geopolitical importance of a country to the US government. In fact, loan size and conditionality have varied widely even within the subset of borrower countries in which American geopolitical or strategic interests would seem to be most likely to have an effect on IMF policies (e.g. Argentina, Russia, Mexico, South Korea, Turkey). Thus, the Fund's lending behavior does not appear to conform either to the "technocratic" view of the economists or to the overtly political views of many outside observers.

Similar patterns of variation are evident when examining the IMF's use of conditionality during the last two decades. Conditionality refers to the policies the Fund expects a member to follow in exchange for IMF credit.[46] By explicitly linking the approval or continuation of Fund financing to the implementation of specified economic policies, conditionality helps to mitigate problems of both debtor and creditor moral hazard. Rather than throwing "good money after bad" should the borrower country fail to meet its obligations, conditionality provides a mechanism by which the Fund can temporarily or permanently suspend its lending.[47] Likewise, linking the availability of IMF credit to specific policy changes provides incentives for the borrower

[45] "Report on access to Fund resources, 2003" (http://imf.org/external/np/fin/2004/access/eng/020504.pdf#access). As part of its recent lending reforms in response to the global credit crisis, the IMF has doubled these access limits (www.imf.org/external/pubs/ft/survey/so/2009/new032409a.htm).

[46] Gold (1979). [47] IMF (2005).

country to adhere to its end of the bargain by guaranteeing loan disbursement if conditions are met. Finally, conditionality also provides a signal to private markets that a borrower will pursue future policies compatible with long-term debt sustainability.[48] As we will see below, changes in patterns of financial globalization have increased the importance of this signaling aspect of conditionality.

IMF programs contain several different types of conditionality, each differing in content, specificity, and the degree to which it is "binding" on the borrower country. *Performance criteria* (PCs) are the most specific and binding type of conditions. PCs are conditions explicitly specified in IMF program documents that must be met by the borrower country in order for the agreed amount of credit to be disbursed.[49] PCs typically specify quantitative targets for key macroeconomic policy variables, such as international reserves, government budget balances, or limits on external borrowing. For example, a program might specify a minimum level of net international reserves, a maximum level of central bank net domestic assets, or a maximum level of government borrowing. Increasingly, IMF programs have also incorporated "structural" PCs, which include such measures as requirements to privatize state-owned enterprises, reform social welfare policies, remove price controls, or strengthen financial regulation. In part, the shift toward greater structural conditionality reflects the increase in medium- and long-term IMF lending; as the Fund has lent more money to low-income countries through the PRGF instrument and its predecessors, structural reforms have become increasingly common. Nonetheless, even within non-concessional IMF programs, the number and type of conditions has varied widely (figure 1.1).

In addition to PCs, IMF programs generally contain one or more additional types of conditionality. As figure 1.1 shows, these conditions account for nearly all the expansion in Fund conditionality in recent years. Non-PC conditions consist of three types: prior actions, quantitative indicative targets, and structural benchmarks. *Prior actions* (PAs) are measures that a country agrees to take before the IMF approves a loan; they are designed to "ensure that the program has the necessary foundation to succeed."[50] Furthermore, prior

[48] Bird and Willett (2004). [49] IMF (2005). [50] Ibid.

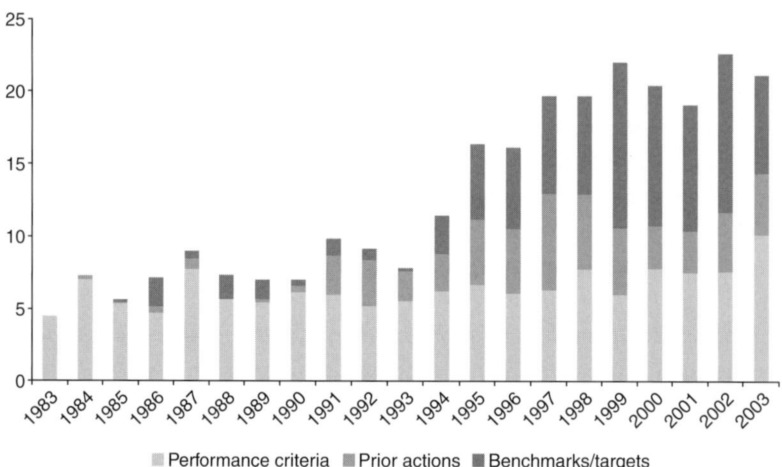

Figure 1.1 IMF conditionality: average number of conditions by type, non-concessional IMF loans, 1983–2003
Source: IMF archives.

actions are intended as a signal to the IMF and private markets that a borrower government has made a firm "upfront" or *ex ante* commitment to reforming its economic policies and resolving its financial problems. Like PCs, prior actions are "hard" conditions; that is, their implementation is compulsory if a borrower country wishes to receive IMF credit. Indeed, PAs are, to some extent, "harder" conditions than PCs, since they must be implemented *prior* to receiving the first installment ("tranche") of an IMF loan. PCs, in contrast, must be implemented only at subsequent interim reviews.

In contrast to both PCs and PAs, the remaining varieties of IMF conditionality are less stringent, or "soft" types. *Indicative targets* are similar in content to quantitative PCs, but are non-binding on the borrower country; that is, failure to meet targets does not automatically result in the suspension of loan disbursement. According to the Fund, indicative targets are utilized when there is substantial uncertainty about economic trends beyond the first months of the program, after which they are often transformed into PCs for the remainder of the Fund program.[51] Likewise, *structural benchmarks*

[51] Ibid.

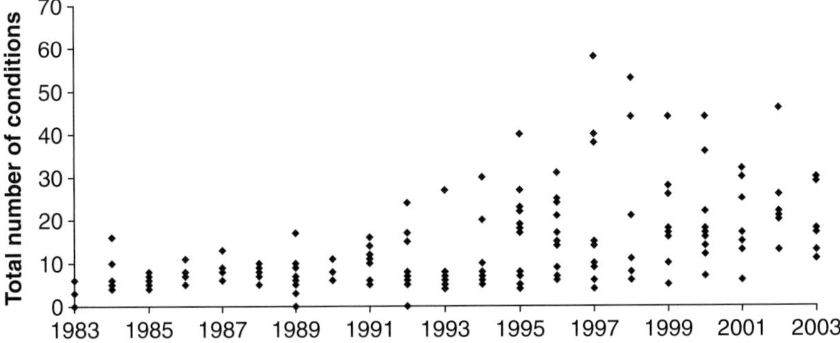

Figure 1.2 Total conditions, non-concessional IMF loans, 1983–2003
Source: IMF archives.

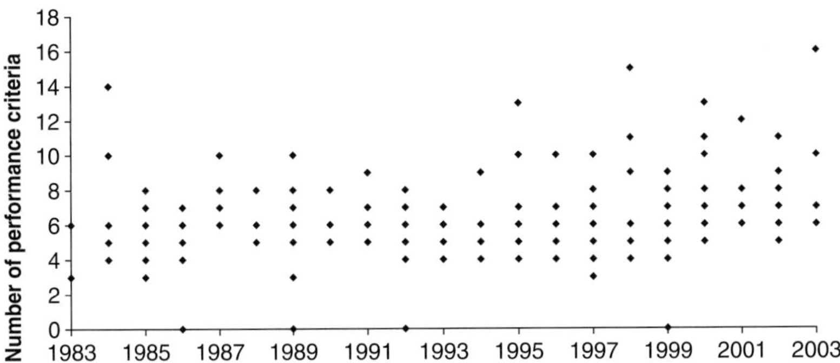

Figure 1.3 Performance criteria, non-concessional IMF loans, 1983–2003
Source: IMF archives.

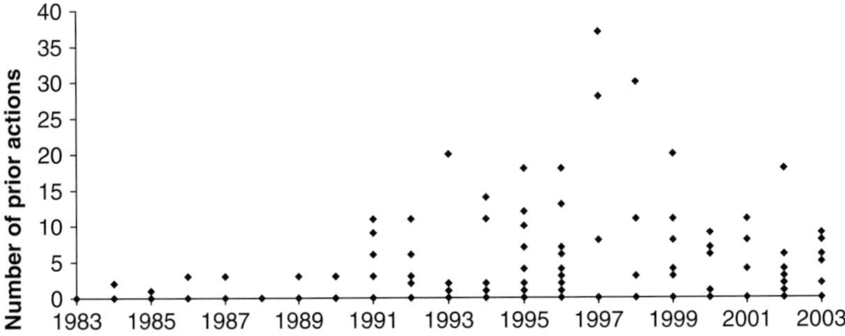

Figure 1.4 Prior actions, non-concessional IMF loans, 1983–2003
Source: IMF archives.

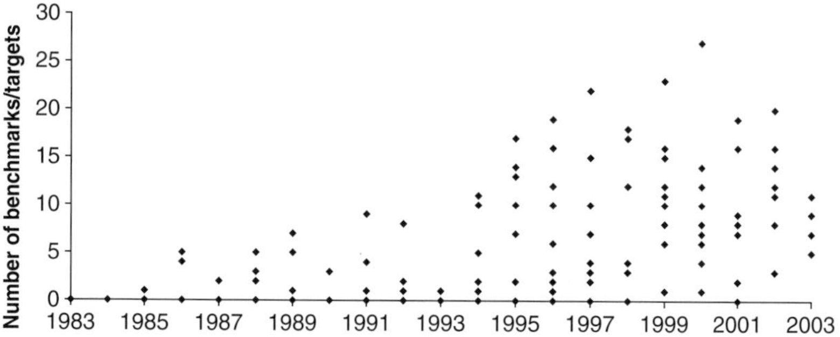

Figure 1.5 Benchmarks/targets, non-concessional IMF loans, 1983–2003
Source: IMF archives.

are similar to structural PCs in substance but not stringency. Benchmarks are often used "for measures that cannot be monitored objectively enough to be PCs, or for small steps in a critical reform process that would not individually warrant an interruption of Fund financing."[52] The IMF monitors a borrower's adherence to conditionality through periodic program reviews. Reviews typically occur at four- to twelve-month intervals, depending on program length. At each review, a borrower may request a waiver for PCs it has failed to meet; if the Fund approves the waiver, the missed PC is generally included in the new set of conditions specified for the subsequent stages of the program.

Figures 1.1 to 1.5 illustrate the substantial variation in the number and type of conditions attached to non-concessional IMF loans during the last two decades.[53] While there has been only a slight increase in recent years in the average number of PCs, there has been substantial cross-sectional variation in the IMF's use of these binding conditions, with the number ranging from zero to sixteen during the 1984–2003 period. In contrast, the IMF's use of prior actions and the less stringent forms of conditionality (benchmarks and targets) has increased notably since the late 1980s. Both the number and type of conditions included in IMF loans have grown significantly over time, therefore.

[52] Ibid.

[53] Appendix 1 provides a complete overview of the substantial variation in both loan size and conditionality for all non-concessional IMF loans from 1984 to 2003.

As with loan size, the reasons for variation in IMF conditionality are not immediately obvious. Larger loans do not always have more extensive conditionality, nor is there a clear relationship between country-specific macroeconomic characteristics and the Fund's use of conditionality. For example, some very large loans (e.g. the SDR 13 billion Brazilian loan in 1998) have had relatively few conditions (five PCs, eleven conditions in total), while some small packages (e.g. Ecuador's SDR 151 million loan in 2003) have had substantially more (sixteen PCs, thirty conditions in all). Moreover, correlations between the total number of conditions and both loan size (amount/quota) and country size (GDP) are quite weak over the 1984–2003 period (0.16 and 0.04, respectively).[54] Existing statistical analyses of IMF conditionality also suggest only weak relationships between a borrower's external debt and macroeconomic characteristics and the number of conditions attached to a loan.[55] Thus, as with variation in loan size, cross-national and cross-temporal differences in IMF conditionality present an important empirical puzzle.

The existing literature

What explains this variation in IMF lending? In deciding how much and on what terms to lend, the IMF faces a central trade-off between *liquidity* and *moral hazard*. This trade-off arises because IMF loans have two simultaneous effects. On the one hand, Fund lending benefits a country directly by providing it with the financing ("liquidity") needed to service its debts. Indirectly, it may also enhance global financial stability by preventing a crisis in one country from becoming a larger systemic problem. On the other hand, IMF loans also create "moral hazard" – incentives for borrower countries and international lenders to assume additional risk in the expectation that the Fund will provide additional "bailouts" in the future.[56] As a result, IMF lending

[54] The relationship is similarly weak for performance criteria: the correlations with amount/quota and GDP are 0.18 and 0.01, respectively.

[55] See, for example, Dreher and Vaubel (2004a).

[56] Crockett (1997). The classic example of moral hazard is in insurance, in which insurers assume two types of risk: the "real hazard" (e.g. auto accident, theft) and the "moral hazard" arising from risky actions an individual may take once he or she is insured (e.g. more reckless driving, not locking his or her home).

may actually exacerbate rather than enhance financial instability. This trade-off presents the IMF with a difficult choice: to lend freely (i.e. large amounts on lenient terms), at the risk of increasing future demand for bailouts, or to limit current lending (i.e. smaller loans with more extensive conditionality), at the risk of having a country default, thereby triggering a broader financial crisis.

The existing literature offers several explanations of how the IMF weighs this trade-off between liquidity and moral hazard as it makes lending decisions. From a purely economic perspective, this choice depends on whether a borrower is insolvent or illiquid – that is, whether the country is "bankrupt," due to bad economic policies, or whether it faces a temporary liquidity problem, caused by an unforeseen macroeconomic shock or a "financial panic" resulting in capital flight by international investors.[57] From this standpoint, IMF lending is a largely technocratic exercise: the Fund's professional economists design and propose lending programs based on a variety of country-specific macroeconomic and external debt indicators. These economic indicators determine the borrowing country's financing needs, as well as the amount of policy adjustment necessary to ensure that the country will be able to repay its private external debt in the future. To be sure, economic factors play a large role in shaping Fund lending decisions. Indeed, past studies have found robust evidence that IMF loans are larger and/or contain more conditions when a country has fewer foreign exchange reserves, higher levels of external debt, and a record of past Fund borrowing.[58] Nonetheless, the empirical record of this technocratic view of IMF behavior is mixed: many macroeconomic variables emphasized in the literature, including GDP, GDP per capita, and government spending, have weak or indeterminate effects on IMF lending.[59] Furthermore, the fact that the IMF has provided large-scale financing in a number of high-profile cases in which the

[57] Chang (1999). Unlike a firm, a country technically cannot be declared bankrupt. The analogy is commonly used to refer to an unsustainable level of sovereign debt, however.

[58] Knight and Santaella (1997); Bird and Rowlands (2003); Joyce (2004).

[59] Joyce (2004). One suggested reason for these results is that the Fund uses a range of indicators, rather than a single "trigger" variable, in making decisions (Bird and Rowlands 2003). It also suggests, however, as I emphasize throughout this book, that politics plays a critical role in shaping IMF lending decisions.

borrowing country appeared to be "insolvent" based on its macroeconomic characteristics – most notably to Russia in the late 1990s and to Argentina in the early 2000s – suggests that political factors also influence IMF lending decisions.[60]

The politics of IMF lending: existing explanations

Recognizing these limitations of a purely economic approach, a number of scholars have sought recently to identify the political determinants of IMF lending. In general, this literature offers two competing explanations of Fund behavior. On the one hand, some scholars argue that the IMF is the servant of the United States, which utilizes its position as the Fund's largest shareholder to direct credit toward countries it deems important. The main variant of this argument is geopolitical: it claims that US foreign policy allies and countries of strategic importance receive more favorable treatment from the Fund. Along these lines, recent quantitative studies have found a relationship between IMF lending and countries' voting patterns in the United Nations General Assembly (UNGA) and/or levels of US foreign and military aid to a given borrower country.[61] Several recent high-profile IMF lending cases are also frequently cited in support of this argument, including Russia, Turkey, and Pakistan.[62] Most recently, Randall Stone has extended this geopolitical logic further, arguing that the formal rules of IMF governance become irrelevant when American strategic interests are at stake. In such cases, he argues, the United States assumes "temporary control" of Fund decision-making and ensures that its "valued client" states receive favorable IMF lending, in the form of reduced conditionality.[63] An alternative but related perspective is that the United States utilizes IMF lending to protect its domestic financial interests. Studies in this vein have found that IMF loans tend to be larger when a borrowing country owes large amounts of debt to private creditors – primarily commercial banks – located within the United States and other major IMF shareholders.[64] Still others, such as Erica Gould, have argued that private international

[60] See, for example, Mussa (2002).
[61] Vreeland (2005); Stone (2004, 2002); Barro and Lee (2002); Thacker (1999).
[62] Stone (2004, 2002). [63] Stone (2008, 590).
[64] Broz and Hawes (2006); Broz (2005); Oatley and Yackee (2004).

creditors influence the IMF independently, rather than as interest groups within the United States and other advanced industrialized countries.[65]

On the other hand, scholars in the "public choice" tradition argue that bureaucratic politics, rather than US interests, is the key political factor in IMF lending.[66] These scholars view the Fund not as the servant of its shareholders, but, rather, as a highly independent actor in its own right. Drawing on principal–agent theory, this alternative approach portrays the IMF staff as a group of "rent-seeking" bureaucrats eager to exploit "agency slack" and maximize its autonomy, budget, and/or the likelihood of program success.[67] From this perspective, we should observe the staff consistently favoring larger loans with more extensive conditionality, since more lending and a larger role for the Fund in monitoring its borrowers' economic policies enhances the staff's own influence. A key proponent of this approach is Roland Vaubel, who finds that the staff engages in "hurry-up lending" during quota reviews in order to obtain quota increases that will facilitate more extensive future lending.[68] Similar studies have found these rent-seeking incentives to be greater when the Fund has more resources available to lend.[69]

As with purely economic explanations of IMF lending, neither of these political approaches fits closely with the empirical evidence. Although bureaucratic politics theories generate clear predictions about variation in IMF lending over time, they provide little, if any, explanation of variation between cases within time periods. For example, although it may be the case that the staff proposes larger loans during quota reviews, this prediction does not explain variation in IMF loan size within years in which a quota review is under way. Furthermore, the public choice logic begs the question of when the IMF staff is able to "get away" with this type of rent-seeking behavior. While bureaucratic arguments draw explicitly on principal–agent theory, however, they tend to leave unspecified both the identity and interests

[65] Gould (2006, 2003).
[66] See, for example, Dreher and Vaubel (2004b) and Willett (2000).
[67] The "rents" accruing to the staff in this approach are defined broadly to include all these factors; strictly speaking, staff members do not receive personal financial gains from more extensive IMF lending or conditionality.
[68] Vaubel (1994, 1991). [69] Dreher and Vaubel (2004b).

of the IMF staff's principal(s). As a result, they offer few predictions about the conditions under which staff behavior will be constrained by member states' monitoring and enforcement.

At the same time, arguments that the United States controls the IMF, or that it can – either temporarily or systematically – bypass the Fund policymaking process when it believes its geopolitical interests are at stake, pay insufficient attention to both the role of the IMF staff and the influence of other large shareholder countries. To be sure, the United States exercises disproportionate influence within the Fund: it holds an appointed seat on the executive board and 16.77 percent of the IMF's votes, which enables it to unilaterally veto certain decisions requiring 85 percent supermajorities, including changes in the Fund's articles of agreement. Nevertheless, US influence is circumscribed in two ways. First, the Fund staff retains significant control over the negotiation and design of IMF programs, and it enjoys agenda-setting power over the executive board: the board cannot approve a lending arrangement without first receiving a staff proposal. Thus, even in cases in which the United States is able to exercise the greatest influence, the staff and other large shareholders still play a key role in shaping lending decisions. Second, US veto power within the IMF does not extend to lending decisions, since executive board approval of loans formally requires the support of only a simple majority of votes rather than an 85 percent supermajority. Moreover, in practice the board does not formally vote to approve IMF programs but, rather, makes decisions on a "consensus basis with respect given to the relative voting power of the states."[70]

As a result, although the IMF's formal rules and informal decision-making norms clearly give the United States a powerful say over Fund policies, they also grant other large member states a significant voice. In particular, the Fund's four next largest shareholders (Japan, Germany, the United Kingdom, and France) also exercise substantial influence within the IMF by virtue of their own appointed seats on the executive board, which grant them a combined voting share of 21.62 percent.[71] It is therefore extremely unlikely that we can

[70] Mussa and Savastano (1999); van Houtven (2002); Vreeland (2005).

[71] China, Russia, and Saudi Arabia also hold their own "elected" seats, with a combined 9.51 percent of the votes. The other sixteen executive directors are elected and represent regional subgroups of the remaining member states (www.imf.org/external/np/sec/memdir/eds.htm).

accurately explain variation in Fund lending policies without also considering the interests of these other powerful states, as well as the extent to which their interests are in harmony or conflict with those of the US. Recent empirical work has partially addressed this problem, by focusing on measuring the aggregate interests of the advanced industrialized countries rather than focusing solely on United States interests.[72] Similarly, J. Lawrence Broz and Michael Hawes (2006) separately measure the bank exposure of each of the G-5 countries in their study. Neither of these approaches, however, addresses the problem of *preference heterogeneity* among the IMF's largest shareholders. Given the collective nature of executive board decision-making, this is a critical oversight in the literature. Indeed, one of this book's central findings is that the distribution of preferences between the Fund's largest shareholders is a key determinant of IMF lending decisions.

The plan of the book

Ultimately, although the existing international political economy literature strongly suggests that IMF policymaking is not simply a technocratic process, it leaves many key questions about the politics of Fund decision-making unanswered. To what extent is the IMF the servant of its shareholders? Under what conditions does the staff exercise the greatest autonomy? What factors determine the interests of the IMF's shareholders and its bureaucrats, and how do these actors' preferences vary over time and between cases? In this book, I develop an analytical framework that provides answers to these critical questions and tests its hypotheses using both quantitative and qualitative analyses of IMF lending since the 1980s.

Chapter 2 further develops the book's analytical framework and core argument. First, it discusses in greater detail several critical changes in the composition of international capital flows during the last two decades. It then introduces the key actors involved in IMF decision-making and the rules and institutions that structure internal IMF policymaking. Drawing on principal–agent theories of international institutions, the chapter sets forth a "common agency" theory of Fund policymaking, in which G-5 governments (the "collective principal") and the IMF staff (the "agent") jointly determine Fund

[72] See Dreher and Sturm (2006).

lending decisions. Thus, in contrast to most scholars and critics, I argue that the IMF is neither the servant of the US government nor an out-of-control bureaucracy. Rather, states and the IMF staff both enjoy partial, but incomplete, control over Fund decision-making. Furthermore, state influence within the IMF lies not with a single country (the United States) or with all member states but, rather, is held collectively by the Fund's largest shareholders. In the remainder of chapter 2, I then develop a set of testable hypotheses linking variation in these actors' preferences – and, therefore, variation in Fund loan size and conditionality – to changes in patterns of financial globalization over time and across cases.

Chapter 3 presents an initial empirical test of my argument and its hypotheses using time-series cross-sectional statistical analysis. The chapter introduces and analyzes an original data set of IMF lending to forty-seven developing countries from 1984 to 2003, which I have assembled primarily from internal Fund documents gathered at the IMF archives. The statistical analysis offers substantial empirical evidence in support of the hypothesized linkages between changes in the composition of international capital flows, shifts in the preferences of G-5 governments and the IMF staff, and variation in IMF loan size and conditionality. In addition, the chapter explores the complex patterns of interaction between the key explanatory variables in the analysis.

Chapters 4 and 5 complement the quantitative evidence with a paired case study analysis of IMF lending to South Korea and Mexico from 1983 to 1997. Although the statistical analysis finds strong correlations between changes in patterns of financial globalization and variation in IMF lending, it does not offer much insight into the actual process of Fund decision-making. Indeed, time-series cross-sectional statistical analysis does not elucidate the causal chain linking changes in international capital flows to variation in IMF policies, nor does it explain how and to what extent the Fund's G-5 principals and its staff take these changes into account in specific cases. By contrast, case studies shed light on the step-by-step chain of events in IMF policymaking. Moreover, they help us to understand the sequencing of – and interaction between – the key economic and political factors explaining variation in IMF lending policies.

Given the vast economic and political diversity of the IMF's borrowers, it is very difficult to choose one or two representative country cases to analyze. Nevertheless, I have chosen to focus on Mexico and

South Korea for several reasons. First, these countries have been two of the IMF's largest borrowers over the last two decades. Second, the Fund's loans to Mexico and South Korea in the mid-1990s were, at the time, the largest loans it had ever provided. Thus, these loans are critical cases for understanding how and why the IMF makes decisions. Third, Mexico and South Korea each borrowed from the IMF in both the 1980s and 1990s, with a multi-year break between their two episodes of borrowing. Studying these two countries therefore sheds light on the impact of historical changes in the composition of international capital flows on IMF behavior. Furthermore, focusing on these two countries' loans offers within-country variation along both the independent and dependent variables, while at the same time controlling for many country-specific factors that complicate interpretation of the time-series cross-sectional statistical results. As with the quantitative analysis, these case studies draw heavily on primary source documents gathered at the IMF archives. These documents include IMF staff reports and executive board minutes, which shed light on the key factors driving Fund lending policies to South Korea and Mexico during the 1980s and 1990s.

Finally, chapter 6 reviews the theory and evidence presented in the book. In addition, it discusses possible research extensions, as well as additional implications for our understanding of the political economy of international finance. The chapter also addresses the important policy implications of my research. Specifically, it assesses several recent proposals to reform the IMF and suggests a number of ways in which the book's findings cast doubt on the merits of these proposals. In so doing, the book seeks to make an analytically informed contribution to the debate about the future of global financial governance and the need to reform the IMF in response to the current global financial crisis. The book concludes with some final thoughts on the implications of my research for our broader understanding of international cooperation and policymaking within international organizations.

2 Global finance and the politics of IMF lending: theory

In this chapter, I develop in greater detail my argument that changes in the composition of international capital flows constitute the key factor explaining variation in the International Monetary Fund's lending policies. I begin by discussing the key dimensions of variation in financial globalization in the contemporary world economy. Specifically, I illustrate the substantial changes in the composition of borrowers and lenders in international finance during the last two decades, as well as the sizeable variation in the geographic distribution of private international creditors. After outlining these changes in the composition of developing countries' international debt, I then discuss the IMF decision-making process in detail. Drawing on principal–agent theories of international institutions, I develop a "common agency" theory of IMF policymaking in which two key actors – the Fund's largest member states (the "collective principal") and the IMF's bureaucratic staff (the "agent") – jointly determine lending decisions. In contrast to most existing theories of IMF lending, this framework explicitly accounts for both actors' key roles in Fund policymaking. Moreover, it also takes into account the importance of preference heterogeneity among the Fund's principals in shaping IMF lending decisions. Finally, using this common agency framework, I explain how changes in the composition of private international capital flows shape the politics of IMF lending. I develop a set of testable hypotheses linking changes in private international debt composition to variation in the preferences of both the Fund's largest shareholder countries and the IMF staff over the size and terms of Fund lending arrangements. These hypotheses yield clear, observable implications about how and why IMF loan size and conditionality vary systematically in accordance with changes in patterns of financial globalization.

Banks and bondholders: the evolution of private international finance

Since the 1970s private capital flows have become the dominant feature of international finance. Private international capital flows to developing countries have grown exponentially, from nearly zero in 1970 to $491 billion in 2005, while the stock of outstanding external debt in developing countries has increased from $748 billion in 1982 to $2.8 trillion in 2005.[1] These aggregate data mask two broad changes in the composition of international capital flows, however: a shift in the composition of *international lenders*, from commercial banks to bondholders; and a shift in the composition of *international borrowers*, from sovereign governments to private actors. These changes in the structure of global financial markets, I argue, are the key to understanding and explaining variation in IMF lending policies.

Figure 2.1 illustrates these substantial changes over time in the composition of borrowers and lenders in the international financial system. In the early 1980s private capital flows to developing countries consisted almost entirely of lending to sovereign governments. Prior to 1990 the primary providers of this "public and publicly guaranteed" (PPG) debt were large commercial banks located in the advanced industrialized countries.[2] In recent years, however, bond financing has largely replaced bank lending as the primary form of sovereign borrowing in global financial markets. At the same time, an increasingly large share of international capital flows consists of lending directly from international banks and bondholders to private entities within developing countries. The vast majority of this "private non-guaranteed" (PNG) debt consists of *interbank* lending – lending from commercial banks in the advanced industrialized countries directly to private banks in the developing world. More recently, however, some private firms in developing countries have also begun to borrow directly from international commercial banks, while other firms have begun to issue bonds in international markets.

[1] World Bank (2006a).

[2] Ibid. As defined by the World Bank, publicly guaranteed debt is debt accumulated by private actors or state-owned enterprises that has been guaranteed by the national government. As such, it is effectively sovereign debt, since the government is ultimately responsible for ensuring its repayment if the borrower is unable to pay.

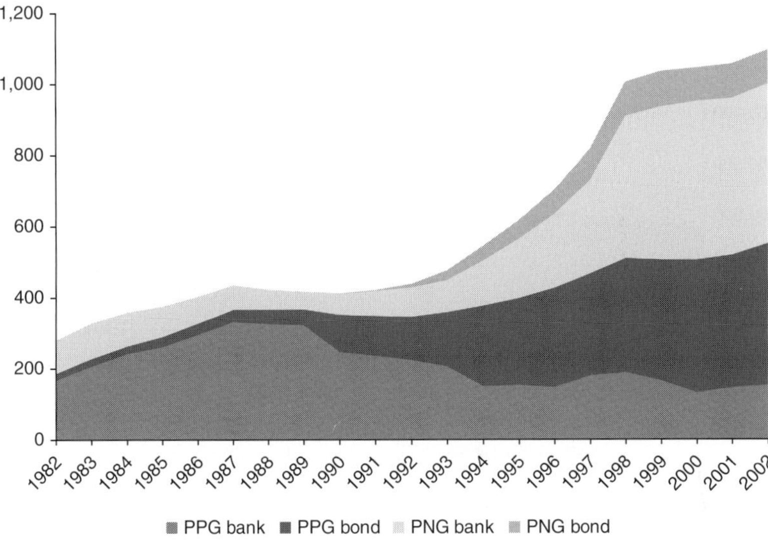

Figure 2.1 Composition of private external debt, all developing countries, 1982–2002 ($ billions)
Source: World Bank (2003).

These general trends in international capital flows nonetheless mask substantial cross-country variation in the composition of developing countries' private external debt. As figures 2.2 to 2.6 illustrate clearly, there has been substantial diversity in developing countries' ties to global financial markets during the last two decades. Indeed, the identity of international borrowers (sovereign governments versus private actors) and lenders (commercial banks versus bondholders) has varied widely over time and across countries since the 1980s.

As these charts illustrate, sovereign governments remain the primary borrowers in many developing countries, although in many cases (e.g. Argentina, Mexico) the creditor base has shifted almost entirely from commercial banks to international bondholders. At the same time, non-sovereign (PNG) debt has become the dominant form of international lending to some countries (e.g. Thailand, South Korea). Finally, as the Moroccan chart illustrates, international capital flows to many developing countries continue to consist primarily of sovereign bank lending, although interbank (PNG bank) lending has increased notably in recent years.

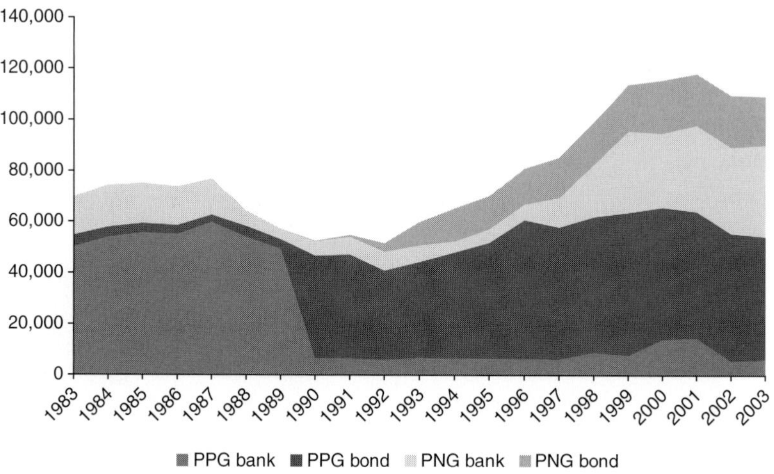

Figure 2.2 Composition of private external debt, Mexico, 1983–2003 ($ millions)
Source: World Bank (2003).

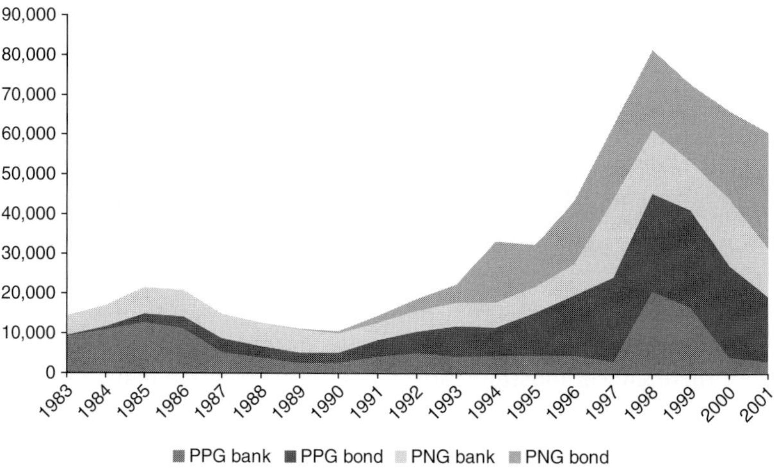

Figure 2.3 Composition of private external debt, South Korea, 1983–2001 ($ millions)
Source: World Bank (2003).

Although explaining the causes of this substantial variation in international capital flows is beyond the scope of this study, the existing literature offers several possible explanations. First, a large

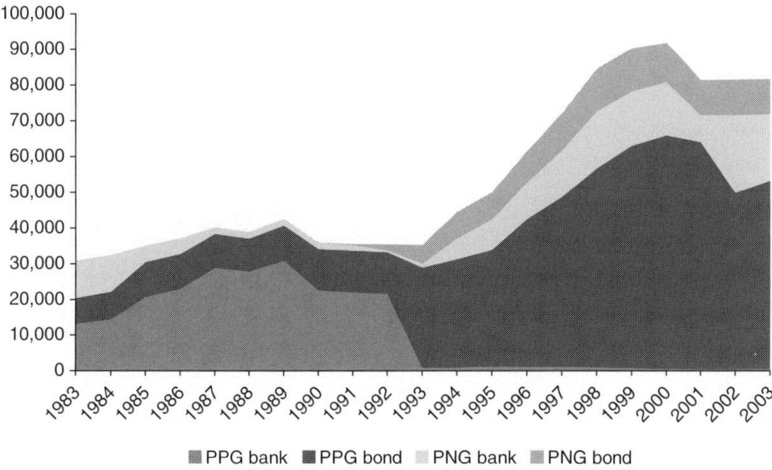

Figure 2.4 Composition of private external debt, Argentina, 1983–2003 ($ millions)
Source: World Bank (2003).

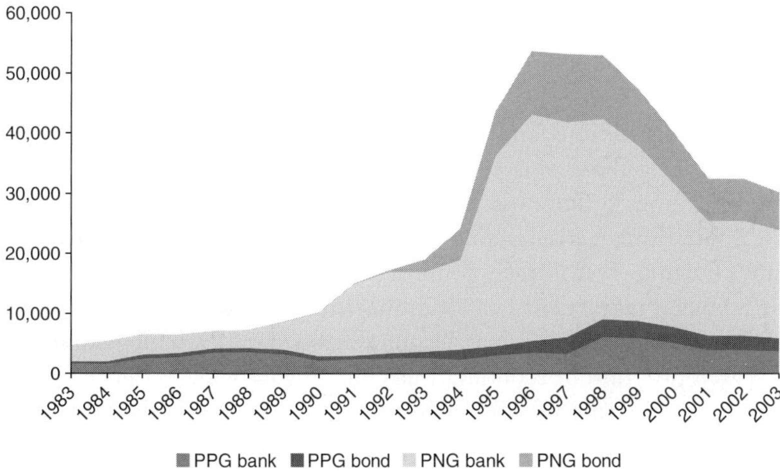

Figure 2.5 Composition of private external debt, Thailand 1983–2003 ($ millions)
Source: World Bank (2003).

portion of these differences is probably a consequence of variations in levels of economic development; poorer developing countries such as Morocco tend to be more dependent on commercial bank lending,

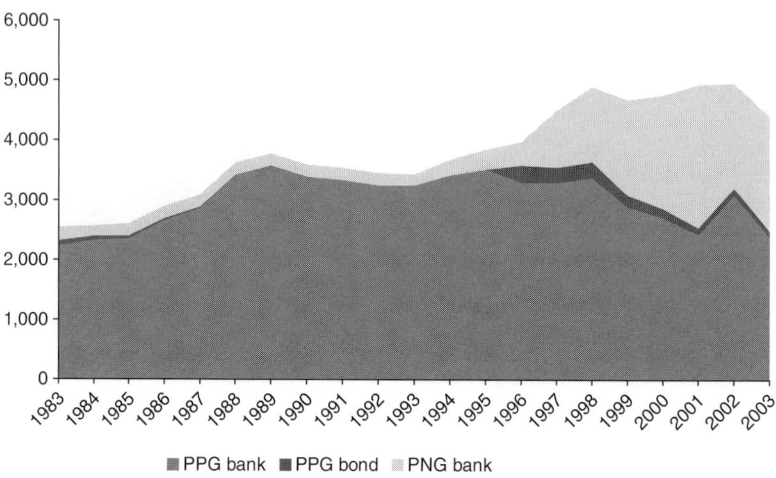

Figure 2.6 Composition of private external debt, Morocco, 1983–2003 ($ millions)
Source: World Bank (2003).

while richer "emerging markets" such as Mexico and Argentina have shifted much of their borrowing toward international bond markets. Second, the growth in private non-guaranteed flows to some developing countries is probably attributable to the emergence of large private financial institutions and multinational corporations. For example, an increasing share of capital flows to South Korea consists of interbank lending to domestic financial institutions and bond issues by the South Korean chaebol (industrial conglomerates) such as Samsung and Hyundai. In contrast, countries without well-developed domestic financial markets or large manufacturing sectors are less likely to attract these "private–private" capital flows. Finally, a long-standing research program in economics has identified a wide variety of additional macroeconomic and microeconomic variables that contribute to differences in country- and firm-level borrowing patterns.[3] Past IMF lending itself may be one of these variables. Indeed, recent work has found that Fund programs enable countries that have previously borrowed on sovereign bond markets to borrow again at lower interest rates.[4] Thus, while IMF policies alone are unlikely to be the underlying

[3] Modigliani and Miller (1958); Rajan and Zingales (1995); Gelos, Sahay, and Sandleris (2004).
[4] Eichengreen, Kletzer, and Mody (2005).

reason for changes in the composition of international financial flows, they might help to maintain or reinforce existing trends.

The geographic distribution of international creditors

Along with these changes in the identity of borrowers and lenders, the geographic distribution of international lenders constitutes a third dimension of change in financial globalization. Private international creditors, whether commercial banks or bondholders, are overwhelmingly located in a handful of advanced industrialized countries. In 2003 commercial banks headquartered in the "G-10" countries held claim to 87 percent of international bank loans.[5] Banks headquartered in the "G-5" (the United States, United Kingdom, Germany, Japan, and France) countries held roughly two-thirds of these G-10 claims, with a global market share of 64 percent; this number has declined since the early 1990s, when G-5 market share exceeded 80 percent, as lenders in countries such as Australia, Ireland, the Nordic countries, and Spain have entered the global banking market. Nonetheless, as figure 2.7 clearly illustrates, G-5 financial institutions continue to dominate international bank lending to developing countries.

Until the 1990s the most common type of international commercial bank lending was the medium-term *syndicated loan*.[6] Syndicated lending involves the cooperation of multiple commercial banks, often from several countries, that negotiate a single loan with a single emerging market borrower.[7] Commercial banks pursue syndication for several reasons. First, syndication reduces default risk through the use of cross-default clauses in the terms of the loan: if a borrower defaults on a syndicated loan, it effectively defaults on all banks participating

[5] BIS (2003). The Group of Ten (G-10) is actually made up of eleven industrial countries (Belgium, Canada, France, Germany, Italy, Japan, the Netherlands, Sweden, Switzerland, the United Kingdom, and the United States) that are the dominant players in the international financial system. These countries consult and cooperate on economic, monetary and financial matters through regular meetings at the Bank for International Settlements (BIS) in Basel, Switzerland. In addition, the ministers of finance and central bank governors of the G-10 usually meet once a year in connection with the autumn meetings of the IMF.

[6] The World Bank classifies medium-term lending to encompass all lending with a maturity of greater than one year (World Bank 2006a).

[7] Smith and Walter (2003).

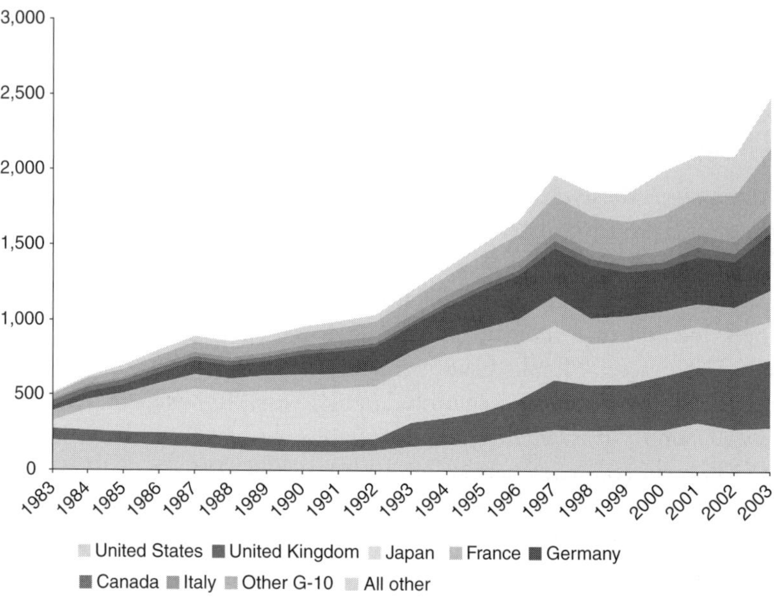

Figure 2.7 International commercial bank lending (consolidated foreign claims), by nationality of reporting banks, 1983–2003 ($ billions)
Source: BIS, consolidated international banking statistics, 2006.

in the syndicate. As a result, a country that defaults on its commercial bank loans risks the possibility that none of the banks involved in the syndicate will provide it with future loans. By eliminating the possibility of selective default, syndication increases the borrower's incentives to pay its debts. Second, syndication allows banks to participate in lending that they might not otherwise have access to on their own; by pooling multiple banks' relationships and resources, all banks in the syndicate can take advantage of additional international lending opportunities. Third, syndicated bank lending reduces the transactions costs and collective action problems associated with private creditor cooperation during times of financial crisis.

In addition to providing loans to sovereign borrowers, commercial banks frequently have further ties to developing countries. As providers of short-term trade credits, banks facilitate cross-border trade and payments, and some commercial banks also serve as managers of central bank reserves for some developing countries.[8] Increasingly,

[8] Tomz (2001).

commercial banks have also engaged in short-term interbank lending directly to private financial institutions in emerging market countries. In some cases this lending is syndicated, while in others individual banks provide financing to a single borrower. Commercial banks therefore have long-standing, multidimensional ties to particular developing countries.

Like commercial banks, international bondholders are also heavily concentrated in the G-5 countries.[9] Although fewer than 100 firms control the vast majority of the international banking market, however, bondholders are significantly more heterogeneous and disaggregated. Recent events in Argentina are illustrative: the Global Committee of Argentina Bondholders (GCAB), which organized in the aftermath of Argentina's default on $155 billion of external debt in December 2001, represented over 500,000 retail investors and over 100 institutional investors.[10] By contrast, debt rescheduling during the 1980s Latin American debt crisis – as discussed in chapter 4 below – involved fewer than 500 commercial banks.

The primary instrument of international bond financing is the *Eurobond*, an unsecured promissory note issued by sovereign governments or private institutions.[11] These bonds are almost universally

[9] The ten largest investment banks and ten largest asset management firms – the underwriters and primary investors in international bonds – are all located in the G-5 countries plus Switzerland (Dobson and Hufbauer 2001).

[10] See www.gcab.org. Retail investors are wealthy individuals whose deposits are invested in emerging markets by banks and other wealth managers such as hedge funds; institutional investors, by contrast, control billions of dollars in assets as the managers of pension funds, mutual funds, central bank portfolios, and insurance companies. Prominent examples of institutional investors include mutual fund companies such as Vanguard and Fidelity Investments, and CALPERS, the California public employees' pension fund. These investors, in turn, represent hundreds of thousands of individual citizens, shareholders, and policyholders both in the advanced industrialized countries and throughout the developing world. In contrast to commercial banks, most international bondholders do not have long-standing, multidimensional ties to particular borrower countries; rather, bondholders tend to invest in a broad portfolio of assets and countries, and they reallocate these investments more frequently in search of the highest rates of return in global markets.

[11] Smith and Walter (2003). To date, sovereign governments have issued the vast majority of international bonds. Private bond issues by multinationals and financial institutions are becoming increasingly commonplace, however, in larger emerging markets such as South Korea. For example, Samsung, the Korean industrial conglomerate, issued $390 million in bonds in 2001, while Hyundai Motor Company issued $400 billion in bonds in 2003.

denominated in one of the major international currencies (dollar, euro, pound, yen).[12] Eurobonds are generally medium-term or long-term investments, although in recent years a growing number of emerging market countries have issued short-term, dollar-denominated paper akin to US Treasury bills (e.g. the Mexican *tesobonos*, which played a central role in the 1994/5 Mexican financial crisis). Like syndicated commercial bank loans, most international bond issues contain cross-default clauses preventing a sovereign debtor from selectively defaulting against individual creditors. Nevertheless, because bondholders are far more heterogeneous and disaggregated than commercial banks, these clauses may not ensure effective creditor cooperation in the case of a financial crisis.[13]

While both bondholders and commercial banks are heavily concentrated within the G-5 countries, there is substantial variation, both over time and across countries, in the geographic distribution of lending from these private international creditors. As figures 2.8 to 2.12 illustrate, some developing countries borrow primarily from private lenders in a single G-5 country. For example, Mexico has depended largely on financing from US lenders since 2000, while Thailand relies heavily on Japanese lending, and Morocco borrows primarily from French banks.[14] In contrast, other countries borrow widely from all the major creditor countries: South Korea, Mexico (pre-2000), and Argentina borrowed extensively from banks in all the G-5 countries throughout much of the last two decades.

[12] In 2001 over 90 percent of international bond issues were denominated in one of these four currencies (Dobson and Hufbauer 2001). International investors are rarely willing to invest in "local currency" bonds given the potentially substantial risk of large exchange rate fluctuations in foreign currency markets.

[13] On the issue of collective action clauses in international bond issues, see Eichengreen and Portes (1995) and Roubini and Setser (2004).

[14] Given the substantially larger number of creditors involved in international bond issues, accurate cross-national data on G-5 bond distribution is not readily available. In most recent international financial crises, however, the geographic distribution of bond debt between G-5 creditors has closely mirrored that of bank exposure (e.g. Argentina 2001, South Korea 1997, Mexico 1995). Moreover, for the reasons described below, commercial banks are politically and economically more important in the eyes of G-5 governments than non-bank institutions and bondholders. In the analysis below, I therefore utilize commercial bank exposure as the best available proxy for the distribution of G-5 governments' domestic financial interests in particular IMF borrower countries.

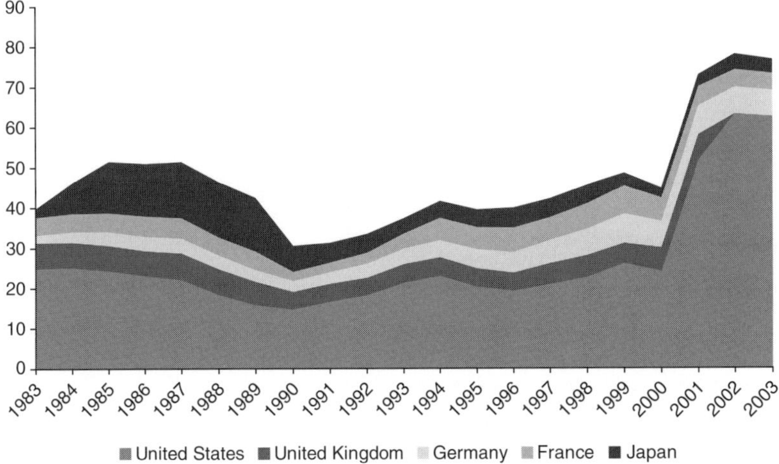

Figure 2.8 G-5 commercial bank exposure to Mexico, 1983–2003 ($ billions)
Source: BIS, consolidated international banking statistics, 2006.

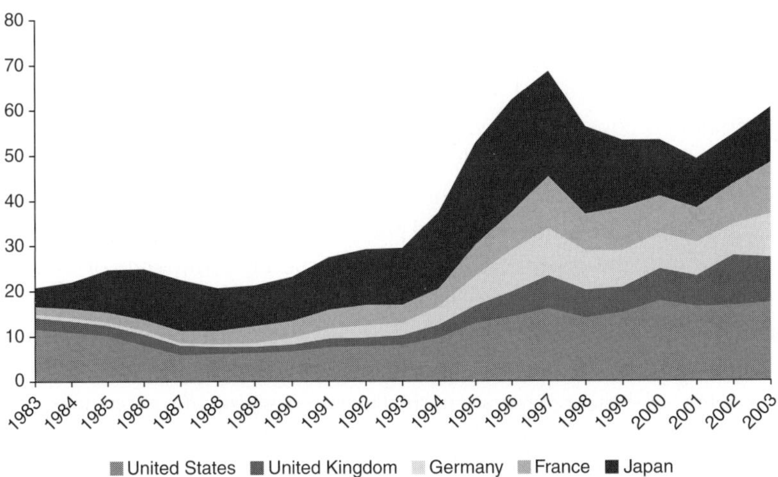

Figure 2.9 G-5 commercial bank exposure to South Korea, 1983–2003 ($ billions)
Source: BIS, consolidated international banking statistics, 2006.

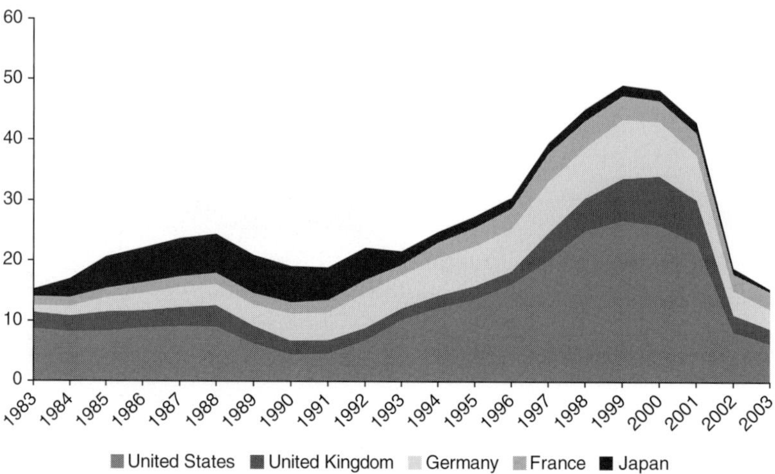

Figure 2.10 G-5 commercial bank exposure to Argentina, 1983–2003 ($ billions)
Source: BIS, consolidated international banking statistics, 2006.

As with variation in the composition of borrowers and lenders, there are a number of possible of reasons for this variation in the geographic distribution of developing countries' international debt. Clearly, proximity plays a substantial role: Asian countries such as South Korea and Thailand borrow more heavily from Japan, while Latin American countries borrow more extensively from US creditors, and the countries of central and eastern Europe borrow disproportionately from German lenders. In addition, historical and political ties probably play an important role in some countries. For example, the predominance of French lending to Morocco and Algeria is quite likely linked to these countries' status as former French colonies. Finally, levels of economic development also appear to play an important role. Indeed, aggregate G-5 lending tends to be most extensive in the largest emerging markets, including South Korea, Mexico, and Argentina. Nonetheless, as the figures below illustrate, important variation in the distribution/heterogeneity of G-5 lenders' exposure exists even in these most prominent cases.

Global finance and the politics of IMF lending

How does this substantial variation in patterns of financial globalization influence the IMF and its lending behavior? In order to answer this question, it is necessary first to understand the multiple steps involved in the Fund's lending process, as well as the Fund's internal

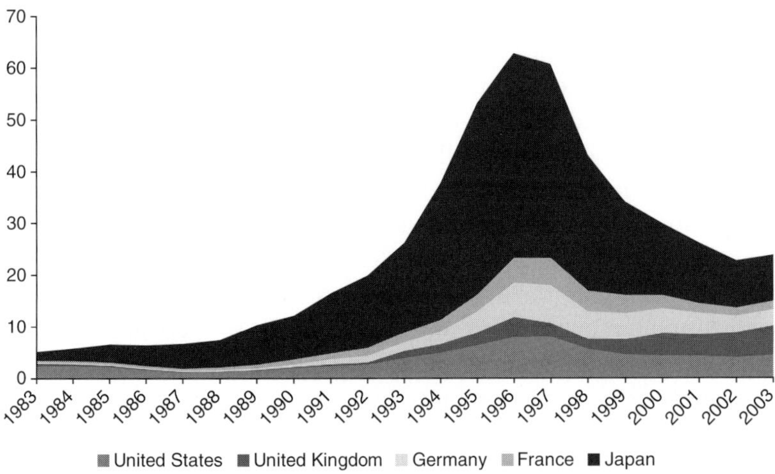

Figure 2.11 G-5 commercial bank exposure to Thailand, 1983–2003 ($ billions)
Source: BIS, consolidated international banking statistics, 2006.

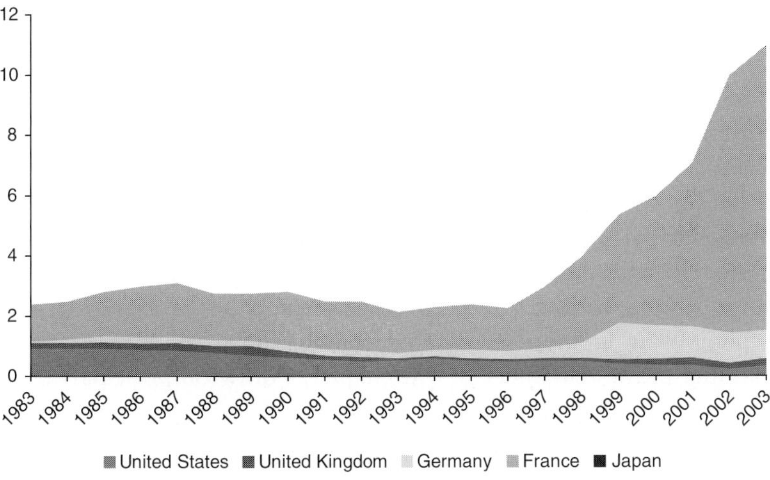

Figure 2.12 G-5 commercial bank exposure to Morocco, 1983–2003 ($ billions)
Source: BIS, consolidated international banking statistics, 2006.

decision-making rules. The IMF's lending process begins when one of the Fund's member states requests external financing assistance. Once a country requests IMF credit, the Fund staff enters into negotiations with the borrower government's finance ministry over the amount and terms of the loan.[15] Once the staff and the borrowing country have agreed on the terms of a Fund loan, the borrower's financial authorities sign a "letter of intent" detailing the loan package and the reforms the borrower will undertake as conditions of the loan ("conditionality"). Subsequently, the staff formally proposes the program to the executive board, a twenty-four-member body composed of executive directors representing the Fund's member states, which holds ultimate authority over all IMF lending decisions. If the loan package is approved, the Fund disburses the first "tranche" of the loan and the IMF staff begins to monitor the borrower's performance to see whether or not the conditions of the program are being met. Decisions about the disbursement of subsequent tranches are made at periodic intervals and must also be approved by the executive board, following the completion of a formal program review by the staff. Once an IMF loan has been disbursed, private creditors react in international markets, either by continuing to lend to a borrower country or by seeking to liquidate their holdings and investing their resources elsewhere.

Thus, the IMF decision-making process formally involves two actors: the Fund's member states, acting through the executive board, and the IMF staff. Each enjoys partial, but incomplete, control over Fund decisions. Explaining variation in IMF lending requires a careful understanding of both actors' roles in the Fund policymaking process, as well as the preferences of each over the size and terms of Fund lending arrangements. Unfortunately, as noted above, most existing studies of the IMF have not adequately explored the consequences of this principal–agent relationship for Fund lending decisions. Rather, past studies have generally ascribed "control" of the Fund to a single actor (e.g. the United States, the staff). Although this strategy is parsimonious, it does not accurately model the dynamics of IMF policymaking. In the remainder of this chapter, I draw on principal–agent theory to develop an alternative model of IMF policymaking, which explicitly incorporates the common agency relationship between G-5 governments and the Fund staff. I then show how both actors' preferences – and, therefore, IMF choices about loan size and conditionality – vary systematically in accordance with changes in the composition of international capital flows to developing countries.

[15] IMF loans are formally referred to as "programs" or "lending arrangements."

A common agency theory of IMF policymaking

In recent years international relations scholars have adopted principal–agent theory as a framework for studying international institutions in general and the IMF in particular.[16] Agency theory provides a useful tool for understanding international organizations, since it focuses on situations of *delegation*, which exist when one or more actors authorized to make a decision or take some action conditionally designate some other actor(s) to make that decision or take that action.[17] Despite the rising importance of non-state actors, states remain the primary decision-making actors in international relations and within international institutions. Thus, the delegation of authority to international organizations generally implies that states are acting as *principals* and that international organizations act as their *agents*. More broadly, *principals* are the actors within a hierarchical relationship in whom authority ultimately rests, while *agents* are the actors who are conditionally designated to perform tasks in the name of the principals.[18]

A central tenet of delegation theory is the assumption that agents pursue their own interests, subject to the constraints imposed upon them by their principals.[19] Principals will try to control their agents, but doing so is costly and some degree of "agency slack" is inevitable: agents always possess some degree of autonomy due to incomplete contracting and/or the costs associated with monitoring and enforcement of the principal–agent contract.[20] Agency slack occurs when agents pursue policies that the principal(s) would not have chosen if it (they) had been acting directly. The problem of agency slack is even more severe in cases of *common agency* (i.e. collective or multiple principals), because the multiple members comprising the agent's principal may have heterogeneous preferences about the agent's behavior.[21] When the members of the collective principal have strongly

[16] See Hawkins *et al.* (2006) and Lyne, Nielson, and Tierney (2006) for overviews of principal–agent theory and its application to international institutions. For specific applications to the IMF, see Martin (2006) and Gould (2006, 2003).

[17] Lyne and Tierney (2002).

[18] Hawkins *et al.* (2006).

[19] Kiewiet and McCubbins (1991).

[20] Hawkins *et al.* (2006).

[21] Ferejohn (1986).

unified preferences over policy outcomes, their ability and willingness to monitor and control the agent's behavior will be extremely high; by contrast, when principals' preferences are heterogeneous, the agent can exploit these differences between the members of the collective principal to pursue its own interests and policies. Similarly, the intensity of the principals' preferences affects agent discretion. When the principal has strong preferences over a particular decision, it has greater incentives to monitor the agent's behavior; conversely, the principal is likely to allow greater discretion to the agent when it has little direct interest in a given policy decision.

Conceiving of IMF decision-making as a principal–agent relationship highlights two critical points about the political economy of IMF lending. First, one-dimensional explanations ascribing control of the IMF to a single actor are overly simplistic and unlikely to generate accurate predictions about the Fund's lending behavior. Contrary to the currently prevailing views in the literature, the IMF is not the servant of its most powerful member states, nor is it the independent master of global finance. Rather, Fund behavior is jointly determined by the preferences of both member states and the IMF staff, which in turn are shaped by the composition and expected behavior of private international creditors. Thus, in order to explain variation in IMF lending, we need to move beyond "ideal type" theories that ascribe control of the Fund to a single actor in favor of clear, case-specific predictions about the relative influence of states and IMF bureaucrats.

Second, distinguishing between agency and influence emphasizes the limits of private actors' authority over the IMF. While some scholars have argued that private creditors have replaced states as the Fund's political principals, these private actors enjoy no formal role in IMF policymaking, nor have they "delegated" political authority to the Fund staff in any meaningful sense.[22] Certainly, private creditors strongly influence IMF behavior, but they do so only indirectly through their ability to affect the interests of the two formally involved political

[22] Gould (2006, 2003). Gould argues that the IMF has become more responsive to the demands of private creditors than Fund member states, citing the increasing prevalence of "bank-friendly" conditions in Fund loans over time. While this finding can be interpreted as evidence of private lenders' increasing influence in international finance, it is misleading to characterize this influence as indicative of a formal delegation/agency relationship between the IMF and private international creditors.

actors. As domestic interests within the Fund's most powerful member states, private lenders shape the preferences of national political representatives (the executive directors) within the executive board. At the same time, as independent actors in global markets, private creditors influence the decisions of the IMF's professional staff as it negotiates and designs Fund lending arrangements. These lines of influence are critically important for understanding IMF policies, but they have not allowed private actors to supersede or replace member states and the IMF staff as the Fund's key political decision-makers.

G-5 governments: the Fund's de facto collective principal

The IMF's member states are its shareholders and formal political principals. Acting through the executive board, a body composed of executive directors representing shareholder governments, member states have the final say over all IMF policy decisions. Because member states' voting power is directly proportional to their quota contributions to the Fund's general resources, however, the advanced industrialized countries' preferences carry the most weight in Fund decision-making. As the Fund's five largest shareholders, the G-5 countries are entitled to appoint their own executive directors, who hold a combined 38.39 percent of the quota-based votes.[23] Three additional countries (China, Russia, Saudi Arabia) "elect" their own board seats, with a combined 9.51 percent of the votes, while the remaining twenty-four board seats are held by elected executive directors representing various regional subgroups of the remaining member states. For example, the Belgian executive director also represents Austria, Luxembourg, Turkey, and several central and eastern European countries, and he/she casts these countries' combined votes (5.14 percent) on his/her constituencies' behalf. Similarly, the Argentine executive director also represents Bolivia, Chile, Paraguay, Peru, and Uruguay, thereby casting a combined 1.96 percent of board votes. In some constituencies the largest country traditionally holds the director's seat, while in others the seat rotates between several countries.[24]

[23] See www.imf.org/external/np/sec/memdir/eds.htm.

[24] For example, Canada has always held the board seat representing Ireland and ten Caribbean nations, while the Nordic and Baltic states typically rotate their executive director every two years. See Martin and Woods (2005) for

As table 2.1 illustrates, this voting structure gives the advanced industrialized countries overwhelming influence within the IMF. The G-5, as mentioned previously, hold 38.39 percent of the votes, while executive directors from constituencies encompassing the G-7 (the G-5 plus Canada and Italy) cast a combined 46.13 percent of executive board votes, and those representing the G-10 (the G-7 plus Belgium, the Netherlands, Sweden, and Switzerland) collectively cast nearly two-thirds (62.28 percent).[25]

Since many of the Fund's non-lending decisions require executive board supermajorities of 70 to 85 percent, the advanced industrialized countries hold collective (or the United States, with 16.77 percent of the votes, unilateral) veto power over a wide range of Fund policies, including quota increases, the sale of IMF gold reserves, and amendments to the articles of agreement.[26] This veto power does not extend to IMF lending decisions, however: formally, approval of an IMF loan requires the support of only a simple majority of executive board votes, rather than a supermajority. Moreover, the executive board's norm is to avoid formal votes on IMF lending decisions whenever possible. Rather, the board makes lending decisions on a "consensus basis with respect given to the relative voting power of the states."[27] This informal norm of IMF policymaking suggests that the interests of the advanced industrialized countries are the dominant factor influencing board decisions about the size and terms of IMF loans.

Put simply, the Fund's formal rules and informal decision-making norms give the IMF's largest shareholders de facto control over IMF decision-making. Indeed, the G-5 countries need to garner the support of only three other executive directors from rich countries (Canada, Switzerland, a handful of fellow EU members) in order to assemble a board majority and control IMF lending decisions. Given the deep economic and political ties between these countries, such cooperation and coordination between the G-5 and their G-7/10 counterparts is

a detailed discussion of the dynamics of delegation and agency within these multiple-state board constituencies.

[25] The eleven countries comprising the G-10 participate in the major global financial regulatory institutions at the BIS and have made supplementary credit commitments to the IMF through the General Arrangements to Borrow (GAB) and the New Arrangements to Borrow (NAB): see www.imf.org/external/np/exr/facts/gabnab.htm.

[26] See IMF (2001) for a detailed description of these special majority rules.

[27] Mussa and Savastano (1999); IMF (2002); van Houtven (2002).

Table 2.1 *IMF Executive Board voting shares, March 2009*

Country	Percentage share
United States	16.77
Japan	6.02
Germany	5.88
France	4.86
United Kingdom	4.86
G-5 total	***38.39***
Italy	4.10
Canada	3.64
G-7 total	***46.13***
Belgium	5.14
Netherlands	4.78
Sweden	3.44
Switzerland	2.79
G-10 total	***62.28***
Spain	4.45
China	3.66
Indonesia	3.52
South Korea	3.44
Egypt	3.20
Saudi Arabia	3.16
Sierra Leone	3.01
Russia	2.69
Iran	2.42
Brazil	2.42
India	2.35
Argentina	1.96
Rwanda	1.35
Other total	***37.63***

Note: Does not sum to 100 percent because of rounding.

highly likely to occur within the IMF. Furthermore, since three G-10 members (Belgium, the Netherlands, and Italy) share a common currency with France and Germany as members of the Eurozone (and a fourth, Sweden, is also a member of the European Union), these countries are very likely to share common preferences over international financial issues such as IMF lending. Finally, it is highly unlikely that the remaining board members will override the collective objections of the Fund's five largest quota contributors and vote to approve a loan without their consent.

For these reasons, I focus in the remainder of this book on G-5 government interests as a strong proxy for the overall interests of the key players within the executive board. Focusing on the G-5 also allows me to control for the fact that G-7/G-10 representation within the executive board has changed over time, as different countries have held these director seats; in contrast, each of the G-5 countries has had a seat at the table for all IMF lending decisions during the last two decades. Treating the G-5 as the Fund's de facto collective principal is therefore a valuable shorthand that makes cross-case identification and comparison of the intensity and heterogeneity of preferences among the Fund's largest shareholders more tractable. Nonetheless, I also consider the interests of a broader set of Fund member states, including the remaining G-7 and G-10 countries, in the statistical analysis presented in chapter 3. Furthermore, in the case studies (chapters 4 and 5), I take into account the views of all board members during the discussions about the terms of IMF loans to Mexico and South Korea from 1983 to 1997. Ultimately, I find evidence that some non-G-5 executive directors – particularly those from other G-10 countries – played important roles in board debates over lending to Mexico and South Korea, although the views of the G-5 clearly carried the greatest weight in these discussions.

The IMF staff as agent

Although the Fund's largest member states hold ultimate authority over IMF policymaking, they have delegated authority to negotiate, design, and propose lending arrangements to the Fund's bureaucratic staff based in Washington, DC. Consisting of approximately 2,400 members (half of whom are economists) from 143 countries, the IMF staff acts as the agent of the Fund's member states in executing the day-to-day operations of the Fund.[28] When a borrowing country requests financial assistance, an IMF staff team is dispatched to the country to negotiate with the borrower government over the amount and terms of the program. Following the signing of the "letter of

[28] See www.imf.org/external/np/exr/facts/glance.htm.

intent" detailing the amount of the loan and the conditionality included in the program, the IMF staff proposes a lending arrangement to the executive board for approval.[29] Along with the draft program, the staff also circulates a "staff report" to the board, which provides further details about the borrower country's economic performance, contains additional information about the program's conditionality, and recommends a proposed amount of financing for the board's approval. Although the staff may consult with the board throughout the process, the board cannot approve a program without first receiving a proposal from the staff. Moreover, while the executive board retains formal authority to amend staff proposals, it hardly ever exercises this power.[30] Indeed, "there are only a few instances in the Fund's entire history of the board turning down or even modifying a request for a conditional loan arrangement."[31] This agenda-setting power gives the Fund staff significant influence over the IMF decision-making process.[32] Nevertheless, as it operates "in the shadow" of an executive board vote, the staff does not enjoy complete autonomy; rather, it must take the executive directors' preferences into account if it is to design and propose a program that will secure approval by the board.

Global finance and G-5 preferences over IMF lending

As noted earlier, the IMF faces a central trade-off between *liquidity* and *moral hazard* when deciding how much and on what terms to lend. On the one hand, Fund lending directly benefits a country by providing it with the financing (liquidity) needed to service its debts. Indirectly, it may also enhance global financial stability by preventing a crisis in one country from becoming a larger systemic problem.

[29] See Mussa and Savastano (1999).
[30] Gould (2006); Martin (2006); Southard (1979).
[31] Gould (2006, 286).
[32] As Martin explains, the rarity of such events is itself evidence of the staff's "gatekeeping power": "If the staff anticipates that the outcome of board decisions will not be to its liking, it can refuse to present a program in the first place" (2006, 149). Martin also argues that the staff has informational advantage over the executive board, since directors are replaced more frequently than staff bureaucrats; these advantages further increase the likelihood that staff proposals will be accepted by the board (2006, 145–7).

On the other hand, IMF loans also create moral hazard – incentives for borrower countries and international lenders to assume additional risk in the expectation that the Fund will provide additional "bailouts" in the future.[33] How do G-5 governments and the IMF staff weigh this trade-off and make IMF lending decisions? I argue that these actors' preferences over the size and terms (conditionality) of IMF loans vary based on the composition of private international capital flows to developing countries. In the remainder of this chapter, I further develop this logic, which yields a set of testable hypotheses linking IMF loan characteristics to variation in patterns of financial globalization since the 1980s.

The substantial variation in the composition of international capital flows to developing countries heavily influences G-5 governments' preferences over IMF lending policies. For G-5 governments, the IMF's trade-off between liquidity and moral hazard entails the choice between potentially conflicting domestic and international interests. On the one hand, G-5 governments have a clear interest in utilizing IMF lending to maintain international financial stability. As the dominant players in international trade and finance, the G-5 countries stand to benefit the most from managing and preventing financial crises.[34] In particular, G-5 governments are interested in minimizing "contagion," the negative spillover effects of an international financial crisis, on the economies of their key trading partners or on their own domestic financial stability. To the extent that IMF lending contributes to limiting contagion and enhancing global financial stability, G-5 governments should generally favor larger loans on more lenient terms. Indeed, because financial stability is a public good, all actors within the G-5 countries enjoy these positive domestic benefits of IMF liquidity.[35] On the other hand, as the largest shareholders and primary financial contributors to the IMF, G-5 governments also have an interest in minimizing the use of Fund resources. More extensive IMF lending places a strain on the Fund's scarce resources and may increase the demand for IMF quota increases – demands that are likely to be met primarily by additional quota contributions from the

[33] Crockett (1997).

[34] In 2002 the G-5 countries accounted for 38.9 percent of world trade and 59.7 percent of global GDP (World Bank 2003). As noted above, creditors in the G-5 countries also hold a majority of private international debt.

[35] Wyplosz (1999); Crockett (1997).

G-5 countries. Moreover, frequent, large-scale IMF lending creates moral hazard and may increase borrowing countries' demands for future IMF credit. Consequently, G-5 governments also have an interest in conserving IMF resources by restricting the amount of Fund lending and requiring loans to contain more extensive conditionality.

In addition, the Fund's trade-off between liquidity and moral hazard also creates a *domestic* political dilemma for G-5 governments. Specifically, it presents them with a trade-off between pursuing the aggregate welfare interests of national taxpayers and catering to the special interests of the domestic financial sector. This trade-off arises because IMF loans – even if they benefit the borrowing country and enhance international financial stability – allow private creditors to benefit from international lending without bearing the full risks involved.[36] When the IMF provides credit to a borrowing country, these funds are frequently transferred directly and immediately to private creditors in the form of debt service payments.[37] For this reason, G-5 governments may face domestic pressure from private creditors to support larger IMF loans on more lenient terms for countries to which they are highly exposed, in the hope that these loans will prevent the country from defaulting and thereby protect their investments.

At the same time, however, voters and their representatives widely perceive Fund programs to be costly "bailouts" or "welfare for banks" that divert taxpayer funds that could otherwise be earmarked for domestic priorities. Technically, IMF lending has no direct impact on G-5 government budgets: IMF quota contributions – and, therefore, Fund loans – take the form of asset transfers, and these loans are almost always repaid in full at interest.[38] Nonetheless, as evidenced by the political uproar surrounding IMF lending during the Mexican and Asian financial crises in the 1990s, IMF lending is perceived by the public to be an international transfer of domestic resources. Moreover, G-5 taxpayers do bear the ultimate risk of IMF lending, inasmuch as a default on a loan reduces available quota resources and may lead to pressures for new quota contributions by the IMF's member states. Thus, G-5 governments also have strong domestic incentives to reduce the number and size of IMF loans, and to impose more extensive conditionality when the Fund does provide liquidity.

36 Broz and Hawes (2006). 37 Bird (1996).
38 Broz (2005, 2002).

How do G-5 governments weigh these relative domestic costs and benefits of IMF lending? Building on an extensive body of research in political economy, I argue that G-5 officials make international economic policy decisions in response not only to the aggregate welfare concerns of voters but also to the pressures applied by organized interest groups with clear stakes in specific policies. This view of economic policymaking, in which governments seek to maximize a weighted function of "votes" (via policies aimed at improving aggregate welfare) and "campaign contributions" (via policies tailored to special interests), is best exemplified by the "endogenous protection" literature on the political economy of trade policy.[39] In this view, the domestic distributional effects of IMF programs on organized economic interests heavily influence G-5 governments' preferences over IMF loan size and conditionality. In other words, G-5 governments prefer certain IMF policies not just because they may enhance international financial stability but, primarily, because they serve their own domestic financial interests. This is not to say that G-5 governments disregard a country's importance for the stability of the global financial system. Rather, my claim is that these systemic concerns are secondary, in the eyes of G-5 governments, to the domestic political economy benefits of IMF lending.

Within the G-5 countries, the interest group that benefits most directly from IMF lending is the group of large, internationally active financial institutions – primarily "money center" commercial banks, but also including institutional investors such as mutual funds and pension funds – that are heavily invested in emerging market countries.[40] For these large banks, IMF lending provides a form of insurance against their international investments. Simply put, IMF programs provide "bailouts" for private lenders to emerging markets, thereby allowing international creditors to benefit from foreign lending without bearing the full risks involved: the banks reap significant profits if borrowers repay their debt and avoid losses when financial crises occur. This risk

[39] See Stigler (1971), Hillman (1982), Grossman and Helpman (1994), and Gawande and Krishna (2003).

[40] Broz and Hawes (2006); Broz (2005); Oatley and Yackee (2004). Other interest groups, such as large exporters of tradable goods, also benefit significantly from IMF lending, but these benefits are only indirect, inasmuch as Fund liquidity enhances international financial stability and facilitates greater international trade. I therefore focus here on the interest group that benefits most directly from IMF loans.

subsidy leads to the aforementioned problem of moral hazard: private creditors are able to increase their international lending and increase their profits without having to take into account the potential negative impact of this excessive lending on their profitability or solvency in the case of a major financial crisis. These direct and sizeable benefits from IMF lending give private creditors in the G-5 countries – in contrast to individual voters and taxpayers – strong incentives to organize and lobby their governments to support the provision of IMF "bailouts." Otherwise stated, domestic financial institutions in the G-5 countries view the moral hazard of IMF lending as a positive externality, whereas voters and taxpayers see it only as a negative cost.

G-5 preference intensity: the importance of commercial bank exposure

How do G-5 policymakers balance these competing incentives over the liquidity/moral hazard trade-off as they decide how to exercise their influence within the IMF's executive board? The answer, I argue, depends on the composition of a borrowing country's private external debt. More specifically, G-5 governments' preferences depend on the extent to which their domestic commercial banks are exposed to an IMF borrower country. Since international lenders to developing countries are overwhelmingly located within the G-5 countries, debt problems in emerging markets are of particular interest to the Fund's political principals; in particular, developing countries' financial crises can threaten the profitability or solvency of major G-5 private financial institutions. In the extreme (e.g. in the event of a major commercial bank failure), these negative spillover effects on individual G-5 financial institutions can trigger broader domestic financial instability within the major creditor countries.

For national politicians, commercial bank failures are more costly than the collapse of other types of financial institutions, for two reasons. First, commercial banks occupy a central role in the domestic political economy as both financial intermediaries and providers of domestic credit; therefore, a failure of one or more large commercial banks may seriously disrupt the payments system and trigger a systemic domestic financial crisis.[41] Second, commercial banks represent

[41] On the unique importance of commercial banks for systemic financial stability, see Crockett (1997).

a highly organized, well-financed political lobby with significant influence over economic policymaking. In contrast, bondholders, mutual funds, and investment banks – the institutions that underwrite bonds – occupy important but less central roles in the domestic financial system.[42] Because investment banks do not issue deposits and hold little or no actual debt on their books, they are less likely to be directly affected by a borrowing country default. Furthermore, the collapse of an investment bank or investment fund is less likely to have systemic effects on domestic financial stability than the failure of a large commercial bank. Similarly, while individual bondholders may suffer significant losses in the event of an emerging market default, they are far less equipped to organize and lobby the government for assistance. Indeed, as noted earlier, bondholders constitute a much larger group with far more heterogeneous interests than commercial banks. As predicted by collective action theory, these two factors – large numbers and heterogeneity of interests – make it significantly less likely that bondholders will organize and lobby G-5 governments on behalf of certain types of IMF lending policies.[43]

In short, because commercial banks occupy a more central economic and political role than other types of financial institutions, G-5 policymakers will most strongly favor IMF "bailouts" when an emerging market financial crisis threatens their profitability or solvency. Of course, G-5 governments may also support IMF bailouts when other types of large financial institutions are highly exposed to a particular country, since the failure or near-collapse of large non-bank institutions (e.g. Long-Term Capital Management in 1998, Lehman Brothers in 2008) can also have substantial negative effects on domestic financial stability. My claim is simply that commercial bank exposure to a developing country in crisis poses the greatest threat to G-5 domestic financial stability. *All else equal, I expect that G-5 governments will support larger IMF loans on more lenient terms when their commercial banks are highly exposed to a prospective borrower country.* In these situations, the economic and political benefits of providing IMF liquidity – specifically, preventing a large domestic bank failure resulting from an international financial crisis – will outweigh concerns about IMF-driven moral hazard and the opposition of domestic voters. Conversely, when domestic commercial banks are less exposed

[42] Oatley and Yackee (2004). [43] Olson (1971).

to a potential Fund borrower, G-5 policymakers will be more inclined to take into account the moral hazard costs of IMF lending and the political costs (in terms of voters' support) of providing "bailouts" for the domestic financial sector. In these cases, they will be less inclined to approve large-scale loans, and they will insist on the inclusion of more extensive conditionality when they do support the use of IMF resources.

Preference heterogeneity among G-5 governments

Thus, both individually and collectively, the intensity of G-5 governments' preferences over IMF loan size and conditionality will vary based on the total exposure of their commercial banks to a borrowing country. At the same time, however, individual G-5 governments may disagree with each other about the importance of IMF lending in a particular case. When a borrowing country's debt is distributed evenly among private creditors in each of the G-5 countries, their executive directors are more likely to agree on the relative costs and benefits of liquidity and moral hazard – and, therefore, to agree on the amount and terms of an IMF loan. In contrast, when G-5 exposure to a prospective borrower is more heterogeneous, summoning an executive board majority in support of a lending arrangement will be more difficult. G-5 policymakers whose domestic commercial banks are at risk will support larger IMF loans on more lenient terms, while G-5 executive directors from countries with few or no direct banking ties to the prospective borrower will be less inclined to support these "bailouts." In such cases, the IMF staff is likely to propose smaller loans on more stringent terms in order to maximize the likelihood of loan approval by the executive board. Thus, the size and terms of IMF loans should depend not only on the *intensity* of G-5 bank exposure but also on the *heterogeneity* of G-5 lending. *All else equal, greater heterogeneity of interests among the Fund's G-5 principals will lead to more serious concerns about moral hazard and the approval of smaller loans with more extensive conditionality.*

In addition, greater G-5 preference heterogeneity may also increase the scope for agency slack in IMF policymaking. By diluting the collective power of the G-5 as a voting bloc, disagreements between G-5 governments within the executive board may increase the autonomy of the IMF staff. In these situations, when G-5 governments disagree over the importance of the liquidity/moral hazard trade-off at the heart of IMF lending, their ability to act in a unified manner and exert control over Fund decision-making should decline. Consequently, the IMF staff should enjoy greater autonomy in such cases, and Fund lending decisions should more closely reflect its preferences.[44]

Which of these effects of G-5 preference heterogeneity – greater executive board conflict between the Fund's principals, or greater staff autonomy – will predominate in particular cases? I argue that the effects of G-5 preference heterogeneity are conditional on G-5 preference intensity; in other words, there is an interactive relationship between the two variables. When G-5 governments, as a group, have a strong interest in an IMF borrower (i.e. high intensity), greater preference heterogeneity should create conflict within the executive board over the liquidity/moral hazard trade-off, and IMF loans should strongly reflect these differences in the interests of the Fund's principals; in other words, they should be smaller and contain more extensive conditionality. In contrast, when G-5 governments collectively have a weak interest in a particular country, preference heterogeneity should create greater scope for the staff to act autonomously, and the influence of G-5 preferences should decline significantly. In the limit (i.e. in cases in which G-5 governments have no domestic financial interests), the IMF staff should exercise nearly total autonomy: executive board oversight and approval of the staff's lending proposals in these instances are likely to be no more than a "rubber stamp." Thus, if public choice scholars are correct in their claims that the Fund staff engages in bureaucratic rent-seeking by proposing larger loans with more extensive conditionality, such behavior should be most visible in these types of cases.

Global finance and IMF staff preferences

In focusing on the determinants of G-5 governments' preferences over Fund lending policies, the common agency framework improves upon existing political economy theories of IMF lending, which overemphasize US interests and overlook the importance of preference heterogeneity among the Fund's largest shareholders. Nevertheless,

[44] As discussed in the following section, changes in financial globalization are also a key determinant of these preferences.

this perspective also highlights the important role and substantial autonomy of the IMF staff in determining the size and terms of Fund lending arrangements. A complete theory of IMF decision-making must also account, therefore, for the sources of (and variation in) the preferences of the Fund staff in particular lending cases.

As with G-5 governments, the staff's preferences over loan size and conditionality also depend critically on variation in patterns of financial globalization. For the Fund staff, as with G-5 governments, the liquidity/moral hazard trade-off also entails a choice between potentially competing goals. On the one hand, the IMF staff has clear incentives to favor larger and more frequent IMF loans. As professional economists and international civil servants, IMF staff members seek to utilize Fund credit and conditionality "to enable countries to rebuild their international reserves, stabilize their currencies, continue paying for imports, and restore conditions for strong economic growth."[45] In short, the staff wants to use its primary policy tool – the conditional loan – for the economic benefit of borrowing countries and the accomplishment of the IMF's institutional goals. In addition, IMF staff members may also be susceptible to bureaucratic incentives to engage in "rent-seeking" behavior.[46] From this perspective, Fund staff members will design and propose larger IMF loans with more extensive conditionality (whether or not such programs are warranted by the borrower's economic situation) in order to maximize their power, autonomy, and budgets. Thus, IMF staff members have both economic and bureaucratic incentives to maximize the amount of financing and the number of conditions included in a Fund program.

On the other hand, like its executive board principals, the Fund staff also has incentives to limit both conditionality and the size of IMF loans. More extensive conditionality may actually be counterproductive to the Fund's policy goals, since a borrowing country may find the implementation of severe economic policy reform politically infeasible.[47] From an economic perspective, the Fund may therefore actually maximize its ability to help a borrower country by exercising restraint in its use of conditionality. Put simply, moderate policy

[45] IMF (2004). [46] Vaubel (1994, 1991); Willett (2000).

[47] See Vreeland (2003) for a detailed discussion of the role of domestic institutions and political opposition in shaping IMF borrowing countries' decisions to request IMF financing.

reforms that are implemented may be more successful in resolving a country's balance of payments problems than more extensive conditionality that a borrower government quickly disregards as economically unattainable or politically infeasible. In addition, extensive conditionality may send an undesired message to private international creditors: by signaling that a country's financial situation is extremely dire, it might lead investors to "cut and run," thereby exacerbating rather than alleviating the country's problems. For this reason, the IMF staff may choose to limit its use of conditionality in order to maximize the probability that private creditors continue lending.

Similarly, the IMF staff also has incentives to limit the size of the loans it proposes to the executive board. Large-scale IMF lending places a severe strain on Fund resources and may also create serious moral hazard. Moreover, such lending is at odds with the Fund's stated policy goal of "catalytic financing." As noted earlier, the purpose of non-concessional IMF lending is not to replace private capital flows; rather, Fund programs are intended to be a signal to private creditors of a borrowing country's future creditworthiness: "[B]ecause IMF lending signals that a country's economic policies are on the right track, it reassures investors and the official community and helps generate additional financing. Thus, IMF financing can act as a catalyst for attracting Funds from other sources."[48] For a Fund program to be deemed successful, it must therefore generate a subsequent inflow of private lending to a borrower country. In other words, the likelihood that private lenders will provide such "catalytic financing" is a key determinant of IMF staff preferences as they negotiate, design, and propose Fund loans.

Debt composition and the catalytic effect of IMF lending

The probability that IMF lending will successfully trigger a catalytic effect on capital inflows, I argue, is a function of the composition of a country's private external debt. In the 1980s, when the vast majority of international debt consisted of syndicated sovereign bank lending, generating this catalytic effect on private lending was fairly straightforward: the IMF managing director and teams of Fund staff members negotiated directly with the heads of major G-5 commercial

[48] See www.imf.org/external/pubs/ft/exrp/what.htm.

banks in order to secure new private lending commitments in tandem with the Fund's own lending programs.[49] To encourage the banks to provide this new lending, the IMF employed a combination of "carrots" and "sticks." The "carrots" consisted of a large Fund loan that would enable the borrowing country to avoid defaulting on its debt to the commercial banks, along with a set of macroeconomic policy reforms (conditionality) aimed at ensuring that the country could continue servicing its debts in the future. The primary "stick" was the IMF's firm pledge to withhold its own lending until the banks themselves committed to providing new credit and/or to rescheduling existing debts. In other words, the Fund would "bail out" the banks, but only on the condition that the banks themselves would "bail in."[50] As described in detail in chapter 4 below, this strategy of "concerted lending" became the IMF's standard recipe for dealing with financial crises in developing countries in the 1980s.

In the global financial system of the 1980s, in which a very small number of large commercial banks lent collectively through syndication to sovereign governments, IMF-led concerted lending was highly effective in both managing financial crises and generating catalytic financing. Since the 1980s, however, two major shifts in the composition of private international capital flows to developing countries have occurred, both of which have complicated the dynamics of catalytic financing. First, the number and composition of *international creditors* have changed, as bondholders have increasingly replaced commercial banks in global financial markets. Second, the composition of *international borrowers* has also evolved, as private firms have joined sovereign governments in search of foreign capital. Both these changes have had important implications for IMF lending. The shift from bank lending to bond financing has sharply increased the number of international lenders, from a few hundred large commercial banks to tens (and in some cases, hundreds) of thousands of heterogeneous bondholders. Furthermore, this shift has decreased creditors' ties to each other, since bond financing is not syndicated; rather, each bond constitutes a separate contract between a sovereign government (or firm) and an individual creditor who has purchased

[49] See chapter 4 below, as well as Boughton (2001), for a detailed discussion of this concerted lending process.

[50] Roubini and Setser (2004).

the bond independently of other investors. Argentina is an illustrative case. In the 1980s several hundred commercial banks lent collectively as a single syndicate to the Argentine government; this syndicated bank lending constituted over 90 percent of Argentina's private external debt. In 2001, when Argentina defaulted on $81 billion in international bond debt, its creditors numbered in the hundreds of thousands and held 152 different bonds issued over more than ten years, denominated in seven currencies, and governed by eight separate jurisdictions.[51]

Similarly, the shift from "private–public" flows (from private lenders to sovereign governments) to "private–private" lending (lending directly to developing countries' firms and financial institutions) has both sharply increased the number of international borrowers and further weakened the ties between international creditors, which no longer share interests by virtue of their ties to a common sovereign borrower.[52] Together, these changes in private international debt composition have significantly complicated the IMF's central policy goal of "catalyzing" private capital flows. Indeed, the shift from bank lending to bond financing, as well as the shift from sovereign borrowing, or "public and publicly guaranteed" debt, to "private non-guaranteed" (private–private) flows, has increased collective action problems among private international creditors and made it less likely that they will respond to an IMF loan with new lending of their own. At the same time, the shift from sovereign borrowing to private non-guaranteed debt has decreased the efficacy of IMF conditionality. In sovereign borrowing cases, the logic of conditionality remains intact: the Fund can provide a loan covering part of a government's payments deficit, while requiring it to undertake policy reforms aimed at closing the rest of the financing gap. In cases in which non-sovereign debt predominates, however, traditional macroeconomic

[51] "Argentina's restructuring guidelines," speech of the secretary of finance, Dr. Guillermo Nielsen, Dubai, United Arab Emirates, September 22, 2003 (www.argentinedebtinfo.gov.ar/documentos/discurso_gn_dubaI_con_diap_english.pdf).

[52] In cases of sovereign lending, whether in the form of bank lending or bonds, a single creditor – the borrowing government – is ultimately responsible for repayment of the debt. In non-sovereign lending, however, many banks and firms in developing countries each borrow independently and on different terms in global financial markets.

conditionality (e.g. balancing budgets, raising interest rates) is less effective. Even if the government undertakes these policy reforms, they will not necessarily solve the country's debt problems, which are driven primarily by private firms' behavior rather than government policy choices. In fact, more extensive conditionality may actually be counterproductive: IMF-driven macroeconomic austerity might transform private sector financial problems into a full-blown sovereign balance of payments crisis.

In sum, the core logic of IMF conditional lending since the 1980s – in which the IMF provides partial "bailouts" (i.e. modest loans with relatively few conditions) in exchange for commercial banks' upfront commitments to provide new syndicated loans to sovereign governments – no longer applies in many cases of contemporary international lending. Indeed, in a world in which international borrowing and lending no longer consists only of sovereign governments and a handful of major commercial banks, concerted lending is often no longer even feasible: the Fund cannot negotiate quickly and directly with tens of thousands of heterogeneous, disaggregated bondholders, nor can these creditors organize rapidly amongst themselves to agree on the provision of catalytic financing. Moreover, even in contemporary cases involving a limited number of commercial banks, the shift toward non-sovereign lending has further undermined the Fund's ability to secure catalytic financing pledges from private creditors before it makes its own lending commitments.

These new dilemmas arising from changes in the composition of international capital flows, I argue, factor heavily into the IMF staff's decision-making calculus as it designs and proposes Fund loans to the executive board. All else equal, I expect that the Fund staff will propose larger loans with more extensive conditionality to countries whose external debt consists of larger shares of bond financing and non-sovereign borrowing. The key reason for this, as I elaborate in the remainder of this chapter, is the increasing collective action costs among private international creditors that have decreased their ability and willingness to provide catalytic financing. Simply put, the IMF has been forced to change the characteristics of its loans in order to "move markets" and ensure that borrowing countries can access international capital in today's global financial system.

From banks to bonds: new lenders and catalytic financing

Just as G-5 governments face coordination problems in controlling IMF lending decisions based on differences in preference heterogeneity and intensity, private creditors also face collective action problems that may hinder their ability and willingness to cooperate in the provision of catalytic financing to IMF borrowing countries. Although private creditors as a group have a collective interest in making new loans to a Fund borrower to defend their existing claims and prevent a default, individual lenders have incentives to defect, leaving others to bear the costs of default and debt rescheduling.[53] This is a textbook case of the classic "prisoner's dilemma" game: individually rational behavior by each creditor leads to suboptimal outcomes for the group as a whole.

For a number of reasons, such coordination problems are more severe for bondholders than for commercial bank lenders.[54] First, commercial banks are few in number relative to bondholders, who are far more numerous and heterogeneous.[55] Second, as discussed earlier, the actors involved in commercial bank lending are easily identified and interact repeatedly through syndicated lending.[56] In addition, there is little turnover among the players in commercial bank lending: major internationally active money center banks in New York, London, and other large financial centers have long-standing ties to each other and particular borrowing countries. By contrast, large, heterogeneous groups of bondholders rarely have long-standing relationships with a particular borrowing country or with each other; rather, they frequently move their investments across borders in search of the highest rate of return. Finally, commercial banks have established a standing institution (the London Club) to facilitate the rescheduling of syndicated commercial bank loans.[57] In contrast, no such permanent framework is in place for the rescheduling of international bond debt. Although the absence of a clear forum for creditor cooperation does not preclude such interactions between bondholders, ad hoc cooperation is historically more difficult to achieve.[58] Consequently, rescheduling large amounts of

[53] Cline (1983). [54] Tomz (2001). [55] Spiegel (1996); White (2000).

[56] Lipson (1985); Smith and Walter (2003).

[57] On the London Club debt rescheduling process, see Rieffel (2003) and Uppal and van Hulle (1997).

[58] On the role of bondholder committees in the interwar and pre-WWI eras, see Eichengreen (1991). For a discussion of the potential effectiveness of standing

international bond debt is generally more difficult and time-consuming than organizing debt rescheduling among banks.[59]

As a result of these factors, international bondholders are generally less likely than commercial banks to provide catalytic financing in the days, months, and weeks following an IMF loan. In the absence of new private lending, a borrowing country's need for Fund credit in order to continue servicing its external debt becomes even more acute; without access to new private credit, IMF financing may be the only thing standing between a borrowing country and a costly default. As it designs and proposes loans to the executive board for approval, the Fund staff necessarily takes this possibility into account. Moreover, the staff recognizes that borrowing countries are unlikely to implement extensive conditionality in the absence of catalytic financing, as costly adjustment policies (e.g. raising interest rates, slashing budget deficits) are less likely to bring a reward of fresh financing from the markets. Thus, in cases involving international bonds, IMF financing plays a very different role from cases of commercial bank lending. Rather than credibly withholding its own credit while it negotiates "new money" commitments from banks, the Fund must now pledge its own financing *ex ante*, in the hopes of convincing a large group of heterogeneous bondholders to overcome their collective action problems and follow suit.[60] Large-scale IMF "bailouts," in other words, are a *precondition* for catalytic financing in cases of international bond lending, rather than a reward provided by the Fund in exchange for banks' upfront commitment to "bail in" by providing new money. Moreover, conditionality is more important in these new bond-oriented scenarios: more extensive economic policy reform is required as a clearer and stronger signal to heterogeneous and disaggregated bondholders of a country's future creditworthiness.

creditor committees in contemporary bond markets, see IMF (2000) and Eichengreen and Portes (1995). The difficulties faced by Argentina in rescheduling its defaulted bond debt from 2001 to 2005 illustrate the difficulty in reaching cooperative agreements between tens or hundreds of thousands of fragmented bondholders.

59 Rieffel (2003).

60 While private creditors often provide actual "new money" (fresh loans or bond purchases) in the aftermath of an IMF lending arrangement, this financing most often involves the write-down or rescheduling of existing debts. The "new" portion of the financing, in these situations, is therefore the reduction (in net present value terms) of the creditors' existing claims on the IMF borrower country.

In sum, the Fund staff's expectations about the availability of catalytic financing – as well as the types of policies necessary to secure it – are significantly different in cases of bond financing from those in cases of commercial bank lending. As a result, the characteristics of the lending programs they propose will also be very different. *All else equal, the Fund staff should design and propose larger loans with more extensive conditionality to countries whose external debt consists of larger shares of bond financing.* In addition, given the need for clearer *ex ante* signals to private creditors in a world of bond financing, this increased conditionality is more likely to be "front-loaded" in the form of prior actions, rather than imposed *ex post* in the form of performance criteria.

The decline of sovereign debt: new borrowers and catalytic financing

The shift from sovereign lending to non-sovereign external debt raises a similar set of problems for the IMF staff as it makes decisions about Fund loan size and conditionality. Even though the vast majority of non-sovereign lending to developing countries is provided by commercial banks, the lack of a common borrower creates similar dilemmas of creditor collective action to those arising in cases of bond financing. Indeed, just as sovereign bondholders own a wide array of different instruments of varying interest rates and maturities, non-sovereign lenders hold claims on a variety of private financial institutions and corporations. Moreover, most non-sovereign bank lending is short-term (i.e. with a maturity of less than one year), whereas syndicated sovereign bank lending is generally of longer maturity (i.e. one to five years).[61] As a result, non-sovereign bank lenders can more easily "cut and run" in times of financial crisis.[62]

To reiterate, the shift from sovereign lending to private–private international capital flows has resulted in three key changes that have further undermined the traditional logic of IMF catalytic lending: (1) the decline of commercial bank cooperation through

[61] In 2002 82.5 percent of private non-guaranteed external debt owed by developing countries was provided by commercial banks (World Bank 2003). To a large extent, then, the shift from PPG external debt to PNG debt is one from medium-term sovereign bank lending to short-term interbank financing.

[62] Lipworth and Nystedt (2001).

syndicated lending; (2) an abbreviation of banks' time horizons; and (3) a multiplication of the number of borrowers. Together, these changes present the IMF staff with a similar set of problems to those faced in bond crises: rather than credibly withholding its own credit while it negotiates catalytic financing from a bank syndicate with sovereign claims and long-term ties to a country, the Fund must now pledge its own financing *ex ante*, in the hopes of convincing a less unified group of banks (and in some cases, bondholders) to "roll over" their short-term claims on a wide variety of private borrowers, few of whom have long-standing relationships with their international creditors.

Consequently, as in cases of international bond lending, large-scale IMF loans are a precondition for catalytic financing when non-sovereign capital flows predominate. Moreover, as noted above, traditional IMF conditionality is also less effective in non-sovereign lending episodes, since governments' macroeconomic policies are generally not the root cause of private firms' financial difficulties. Rather, more extensive "structural" policy reforms (e.g. reforming banking regulation, privatizing state-owned industries) are likely to be necessary to resolve financial crises arising from private–private international borrowing. Therefore, as with the shift from bank lending to bond financing, the shift from sovereign to private borrowing in global financial markets has altered IMF staff preferences over the size and terms of Fund loans. *All else equal, the Fund staff should design and propose larger loans with more extensive conditionality to countries whose external debt consists of larger shares of non-sovereign debt.* As in cases involving bonds, this increased conditionality is also more likely to be "front-loaded," in the form of prior actions, rather than imposed *ex post* as performance criteria.

Ultimately, just as they shape the preferences of G-5 governments, changes in the composition of international capital flows also determine the IMF staff's preferences over the size and terms of Fund lending arrangements. In particular, shifts in the composition of international lenders (banks versus bondholders) and borrowers (sovereign governments versus private actors) alter the staff's expectations about the potential for IMF loans to have a catalytic effect on private capital flows. Given the Fund staff's substantial autonomy over the negotiation, design, and proposal of IMF programs, these preferences will also be a key determinant of variation in Fund lending outcomes.

Conclusions

In this chapter, I have developed a new analytical framework for understanding and explaining the political economy of IMF lending. Drawing on principal–agent theories of international institutions, I argue that IMF lending policies are determined jointly by the Fund's five largest shareholders (its de facto "collective principal") and the IMF's professional staff (the "agent"). Each of these actors exercises partial, but incomplete, control over Fund lending decisions. In turn, I argue that the preferences of both G-5 governments and the Fund staff vary systematically in accordance with changes in patterns of financial globalization. G-5 governments care about IMF lending largely for domestic political economy reasons. In particular, they will favor larger loans on more lenient terms when a borrowing country is of greater importance to their domestic banking system. As a result, IMF lending decisions will vary based on the intensity and heterogeneity of G-5 bank exposure to particular borrowing countries. At the same time, the Fund staff's concerns about catalytic financing – the likelihood that a loan will trigger subsequent private capital inflows – are also a key determinant of IMF lending decisions. Consequently, IMF loan size and conditionality will also vary based on the composition of a country's lenders (banks versus bondholders) and borrowers (sovereign governments versus private institutions).

In summary, this theoretical framework yields the following testable hypotheses.

- IMF loans will be larger and contain fewer conditions when aggregate G-5 commercial bank exposure is higher (*G-5 preference intensity*).
- IMF loans will be smaller and contain more conditions when G-5 commercial bank exposure is more unevenly distributed (*G-5 preference heterogeneity*).
- The relationship between the intensity and heterogeneity of G-5 commercial bank exposure is conditional and interactive (*common agency/agency slack*).
- IMF loans will be larger and contain more conditions when bond financing constitutes a larger share of a country's private external debt (*staff expectations about catalytic financing*).

- IMF loans will be larger and contain more conditions when non-sovereign borrowing constitutes a larger share of a country's private external debt (*staff expectations about catalytic financing*).
- The increased conditionality imposed in bond and non-sovereign financing cases is most likely to be in the form of prior actions (*staff expectations about catalytic financing*).

The first two hypotheses illustrate the expected relationship between the intensity and heterogeneity of G-5 governments' preferences and IMF lending decisions, while the third hypothesis tests the common agency framework's expectation that G-5 governments' influence over Fund lending (and, by extension, the IMF staff's autonomy) will be conditional on both the intensity and heterogeneity of their preferences in a particular borrower country. The final three hypotheses account for the IMF staff's concerns about the likelihood that Fund lending will have a catalytic effect on private capital inflows. In particular, they emphasize the need for larger IMF loans, with more extensive (and upfront) conditionality, in cases in which market actors are less willing to provide catalytic financing. Together, these hypotheses account for the principal–agent relationship at the heart of IMF policymaking, as well as the multiple ways that patterns of financial globalization influence Fund lending decisions. In the chapters that follow, I subject these hypotheses to a series of empirical tests, using both quantitative and qualitative analysis.

This common agency framework, along with the hypotheses and observable implications it provides, substantially improves our understanding of the political economy of IMF lending. In particular, it demonstrates that both states and international bureaucrats play important roles in determining the policy "outputs" of international organizations such as the IMF, and it emphasizes that we cannot explain the sources of these outputs – or the reasons for changes in them over time and across cases – without considering the interests and influence of both sets of actors. Therefore, in addition to explaining an important empirical puzzle about the IMF and global financial governance, this theoretical approach also enhances our broader understanding of international relations and policymaking within international organizations.

3 Global finance and the politics of IMF lending: evidence

In this chapter, I conduct a series of empirical tests of my argument that changes in patterns of financial globalization are the key determinant of IMF lending policies. Using time-series cross-sectional statistical methods, I analyze a new data set of 197 non-concessional IMF loans to forty-seven countries from 1984 to 2003. These countries are middle-income developing nations that typically borrow on private international markets but periodically and temporarily seek loans from the IMF when facing balance of payments problems. As noted earlier, the IMF also lends on a longer-term, concessional basis to extremely poor countries that rarely borrow on private markets. These loans differ notably from non-concessional Fund programs, however: they are intended to fund long-term development and structural adjustment rather than short-term payments imbalances; they are not linked to specific repayment timetables; they are fully financed from a trust fund entirely separate from the IMF's quota resources; and they are available only to a specified set of extremely poor countries. While many studies of IMF lending pool these two types of loans and countries, doing so is likely to result in biased predictions about the Fund's non-concessional lending behavior.[1]

The original data set analyzed in this chapter has been assembled from official Fund documents available at the IMF archives in Washington, DC. For each loan, data on loan size and conditionality are taken from several categories of documents: the "letter of intent" declaring the borrower country's intent to enter into a Fund program, the attached "memorandum of economic policies" specifying the policy reforms and conditionality a country will implement during the

[1] Previous studies have generally included samples of both short-term and long-term (concessional) IMF loans (e.g. Dreher and Jensen 2007; Gould 2006, 2003). Oatley and Yackee (2004) and Broz and Hawes (2006) are notable exceptions.

course of the IMF loan, and the "staff report" to the executive board that outlines the draft program and provides further details on conditionality. For most IMF loans since 1997, letters of intent and memoranda of economic policies are also available through the IMF's website. Each observation in the data set is a unique country-year loan. The data set is therefore "unbalanced," in the sense that not all country-years are present in the sample.[2] For each of these observations, I code both the size of the loan and the number of conditions it includes.[3]

Dependent variables

Loan size

In the statistical analysis, the first dependent variable is loan size, measured as a share of a country's IMF quota. This variable (*AMTQTA*) is the total amount of new non-concessional IMF lending approved for country *i* in year *t*, divided by the country's Fund quota.[4] *AMTQTA* enters the regressions as a natural log, to control for outlier observations and to ensure that the data correspond as closely as possible to the linear regression model's assumption of a normally distributed dependent variable. Summary statistics for *AMTQTA* and all other variables described below are presented in table 3.1. As a robustness check, I also test two alternative measures of loan size: the loan amount relative to GDP (*AMTGDP*) and the absolute loan size in millions of SDRs (*AMTSDR*).[5] I focus on *AMTQTA* as the primary dependent variable, however, for two reasons: access to non-concessional IMF credit is

[2] The full data set of all country-years for these countries, as well as eligible countries (i.e. the remaining countries not eligible for concessional IMF loans) that did not borrow from the IMF during the 1984–2003 period, consists of 892 observations and fifty-five countries. This larger sample is used in the propensity-score-matching estimation, described below, to control for possible selection effects. Missing data on some independent variables reduces the actual sample to 177 loans for forty-three countries.

[3] See appendix 1 for a complete list of the IMF loans included in the data set, as well as summary information on their characteristics (loan size, conditionality, date, length).

[4] Disbursements of credit from loans approved in prior years are not included in *AMTQTA*.

[5] As with *AMTQTA*, each of these alternatives enters as a natural log.

explicitly linked to country quotas rather than GDP, and absolute loan size is almost perfectly correlated (0.87) with country size (log of GDP). In short, since larger countries almost always receive larger IMF loans in dollar or SDR terms, measuring sizes in relation to quotas provides a more accurate measure of an "oversized" loan.

Conditionality

To measure variation in the level of IMF conditionality, I count the number of conditions included in a Fund program. This strategy follows in the tradition of most recent quantitative analyses of IMF conditionality.[6] Although the number of conditions is, admittedly, a fairly rough proxy of the level of conditionality, it does provide an overall picture of the stringency of the terms of an IMF loan. A larger number of conditions indicates a more extensive commitment by a borrowing country to significant economic reform during the lifetime of the loan, and it indicates the Fund's greater concern about the potential moral hazard effects of lending to countries requiring significant reform in order to achieve long-term debt sustainability. While data on the specific content of conditionality are available in the IMF archival documents, it is extremely difficult to compare the relative stringency of individual conditions (such as current account balance targets or foreign exchange reserve requirements) between loans, given the vastly different macroeconomic and external debt characteristics of IMF borrowers. In contrast, the number of conditions is a more readily comparable metric across IMF lending cases.

When counting the number of conditions, I focus on the number specified at the initial stage of a loan's approval. Although the IMF staff and executive board review conditionality prior to each stage of a program, they hardly ever alter the number of conditions from stage to stage, even if they modify the specific quantitative targets and policies specified in these conditions. For example, if the initial program includes performance criteria governing central bank reserves and the overall government budget balance, these criteria customarily remain throughout the lifespan of the loan, even if the specific numerical targets are adjusted over time. Thus, the basic parameters of conditionality are established when the Fund first approves a loan, rather than at later stages. Moreover,

[6] Gould (2006, 2003); Dreher and Jensen (2007).

since the number of conditions rarely varies from stage to stage of a Fund program, counting each stage as a separate "case" would overweight the influence of longer loans in the IMF lending data set without actually multiplying the number of relevant observations.[7]

Based on these parameters, I create four dependent variables for the conditionality models. The first variable, *TC*, measures the total number of conditions, including the two "hard" forms of conditionality (prior actions, performance criteria), as well as the less stringent types of conditionality (e.g. structural benchmarks, indicative targets) discussed earlier. The second variable, *PC*, is the number of performance criteria included in the IMF program. PCs, as noted above, are the most "binding" form of conditionality, as the disbursement of IMF credit is explicitly linked to their implementation. The third variable, *PA*, is a count of the number of prior actions included in the program. Like PCs, prior actions are "hard" conditions, in that their implementation is mandatory in order for the borrower to receive IMF credit. Unlike performance criteria, however, PAs are preconditions: they have to be implemented before the first tranche of an IMF loan is disbursed. As such, they constitute a firmer upfront commitment by the borrower. Furthermore, prior actions also provide a clearer *ex ante* signal to international creditors that a country intends to implement Fund-mandated economic policy reforms. The final variable, benchmarks/targets (*BT*), counts the number of "soft" conditions included in an IMF loan, including quantitative benchmarks, indicative targets, and structural benchmarks.

Testing these four variables independently is important, since it allows us to assess whether the key explanatory variables outlined below have different effects on different types of conditionality. The data utilized in coding these measures of conditionality are taken from the aforementioned policy documents collected and analyzed at the IMF archives; specifically, the IMF staff report and the letter of intent/memorandum of economic policy associated with each Fund loan in the data set include detailed tables and discussions of the conditionality included in each lending arrangement. Table 3.1 provides summary statistics for each of these dependent variables, as well summary data for the independent variables described below.

[7] For example, a thirty-six-month extended arrangement containing six reviews would count as seven cases (each with an identical number of conditions), while a twelve-month stand-by arrangement with a single program review would count as only two cases.

Table 3.1 *Summary statistics, IMF lending data set*

Variable	Number of observations	Mean	Standard deviation	Minimum	Maximum
Amount/quota (not logged)	197	1.21	2.11	0.15	19.38
Amount/GDP (not logged)	197	1.40	2.27	0.20	14.81
Amount (SDR millions)	197	1,222.78	3,218.43	7.10	22,821.12
Total conditions	190	13.40	10.40	0	58
Performance criteria	192	6.40	2.45	0	16
Prior actions	191	2.84	5.64	0	37
Benchmarks/targets	190	4.17	5.80	0	27
G-5 bank exposure ($ billions)	902	8.79	14.04	0.00	78.05
Coefficient of variation, G-5 bank exposure	902	116.13	46.29	0.00	223.61
US share, G-5 bank exposure	902	0.28	0.23	0.00	1.00
UK share, G-5 bank exposure	902	0.11	0.14	0.00	1.00
Japanese share, G-5 bank exposure	902	0.14	0.19	0.00	0.94
German share, G-5 bank exposure	902	0.23	0.24	0.00	1.00
French share, G-5 bank exposure	902	0.19	0.22	0.00	1.00
Percent bond debt	902	22.73	27.84	0.00	95.63
Percent private non-guaranteed debt	902	23.38	24.90	0.00	100.00
Extended Fund Facility	197	0.17	0.37	0	1
GDP (log)	902	10.05	1.62	5.68	14.05
GDP per capita (log)	902	8.61	0.44	6.83	9.71
GDP growth (%)	902	3.12	5.57	–42.45	38.20

Table 3.1 *(cont.)*

Variable	Number of observations	Mean	Standard deviation	Minimum	Maximum
Current account/GDP (%)	902	−2.20	6.72	−56.20	25.60
External debt/GDP (%)	902	50.94	29.77	0.65	231.33
Short-term debt/reserves (log)	902	−0.68	1.33	−4.61	5.03
Currency crash	902	0.12	0.32	0	1
Veto players (log)	902	0.89	0.63	0.00	2.08
G-5 UN voting affinity (mean "S" score)	902	1.32	0.21	0.90	2
Standard deviation, G-5 "S" scores	902	0.32	0.07	0.00	0.56
Propensity score	181	0.33	0.17	0.04	0.81
IMF liquidity ratio	902	0.31	0.07	0.20	0.46
IMF quota review	902	0.60	0.49	0	1
Number of currency crises globally	902	6.15	2.84	1	12
LIBOR	902	5.94	2.16	1.73	10.75

Independent variables

In order to test my hypotheses about the relationship between private international capital flows, the interests of G-5 governments and the IMF staff, and Fund loan characteristics, I include several measures of borrowing countries' private external debt composition. These variables serve as proxies for the domestic financial interests of the G-5 countries and for IMF staff concerns about the availability of catalytic financing. These explanatory variables are taken or derived from publicly available data gathered from the World Bank's *Global Development Finance* database and the BIS's consolidated international banking statistics. I also include a battery of additional explanatory variables to control for other economic and political factors identified in the literature as potential determinants of IMF lending policies.

G-5 domestic financial interests: the intensity and heterogeneity of bank exposure

As a proxy for G-5 governments' domestic financial interests, I follow the existing literature in utilizing commercial bank exposure data. Although other economic links between G-5 countries and IMF borrowers are also important (e.g. bond/equity financing, foreign direct investment, trade), these flows are highly correlated with bank lending in most cases. Moreover, banks and other institutional investors stand to benefit most directly from IMF lending, since Fund credit is frequently transferred immediately from the borrower to private creditors in the form of debt service payments. Finally, as discussed above in the previous chapter, banks occupy a role of unique economic and political importance in the eyes of G-5 government officials. Bank exposure therefore provides a strong measure of a country's overall financial importance to the G-5. Data on bank exposure are taken from the BIS's consolidated international banking statistics, which provide annual data on the total foreign claims by commercial banks in twenty-three countries (including the G-5).

Utilizing these BIS data, I calculate two variables. The first, *G5BANK*, measures total, or aggregate, commercial bank lending by all banks located in the G-5 countries to an IMF borrower country. This variable serves as a proxy for the collective *intensity* of G-5 governments' domestic financial interests in a particular IMF lending case. *G5BANK* is the natural log of total G-5 commercial bank exposure to country i in year t, in billions of dollars.[8] It is intended to measure the importance assigned by the Fund's largest shareholders, as members of the IMF's de facto collective principal, to the prospective borrowing country. Otherwise stated, this variable measures the extent to which the G-5 countries are willing to tolerate the increased moral hazard resulting from a "bailout" (i.e. a larger IMF loan on more lenient terms), in exchange for safeguarding the profitability

8 Since the minimum non-zero value of G-5 bank exposure is \$0.001 billion, I add 0.0009 to the zero values to calculate the natural log. The results are not sensitive to the use of alternative constant values.

and stability of their domestic banking sectors. All else equal, I expect larger values of *G5BANK* to be associated with larger IMF loans and fewer conditions.

The second variable measures the *heterogeneity* of G-5 financial interests in a particular case. Using the individual BIS data for each G-5 country, I calculate the coefficient of variation of bank exposure (*COVG5BANK*). The coefficient of variation, which is the ratio of the standard deviation to the mean, expressed as a percentage, measures the relative dispersion of G-5 bank exposure to a particular IMF borrower. Higher values indicate a more uneven, or heterogeneous, distribution of bank exposure between the G-5 countries. This heterogeneity, in turn, serves as a proxy for the expected degree of conflict among the G-5 countries over the appropriate size and conditionality of non-concessional IMF loans. All else equal, I expect larger values of *COVG5BANK* to be associated with smaller IMF loans and more extensive conditionality, as G-5 governments disagree over the merits of providing "bailouts" in such cases. I also test the interaction between *G5BANK* and *COVG5BANK* by including a multiplicative interaction term (*G5BANK* × *COVG5BANK*) in several of the models detailed below.

While *G5BANK* and *COVG5BANK* measure the aggregate intensity and heterogeneity of G-5 domestic financial interests in a particular IMF borrower country, they do not tell us which G-5 country has the most at stake in a given lending case. Consequently, I also calculate a third set of variables: the share of total G-5 commercial bank lending provided by banks in each individual G-5 country. These five variables (*USSHARE*, *UKSHARE*, *GRSHARE*, *FRSHARE*, *JPSHARE*) measure the extent to which each G-5 government (the United States, the United Kingdom, Germany, France, and Japan) has strong domestic financial interests in supporting IMF lending in a particular case. All else equal, I expect that each of these variables will be associated with larger IMF loans and less extensive conditionality, although I also expect that US influence will be stronger than that of the other G-5 countries, given the United States' pre-eminent position within the Fund.

Staff expectations about catalytic financing: bond and private non-guaranteed debt

In addition to including variables measuring the G-5 countries' interests in IMF lending, I also include two variables as proxies for the IMF staff's concerns about the probability of catalytic financing. The first, *PCTBOND*, is the percentage of a borrower country's total private external debt owed to bondholders rather than commercial banks.[9] The second variable, *PCTPNG*, is the country's share of total private external debt that is "private non-guaranteed debt" rather than sovereign, or "public and publicly guaranteed," debt.[10] Data for these variables are taken from the World Bank's *Global Development Finance* database. All else equal, I expect larger values of both *PCTBOND* and *PCTPNG* to be associated with larger IMF loans and more extensive conditionality. To reiterate, the logic is that private creditors' collective action problems become more severe – and, consequently, the likelihood of catalytic financing declines – in cases in which an IMF borrower country's external debt is owed to bondholders and non-syndicated interbank lenders. In these cases, larger IMF loans and more extensive conditionality should be required as a signal to private markets and a trigger for new private capital inflows. Moreover, as noted above, this increased conditionality is more likely to be "front-loaded" in the form of prior actions, since these *ex ante* conditions provide a stronger signal to private markets (compared to *ex post* conditionality) of a country's intention to implement the economic policy reforms necessary to ensure its long-term solvency and stability.

Control variables

In addition to testing my argument that variation in the composition of private international capital flows influences IMF lending, I include an extensive battery of additional controls for the alternative economic and political explanations of IMF lending identified in the existing literature. The first set of variables controls for both relevant characteristics of IMF programs and a borrower's past history with the Fund. These include a dummy variable (*PASTLOAN*) if a country is already under an IMF program at the time of the new loan, as well as a dummy if a loan is an Extended Fund Facility (*EFF*) arrangement. Although tests

[9] World Bank (2006b) *PCTBOND* is calculated as follows: 100 × (public and publicly guaranteed bond debt + private non-guaranteed bond debt)/(total public and publicly guaranteed debt owed to private creditors + total private non-guaranteed debt).

[10] World Bank (2006b). *PCTPNG* is calculated as follows: 100 × (total private non-guaranteed debt)/(total private non-guaranteed debt + total public and publicly guaranteed debt owed to private creditors).

indicate that serial correlation is not a problem in the loan size models, *PASTLOAN* acts as a modified lagged dependent variable controlling for a country's prior experience with the IMF.[11] In the conditionality regressions, as well as in the binary logit model employed in the propensity-score-matching exercise discussed below, I model temporal dependence by replacing *PASTLOAN* with an alternative variable (*LASTLOAN*) that measures the number of years since a country last borrowed from the Fund. In addition, I include three cubic splines that further model temporal dependence in event count and binary models.[12] The dummy for loans under the EFF controls for the fact that these programs are intended for countries with more severe balance of payments problems and are generally of longer duration than stand-by arrangements. Consequently, they are likely to be larger in per quota terms and contain more extensive conditionality.

The second set of control variables includes a variety of country-specific macroeconomic factors consistently identified in the existing literature as the key "technocratic" criteria utilized by the IMF staff in designing Fund programs.[13] These variables include: the borrower country's external debt to GDP ratio (*DEBTGDP*); the log of GDP in millions of current dollars (*GDP*); the log of GDP per capita (*GDPPC*); the GDP growth rate (*GROWTH*); the current account as a percentage of GDP (*CURRGDP*); and the logged ratio of short-term debt to reserves (*STDRES*).[14] I also include a dummy variable, *CRASH*, which takes a value of 1 if a country experienced a sharp depreciation, or "currency crash," in the year prior to the IMF loan. This variable follows the widely used definition of Frankel and Rose in defining a currency crash as a nominal depreciation of the currency of at least 25 per cent that is also at least a 10 per cent increase over the previous year's depreciation rate.[15]

The third group of control variables includes proxies for a number of domestic and international political factors identified in the literature

[11] In the models discussed below, substituting the actual amount of outstanding credit or credit relative to a country's quota as alternative controls for temporal dependence does not alter the substantive results.

[12] See Beck, Katz, and Tucker (1998) for a detailed discussion of the treatment of temporal dependence in non-linear models.

[13] Knight and Santaella (1997); Bird and Rowlands (2003); Joyce (2004).

[14] Data are from the World Bank's *World Development Indicators* and *Global Development Finance* and from the Economist Intelligence Unit's *Country Data* reports.

[15] Frankel and Rose (1996).

as important determinants of IMF lending. Following Vreeland, I include the natural log of the number of veto players in a borrower country (*CHECKS*), as a control for the impact of a borrowing country's domestic political institutions on IMF lending.[16] Vreeland finds this variable to be a key determinant not just of a country's decision to seek IMF financing but also of the Fund's decision to lend. Thus, there is good reason to believe that veto players also influence the characteristics of IMF loans.

I also include several variables as proxies for a borrowing country's geopolitical or foreign policy importance to the Fund's largest shareholder countries. Past studies have found robust evidence that countries with close foreign policy ties to the United States receive more favorable treatment from the IMF.[17] These studies commonly utilize measures of United Nations General Assembly voting affinity (i.e. the similarity in voting between the borrower country and the United States in a given year) as a proxy for foreign policy ties and/or a country's geopolitical importance to the United States government. Following this work, I utilize UN voting affinity data available through the "Affinity of nations" data set.[18] Drawing on roll call votes in the UNGA Gartzke calculates "S scores" that measure "the similarity between two [countries' UN] voting profiles as the length of a line between two points in a multidimensional issue space."[19]

Whether these "S" scores accurately capture similarities in foreign policies between countries – let alone indicate a borrower's geopolitical importance to the IMF's largest shareholders – is open to debate. Indeed, some countries of clear strategic importance to the US and other G-5 governments, such as Russia and Turkey, do not score highly on the UN affinity measure. Although I share these concerns about the suitability of this metric as a proxy for states' geopolitical interests, I nevertheless include it in the analysis as a control variable

[16] Vreeland (2005, 2003). The variable is logged to account for the possibility of diminishing returns to additional veto players. The data are taken from the World Bank's "Database of political institutions" (Beck *et al.* 2001).

[17] Vreeland (2005); Stone (2004); Barro and Lee (2002); Thacker (1999).

[18] Gartzke (2006).

[19] Stone (2004, 580). The specific variable is S2UN, which ranges from –1 to 1 and is coded based on a yes/abstain/no voting record (Gartzke 2006). To avoid complications arising from the inclusion of negative values when calculating the standard deviations discussed below (*SDS*), I rescale S2UN from 0 to 2.

in order to test past IMF scholars' arguments directly. In contrast to existing work, however, I use the mean "S" score (*G5S*) of the G-5 countries rather than the United States' score, since the United States is not the only large shareholder with strong influence within the IMF executive board.[20] In addition, I include the standard deviation of G-5 "S" scores (*SDS*) as a measure of the heterogeneity of geopolitical/foreign policy interests among the Fund's principals. Like the coefficient of variation of G-5 bank exposure (*COVG5BANK*), this variable is intended to capture the extent to which G-5 governments disagree about the importance of a particular IMF borrower country.[21] I also include the interaction between these variables (*G5S* X *SDS*), since there is good reason to believe that a conditional, interactive relationship between G-5 preference intensity and heterogeneity also exists when focusing on geopolitical rather than financial interests.

As an additional set of political controls, I include variables identified by public choice scholars as key determinants of the IMF staff's bureaucratic incentives. As noted earlier, such scholars argue that the IMF staff has strong organizational incentives to increase loan size and conditionality in order to maximize its budget, autonomy, and/or IMF program success.[22] Past studies in this vein have found that these bureaucratic incentives are particularly strong when the Fund has more resources to spare, and when the IMF's member states are reviewing the Fund's quotas and considering whether to increase the size of its "war chest." As a test of this logic, I include two variables. The first, *LIQRATIO*, is the IMF's "liquidity ratio," or the ratio of outstanding IMF loans and administrative expenses to total Fund quotas. This variable is generated by dividing the sum of the IMF's outstanding loans and used administrative resources by the Fund's total quota resources, then subtracting this value from one.[23] The expectation of the public choice logic is that the Fund's liquidity ratio will be positively associated with both loan size and conditionality.

[20] The individual G-5 "S" scores are extremely collinear; correlations between the five variables range from 0.75 to 0.94 in the IMF lending data set utilized in this chapter. Utilizing weighted averages of "S" scores (rather than the simple mean), based on the relative voting power of the G-5 countries within the executive board, yields substantively identical results.

[21] The standard deviation is used here, rather than the coefficient of variation, because the "S" scores are already normalized between –1 and 1.

[22] Vaubel (1994, 1991).

[23] Dreher and Vaubel (2004a).

The second variable, *REVIEW*, is a dummy indicating years in which a quota review was under way. *REVIEW* tests the aforementioned "hurry up" lending hypothesis. According to this argument, the Fund staff will propose larger loans during quota reviews in order to exhaust the Fund's available resources and generate pressure on the executive board to approve new quota increases.[24]

Finally, I include dummy variables for each borrowing country's geographic region, as well as the propensity score (*PSCORE*), which controls for the possibility of non-random selection into IMF programs.[25] In addition, I include two variables to capture the effects of broader global macroeconomic trends on IMF lending decisions. The first variable, *CRISES*, is the lagged count of the number of currency crashes in the forty-seven-country sample in a given year.[26] It serves as a proxy for the level of global financial instability at the time when a country seeks IMF financing. The logic here is that concerns about financial contagion stemming from previous or ongoing crises in global markets might influence the Fund's current lending decisions. The second variable, *LIBOR*, is the three-month London Interbank Offer Rate – the interest rate that banks charge each other on interbank loans, which serves as the primary benchmark on private international capital markets. Since higher interest rates may increase a country's external debt service and its new borrowing costs, IMF loan characteristics are likely to be influenced by fluctuations in LIBOR. The data are taken from the IMF's *International Financial Statistics* and Dreher and Vaubel (2004a).

Preliminary evidence

Although the multivariate statistical analysis presented below provides a more rigorous test of my argument and its hypotheses, tables 3.2 and 3.3 conduct a preliminary assessment of the connection between changes in the composition of international capital flows

[24] Both *LIQRATIO* and *REVIEW* are taken from Dreher and Vaubel (2004b).

[25] I discuss selection effects and the propensity score further below (p. 86). These geographic variables are based on the World Bank's regional classifications. The five dummy variables are: Americas (North/South America/Caribbean), central Asia/Europe, Middle East/north Africa, east/south Asia, and sub-Saharan Africa.

[26] Frankel and Rose (1996).

Table 3.2 *Average IMF loan characteristics by G-5 commercial bank exposure, 1984–2003*

G-5 preference heterogeneity Coefficient of variation, G-5 bank exposure (standard deviation/mean)	*G-5 preference intensity* Aggregate G-5 bank exposure ($ billions)	
	Low	**High**
Low	• Amount/quota: 0.8 • Amount (SDR millions): 282.1 • PCs: 6.4 • PAs: 2.5 • (TCs): 12.1 • N = 70	• Amount/quota: 3.6 • Amount (SDR millions): 5,127.3 • PCs: 6.8 • PAs: 1.1 • TCs: 12.2 • N = 35
High	• Amount/quota: 0.6 • Amount (SDR millions): 201.2 • PCs: 6.3 • PAs: 3.9 • TCs: 15.3 • N = 80	• Amount/quota: 1.2 • Amount (SDR millions): 2,132.9 • PCs: 6.1 • PAs: 3.2 • TCs: 11.9 • N = 12

Notes: Based on 197 non-concessional IMF loans to forty-seven countries. Observations were classified as "high" or "low" along each dimension based on whether the observed values are above or below the sample mean.

and IMF lending policies. Table 3.2 presents a simple cross-tabulation of IMF loan size and conditionality by G-5 bank exposure intensity (*G5BANK*) and heterogeneity (*COVG5BANK*), while table 3.3 presents the cross-tabulation results of loan size and conditionality by levels of bond (*PCTBOND*) and private non-guaranteed debt (*PCTPNG*). Several patterns in the data are clearly evident from these charts. First, for a given level of G-5 preference heterogeneity, IMF loans markedly increase in size as G-5 preference intensity increases

Table 3.3 *Average IMF loan characteristics by composition of private borrowers and lenders, 1984–2003*

Borrowers Percent PNG debt	*Lenders* Percent bond debt	
	Low (Primarily banks)	High (Primarily bondholders)
High (primarily non-sovereign)	• Amount/quota: 0.9 • Amount (SDR millions): 794.2 • PCs: 7.3 • PA: 1.8 • TCs: 15.3 • N = 32	• Amount/quota: 2.9 • Amount (SDR millions): 3,939.0 • PCs: 6.6 • PAs: 4.5 • TCs: 18.1 • N = 39
Low (primarily sovereign)	• Amount/quota: 0.7 • Amount (SDR millions): 513.4 • PCs: 6.0 • PAs: 2.0 • TCs: 9.7 • N = 87	• Amount/quota: 0.9 • Amount (SDR millions): 440.8 • PCs: 6.5 • PAs: 3.9 • TCs: 15.5 • N = 39

Note: See notes to table 3.2.

(i.e. moving from the left-hand column to the right-hand one in table 3.2); this result holds for both absolute loan size and loan amount relative to a country's quota in the Fund. Second, for a given level of G-5 preference intensity, IMF loans are notably smaller in size as G-5 bank exposure heterogeneity increases (i.e. moving from the top row to the bottom one in table 3.2). Thus, at least when focusing on loan size, the basic parameters of my argument hold: IMF loans are larger when the Fund's largest shareholders, as a group, have strong domestic financial interests in a borrowing country and smaller when these countries' interests diverge.

The relationship between G-5 bank exposure and conditionality is less clear, although table 3.2 does provide some evidence of a link between G-5 domestic financial interests and the number and type of conditions included in IMF loans. On the one hand, the average number of performance criteria varies little between the four cells of the table, and the only notable difference in total conditions exists in cases in which G-5 interests are weak and divided. In these cases (lower left cell), the IMF imposes substantially more total conditions (15.3), on average. On the other hand, it does appear that higher levels of aggregate G-5 bank exposure are associated with fewer prior actions (right column), and this trend is particularly noticeable in cases in which G-5 preferences are more homogeneous (top right cell). In contrast, the IMF appears to impose the most prior actions on its loans in cases in which G-5 preferences are weak and divided (lower left cell). Thus, table 3.2 offers initial evidence that the intensity and heterogeneity of G-5 governments' domestic financial interests also play an important role in shaping IMF lending policies.

Table 3.3 provides preliminary evidence that IMF lending policies have also shifted in response to changes in the Fund staff's expectations about the availability of catalytic financing, as measured by variation in the composition of borrowers and lenders in international capital markets. Two patterns in particular are most evident from the chart. First, IMF loans, on average, are smallest and contain the fewest conditions in cases of syndicated commercial bank lending to sovereign governments (lower left cell). This finding reinforces the idea that catalytic financing is a key concern of the IMF as it designs lending programs. Since private creditors' collective action problems are least severe in these cases of 1980s-style sovereign bank lending, relatively small loans with modest conditionality are sufficient to generate a catalytic effect on private capital flows. Second, table 3.3 suggests that changes in the composition of both borrowers and lenders in private international capital markets have been a key determinant of variation in IMF lending policies over the last two decades. Indeed, IMF loan size and conditionality have increased as a result of both the shift to non-sovereign borrowing (i.e. moving from the lower row to the upper one in the table 3.2) and the shift from bank lending to bond financing (i.e. moving from the left-hand column to the right-hand one). As expected, these trends are particularly pronounced with respect to the IMF's use of prior actions, since these *ex ante* conditions are most likely to trigger catalytic private capital inflows. In addition, the increases in both loan size and conditionality are most visible in cases in which both types of debt composition changes have occurred (the top right cell) – that is, when both borrowers and lenders have become more numerous and heterogeneous as a result of a "double shift" from public to private borrowing and from bank lending to bond financing. In these cases, as discussed above, private creditor collective action problems are likely to be most severe, and IMF staff concerns about the availability of catalytic financing will be strongest.

Multivariate analysis

While these cross-tabulations provide initial evidence in support of my argument, multivariate analysis offers a more rigorous test of the connection between patterns of financial globalization, the preferences of G-5 governments and the IMF staff, and Fund loan characteristics. In the remainder of this chapter, I present the structure and results of this analysis, which provide further support for the common agency theory of IMF lending and its empirical predictions.

Model selection

Because time-series cross-sectional (TSCS) data often exhibit properties (heteroskedasticity, serial autocorrelation, panel heterogeneity, and spatially correlated errors) incompatible with the assumptions of standard ordinary least squares (OLS) regression, it is necessary to test for and model these conditions when estimating such models.[27] Inspection of the data suggests that heteroskedasticity (unequal variance of the error terms between units) and both serial and spatial autocorrelation (correlation of the error terms both over time within units and contemporaneously between units) are evident in the IMF lending data set. To account for these violations of the standard OLS model in the loan size regressions, I specify a model with panel-corrected standard errors and include the aforementioned variant of the lagged dependent variable, *PASTLOAN*.[28] Although there is an ongoing debate about

[27] Beck (2004).

[28] Beck and Katz (1995); Beck (2001). Stata's *xtserial* test for TSCS regressions indicates that including *PASTLOAN* resolves the serial correlation problems in the data. The F-test for first-order autocorrelation in the loan size regressions (model 3, table 3.4) generates a value of 0.36 (Pr > F = 0.58).

the appropriateness of the "Beck and Katz solution" for analyzing TSCS models, there is a strong case for choosing this specification in the present case.[29] In particular, past studies provide substantial empirical evidence that the previous use of IMF credit influences Fund decision-making.[30]

For the conditionality regressions, which involve discrete counts of the number of conditions included in an IMF loan, linear regression is not appropriate. Therefore, I utilize a series of event count models for panel data.[31] For the performance criteria regressions, the specification is a Poisson model with robust standard errors. For the other types of conditionality, the Poisson model is not appropriate, given the overdispersion of these dependent variables.[32] For these models, I specify a negative binomial regression model with robust standard errors.[33] Each of these models includes the controls for temporal dependence (three cubic splines and *LASTLOAN*) described above to account for the possibility of serial correlation in the data.

In both the loan size and conditionality regressions, each of the models is estimated without country-specific or yearly fixed effects. I adopt this strategy for several reasons. First, Hausman tests for fixed effects are statistically insignificant, suggesting that this model is not appropriate for the current analysis.[34] Thus, the primary reason for including country-specific fixed effects – the existence of unobserved panel heterogeneity (i.e. the fact that countries differ in ways not explained by the observed independent variables) – does not appear to be a major problem in my data set. Second, including country-specific

[29] Wilson and Butler (2007). [30] Joyce (2004); Conway (2005).

[31] Long and Freese (2001).

[32] A central assumption of the Poisson model is that the variance equals the mean. This is a reasonable assumption for performance criteria (mean = 6.38, variance = 6.01), but not for total conditions (mean = 12.97, variance = 109.53), prior actions (mean = 2.81, variance = 5.62), or benchmarks/targets (mean = 4.13, variance = 5.79).

[33] See http://data.princeton.edu/wws509/stata/overdispersion.html for an overview of methods for dealing with overdispersion in count models. The results of the negative binomial models are substantively identical when using an alternative event count specification for overdispersion, the generalized linear model (GLM).

[34] For example, in the loan size regressions (model 3, table 3.4), the Hausman test for fixed effects generates a chi^2 value of 34.36 ($Pr > chi^2 = 0.13$). For the total conditions regression (model 1, table 3.6), the values are 28.01 and 0.52, respectively.

fixed effects saps the model of its ability to estimate the effects of variables, such as those measuring differences in the composition of borrowers and lenders in global financial markets, that vary primarily across countries, rather than within countries over time.[35] Since I am concerned with the effects of both cross-national and cross-temporal variation in patterns of financial globalization on IMF lending behavior, the fixed effects specification is therefore not appropriate. Likewise, including temporal fixed effects makes it impossible to test the significance of year-specific factors that do not vary across countries, such as the IMF's liquidity ratio and the number of currency crises in a given year – variables that have been identified previously by public choice scholars and economists as key determinants of IMF lending. Finally, the fixed effects model incurs an enormous tax on degrees of freedom and creates severe problems of multicollinearity, since these models include forty-six country dummy variables and nineteen temporal (year) dummy variables.[36]

Addressing endogeneity and selection effects

Given the duration of both the economic problems leading a country to seek IMF financing and the loan negotiations themselves, the time at which the independent variables are measured in studies of IMF lending involves difficult problems of interpretation and the potential for endogeneity.[37] To mitigate these issues, I follow most previous studies in lagging the explanatory variables by one period.[38] This one-period lag also reflects IMF officials' assessments about the timing and nature of the lending process. As Knight and Santaella explain, "Programs approved by the end of the second quarter of a calendar year will normally have been designed on the basis of information about the macroeconomic picture for the preceding

[35] In fact, as Beck and Katz note, including country-specific fixed effects removes "any of the average unit to unit variation from the analysis, and simply ask[s] whether intra-unit changes in y are associated with intra-unit changes in x... [Therefore] a fixed effects analysis should not conclude anything about the inter-unit effects of the independent variables, since such effects have been removed" (2004, 5–6).

[36] See www.nyu.edu/its/pubs/connect/fall03/yaffee_primer.html.

[37] Knight and Santaella (1997).

[38] See, for example, Thacker (1999), Dreher and Vaubel (2004b), and Stone (2002).

calendar year, while arrangements approved in the second half of the calendar year will generally be based on information that extends through the first half of the same year."[39] In the data set, ninety-two of the 197 IMF loans were approved on or after July 1 of the given year (i.e. on the basis of current-year data), while the remaining 105 were approved in the first half of the year. Therefore, lagging the explanatory variables by one year for all observations is actually a quite conservative estimate of the time lag between the initiation of the Fund lending process and the ultimate approval of a loan by the executive board.[40]

In addition to addressing endogeneity concerns, statistical analyses of IMF lending must also address the problem of selection effects.[41] The basic problem is that selection into IMF programs may be non-random – that is, the same variables that explain variation in loan size and conditionality may also explain a country's initial decision to request an IMF loan. If these effects are not taken into account in the statistical model, estimates of IMF loan characteristics may be biased. The most common method of addressing selection bias is the Heckman selection model, which has become increasingly popular in the political science literature.[42] Recent studies have highlighted a number of significant weaknesses with this model, however, including its sensitivity to specification and strong reliance on distributional assumptions about the model's residuals.[43] Most importantly, the Heckman model requires that at least one "extra" explanatory variable influences selection but not the subsequent outcome of interest in the second stage of the model; if this "exclusion restriction" is not met, then the model is

[39] Knight and Santaella (1997, 413). The staff also considers "the latest annual estimates for the country's main macroeconomic variables and preliminary projections for at least one year ahead" (Mussa and Savastano 1999, 87).

[40] Moreover, my goal is not to explain a country's decision to request a loan, which often evolves over several years, but, rather, to explain the Fund's subsequent choices about the loan's characteristics. While the anticipation of an IMF agreement may have large effects on the factors treated as independent variables in this analysis, these effects generally occur prior to or immediately following the signing of a letter of intent but before the staff proposes a program to the board. Consequently, they are likely to be "built into" the data used in the staff's proposals.

[41] Przeworski and Vreeland (2000); Vreeland (2003).

[42] Heckman (1979); Berinsky (1999); Vreeland (2003); von Stein (2005).

[43] Simmons and Hopkins (2005); Sartori (2003); Winship and Mare (1992).

identified solely on its distributional assumptions.[44] Ideally, one could identify the exclusion restriction(s) from theory. In the case of IMF lending, however, it is not clear which economic and political variables influence selection but not IMF loan characteristics. The analyst is left with a difficult choice, therefore: risking specification error by including potentially inappropriate exclusion restrictions, or relying exclusively on the model's distributional assumptions.[45]

To avoid these problems associated with Heckman selection models, I utilize an alternative method of dealing with selection effects: propensity score matching.[46] Briefly, the key advantage of matching estimators is that they do not require the identification of exclusion restrictions, nor do they depend on modeling and distributional assumptions. Rather, matching allows the analyst to "preprocess" the available data to minimize selection effects, after which standard single-stage regression analyses can be conducted.[47] The critical idea behind matching is to match each "treated" observation (in this case, each country-year observation of an IMF loan) with a "control" observation (i.e. a non-loan country-year observation) for which all the values of the explanatory variables are as close to identical as possible. This strategy is known as "nearest neighbor" or "one-to-one" propensity score matching.[48] The propensity score estimation procedure employs a binary logit model and a "common support" constraint, which discards treated (IMF loan) observations that do not have like

[44] Achen (1986). The central assumptions of the Heckman model are that both *Y* (the variable of interest in the second stage) and *Z* (the underlying latent variable determining selection in the first stage) are distributed normally (Sartori 2003). Winship and Mare (1992) show that the Heckman model's results are highly sensitive to the fit of this assumption with the actual data.

[45] Sartori (2003).

[46] For a more detailed discussion of matching estimators, see Ho *et al.* (2007), Simmons and Hopkins (2005), and Abadie *et al.* (2004). The key disadvantage of matching is that, like the Heckman approach, it controls only for bias on observable variables but not for selection based on unobserved heterogeneity.

[47] Ho *et al.* (2007).

[48] Other matching methods are also available, although the results presented here do not vary based on the choice of matching estimators. Matching was done using the PSMATCH2 module for Stata (Leuven and Sianesi 2003). Matching estimation diagnostics are presented in appendix 3. Robustness checks using Heckman selection models yield substantively identical results, despite the aforementioned concerns about their limitations.

counterparts in the non-treated sample in order to ensure that the estimated treatment effects themselves are not subject to bias. Fortunately, in the IMF lending data set, this common support constraint does not result in the loss of any observations, as suitable matches are available for all country-years of IMF loans. For each observation, this process generates a "propensity score" (*PSCORE*) ranging from 0 to 1, which measures the predicted probability that a country will enter an IMF program given the observed values of the explanatory variables. Including *PSCORE* in the subsequent loan size and conditionality regressions controls for potential selection bias in the data without requiring us to identify exclusion restrictions or make the strong modeling assumptions required of Heckman-style selection models.

Results

Loan size models

Table 3.4 presents the results of five multivariate regression models analyzing IMF loan size. Model 1 presents the results of the propensity-score-matching analysis described above, which controls for non-random selection into IMF programs. In this model, the dependent variable is binary, taking a value of 1 if a country received an IMF loan in a given year and a value of 0 otherwise.[49] The predicted probabilities from this analysis are utilized to calculate *PSCORE*, the probability that a country will request an IMF loan. This variable is subsequently included in the loan size and conditionality regressions to mitigate concerns about selection bias in these models.

The results of the propensity-score-matching estimation (model 1) highlight two key points about the political economy of IMF lending. First, in line with past studies, the key determinants of whether or not a country requests an IMF loan are economic: countries with lower growth rates, larger current account deficits, higher levels of external debt relative to GDP, and higher levels of short-term debt in relation to reserves are more likely to request and receive IMF loans. Second, the variables capturing variation in patterns of financial globalization are not significant in the logit/matching analysis. Indeed, the insignificance of both the G-5 bank exposure variables (*G5BANK*,

[49] The model presented here is a logit specification, although the results are substantively identical when utilizing a probit model.

COVG5BANK) and the measures of bond and private non-guaranteed debt (*PCTBOND*, *PCTPNG*) suggest that neither G-5 domestic financial interests nor IMF staff expectations about catalytic financing play a major role in the decision as to whether or not a country seeks and receives an IMF loan. Rather, this initial decision appears to be driven primarily by the borrower's economic characteristics, as well as broader global macroeconomic conditions. Thus, while politics does play an important role in shaping the *characteristics* of IMF programs (loan size, conditionality), "technocratic" economic factors are the most significant determinants of whether or not a country borrows from the Fund in the first place. Ultimately, countries are most likely to seek IMF assistance – and the Fund is most likely to agree to lend – in times of dire financial need and global financial crises.

In the remainder of table 3.4, models 2 to 5 present several alternative specifications of the loan size regressions. Model 2 presents the non-interactive model using *AMTQTA*, while model 3 shows the preferred specification, which includes *AMTQTA* as the dependent variable and adds the multiplicative interaction term (*G5BANK* × *COVG5BANK*), which models the hypothesized complex relationship between the intensity and heterogeneity of G-5 domestic financial interests. Finally, models 4 and 5 illustrate robustness checks using the two alternative specifications of the dependent variable: loan amount relative to GDP (*AMTGDP*) and absolute loan size (*AMTSDR*).

On the whole, the loan size models provide strong support for the book's core argument linking patterns of financial globalization to variation in IMF lending behavior. First, the results provide clear evidence that the intensity and heterogeneity of G-5 financial interests play a significant role in determining IMF lending decisions. At first glance, this does not appear to be the case: in the non-interactive specification (model 2), neither *G5BANK* nor *COVG5BANK* is statistically significant. The results of the fully interactive model (model 3) clarify this initial result, however, and provide clear and robust support for the empirical predictions of my theory of IMF lending. In this specification, *G5BANK* is positive, while *COVG5BANK* is negative, and the interaction term (*G5BANK* × *COVG5BANK*) is negative and significant at the 99 percent confidence level. Given the explicitly conditional nature of my argument linking G-5 preference intensity and heterogeneity, this last model is the appropriate and preferred specification for my analysis. In such interactive models, however, one cannot infer

Table 3.4 *IMF loan size regressions*

Model Variable	1 IMF loan	2 Amount/ quota	3 Amount/ quota	4 Amount/ GDP	5 Amount (SDR millions)
G-5 bank exposure ($ billions, log)	−0.1261	−0.0642	0.2271***	0.1579**	0.2711***
(*G5BANK*)	[0.1080]	[0.0407]	[0.0752]	[0.0773]	[0.0791]
Coefficient of variation, G-5 bank exposure	0.0001	−0.0003	−0.0012	0.0003	0.0008
(*COVG5BANK*)	[0.0027]	[0.0019]	[0.0016]	[0.0012]	[0.0013]
G5BANK ×			−0.0018***	−0.0014***	−0.0014***
COVG5BANK			[0.0004]	[0.0004]	[0.0004]
Percent bond debt	0.0008	0.0036*	0.0038**	0.0064***	0.0072***
(*PCTBOND*)	[0.0043]	[0.0019]	[0.0018]	[0.0015]	[0.0016]
Percent private non-guaranteed debt	−0.0065	0.0022	0.0015	−0.0001	−0.0010
(*PCTPNG*)	[0.0055]	[0.0025]	[0.0022]	[0.0018]	[0.0016]
US share, G-5 bank exposure (%)	−0.8417	0.0366	−0.5568	−0.0164	−0.5094
(*USSHARE*)	[0.9952]	[0.7633]	[0.4702]	[0.4335]	[0.4673]
UK share, G-5 bank exposure	−1.4732	−0.2608	−1.0933	−0.6499	−1.0993
(*UKSHARE*)	[1.3081]	[0.9551]	[0.9077]	[0.8519]	[0.8643]
Japanese share, G-5 bank exposure	−1.1978	−0.2195	−1.1863**	−0.3325	−0.9144
(*JPSHARE*)	[1.2989]	[0.7725]	[0.6044]	[0.6248]	[0.6553]
German share, G-5 bank exposure	−0.0046	−0.0603	−1.1336*	−0.4521	−0.7225
(*GRSHARE*)	[1.0106]	[0.7118]	[0.5854]	[0.5272]	[0.5510]
French share, G-5 bank exposure	−1.4631	−0.2764	−1.1377	0.5660	−0.1353
(*FRSHARE*)	[1.1232]	[0.8703]	[0.8807]	[0.8023]	[0.7551]
Years since last IMF loan	1.2256***				
(*LASTLOAN*)	[0.2690]				
Cubic temporal spline 1	0.3676***				
(*IMFSP1*)	[0.0839]				
Cubic temporal spline 2	−0.1457***				
(*IMFSP2*)	[0.0377]				
Cubic temporal spline 3	0.0092*				

Table 3.4 *(cont.)*

Model Variable	1 IMF loan	2 Amount/ quota	3 Amount/ quota	4 Amount/ GDP	5 Amount (SDR millions)
(*IMFSP3*)	[0.0056]				
Past IMF loan (dummy)		−0.1653**	−0.1643**	−0.1265*	−0.0951
(*PASTLOAN*)		[0.0829]	[0.0789]	[0.0753]	[0.0749]
Extended Fund Facility		0.7055***	0.6747***	0.7893***	0.8166***
(*EFF*)		[0.1183]	[0.1208]	[0.1181]	[0.1152]
GDP (log)	0.2341	0.3363***	0.2359***	0.0465	0.9461***
	[0.1472]	[0.0725]	[0.0548]	[0.0678]	[0.0606]
GDP per capita (log)	−0.2620	0.2775	0.1993	0.0656	−0.1206
(*GDPPC*)	[0.2845]	[0.1872]	[0.1762]	[0.1355]	[0.1347]
GDP growth (%)	−0.0694***	−0.0371***	−0.0442***	−0.0516***	−0.0592***
(*GROWTH*)	[0.0183]	[0.0118]	[0.0110]	[0.0109]	[0.0110]
Current account/ GDP (%)	−0.0361**	−0.0251**	−0.0228**	−0.0094	−0.0212*
(*CURRGDP*)	[0.0153]	[0.0120]	[0.0114]	[0.0126]	[0.0120]
External debt/ GDP (%)	0.0071*	0.0046***	0.0043***	0.0112***	0.0075***
(*EDTGDP*)	[0.0041]	[0.0017]	[0.0016]	[0.0018]	[0.0017]
Short-term debt/ reserves (log)	0.2902***	0.1527***	0.1161***	0.0435	0.0414
(*STDRES*)	[0.0944]	[0.0468]	[0.0436]	[0.0472]	[0.0413]
Currency crisis (dummy)	0.0272	0.0764	0.0581	0.1139	−0.0003
(*CRASH*)	[0.2868]	[0.1687]	[0.1581]	[0.1381]	[0.1336]
Veto players (log)	0.0228	0.0884	0.0574	0.1806**	0.1524*
(*CHECKS*)	[0.2018]	[0.0831]	[0.0812]	[0.0823]	[0.0897]
G-5 UN voting affinity (mean "S" score)	0.7860	−0.3202	−0.4297	−0.4713	0.0410
(*G5S*)	[0.7859]	[0.4974]	[1.2397]	[1.0998]	[1.1588]
Standard deviation, G-5 "S" scores	1.9435	1.8315**	0.5412	1.0166	3.1341
(*SDS*)	[1.6202]	[0.8583]	[5.6602]	[5.0605]	[5.2078]
G5S x *SDS*			1.2519	0.7847	−0.5088
			[3.8355]	[3.5077]	[3.5778]
Propensity score		−0.8730*	−0.8833*	−0.7464*	−0.8737*
(*PSCORE*)		[0.4971]	[0.4903]	[0.4392]	[0.4683]

Table 3.4 *(cont.)*

Model Variable	1 IMF loan	2 Amount/ quota	3 Amount/ quota	4 Amount/ GDP	5 Amount (SDR millions)
IMF liquidity ratio (%)	−1.9050	0.2618	0.0996	0.2337	0.3080
(*LIQRATIO*)	[1.6347]	[1.0800]	[1.0319]	[0.7288]	[0.8917]
IMF quota review (dummy)	0.1416	0.1110	0.1251	0.2003*	0.0747
(*REVIEW*)	[0.2432]	[0.1267]	[0.1218]	[0.1030]	[0.1241]
Number of currency crises in year *t*	0.0597	−0.0286	−0.0159	−0.0069	−0.0167
(*CRISES*)	[0.0410]	[0.0270]	[0.0242]	[0.0183]	[0.0209]
LIBOR (%)	0.0187	0.0231	0.0177	0.0302	0.0146
	[0.0625]	[0.0265]	[0.0270]	[0.0243]	[0.0257]
Middle East	0.1195	−0.5302*	−0.6297**	−0.5195	−0.7887***
	[0.5960]	[0.3175]	[0.3188]	[0.4001]	[0.3057]
Africa	0.0734				
	[0.6638]				
Europe/central Asia	0.3526	−0.6466	−0.6082	0.1978	−0.1858
	[0.5869]	[0.4284]	[0.4813]	[0.5473]	[0.4479]
Americas	0.3476	−0.6752*	−0.8705*	−0.1938	−0.6830*
	[0.4500]	[0.4072]	[0.4764]	[0.5493]	[0.4147]
East Asia		−0.1946	−0.3521	0.0242	−0.2783
		[0.6057]	[0.6285]	[0.6183]	[0.5196]
Constant	−2.8701	−5.8418**	−3.1859	−6.2994**	−3.7322
	[3.2955]	[2.3587]	[3.1171]	[2.6017]	[2.5949]
Observations	*902*	*181*	*181*	*181*	*181*
Number of countries	*55*	*44*	*44*	*44*	*44*
R-squared	—	*0.512*	*0.555*	*0.498*	*0.889*
Adjusted R-squared	—	*0.414*	*0.458*	*0.389*	*0.865*
Log-likelihood	*−377.582*	*−170.715*	*−162.337*	*−154.326*	*−156.623*
Percent correctly predicted	*80.27*	—	—	—	—

Notes: Model 1 (logit): robust standard errors in brackets. Models 2 to 4 (OLS): panel-corrected standard errors in brackets. * = significant at 10 percent; ** = significant at 5 percent; *** = significant at 1 percent.

statistical significance simply by reading the regression coefficients. In fact, the separate coefficients on each component of the multiplicative interaction term (*G5BANK*, *COVG5BANK*) are meaningful only when the other component is equal to zero.[50] In model 2, therefore, the negative and significant coefficient on *G5BANK* is meaningful only when *COVG5BANK* = 0, while the insignificant coefficient on *COVG5BANK* is readily interpretable only when *G5BANK* = 0. While theoretically possible, such cases are extremely rare in the real world: *G5BANK* is equal to zero in just eight of the 177 IMF loan observations, while *COVG5BANK* is equal to zero in only six cases. In short, these separate coefficients tell us nothing about the impact of these variables in the remaining 163 lending cases included in the IMF non-concessional lending data set. Rather, in order to ascertain the significance of these variables, as well as the interactive relationship between them, we need to identify the *conditional* effect of each variable (*G5BANK*, *COVG5BANK*) as the other changes. Panels (a) and (b) of figure 3.1, which present graphs of the estimated effect of G-5 bank exposure intensity (*G5BANK*) at different levels of G-5 bank exposure heterogeneity (*COVG5BANK*) – and vice versa – illustrate these complex relationships.[51]

In panel (a), we see that the coefficient of *G5BANK* is positive when *COVG5BANK* is low. In other words, higher levels of G-5 bank exposure result in larger IMF loans when G-5 preference heterogeneity is low. This effect loses significance as *COVG5BANK* increases, however, and ultimately turns negative at very high levels of *COVG5BANK*. Thus, when G-5 preference heterogeneity is highest, higher levels of G-5 bank exposure actually lead to *smaller* IMF loans. Similarly, in panel (b), we see that the coefficient on *COVG5BANK* is positive when *G5BANK* is low; in other words, greater G-5 preference heterogeneity *increases* IMF loan size, but only at low levels of G-5 preference intensity. On the one hand, this finding may be evidence of agency slack and bureaucratic rent-seeking: such loans might be larger

[50] On the correct use and interpretation of interaction terms, see Braumoeller (2004) and Brambor, Clark and Golder (2006).

[51] The histograms in these charts illustrate the distribution of the *x*-axis variable in the data sample. For example, the histogram in panel (a) shows the distribution of *COVG5BANK*. Each of these charts shows the coefficient estimates from each model, as well as the 95 percent confidence intervals (CIs).

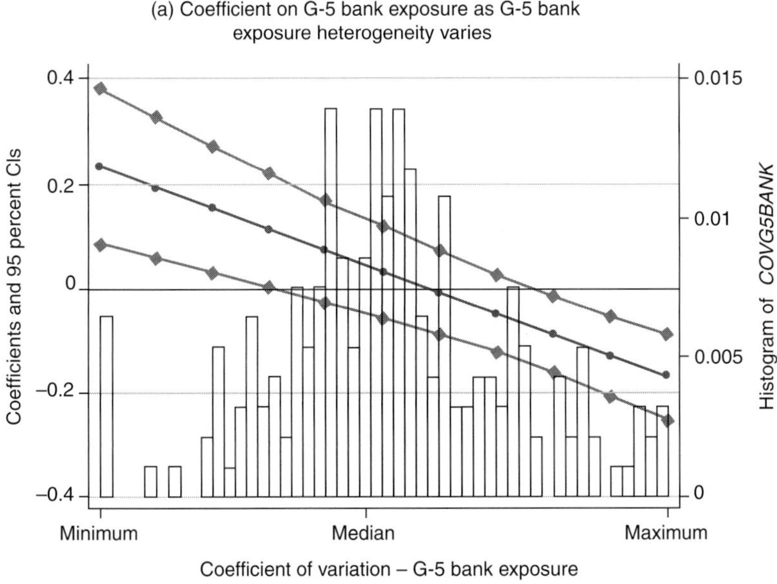

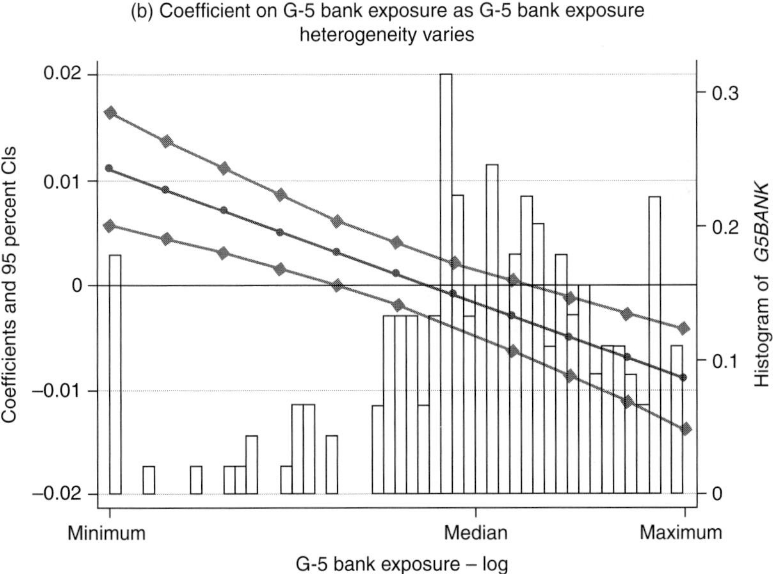

Figure 3.1 Interactions between G-5 bank exposure intensity and heterogeneity, loan size (amount/quota)

as a result of the staff exploiting the executive board's relative lack of interest in these cases in order to push through larger loans. On the other, this result may indicate a "logrolling" dynamic at work within the executive board, as the less interested G-5 governments agree to support their more invested counterparts precisely because the cost of doing so is minimal. Indeed, since these countries are of little importance to either the G-5 as a group or the global financial system, the moral hazard costs of providing an abnormally large loan are minimal. In contrast, greater G-5 preference heterogeneity (*COVG5BANK*) has precisely the opposite effect on loan size in countries of greater importance to the G-5 as a whole. As panel (b) illustrates, the coefficient on *COVG5BANK* becomes negative and statistically significant at high levels of *G5BANK* (i.e. slightly above the median or greater). As expected, therefore, divergent preferences among the Fund's principals lead to conflict within the executive board in "important" country cases and results in the approval of smaller IMF loans.

Taken together, these results of the interactive analysis indicate strongly that both the intensity and the heterogeneity of G-5 governments' preferences play an important role in determining the size of IMF programs, and they illustrate that the effects of each of these variables are conditional on the other. This finding also clarifies further the dynamics of the common agency relationship at the heart of IMF decision-making. In particular, it shows that the ability of powerful states to "control" IMF lending is not a constant but, rather (as predicted by the common agency theory), a variable that changes over time in accordance with shifts in the composition of international capital flows.

In addition to illustrating the nature and extent of G-5 influence over IMF lending decisions, the loan size regressions also provide support for my expectation that IMF staff concerns about catalytic financing are a key determinant of Fund lending decisions. The results are not unequivocal, however. On the one hand, *PCTBOND*, the percentage of private external debt held by bondholders rather than commercial banks, is positive and significant at the 95 percent confidence level in all four of the loan size models. Thus, IMF loans increase in size as bondholders make up a larger share of a country's private international creditors – a result consistent with both my hypothesis and the logic of catalytic financing, in which the IMF provides more extensive credit in cases in which a country's private international creditors face greater collective action problems and are less able and willing to provide new lending. In these cases, more extensive IMF credit is required to meet a country's financing needs and to convince private lenders to provide catalytic financing.

On the other hand, the loan size models do not support the hypothesis linking the composition of a country's borrowers to IMF loan size: *PCTPNG*, the percentage of private non-guaranteed debt (external debt owed by non-sovereign borrowers), is not statistically significant in any of the models in table 3.4. One possible interpretation of this negative result is that the IMF, despite greater concerns about the availability of catalytic financing in these cases, is hesitant to provide "bailouts" to non-sovereign borrowers, given its institutional mandate to assist its member states (rather than private actors) in maintaining financial and monetary stability. Therefore, although the staff's concerns about catalytic financing may increase, as I had hypothesized, as a result of the shift to PNG external debt, the Fund may nonetheless be reluctant to expend its limited resources in non-sovereign crisis cases.[52] Together, these results suggest that, as expected, the composition of international capital flows do shape IMF staff expectations about catalytic financing, although they suggest that *creditor* composition (i.e. the bank versus bondholder distinction) rather than *borrower* composition (sovereign versus non-sovereign) matters more in shaping decisions about the size of Fund loans.

Substantive quantities of interest

Since the raw regression results in table 3.4 are not easily interpretable, table 3.5 presents substantive quantities of interest illustrating the impact of the significant explanatory variables in model 1 (IMF loan occurrence) and model 3 (IMF loan size: amount/quota). The

[52] Another possible explanation arises from the fact that PNG lending consists primarily of short-term interbank financing – lending from commercial banks in the industrialized countries to private firms and banks in the developing world – rather than bond financing. Since these banks have fewer collective action problems than international bondholders, less IMF financing may be needed to convince them to roll over their claims and provide new lending to a Fund borrower. Furthermore, as noted above, commercial banks involved in non-sovereign interbank lending also often have additional, long-term ties to IMF borrower countries (e.g. as holders of central bank reserves, as sovereign lenders, as providers of trade credits) that serve to extend their time horizons during financial crises and may offset their short-term incentives to "cut and run" in the wake of an IMF loan.

Table 3.5 *First differences, loan size models*

IMF loan (model 1)

Predicted probability of loan, all variables at means: 14.25%

Variable	Predicted change in probability of IMF loan	Substantive change in each variable
GDP growth	–3.92%	3.22% to 8.68%
Current account/GDP	–2.65%	–2.25% to 4.44%
External debt/GDP	2.85%	51.25% to 80.99%
Short-term debt/reserves	5.34%	0.52 to 1.90

Amount/quota (model 3)

Predicted loan size, all variables at means: 0.88

Variable	Predicted change in loan size (*AMTQTA*)	Substantive change in each variable
G-5 bank exposure		
G5BANK (*COVG5BANK* = 45.6)	0.44**	$1.6 billion to $20.3 billion
G5BANK (*COVG5BANK* = 115.5)	0.06	$1.6 billion to $20.3 billion
G5BANK (*COVG5BANK* = 185.4)	–0.15**	$1.6 billion to $20.3 billion
G-5 bank exposure heterogeneity		
COVG5BANK (*G5BANK* = $3.4 million)	0.20**	115.53 to 162.60
COVG5BANK (*G5BANK* = $1.6 billion)	–0.07	115.53 to 162.60
COVG5BANK (*G5BANK* = $72.2 billion)	–0.31**	115.53 to 162.60
Percent bond debt	0.10	22.9% to 51.2%
Japanese share, G-5 bank exposure	–0.14	12.1% to 27.7%
German share, G-5 bank exposure	–0.22	27.7% to 54.6%
Extended Fund Facility (dummy)	0.76	0 to 1
Current IMF loan in progress	–0.16	0 to 1

Table 3.5 *(cont.)*

Variable	Predicted change in loan size (*AMTQTA*)	Substantive change in each variable
GDP	0.36	\$25.6 billion to \$108 billion
GDP growth	−0.23	0.78% to 7.72%
Current account/GDP	−0.08	-3.24% to 1.2%
External debt/GDP	0.15	58.5% to 94.3%
Short-term debt/reserves	0.15	0.79 to 3.10
Propensity score	−0.12	0.33 to 0.50
G-5 UN voting affinity heterogeneity		
SDS (G5S = 1)	0.11	0.31 to 0.37
SDS (G5S = 1.36)	0.13**	0.31 to 0.37
SDS (G5S = 1.72)	0.16	0.31 to 0.37

Note: ** = significant at 5 percent.

table presents the effect of a one standard deviation increase (or substantively equivalent change) in each of the significant explanatory variables, holding all other variables constant at their means.[53]

As is evident, G-5 financial interests have quite sizeable effects on loan size, both in absolute terms and in relation to the other economic and political determinants of IMF lending. Since these significant effects are conditional and interactive (as illustrated in figure 3.1), however, rather than constant, I calculate first differences for both *G5BANK* and *COVG5BANK* at three different values of the other variable: the mean and ±1.5 standard deviations from the mean. Once again, the conditional significance of these variables is apparent. At "low" levels of G-5 preference heterogeneity (*COVG5BANK* = 45.6), a one standard deviation increase in G-5 bank exposure (*G5BANK*) increases the IMF loan size by nearly 50 percent of a country's quota (0.44). In contrast, at "high" levels of *COVG5BANK* (185.4), greater G-5 bank exposure

[53] The data were analyzed using Stata 9 and the post-estimation supplementary software modules Clarify (King, Tomz, and Wittenberg 2000) and SPost (www.indianna.edu/~jslsoc/spost.htm) (Long and Freeze 2001).

results in a significant reduction in IMF loan size (−0.16). Together, these results provide strong evidence in support of the common agency theory of IMF decision-making. When G-5 governments' domestic financial interests in an IMF borrower country are both more intense and more unified, the Fund approves substantially larger loans. As the preferences of the Fund's principals diverge, however, more intense interests (i.e. higher levels of *G5BANK*) create conflict within the executive board and result in approval of smaller IMF loans.

Similarly, the effect of G-5 preference heterogeneity on IMF loan size is conditional on preference intensity. At low levels of G-5 bank exposure ($3.4 million), a one standard deviation increase in *COVG5BANK* increases IMF loan size by 20 percent of a country's IMF quota. Once again, this may be evidence of bureaucratic rent-seeking, as the Fund staff exploits divergent G-5 preferences in lending cases in which the Fund's principals, as a group, have weak domestic financial interests. Alternatively, however, this finding may indicate a logrolling dynamic, as the G-5 support each other's preferred borrower countries in cases in which aggregate G-5 interests are weak. In contrast, at high levels of *G5BANK* ($72.2 billion), greater G-5 preference heterogeneity (*COVG5BANK*) reduces loan size by 31 percent. The loan size regressions also provide evidence that some G-5 countries exercise greater influence within the IMF than others. Both *JPSHARE* and *GRSHARE*, Japanese and German bank exposure as shares of total G-5 lending, respectively, are negative and significant in model 2. This result suggests that countries of greater financial importance to Germany and Japan receive less favorable treatment than borrowers with more extensive ties to the remaining G-5 governments. Finally, the effect of a one standard deviation increase in *PCTBOND* is less substantial (0.10 times quota) than these G-5 measures, although its magnitude is still quite large relative to the mean predicted loan size (0.88 times quota). Moreover, both the magnitude and significance of this effect increase in models 3 and 4, the specifications testing alternative measures of IMF loan size. Thus, the evidence linking the composition of international lenders to variation in Fund loan amounts is quite robust.

In sum, the loan size regressions offer substantial evidence in support of my theoretical argument and its hypotheses linking changes in patterns of financial globalization to IMF lending decisions. At the same time, the results also illustrate the importance of several economic and political variables previously identified in the literature;

indeed, many of the control variables are significant and signed as expected across the various specifications in table 3.4. Countries already under IMF programs (*PASTLOAN*) receive smaller new loans, while larger countries (*GDP*) receive larger loans. Likewise, arrangements under the Extended Fund Facility (*EFF*) are larger, given their typically longer duration and the fact that they are provided to countries facing more severe balance of payments problems. Economic growth and current account balances are negatively associated with loan size, while the various measures of external debt levels (external debt/GDP, debt service/exports, short-term debt/reserves) are all significant and associated with larger loans in one or more of the specifications. These results reinforce the notion that, although patterns of financial globalization strongly influence IMF lending behavior, "technocratic" economic factors also play a central role in shaping Fund decisions about loan size and conditionality.

In marked contrast to this robust evidence in support of the book's core argument, the models provide only limited support for the existing alternative political explanations of IMF behavior. The veto players variable (*CHECKS*), measuring the structure of domestic political institutions in a borrowing country, is positive and significant in models 4 and 5, but not significant in model 3. Likewise, the loan size models provide little evidence to support "public choice" theories of IMF lending: the IMF's liquidity ratio is never significant, while the quota review dummy is weakly significant and positive only in model 4. This finding offers limited support in favor of the "hurry up" lending hypothesis, which argues that the Fund staff will propose larger loans during quota reviews in order to create demand for Fund credit and to generate pressure on IMF shareholders to increase the Fund's resources. Overall, however, the models suggest that these existing political theories of Fund lending have not been the primary determinants of variation in IMF loan size during the last two decades.

Similarly, the loan size models provide only limited evidence in favor of the widely held view that geopolitical factors or the foreign policy interests of the Fund's largest shareholders are the key political determinants of IMF lending behavior. In model 2, *SDS*, the measure of G-5 UN voting affinity heterogeneity, is positive and significant. Once we include the aforementioned interaction term (*G5S* X *SDS*) between these two variables in models 3 to 5, however, we see that this variable has only a limited effect on IMF loan size. Indeed, as table 3.5 clearly illustrates, *SDS* is positive and significant in model 3 only when *G5S* is at its mean, whereas it loses statistical significance at both high and low levels of *G5S*. Moreover, the average level of G-5 UN affinity (*G5S*) is not statistically significant at any level of *SDS* in the loan size regressions.[54] Unlike the G-5 financial interest variables, these results suggest that divergent views over the geopolitical importance of an IMF borrower result in a logrolling dynamic within the executive board in some cases. Specifically, this result suggests that the G-5 are willing to support each other's foreign policy allies within the IMF, provided the country in question is of moderate importance to the Fund's principals as a group (i.e. *G5S* is at its mean value). One possible interpretation of this finding is that geopolitics within the IMF operates through a "spheres of influence" dynamic, in which each G-5 government advocates on behalf of certain countries in which it has a significant regional or foreign policy interest (e.g. France in north Africa, Germany in eastern Europe). That said, given that this effect disappears at high levels of *G5S*, as well as the fact that aggregate G-5 UN voting affinity (*G5S*) is insignificant at all values of *SDS*, we should exercise caution in ascribing too much importance to geopolitics as a determinant of IMF lending behavior. Indeed, the loan size models provide strong evidence that G-5 governments' preferences over IMF loan size are shaped far more strongly by financial than by geopolitical interests.

Conditionality models

The loan size regressions provide strong evidence in support of the book's argument that changes in the composition of international capital flows to developing countries are the key determinant of variation in IMF lending. Moreover, they illustrate that both G-5 domestic financial interests and IMF staff concerns about catalytic financing influence Fund lending decisions – a finding that reinforces the common agency theory of IMF policymaking. In table 3.6, I turn to an analysis of conditionality by presenting the results of four statistical models.

[54] As these control variables are not direct tests of the book's core argument, I have omitted the charts of the interactive marginal effects of *G5S* and *SDS* that correspond to figures 3.1 and 3.2 for G-5 financial interests. These charts mirror the results presented in the first differences table (table 3.5) and are available on request from the author.

Table 3.6 *IMF conditionality regressions*

Model Variable	1 Total conditions	2 Performance criteria	3 Prior actions	4 Benchmarks/ targets
G-5 bank exposure ($ billions, log)	−0.0914	−0.0873	−0.5094	−0.2152
(*G5BANK*)	[0.0742]	[0.0610]	[0.3751]	[0.3190]
Coefficient of variation, G-5 bank exposure	−0.0010	−0.0016*	−0.0042	−0.0031
(*COVG5BANK*)	[0.0013]	[0.0009]	[0.0066]	[0.0045]
G5BANK ×	0.0000	0.0003	0.0029**	−0.0003
COVG5BANK	[0.0002]	[0.0002]	[0.0013]	[0.0012]
Percent bond debt	0.0059***	−0.0009	0.0315***	0.0156*
(*PCTBOND*)	[0.0022]	[0.0017]	[0.0092]	[0.0080]
Percent private non-guaranteed debt	−0.0010	−0.0027	0.0214	−0.0001
(*PCTPNG*)	[0.0036]	[0.0021]	[0.0142]	[0.0086]
US share, G-5 bank exposure	−0.3056	−0.1389	5.3050*	−0.1457
(*USSHARE*)	[0.4333]	[0.3363]	[2.8346]	[1.6468]
UK share, G-5 bank exposure	−0.6594	−0.3769	4.1806	−4.5309*
(*UKSHARE*)	[1.0078]	[0.7210]	[3.8507]	[2.6712]
Japanese share, G-5 bank exposure	−0.5882	−0.4872	3.4297	0.3803
(*JPSHARE*)	[0.5663]	[0.5661]	[3.0665]	[1.6742]
German share, G-5 bank exposure	1.2121***	0.5417**	5.9460*	3.7571**
(*GRSHARE*)	[0.4269]	[0.2266]	[3.0385]	[1.8279]
French share, G-5 bank exposure	0.2492	0.0896	6.5700**	−0.3924
(*FRSHARE*)	[0.7479]	[0.5789]	[3.3129]	[2.1139]
Years since last IMF loan	0.6989*	0.4986*	0.1957	1.3739*
(*LASTLOAN*)	[0.3754]	[0.2677]	[1.4465]	[0.8292]
Cubic temporal	0.2289*	0.1420*	0.0400	0.3946
spline 1	[0.1172]	[0.0823]	[0.4362]	[0.2400]
Cubic temporal	−0.0927*	−0.0544*	−0.0196	−0.1465
spline 2	[0.0477]	[0.0330]	[0.1744]	[0.0958]
Cubic temporal	0.0062*	0.0024	0.0034	0.0035
spline 3	[0.0037]	[0.0024]	[0.0128]	[0.0078]
Extended Fund	0.1005	0.0976	−0.0875	0.1799
Facility (*EFF*)	[0.0825]	[0.0619]	[0.3096]	[0.3418]

Table 3.6 *(cont.)*

Model Variable	1 Total conditions	2 Performance criteria	3 Prior actions	4 Benchmarks/ targets
Gross domestic product ($ millions, log)	0.1980**	0.0873	0.3802	0.5285
(GDP)	[0.0892]	[0.0719]	[0.4433]	[0.3558]
GDP per capita	−0.6431***	−0.1971	−1.8656***	−0.9283**
(GDPPC)	[0.1487]	[0.1285]	[0.6560]	[0.3644]
GDP growth (%)	−0.0677***	−0.0319*	−0.0521	−0.1313**
(GROWTH)	[0.0235]	[0.0166]	[0.0916]	[0.0551]
Current account/ GDP (%)	−0.0104	−0.0031	0.0238	−0.0198
(CURRGDP)	[0.0130]	[0.0096]	[0.0513]	[0.0392]
External debt/GDP (%)	0.0037	0.0038**	0.0034	0.0045
(EDTGDP)	[0.0025]	[0.0019]	[0.0101]	[0.0071]
Short-term debt/ reserves (log)	0.1984**	0.1262*	−0.2320	0.5366**
(STDRES)	[0.0943]	[0.0754]	[0.3869]	[0.2650]
Currency crisis	0.1438	0.1350*	0.6421	−0.3094
(CRASH)	[0.0982]	[0.0817]	[0.4331]	[0.2560]
Veto players (log)	0.1340**	−0.0051	0.1025	0.2469
(CHECKS)	[0.0661]	[0.0538]	[0.3180]	[0.2594]
G-5 UN voting affinity (mean "S" score)	−0.0963	0.8161	−1.6671	−2.3692
(G5S)	[0.8547]	[0.5283]	[4.5875]	[2.7490]
Standard deviation, G-5 "S" scores	−0.7664	4.4395	6.4049	−20.4232*
(SDS)	[4.1233]	[2.8353]	[24.6608]	[12.1146]
G5S × SDS	2.0230	−2.8042	−4.7915	19.2364**
	[2.9927]	[2.0666]	[16.1872]	[9.3388]
Propensity score	−3.6061**	−2.0777*	0.4276	−8.8756**
(PSCORE)	[1.5046]	[1.1158]	[6.1173]	[3.5735]
IMF liquidity ratio (%)	−0.4142	−1.0293**	−3.6026	0.5034
(LIQRATIO)	[0.8623]	[0.4931]	[2.7614]	[2.5909]
IMF quota review (dummy)	0.1027	−0.0644	−0.4879	0.6515
(REVIEW)	[0.1002]	[0.0739]	[0.3892]	[0.4815]
Number of currency crises in year *t*	−0.0137	−0.0236	−0.0094	0.0008

Table 3.6 *(cont.)*

Model Variable	1 Total conditions	2 Performance criteria	3 Prior actions	4 Benchmarks/ targets
(CRISES)	[0.0274]	[0.0164]	[0.1001]	[0.0843]
LIBOR (%)	−0.0100	−0.0138	−0.1463	−0.0445
	[0.0293]	[0.0202]	[0.1001]	[0.0632]
Middle East	0.1690	−0.4303*	3.2618*	1.5604**
	[0.2826]	[0.2346]	[1.7718]	[0.7781]
Africa	0.3188	−0.2817	5.0749*	0.4543
	[0.5065]	[0.3475]	[2.8188]	[1.2375]
Europe/central Asia	0.3560	0.0060	4.3716***	−0.5687
	[0.2703]	[0.2094]	[1.6532]	[0.9018]
Americas	0.1904	−0.0020	1.5285	0.1601
	[0.1629]	[0.1327]	[1.2953]	[0.5688]
Constant	6.0072***	2.5493**	7.5440	6.1525
	[2.0757]	[0.9997]	[10.4331]	[7.3275]
Observations	*175*	*177*	*175*	*175*
Number of countries	*44*	*44*	*44*	*44*
Log-likelihood	*−522.236*	*−380.382*	*−255.133*	*−361.626*
Alpha	*0.089*		*1.324*	*1.248*
Poisson goodness of fit (chi²)	*410.571*	*−118.998*	*412.786*	*640.916*
Poisson goodness of fit (Pr > chi²)	*0.000*	*0.911*	*0.000*	*0.000*

Notes: Models 1, 3, and 4 (negative binomial); model 2 (poisson): robust standard errors in brackets. * = significant at 10 percent; ** = significant at 5 percent; *** = significant at 1 percent. East Asian regional dummy dropped.

Model 1 employs the total number of conditions (*TC*) included an IMF loan as the dependent variable, while models 2 to 4 substitute performance criteria (*PC*) , prior actions (*PA*), and benchmarks/targets (*BT*), respectively.

While the loan size regression results were largely consistent across specifications, the results for the conditionality models tell a more complex story about the relationship between changes in the composition of international capital flows and IMF lending. In addition, they shed further light on the nature of the principal–agent relationship between G-5 governments and the IMF staff. On the one hand, the variables measuring G-5 governments' financial interests have no significant effect on the total number of conditions included in IMF loans, on the Fund's use of prior actions, or on its decisions about the number of "soft" conditions (structural benchmarks and indicative targets) included in IMF loans. Once again, however, it is not possible to interpret the raw coefficients directly on either interaction terms or their components. Therefore, we must turn again to the conditional marginal effects graphs in order to see clearly these interactive effects between *G5BANK* and *COVG5BANK*. Figures 3.2 to 3.5, which present graphs of the estimated effect of G-5 bank exposure intensity (*G5BANK*) at different levels of G-5 bank exposure heterogeneity (*COVG5BANK*) – and vice versa – illustrate these complex relationships for each of the four dependent variables in the conditionality analysis.

In addition to these results, the measures of the G-5 countries' individual bank exposure "shares" are not consistently significant across the various specifications in table 3.6. These findings, coupled with the significance of both *PCTBOND* and many of the "technocratic" economic variables discussed below, suggest that the IMF's most powerful member states – in contrast to their prominent role in shaping decisions about Fund loan size – exercise less extensive influence over decisions about conditionality. Rather, the IMF staff appears to enjoy substantial autonomy, or agency slack, in setting the terms of Fund programs.

On the other hand, the results and charts do indicate that G-5 governments exercise some influence over IMF conditionality. In particular, they suggest that the G-5 play a role in determining the Fund's use of performance criteria, the "hardest" type of conditionality included in Fund programs. Panel (a) of figure 3.3 illustrates that aggregate G-5 bank exposure (*G5BANK*) has no significant effect on the number of performance criteria attached to an IMF loan, regardless of the level of G-5 preference heterogeneity (*COVG5BANK*): *G5BANK* is negatively signed, but its coefficient is never significantly different from zero. As illustrated in panel (b) of figure 3.3, however, *COVG5BANK* has a negative and significant effect on the number of PCs, although

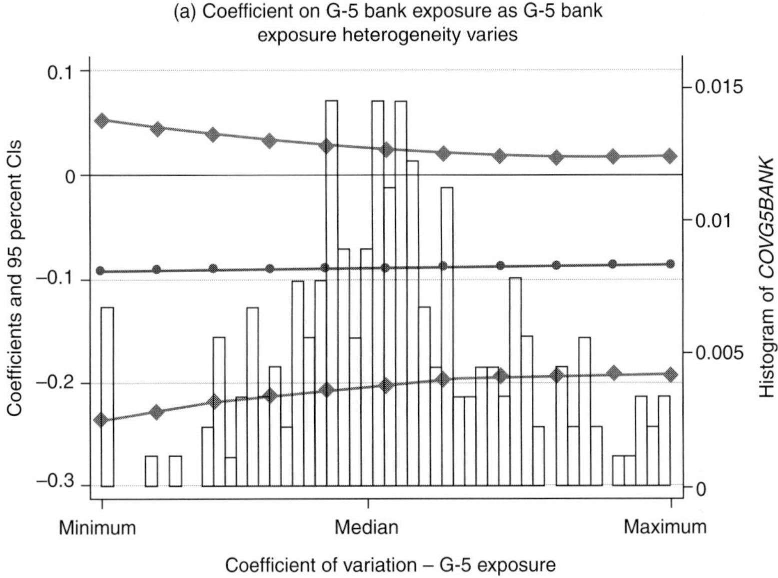

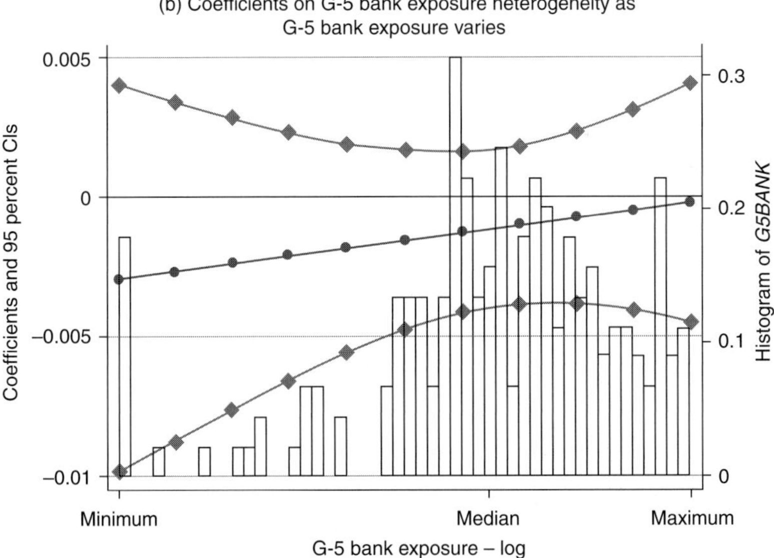

Figure 3.2 Interactions between G-5 bank exposure intensity and heterogeneity, conditionality (total conditions)

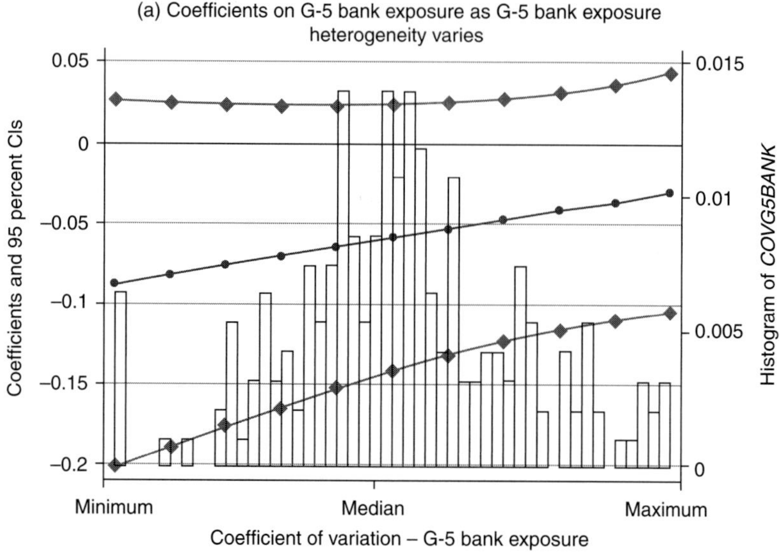

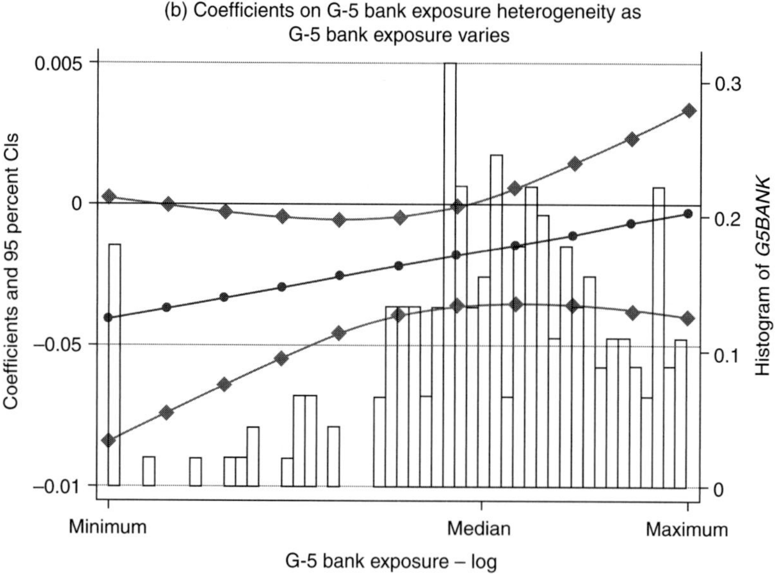

Figure 3.3 Interactions between G-5 bank exposure intensity and heterogeneity, conditionality (performance criteria)

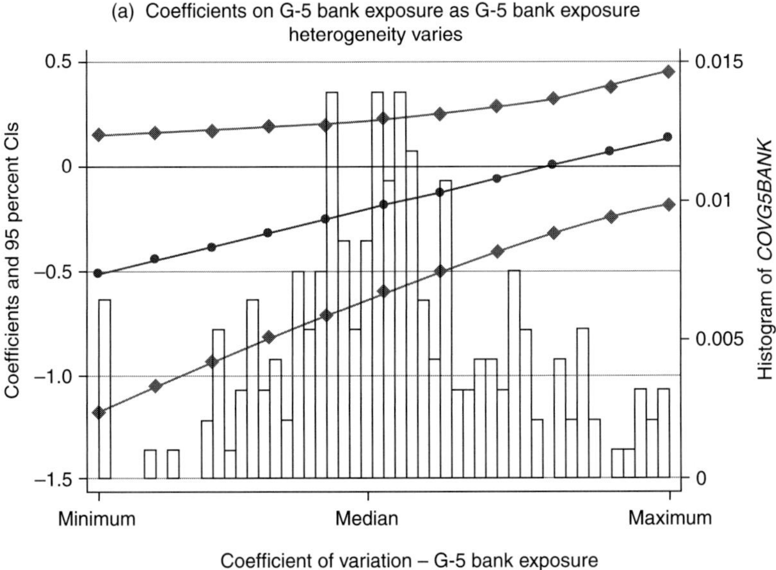

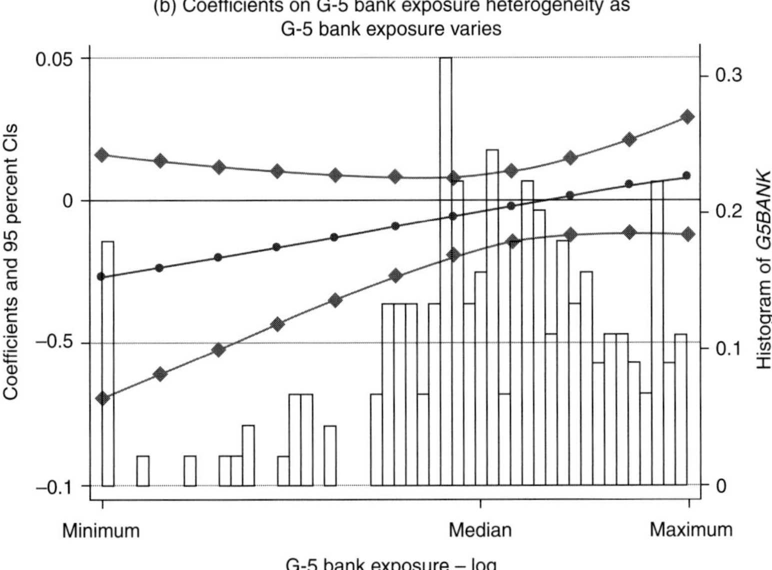

Figure 3.4 Interactions between G-5 bank exposure intensity and heterogeneity, conditionality (prior actions)

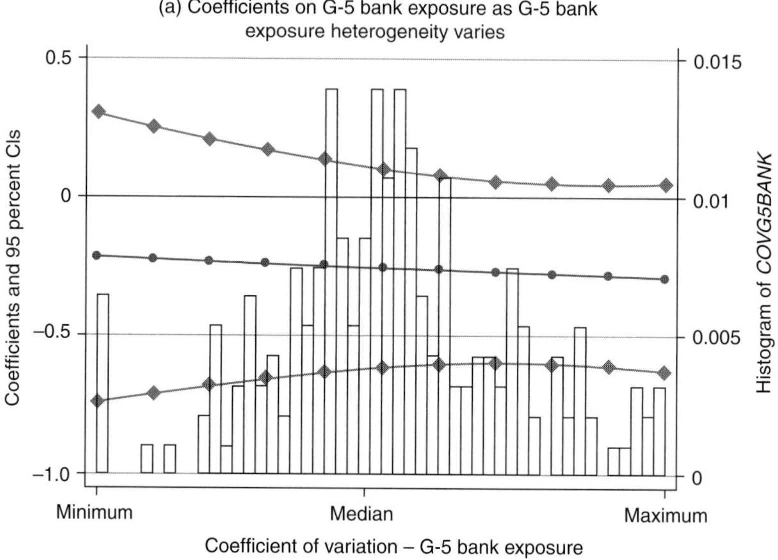

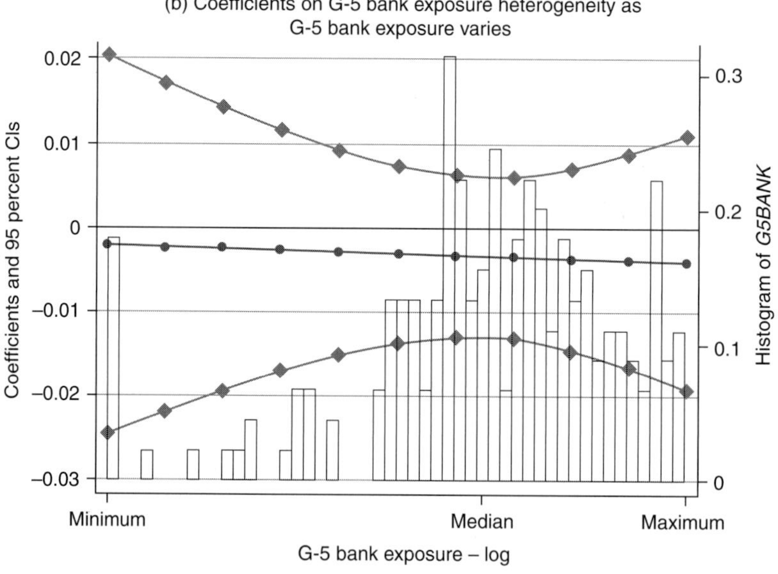

Figure 3.5 Interactions between G-5 bank exposure intensity and heterogeneity, conditionality (benchmarks/targets)

this effect disappears as *G5BANK* increases. Thus, G-5 disagreements about the financial importance of a particular country lead to reductions in conditionality only in cases in which the borrower is of little importance to the G-5 as a group (i.e. when *G5BANK* is below its median value). In cases in which G-5 collective interests are strong (i.e. when *G5BANK* is at or above its median value), greater preference heterogeneity does not result in such leniency about IMF conditionality. Table 3.7 provides first differences illustrating the actual substantive impact of this finding, as well as the substantive impact of the remaining significant variables in the conditionality specifications.[55]

Viewed in conjunction with the findings of the loan size regressions, these results from the conditionality models illustrate that the IMF does not simply "bail out" all countries of financial importance to its largest shareholders. In fact, to the extent that IMF provides such bailouts (i.e. larger loans on more lenient terms) at all, it appears to do so only in very limited circumstances: specifically, when aggregate G-5 bank exposure (*G5BANK*) is low and G-5 preference heterogeneity (*COVG5BANK*) is high. In such cases, when a single G-5 government cares strongly about the lending outcome but its counterparts do not, IMF loans – all else equal – contain fewer performance criteria. In contrast, in the country cases typically seen as bailout candidates – those in which *G5BANK* is high, indicating that the Fund's principals have more intense domestic financial interests – greater preference heterogeneity actually results in *smaller* loans, while the aforementioned negative effect of *COVG5BANK* on the number of PCs loses statistical significance. Put simply, the distribution of preferences among G-5 governments does play an important role in shaping IMF lending decisions, but it does not, as commonly assumed, lead to bailouts in all large-country cases.

[55] One interesting and unexpected finding in the conditionality regressions is that more extensive German bank exposure (*GRSHARE*) appears to result in a larger number of total conditions (model 1). This variable is only weakly significant (90 percent confidence level), however, and it is not significant in the remaining conditionality models. While we should be cautious in inferring too much from this single result, it may suggest that the German government is somewhat less effective than its G-5 counterparts in ensuring that countries it deems financially important receive preferential treatment from the IMF.

Table 3.7 *First differences, conditionality models*

Total conditions (model 1)
Predicted number of conditions, all variables at means: 11.43

Variable	Predicted change (number of conditions)	Substantive change in each variable
Percent bond debt	2.07	22.9% to 51.2%
German share, G-5 bank exposure	4.64	27.7% to 54.6%
GDP	3.91	\$25.6 billion to \$108 billion
GDP per capita	–2.56	\$5,486 to \$8,185
GDP growth	–4.27	0.78% to 7.72%
Short-term debt/reserves	3.64	0.79 to 3.10
Veto players	0.99	3 to 5
Propensity score	–5.10	0.33 to 0.50
G-5 UN voting affinity heterogeneity		
SDS (*G5S* = 1)	0.77	0.31 to 0.37
SDS (*G5S* = 1.36)	1.45**	0.31 to 0.37
SDS (*G5S* = 1.72)	2.71**	0.31 to 0.37

Performance criteria (model 2)
Predicted number of performance criteria, all variables at means: 6.34

Variable	Predicted change (number of conditions)	Substantive change in each variable
G-5 bank exposure heterogeneity		
COVG5BANK (*G5BANK* = \$3.4 million)	–0.90**	115.53 to 162.60
COVG5BANK (*G5BANK* = \$1.6 billion)	–0.43	115.53 to 162.60
COVG5BANK (*G5BANK* = \$72.2 billion)	–0.14	115.53 to 162.60
GDP growth	–1.24	0.78% to 7.72%
External debt/GDP	0.93	58.48% to 94.30%
Short-term debt/reserves	1.23	0.79 to 3.10
Currency crisis	0.93	0 to 1
IMF liquidity ratio	–0.94	0.30 to 0.46
Propensity score	–1.83	0.33 to 0.50

Table 3.7 *(cont.)*

Total conditions (model 1)

Prior actions (model 3)
Predicted number of prior actions, all variables at means: 0.69

Variable	Predicted change	Substantive change in each variable
Percent bond debt	0.97	22.9% to 51.2%
US share, G-5 bank exposure	2.22	29.7% to 53.7%
German share, G-5 bank exposure	3.66	27.7% to 54.6%
French share, G-5 bank exposure	2.23	15.6% to 34.2%
GDP per capita	–0.34	$5,486 to $8,185

Benchmarks/targets (model 4)
Predicted number of benchmarks/targets, all variables at means: 2.04

Variable	Predicted change	Substantive change in each variable
Percent bond debt	1.17	22.9% to 51.2%
UK share, G-5 bank exposure	–0.59	8.5% to 16.1%
German share, G-5 bank exposure	4.05	27.7% to 54.6%
GDP per capita	–0.52	$5,486 to $8,185
GDP growth	–1.19	0.78% to 7.72%
Short-term debt/reserves	2.48	0.79 to 3.10
Propensity score	–1.53	0.33 to 0.50
G-5 UN voting affinity		
G5S (*SDS* = 0.21)	0.62	1.36 to 1.60
G5S (*SDS* = 0.31)	3.11**	1.36 to 1.60
G5S (*SDS* = 0.41)	12.89**	1.36 to 1.60
G-5 UN voting affinity heterogeneity		
SDS (*G5S* = 1)	–0.06	0.31 to 0.37
SDS (*G5S* = 1.36)	0.88**	0.31 to 0.37
SDS (*G5S* = 1.72)	11.64**	0.31 to 0.37

Note: ** = significant at 5 percent.

Along with these aggregate measures of G-5 bank exposure, several of the individual G-5 bank exposure "share" variables are also significant in the conditionality models. Specifically, the results indicate that more extensive German bank exposure (*GRSHARE*) consistently results in more extensive conditionality: *GRSHARE* is positive and statistically significant in all four conditionality models. In contrast, the remaining G-5 "share" variables are only intermittently significant and of varying sign: more extensive American and French bank exposure (*USSHARE*, *FRSHARE*) is correlated with a larger number of prior actions (model 3), while more extensive British bank exposure (*UKSHARE*) is *negatively* associated with the number of benchmarks/targets (model 4). On the whole, these results to seem to indicate that the German government is rather less effective than its G-5 counterparts in ensuring that countries it regards as financially important receive preferential treatment from the Fund. Nevertheless, given that German (and French) banks tend to have greater exposure to the poorest countries in the data sample (the central and eastern European countries and north African/Middle Eastern borrowers, respectively), these results may simply indicate a greater need for structural adjustment by these borrowers, rather than less influence of these Fund principals relative to the United States, United Kingdom, and Japan. Finally, given the fairly high degree of multicollinearity among these G-5 "share" variables, these results may simply be spurious correlations. As with the "share" variable results from the loan size regressions, therefore, we should interpret these results with caution.

In addition to highlighting the nature of (and limits to) G-5 influence over IMF lending decisions, the conditionality models also provide qualified support for the hypotheses linking changes in the composition of international borrowers and lenders to IMF staff expectations about catalytic financing. As in the loan size regressions, *PCTBOND* is positive and statistically significant in model 1 (total conditions), model 3 (prior actions), and model 4 (benchmarks/targets). Moreover, as expected, the largest effect of *PCTBOND* on conditionality occurs in the prior actions model (model 3). This finding lends further support to the catalytic financing logic, since these *ex ante* conditions are explicitly intended to be an outward signal to global financial markets of a borrower government's commitment to future economic reform.[56] In contrast, *PCTBOND* does not have a significant effect on the number of performance criteria included in an IMF loan (model 2). These results shed further light on the IMF staff's calculations as it designs and proposes Fund programs to the executive board for approval. In particular, they suggest that changes in the composition of international capital flows from bank lending to bond financing have influenced staff decisions about both the *amount* and *timing* of the conditionality included in IMF programs: rather than adding more *ex post* conditionality (e.g. performance criteria) in order to address private international creditors' more severe collective action costs and reluctance to provide catalytic financing, the staff has shifted toward the use of more *ex ante* "hard" conditions (prior actions), as well as additional "soft" conditions (benchmarks/ targets), in order to generate the desired catalytic effect on private capital flows.

Although the conditionality models reinforce the importance of the shift from bank lending to bond financing, they suggest that the composition of a country's borrowers (i.e. sovereign versus non-sovereign) is of less importance in shaping Fund decisions about conditionality. As table 3.6 demonstrates, *PCTPNG*, the share of private non-guaranteed debt, is not significant in any of the conditionality specifications, even though it is positively signed, as expected, in each regression and approaches statistical significance ($p = 0.12$) in the prior actions model. As in the loan size models, this unexpected negative result may be due to the fact that the IMF is less willing to exert its influence in non-sovereign lending cases, even though creditors' collective action problems are more severe and a large-scale IMF bailout might have the desired catalytic effect. Thus, while the preliminary two-by-two tables suggest that the increase in non-sovereign capital flows has substantially influenced IMF lending, these findings are not echoed in the multivariate analysis. Nonetheless, the absence of a clear, systematic effect of non-sovereign capital flows on IMF lending in the multivariate regressions does not mean that this change in patterns of financial globalization is unimportant in all Fund lending cases. Indeed,

[56] Thomas and Ramakrishnan (2006) find that the implementation of prior actions is a strong predictor of compliance with subsequent conditionality, thereby reinforcing this "signaling" logic.

as discussed extensively in chapter 5, this shift from sovereign to non-sovereign borrowing played a central role in at least one major IMF lending episode in the last two decades: the Fund's bailout of South Korea in 1997/8.

The statistical analysis also illustrates that catalytic financing concerns are only one factor influencing IMF staff choices about conditionality. Indeed, as expected, a number of the control variables included in the regressions are also significant determinants of conditionality. The substantive effects of these control variables are illustrated in table 3.7. Several interesting patterns emerge from the data. Apart from *PCTBOND*, *GDP*, GDP per capita (*GDPPC*), economic growth (*GROWTH*), and short-term debt/reserves (*STDRES*) are all significant in model 1 (total conditions). In addition, a number of the macroeconomic and external debt measures are also significant in one or more of the remaining models. As with the loan size analysis, these results once again indicate that "technocratic" economic criteria play a key role in shaping IMF lending decisions. In addition, the negative and significant result on the propensity score variable (*PSCORE*) in three of the conditionality specifications (models 1, 2, and 4) is a further indication that strong selection effects exist in IMF lending. In particular, countries that are more likely to request IMF loans are also more likely to receive lenient treatment from the Fund, in the form of less extensive conditionality.

Several additional control variables are also significant in one or more of the conditionality specifications. *CHECKS*, the veto players variable, is positive and significant in model 1, indicating that the Fund imposes more extensive conditionality when a borrower government faces greater domestic political opposition. The currency crisis dummy (*CRASH*) is also positive and significant in the performance criteria regression (model 2), a likely indicator of the Fund's overarching concern with providing clear signals of a country's creditworthiness and liquidity to international investors during financial crises. The IMF liquidity ratio variable (*LIQRATIO*) is negative and significant in model 2, suggesting that the Fund imposes less extensive conditionality when it has greater resources available to lend.

Finally, in contrast to the loan size regressions, the conditionality models provide somewhat greater support for geopolitical theories of IMF lending. Although the component terms of the interaction between mean G-5 UN voting affinity (*G5S*) and its standard deviation (*SDS*) are insignificant in all four models (with the exception of *SDS* in model 4), table 3.7 illustrates that these variables do have a significant conditional effect on some types of conditionality. For example, greater heterogeneity of G-5 UN voting affinity with an IMF borrower country (*SDS*) has a positive and significant effect on both the total number of conditions (model 1) included in a Fund program and the number of benchmarks/targets (model 4) when *G5S* is at or above its mean value. Furthermore, *G5S* is associated with more extensive use of benchmarks/targets (model 4) at medium to high levels of *SDS*. Thus, while the loan size model provided only weak evidence of "geopolitical logrolling," the conditionality specifications suggest that differences between the Fund's principals over the geopolitical or foreign policy importance of a borrower result in the inclusion of more extensive "soft" conditionality in IMF loans. G-5 foreign policy interests do not appear to influence the Fund's decisions about "hard" conditionality (performance criteria, prior actions), however. These results once again cast doubt on the widely held view that the foreign policy interests of the Fund's largest shareholders constitute the dominant political factor shaping IMF lending policies.

Robustness analysis: alternative specifications of the IMF's principals

Ultimately, both the loan size and conditionality models provide substantial and robust evidence in support of the book's core argument that changes in the composition of international capital flows – by shaping both G-5 governments' interests and those of the IMF staff – are a critical determinant of variation in Fund lending behavior over the last two decades. In order to assess the robustness of these findings further, however, I test an additional set of model specifications in this final section. In table 3.8, I substitute "US-only" measures of bank exposure (and UN voting affinity) for the G-5 variables included in the loan size and conditionality models discussed previously. This respecification directly tests my common agency theory of IMF lending against the dominant view

Table 3.8 *Robustness checks, loan size and conditionality (US-only models)*

Model	1	2	4	5	6	7	8
Variable	Amount/ quota	Amount/ GDP	Amount (SDR millions)	Total conditions	Performance criteria	Prior actions	Benchmarks/ targets
US bank exposure ($ billions)	0.0306	−0.0522	0.0503	−0.0275	−0.0172	−0.0895	−0.1298
(USBANK)	[0.0361]	[0.0426]	[0.0412]	[0.0570]	[0.0331]	[0.1833]	[0.1808]
US share, G-5 bank exposure	0.1923	0.2793	−0.1371	−0.0967	0.0681	1.3520	−0.2229
(USSHARE)	[0.3526]	[0.3099]	[0.3494]	[0.3126]	[0.1831]	[1.3723]	[1.1416]
PCTBOND	0.0034**	0.0064***	0.0080***	0.0076***	−0.0002	0.0344***	0.0194***
	[0.0017]	[0.0016]	[0.0017]	[0.0018]	[0.0012]	[0.0071]	[0.0064]
PCTPNG	0.0035	0.0007	0.0016	0.0044**	−0.0004	0.0141	0.0134**
	[0.0023]	[0.0018]	[0.0019]	[0.0021]	[0.0015]	[0.0096]	[0.0062]
PASTLOAN	−0.1278	−0.1192	−0.1101				
	[0.0886]	[0.0837]	[0.0810]				
LASTLOAN				0.1340	0.1972	0.8335	−0.1612
				[0.2337]	[0.1334]	[0.9077]	[0.6627]
Cubic temporal spline 1				0.0601	0.0512	0.2236	−0.0308
				[0.0710]	[0.0412]	[0.2662]	[0.2040]
Cubic temporal spline 2				−0.0265	−0.0183	−0.0909	0.0156
				[0.0288]	[0.0169]	[0.1069]	[0.0835]

Cubic temporal spline 3				0.0025	0.0001	0.0070	−0.0037
				[0.0024]	[0.0015]	[0.0084]	[0.0074]
EFF	0.6986***	0.8203***	0.8540***	0.1430	0.1107	0.0132	0.2920
	[0.1263]	[0.1244]	[0.1263]	[0.0948]	[0.0677]	[0.3515]	[0.3070]
GDP	0.2139***	0.1002	0.9953***	0.0946	0.0313	0.3774	0.2900
	[0.0640]	[0.0698]	[0.0704]	[0.0780]	[0.0507]	[0.2865]	[0.2302]
GDPPC	0.2518	0.0818	−0.1668	−0.5806***	−0.1679	−2.1779***	−0.4463
	[0.1898]	[0.1452]	[0.1516]	[0.1330]	[0.1116]	[0.4560]	[0.3500]
GROWTH	−0.0387***	−0.0448***	−0.0545***	−0.0328**	−0.0152	−0.0847	−0.0489
	[0.0117]	[0.0114]	[0.0118]	[0.0161]	[0.0097]	[0.0570]	[0.0418]
CURRGDP	−0.0241*	−0.0164	−0.0268**	0.0017	0.0071	−0.0012	−0.0036
	[0.0134]	[0.0126]	[0.0127]	[0.0113]	[0.0072]	[0.0355]	[0.0384]
EDTGDP	0.0028	0.0110***	0.0069***	−0.0001	0.0016	0.0019	−0.0022
	[0.0021]	[0.0020]	[0.0019]	[0.0017]	[0.0012]	[0.0062]	[0.0053]
STDRES	0.1094***	0.0646	0.0858**	0.0517	0.0444	−0.0634	0.1033
	[0.0396]	[0.0441]	[0.0426]	[0.0628]	[0.0345]	[0.2371]	[0.1648]
CRASH	0.0815	0.1559	0.0413	0.1426	0.1155	0.7348*	−0.4446
	[0.1673]	[0.1451]	[0.1390]	[0.1199]	[0.0827]	[0.4022]	[0.3427]
CHECKS	0.0999	0.2289***	0.2163**	0.1377*	−0.0026	0.0865	0.1699
	[0.0848]	[0.0795]	[0.0850]	[0.0760]	[0.0552]	[0.3076]	[0.2854]
US UN voting affinity (“S” score)	−0.5216*	−0.5335**	−0.5253**	−0.2058	−0.1698	−1.6177	0.4845
(*USS*)	[0.2870]	[0.2548]	[0.2606]	[0.2429]	[0.1808]	[1.0814]	[0.8868]

Table 3.8 *(cont.)*

Model	1	2	4	5	6	7	8
Variable	Amount/ quota	Amount/ GDP	Amount (SDR millions)	Total conditions	Performance criteria	Prior actions	Benchmarks/ targets
Propensity score	−0.5944	−0.7378*	−0.7542	−1.0798	−0.7786*	−1.0839	−2.5579
	[0.4793]	[0.4408]	[0.4726]	[0.8415]	[0.4719]	[3.4186]	[2.4317]
LIQRATIO	0.2694	0.4437	0.3018	0.3944	−0.5986	−4.6154*	2.9086
	[1.0849]	[0.8287]	[1.0078]	[0.6650]	[0.4707]	[2.4139]	[2.1923]
REVIEW	0.0914	0.1818*	0.0439	−0.0126	−0.0836	−0.4859	0.2740
	[0.1156]	[0.1012]	[0.1211]	[0.0964]	[0.0619]	[0.4162]	[0.2800]
CRISES	−0.0298	−0.0184	−0.0255	−0.0483**	−0.0369***	0.0287	−0.0863
	[0.0250]	[0.0207]	[0.0238]	[0.0201]	[0.0103]	[0.0715]	[0.0675]
LIBOR	0.0122	0.0350	0.0124	−0.0390	−0.0197	−0.1478	−0.1429**
	[0.0237]	[0.0217]	[0.0253]	[0.0243]	[0.0205]	[0.1002]	[0.0634]
Middle East	−0.4469	−0.7747**	−0.9499***	0.6535***	−0.1505	4.3469***	1.2529*
	[0.2854]	[0.3182]	[0.2932]	[0.2510]	[0.1884]	[1.5216]	[0.7416]
Africa				1.0921***	0.0483	6.7050***	1.1729
				[0.3644]	[0.2285]	[2.0697]	[1.1601]
Europe/central Asia	−0.4763	−0.4292	−0.5489**	0.9740***	0.1996	5.3141***	0.8843
	[0.3189]	[0.3090]	[0.2753]	[0.2786]	[0.1870]	[1.6728]	[0.8757]

Americas	−0.6186**	−0.7376**	−1.0814***	0.2906	0.0220	1.8020	−0.0802
	[0.2802]	[0.3442]	[0.3134]	[0.2501]	[0.1442]	[1.6218]	[0.8929]
East Asia	−0.1569	−0.5420	−0.8352*				
	[0.5235]	[0.4539]	[0.4609]				
Constant	−4.0677*	−6.2780***	−2.5543	6.4850***	3.7222***	13.1008***	1.5595
	[2.0862]	[1.5954]	[1.8269]	[1.4016]	[1.0046]	[5.0673]	[4.0007]
Observations	*181*	*181*	*181*	*175*	*177*	*175*	*175*
Number of countries	*44*	*44*	*44*	*44*	*44*	*44*	*44*
R-squared	*0.502*	*0.446*	*0.877*	–	–	–	–
Adjusted R-squared	*0.426*	*0.360*	*0.859*	–	–	–	–
Log-likelihood	*−172.439*	*−163.229*	*−165.426*	*−531.489*	*−384.530*	*−259.403*	*−370.504*
Alpha	–	–	–	*0.124*	*3.11E−20*	*1.549*	*1.458*
Poisson goodness of fit (chi²)	–	–	–	*453.297*	*127.294*	*441.017*	*721.025*
Poisson goodness of fit (Pr > chi²)	–	–	–	*0.000*	*0.901*	*0.000*	*0.000*

Notes: Models 1–3: panel-corrected standard errors in brackets. Models 4–7: robust standard errors in brackets. * = significant at 10 percent; ** = significant at 5 percent; *** = significant at 1 percent.

Table 3.9 *Robustness checks, loan size (G-7 and G-10 models)*

Model	1	2	3	4	5	6
Variable	Amount/ quota	Amount/ GDP	Amount (SDR millions)	Amount/ quota	Amount/ GDP	Amount (SDR millions)
G-7 bank exposure ($ billions)	0.4543***	0.2132	0.3816***			
(*G7BANK*)	[0.1364]	[0.1434]	[0.1436]			
COVG7BANK	0.0001	−0.0003	0.0003			
	[0.0012]	[0.0012]	[0.0012]			
G7BANK ×	−0.0022***	−0.0011*	−0.0014**			
COVG7BANK	[0.0006]	[0.0006]	[0.0006]			
G-10 bank exposure ($ billions)				0.2109**	0.1184	0.2172**
(*G10BANK*)				[0.0927]	[0.0885]	[0.0926]
COVG10BANK				−0.0002	0.0000	0.0001
				[0.0011]	[0.0012]	[0.0013]
G10BANK ×				−0.0012***	−0.0010***	−0.0009**
COVG10BANK				[0.0004]	[0.0004]	[0.0004]
PCTBOND	0.0055***	0.0075***	0.0091***	0.0036**	0.0062***	0.0075***
	[0.0017]	[0.0017]	[0.0018]	[0.0014]	[0.0014]	[0.0016]
PCTPNG	0.0050**	0.0025	0.0023	0.0046*	0.0036	0.0026
	[0.0023]	[0.0021]	[0.0020]	[0.0027]	[0.0024]	[0.0024]

US share, G-7 bank exposure	−3.1386***	−1.2265	−2.0276*
(*US7SHARE*)	[0.8474]	[1.1943]	[1.1770]
UK share, G-7 bank exposure	−2.3075*	−1.4378	−2.0385*
(*UK7SHARE*)	[1.1947]	[1.3191]	[1.2146]
Japanese share, G-7 bank exposure	−3.8436***	−1.4786	−2.3042*
(*JP7SHARE*)	[0.9861]	[1.2547]	[1.2511]
German share, G-7 bank exposure	−3.7267***	−1.5500	−2.3109**
(*GR7SHARE*)	[0.9831]	[1.0965]	[1.0902]
French share, G-7 bank exposure	−3.4903***	−1.1377	−1.9900**
(*FR7SHARE*)	[0.9047]	[0.9724]	[0.9781]
Canadian share, G-7 bank exposure	−3.4768***	−0.9861	−1.8957
(*CN7SHARE*)	[0.8966]	[1.1865]	[1.2121]
Italian share, G-7 bank exposure	−4.8861***	−2.1889*	−2.9061**
(*IT7SHARE*)	[1.0452]	[1.2125]	[1.2176]

Table 3.9 *(cont.)*

Model	1	2	3	4	5	6
Variable	Amount/ quota	Amount/ GDP	Amount (SDR millions)	Amount/ quota	Amount/ GDP	Amount (SDR millions)
US share, G-10 bank exposure				0.4147	0.8089**	–0.0383
(*US10SHARE*)				[0.4384]	[0.4019]	[0.3800]
UK share, G-10 bank exposure				1.7108*	1.1890	0.0628
(*UK10SHARE*)				[0.9792]	[1.0411]	[1.0030]
Japanese share, G-10 bank exposure				–0.0455	0.6986	–0.2858
(*JP10SHARE*)				[0.6969]	[0.6020]	[0.5599]
German share, G-10 bank exposure				0.2158	0.9244*	0.3069
(*GR10SHARE*)				[0.5251]	[0.5267]	[0.5184]
French share, G-10 bank exposure				–0.0354	0.7309	–0.0860
(*FR10SHARE*)				[0.5862]	[0.5987]	[0.5863]
Canadian share, G-10 bank exposure				0.0665	1.1457**	0.1341
(*CN10SHARE*)				[0.4900]	[0.4486]	[0.4924]

Italian share, G-10 bank exposure				−1.4240**	−0.3905	−1.0554
(*IT10SHARE*)				[0.6035]	[0.6886]	[0.6875]
Other G-10 countries' share				0.0149	0.2524	−0.3037
(*OTH10SHARE*)				[0.4575]	[0.4979]	[0.5111]
PASTLOAN	−0.0548	−0.0648	−0.0376	−0.1204	−0.1350	−0.1036
	[0.0711]	[0.0828]	[0.0845]	[0.0739]	[0.0851]	[0.0863]
EFF	0.6662***	0.7870***	0.8262***	0.6269***	0.7556***	0.7690***
	[0.1285]	[0.1254]	[0.1246]	[0.1363]	[0.1378]	[0.1369]
GDP	0.0618	−0.0509	0.8244***	0.2013**	0.0424	0.9449***
	[0.0838]	[0.1028]	[0.1038]	[0.0807]	[0.0872]	[0.0891]
GDPPC	0.0662	−0.0172	−0.2529*	0.2703	0.1989	−0.0512
	[0.1902]	[0.1547]	[0.1515]	[0.1882]	[0.1516]	[0.1553]
GROWTH	−0.0322***	−0.0453***	−0.0519***	−0.0303***	−0.0446***	−0.0514***
	[0.0112]	[0.0129]	[0.0132]	[0.0112]	[0.0123]	[0.0129]
CURRGDP	−0.0174	−0.0113	−0.0212*	−0.0126	−0.0032	−0.0147
	[0.0115]	[0.0134]	[0.0128]	[0.0117]	[0.0139]	[0.0130]
EDTGDP	0.0024	0.0094***	0.0051**	0.0042*	0.0114***	0.0077***
	[0.0020]	[0.0022]	[0.0021]	[0.0022]	[0.0023]	[0.0021]
STDRES	0.1318***	0.0590	0.0643	0.1128**	0.0315	0.0514
	[0.0508]	[0.0573]	[0.0525]	[0.0459]	[0.0395]	[0.0409]

Table 3.9 *(cont.)*

Model	1	2	3	4	5	6
Variable	Amount/ quota	Amount/ GDP	Amount (SDR millions)	Amount/ quota	Amount/ GDP	Amount (SDR millions)
CRASH	0.1194	0.1914	0.0688	0.0570	0.0922	−0.0263
	[0.1453]	[0.1421]	[0.1328]	[0.1548]	[0.1424]	[0.1442]
CHECKS	0.1121	0.2449***	0.2146**	0.1142	0.2312***	0.2009**
	[0.0815]	[0.0901]	[0.0931]	[0.0790]	[0.0836]	[0.0915]
G-7 UN voting affinity (mean "S" score)	−3.1759**	−2.9583*	−2.7832*			
(*G7S*)	[1.5636]	[1.5277]	[1.4827]			
SD7S	−11.9611*	−10.2477*	−9.9474			
	[6.6163]	[6.2124]	[6.0939]			
G7S × *SD7S*	8.7001**	7.3351*	7.1536*			
	[4.2007]	[4.1006]	[3.9180]			
G10S				−2.6473	−1.6245	−2.0812
				[1.9313]	[1.4766]	[1.5733]
SD10S				−11.3663	−4.7538	−7.2274
				[9.3662]	[7.3956]	[7.5158]

G10S ×				8.6653	4.0106	5.6137
SD10S				[5.7455]	[4.6299]	[4.6123]
PSCORE	−0.6849	−0.5959	−0.6114	−0.7587*	−0.7109*	−0.8520**
	[0.4332]	[0.3931]	[0.4328]	[0.4195]	[0.3759]	[0.4066]
LIQRATIO	−0.1992	0.2066	0.2938	−0.0977	−0.0194	0.1713
	[1.0987]	[0.8732]	[1.0255]	[1.0876]	[0.8708]	[1.0697]
REVIEW	0.0875	0.1583	0.0388	0.0098	0.0680	−0.0423
	[0.1243]	[0.1201]	[0.1342]	[0.1336]	[0.1264]	[0.1433]
CRISES	−0.0269	−0.0191	−0.0283	−0.0311	−0.0188	−0.0273
	[0.0231]	[0.0212]	[0.0228]	[0.0251]	[0.0199]	[0.0236]
LIBOR	0.0173	0.0289	0.0126	−0.0034	0.0080	−0.0045
	[0.0334]	[0.0309]	[0.0327]	[0.0389]	[0.0373]	[0.0374]
Middle East	−0.2440	−0.5392	−0.7125*	−0.1994	−0.1497	−0.1455
	[0.3432]	[0.4508]	[0.3874]	[0.3712]	[0.3714]	[0.3744]
Africa				0.1597	0.4380	0.6523
				[0.5472]	[0.5718]	[0.5584]
Europe/central Asia	−0.0848	−0.0928	−0.2696	−0.1771	0.1723	0.1505
	[0.4028]	[0.5213]	[0.4559]	[0.5223]	[0.3788]	[0.4342]
Americas	−0.5834	−0.6207	−0.9944**	−0.4560	−0.2142	−0.3412
	[0.4157]	[0.5374]	[0.4913]	[0.3620]	[0.2717]	[0.3368]

Table 3.9 *(cont.)*

Model	1	2	3	4	5	6
Variable	Amount/ quota	Amount/ GDP	Amount (SDR millions)	Amount/ quota	Amount/ GDP	Amount (SDR millions)
East Asia	−0.1897	−0.4624	−0.7175			
	[0.5733]	[0.6155]	[0.5843]			
Constant	6.1818	1.2137	5.0831	−1.2370	−5.8304*	−1.2927
	[4.1404]	[4.1368]	[3.9944]	[4.0849]	[3.4308]	[3.7257]
Observations	*181*	*181*	*181*	*179*	*179*	*179*
Number of countries	*44*	*44*	*44*	*44*	*44*	*44*
R-squared	*0.579*	*0.470*	*0.884*	*0.575*	*0.498*	*0.885*
Adjusted R-squared	*0.481*	*0.347*	*0.857*	*0.470*	*0.375*	*0.857*
Log-likelihood	*−157.305*	*−159.135*	*−160.133*	*−156.094*	*−151.262*	*−156.362*

Notes: Panel-corrected standard errors in brackets. * = significant at 10 percent; ** = significant at 5 percent; *** = significant at 1 percent.

Table 3.10 *Robustness checks, conditionality (G-7 and G-10 models)*

Model	1	2	3	4	5	6	7	8
Variable	Total conditions	Performance criteria	Prior actions	Benchmarks/ targets	Total conditions	Performance criteria	Prior actions	Benchmarks/ targets
G-7 bank exposure ($ billions)	−0.2075*	−0.1236*	−1.8049***	−0.2083				
(*G7BANK*)	[0.1121]	[0.0720]	[0.5427]	[0.3538]				
COVG7BANK	−0.0001	0.0007	−0.0076	−0.0050				
	[0.0014]	[0.0008]	[0.0048]	[0.0044]				
G7BANK ×	0.0005	0.0004	0.0066***	−0.0005				
COVG7BANK	[0.0004]	[0.0003]	[0.0018]	[0.0014]				
G-10 bank exposure ($ billions)					−0.0944	−0.0649	−0.6508**	0.0462
(*G10BANK*)					[0.0645]	[0.0441]	[0.2957]	[0.2009]
COVG10BANK					−0.0005	−0.0001	−0.0012	−0.0037
					[0.0011]	[0.0007]	[0.0038]	[0.0036]
G10BANK ×					0.0001	0.0003*	0.0009	−0.0012
COVG10BANK					[0.0002]	[0.0002]	[0.0008]	[0.0009]
PCTBOND	0.0052***	−0.0004	0.0279***	0.0124*	0.0055***	0.0003	0.0364***	0.0142**
	[0.0018]	[0.0012]	[0.0061]	[0.0066]	[0.0018]	[0.0012]	[0.0076]	[0.0066]
PCTPNG	0.0006	−0.0010	0.0207	0.0022	0.0033	−0.0007	0.0104	0.0073
	[0.0027]	[0.0017]	[0.0136]	[0.0071]	[0.0028]	[0.0014]	[0.0125]	[0.0079]

Table 3.10 *(cont.)*

Model Variable	1 Total conditions	2 Performance criteria	3 Prior actions	4 Benchmarks/ targets	5 Total conditions	6 Performance criteria	7 Prior actions	8 Benchmarks/ targets
US share, G-7 bank exposure	0.8420	0.3342	12.4171***	2.3054				
(*US7SHARE*)	[0.7411]	[0.3934]	[4.1542]	[2.5040]				
UK share, G-7 bank exposure	0.4993	0.6949	7.6311**	−1.8087				
(*UK7SHARE*)	[1.0283]	[0.6544]	[3.7672]	[2.9028]				
Japanese share, G-7 bank exposure	0.7431	0.2212	12.9281***	2.7114				
(*JP7SHARE*)	[0.8461]	[0.5055]	[4.3309]	[2.9719]				
German share, G-7 bank exposure	1.6736**	0.4344	13.6526***	4.7005*				
(*GR7SHARE*)	[0.8040]	[0.4523]	[4.0720]	[2.6307]				
French share, G-7 bank exposure	1.4839**	0.5143	12.5670***	2.9199				
(*FR7SHARE*)	[0.7393]	[0.4107]	[3.5205]	[2.5817]				
Canadian share, G-7 bank exposure	0.3059	−0.1434	−13.1934	0.9574				
(*CN7SHARE*)	[0.7242]	[0.4160]	[8.7114]	[2.9199]				

Italian share, G-7 bank exposure	1.1349	0.3653	12.7574***	2.5588				
(*IT7SHARE*)	[0.8997]	[0.5135]	[4.2098]	[2.7441]				
US share, G-10 bank exposure					−0.3699	−0.4855**	−0.9052	−0.5841
(*US10SHARE*)					[0.4075]	[0.2371]	[2.2192]	[1.3339]
UK share, G-10 bank exposure					−0.9194	−0.6813	−3.9399	−4.2076*
(*UK10SHARE*)					[1.1126]	[0.7540]	[3.0083]	[2.5007]
Japanese share, G-10 bank exposure					−0.6319	−0.8845*	−2.2704	−0.1243
(*JP10SHARE*)					[0.6056]	[0.4540]	[2.7644]	[1.7678]
German share, G-10 bank exposure					0.6326	−0.2880	1.0867	2.3986**
(*GR10SHARE*)					[0.3881]	[0.2453]	[2.0571]	[1.0429]
French share, G-10 bank exposure					0.4399	−0.0407	0.5825	0.5059
(*FR10SHARE*)					[0.4570]	[0.2864]	[1.4749]	[1.3248]
Canadian share, G-10 bank exposure					−0.6021	−0.8527***	−15.8971	−0.8478
(*CN10SHARE*)					[0.4050]	[0.2872]	[9.6707]	[1.9396]

Table 3.10 *(cont.)*

Model Variable	1 Total conditions	2 Performance criteria	3 Prior actions	4 Benchmarks/ targets	5 Total conditions	6 Performance criteria	7 Prior actions	8 Benchmarks/ targets
Italian share, G-10 bank exposure					−0.0645	−0.4137	1.9605	0.5726
(*IT10SHARE*)					[0.5874]	[0.3881]	[2.1690]	[1.6677]
Other G-10 countries' share					0.3642	−0.2306	3.3884*	1.4555
(*OTH10SHARE*)					[0.4140]	[0.2665]	[1.9227]	[1.1448]
Years since last IMF loan	0.4361	0.2373	0.8072	0.8487	0.4064	0.1920	1.6493	1.0883
(*LASTLOAN*)	[0.2887]	[0.1798]	[1.5871]	[0.8183]	[0.2686]	[0.1772]	[1.2021]	[0.8904]
Cubic temporal spline 1	0.1516*	0.0667	0.1707	0.2465	0.1423*	0.0566	0.4083	0.3219
	[0.0885]	[0.0549]	[0.4874]	[0.2478]	[0.0809]	[0.0541]	[0.3492]	[0.2690]
Cubic temporal spline 2	−0.0635*	−0.0248	−0.0675	−0.0933	−0.0594*	−0.0211	−0.1517	−0.1238
	[0.0362]	[0.0222]	[0.1991]	[0.1014]	[0.0328]	[0.0219]	[0.1392]	[0.1100]
Cubic temporal spline 3	0.0052*	0.0006	0.0056	0.0032	0.0048*	0.0006	0.0056	0.0053
	[0.0031]	[0.0017]	[0.0160]	[0.0088]	[0.0027]	[0.0018]	[0.0100]	[0.0099]
EFF	0.1092	0.1259*	−0.1723	0.0652	0.0900	0.1267*	−0.1751	0.0012
	[0.0976]	[0.0690]	[0.3513]	[0.2943]	[0.0940]	[0.0648]	[0.3421]	[0.3193]
GDP	0.2322**	0.1141*	1.3135***	0.4286	0.1699**	0.0782	0.9933**	0.3091
	[0.0959]	[0.0681]	[0.5051]	[0.2971]	[0.0772]	[0.0612]	[0.4100]	[0.2355]
GDPPC	−0.4854***	−0.1301	−1.3262**	−0.6547	−0.4469***	−0.1591	−1.3018**	−0.6834
	[0.1480]	[0.1143]	[0.6202]	[0.4044]	[0.1364]	[0.1142]	[0.6444]	[0.4173]
GROWTH	−0.0483***	−0.0165	−0.0896	−0.1058**	−0.0527***	−0.0170	−0.1631**	−0.1136**
	[0.0167]	[0.0117]	[0.0840]	[0.0480]	[0.0164]	[0.0119]	[0.0654]	[0.0524]

CURRGDP	−0.0047	0.0025	−0.0114	−0.0209	−0.0034	0.0011	−0.0274	−0.0222
	[0.0110]	[0.0078]	[0.0415]	[0.0374]	[0.0118]	[0.0082]	[0.0358]	[0.0401]
EDTGDP	0.0041*	0.0038**	0.0153	0.0048	0.0045**	0.0037**	0.0183	0.0070
	[0.0025]	[0.0016]	[0.0121]	[0.0071]	[0.0022]	[0.0017]	[0.0117]	[0.0072]
STDRES	0.1103	0.0633	−0.1942	0.2881	0.0661	0.0434	−0.1074	0.2579
	[0.0768]	[0.0505]	[0.4431]	[0.2101]	[0.0672]	[0.0433]	[0.2920]	[0.1858]
CRASH	0.1556	0.0925	1.0865***	−0.2452	0.0984	0.0992	1.0562**	−0.4211
	[0.1177]	[0.0761]	[0.4189]	[0.3159]	[0.1211]	[0.0726]	[0.4207]	[0.3298]
CHECKS	0.1406*	0.0102	0.1491	0.1878	0.1541**	0.0192	0.4085	0.2013
	[0.0723]	[0.0567]	[0.2958]	[0.2736]	[0.0756]	[0.0558]	[0.2983]	[0.2867]
G-7 UN voting affinity (mean "S" score)	0.5466	1.7872**	−6.0012	−1.5052				
(*G7S*)	[1.5091]	[0.7775]	[6.0092]	[5.1283]				
SD7S	1.3775	9.0857**	−15.5255	−18.3420				
	[6.5560]	[3.5882]	[28.0947]	[21.5285]				
G7S × *SD7S*	0.7764	−5.6713**	14.9074	16.4395				
	[4.2268]	[2.2326]	[17.9620]	[14.0296]				
G10S					−0.7053	0.9386	−17.8137***	−2.1327
					[1.5853]	[0.8717]	[6.4785]	[5.3158]
SD10S					−5.6172	6.2002	−81.8112***	−29.1634
					[7.6197]	[4.1176]	[31.7321]	[25.5701]
G10S × *SD10S*					4.3422	−3.9848	54.6940***	20.6553
					[4.6278]	[2.4646]	[19.7908]	[15.5933]

Table 3.10 *(cont.)*

Model	1	2	3	4	5	6	7	8
Variable	Total conditions	Performance criteria	Prior actions	Benchmarks/ targets	Total conditions	Performance criteria	Prior actions	Benchmarks/ targets
PSCORE	−2.3793**	−1.1060	−2.1250	−5.9570**	−2.2971**	−0.9446	−4.6132	−6.7759**
	[1.0854]	[0.7068]	[5.6616]	[2.9686]	[0.9987]	[0.6976]	[4.1122]	[3.2161]
LIQRATIO	0.2146	−0.5816	−4.2463	2.1086	0.0352	−0.6273	−4.7152**	1.5482
	[0.6654]	[0.4880]	[2.6538]	[2.2037]	[0.6415]	[0.4984]	[2.3908]	[2.3119]
REVIEW	−0.0060	−0.0848	−0.3986	0.2208	0.0411	−0.0145	0.0409	0.2954
	[0.0935]	[0.0619]	[0.4272]	[0.2913]	[0.0951]	[0.0561]	[0.3898]	[0.3129]
CRISES	−0.0342*	−0.0330**	0.0372	−0.0680	−0.0227	−0.0308**	0.1492*	−0.0257
	[0.0207]	[0.0133]	[0.0967]	[0.0758]	[0.0222]	[0.0142]	[0.0889]	[0.0788]
LIBOR	−0.0362	−0.0277	−0.0987	−0.1199*	−0.0074	0.0060	0.1357	−0.0693
	[0.0260]	[0.0208]	[0.0917]	[0.0694]	[0.0289]	[0.0186]	[0.1202]	[0.0891]
Middle East	0.0793	−0.3890*	3.0664	0.6720	0.1079	−0.2086	2.4860	0.6328
	[0.3283]	[0.2264]	[1.8832]	[0.9523]	[0.3763]	[0.2123]	[1.9192]	[1.1231]
Africa	0.3114	−0.1671	6.5382**	−0.0145	0.3506		4.9637*	0.1488
	[0.4817]	[0.3171]	[3.0558]	[1.4101]	[0.5715]		[2.9971]	[1.6833]
Europe/central Asia	0.4290	0.1398	3.5250*	−0.4756	0.4237	0.2874	3.0529	−0.1584
	[0.3135]	[0.2044]	[1.8664]	[0.9936]	[0.3103]	[0.2765]	[2.0606]	[1.0139]
Americas	0.1685	0.0438	1.9568	−0.2392	0.0809	0.2207	0.4776	−0.3555
	[0.2416]	[0.1553]	[1.7432]	[0.8684]	[0.2568]	[0.2728]	[1.8469]	[0.9373]
East Asia						0.2480		
						[0.3301]		

Constant	1.9221	−0.8545	−8.3173	2.0930	5.4614*	1.5642	24.2708*	7.1855
	[3.1918]	[1.6004]	[15.8703]	[10.7293]	[3.2635]	[1.7918]	[14.1021]	[10.5255]
Observations	*175*	*177*	*175*	*175*	*173*	*175*	*173*	*173*
Number of countries	*44*	*44*	*44*	*44*	*44*	*44*	*44*	*44*
Log-likelihood	*−520.368*	*−379.921*	*−247.355*	*−360.377*	*−513.450*	*−372.097*	*−240.414*	*−359.891*
Alpha	*0.102*	–	*1.178*	*1.198*	*0.099*	–	*0.972*	*1.270*
Poisson goodness of fit (chi^2)	*404.478*	*118.076*	*375.649*	*620.322*	*396.572*	*109.744*	*348.379*	*642.633*
Poisson goodness of fit ($Pr > chi^2$)	*0.000*	*0.900*	*0.000*	*0.000*	*0.000*	*0.952*	*0.000*	*0.000*

Notes: Robust standard errors in brackets. * = significant at 10 percent; ** = significant at 5 percent; *** = significant at 1 percent.

in the existing literature that the Fund is effectively controlled by the US government alone, rather than by the G-5 countries as a group. In tables 3.9 and 3.10, I reanalyze loan size and conditionality, respectively, by replacing the G-5 variables with corresponding measures for the G-7 and G-10. These specifications are intended as checks to ensure that my findings above are not dependent on my focus on the G-5 as the relevant set of countries comprising the Fund's collective principal.

Several interesting findings emerge from these additional specifications. First and foremost, the results in table 3.8 cast significant doubt on the view that the US government controls IMF policymaking. Across all seven models of loan size and conditionality, neither US bank exposure (*USBANK*) nor the US share of total G-5 bank exposure (*USSHARE*) is statistically significant. These null findings contrast markedly with the earlier results, which showed a strong correlation between the intensity and heterogeneity of G-5 bank exposure and IMF loan characteristics. Similarly, voting affinity in the UN between the US and IMF borrower countries (*USS*) is not significant in the four conditionality models (models 4 to 7), and *negatively* correlated with IMF loan size in models 1 to 3. In contrast to past studies, therefore, my results do not support the view that the United States' foreign policy allies receive more favorable treatment from the Fund. Furthermore, as the goodness-of-fit statistics indicate, the original G-5 specifications, as a whole, are preferable to the "US-only" models.

Altogether, these results offer strong evidence that the common agency theory of IMF decision-making more accurately captures the dynamics of Fund policymaking and better explains variation in the size and terms of IMF loans during the last two decades. In short, despite the fact that the US-centric view of IMF politics is widely held by scholars and Fund critics alike, the statistical analysis emphatically rejects this perspective in favor of the common agency theory. Once again, this is not to say that American interests have no influence over IMF lending. Indeed, as the Mexican and South Korean case studies below illustrate, the US government's preferences are critically important in many high-profile lending cases. Nonetheless, the statistical analysis presented here quite clearly illustrates that American influence is not nearly as dominant as the conventional wisdom suggests, and that we must also consider the interests and influence of other powerful states within the IMF when seeking to explain Fund lending policies.

Second, the results of tables 3.9 and 3.10 show that my earlier findings are highly robust to alternative specifications of the membership of the IMF's "collective principal." To illustrate this clearly, I include charts of the conditional, interactive effects of G-7 and G-10 bank exposure intensity (*G7BANK*, *G10BANK*) and heterogeneity (*COVG7BANK*, *COVG10BANK*) in appendix 3 at the end of the book. As these charts illustrate, the same patterns evident in the earlier G-5 models are largely echoed in these new specifications. In fact, the interactive relationship between the intensity and heterogeneity of bank exposure among the IMF's largest shareholders is even stronger and more significant in the G-7 loan size results than it was in the G-5 analysis. These effects are also evident in the G-10 loan size models, although they are both less substantial and less significant than in the G-5 and G-7 specifications.

Similarly, these new G-7 and G-10 results mirror the earlier finding that the Fund's principals have substantially less influence over IMF conditionality than over decisions about loan size. The new models differ somewhat from the G-5 specifications on the nature of this influence, however. For example, the one significant result from the G-5 conditionality models – the finding that G-5 bank exposure heterogeneity (*COVG5BANK*) is negatively correlated with the number of performance criteria at low levels of aggregate G-5 bank exposure (*G5BANK*) – is no longer evident in the G-7 and G-10 specifications (table 3.10, models 2 and 6). Moreover, in contrast to the earlier results, *G7BANK* is negatively correlated with fewer prior actions at low levels of *COVG7BANK* (and vice versa), in table 3.10, model 3. Finally, *G10BANK* is *negatively* correlated with fewer total conditions at high levels of *COVG10BANK* (table 3.10, model 5) and with fewer prior actions in general (table 3.10, model 7). These slight differences notwithstanding, the results of tables 3.9 and 3.10 strongly indicate that my findings are not contingent on a focus on the G-5 as the Fund's de facto collective principal.

Third, the G-7 and G-10 models illustrate that the previous findings linking levels of bond debt (*PCTBOND*) to both IMF loan size and conditionality are strongly robust across specifications.

PCTBOND is once again positive and significant in each of the loan size specifications in table 3.9. Likewise, as in the earlier analysis, *PCTBOND* is also positive and significant in the conditionality models for total conditions, prior actions, and benchmarks/targets. Thus, alternative specifications of the IMF's "collective principal" do not alter the finding that changes in the composition of private international lenders from banks to bondholders consistently influence Fund decisions about both the size and terms of its lending arrangements.

Finally, in contrast to the earlier models, these new specifications offer partial evidence in support of the hypothesis linking levels of non-sovereign debt (*PCTPNG*) to IMF lending policies. Whereas *PCTPNG* was not statistically significant in any of the G-5 loan size or conditionality models, it is positive and significant in two of the "US-only" conditionality specifications (models 5 and 8). Similarly, *PCTPNG* is positive and significant in model 4 of table 3.9, the G-10 loan size (amount/quota) specification. Although we should exercise caution in ascribing too much significance to these intermittently significant results, these findings nevertheless suggest that the earlier lack of evidence in support of this hypothesis may be due, at least in part, to model specification. Further research is clearly warranted to ascertain the extent to which this particular change in patterns of financial globalization influences IMF lending behavior over time and across cases.

Conclusions

This chapter has presented a series of statistical tests of the book's core argument that changes in patterns of financial globalization are the key determinant of variation in IMF lending. These shifts in the composition of international capital flows to developing countries influence IMF lending through two channels: they determine both the domestic financial interests of the Fund's largest shareholders and the policy preferences of its bureaucrats. On the whole, the results of this analysis offer clear and robust evidence that these actors' preferences – and, therefore, IMF loan size and conditionality – vary systematically in accordance with changes in the composition of developing countries' private international debt. All else equal, IMF programs are larger and include fewer conditions when G-5 domestic financial interests in a borrowing country (as measured by commercial bank exposure) are more intense, while loans are smaller and contain more extensive conditionality when G-5 financial interests are more heterogeneous. These effects are conditional and interactive, however. Moreover, their effects are not uniform across IMF loan characteristics. Rather, the data clearly indicate that G-5 domestic financial interests play a more significant role in shaping decisions about IMF loan size, whereas the Fund's largest shareholders exercise only limited influence over conditionality.

In addition, the statistical analysis provides strong evidence that IMF staff concerns about the potential for catalytic financing also play a key role in determining the characteristics of Fund programs. In particular, there is robust evidence that the extent to which a country depends on international bond financing rather than commercial bank lending is a major determinant of both IMF loan size and conditionality. In contrast, the statistical analysis offers only limited evidence of a systematic connection between the shift from sovereign lending to non-sovereign capital flows and IMF loans; that said, this change in international debt composition, as discussed below in the case study of South Korea, has been of critical importance in selected IMF lending cases. Finally, the analysis also finds support for some alternative economic and political explanations of IMF lending, although the effects of variation in patterns of financial globalization on loan size and conditionality are quite large in comparison to these other factors.

Ultimately, the evidence presented here significantly enhances our understanding of the political economy of IMF lending. First, it highlights the necessity of understanding and accounting for changes in patterns of financial globalization when seeking to explain IMF lending policies. Clearly, as both the loan size and conditionality regressions illustrate, the Fund's loans have varied widely in accordance with changes in the composition of international capital flows to developing countries. In failing to take these important changes in the structure of global financial markets into account, the existing literature has overlooked a critical determinant of variation in IMF behavior.

Second, the evidence plainly indicates that no single economic or political variable can explain all IMF lending decisions. Put simply, there is no "magic bullet" explaining why IMF loans vary so widely in both size and conditionality over time and across cases. Rather, the influence of the debt composition variables emphasized here, as well as that of alternative economic and political factors identified in the existing literature, is highly conditional and case-specific. In some cases, political factors, including the intensity and heterogeneity of preferences among the Fund's largest shareholders, play a critical role in shaping Fund policymaking, while economic factors take precedence in others. One cannot explain variation in IMF lending, therefore, without acknowledging the importance of both types of factors, as well as the conditions under which each most strongly influences Fund decision-making.

Likewise, the statistical analysis strongly supports the common agency theory and its claim that no single actor controls the IMF policymaking process. The regression results provide substantial evidence that both the Fund's "collective principal" (G-5 governments) and its "agent' (the IMF staff) exercise partial but incomplete authority over lending decisions. Perhaps more importantly, the analysis also clarifies the nature and extent of each actor's influence. Specifically, it suggests that G-5 governments exercise greater influence over decisions about loan size, whereas the IMF staff enjoys more autonomy over the design of conditionality. Furthermore, as the robustness analysis illustrates, the data strongly recommend the common agency framework over US-centric theories of IMF politics. Thus, the IMF, despite its critics' contentions to the contrary, is neither the "lapdog" of the United States nor a "runaway bureaucracy" acting without regard for its shareholders' interests. By focusing excessively on a single key variable, these one-dimensional explanations are unlikely to yield accurate predictions about IMF lending behavior.

In sum, the quantitative analysis presented in this chapter significantly enhances our understanding of the political economy of IMF lending by moving beyond overly simplistic explanations in favor of a more complex – yet ultimately more accurate – theoretical framework. This common agency theory takes seriously the importance of economic as well as political variables, as well as the principal–agent relationship at the heart of IMF decision-making. Rather than rejecting existing theories of IMF lending outright, this new approach clarifies the theoretical and empirical limitations of these alternative explanations. At the same time, it also identifies a critical set of variables – changes in the composition of private international capital flows – influencing the preferences of the Fund's key decision-makers and explaining variation in IMF lending over the last two decades.

4 *Global finance and IMF lending to Mexico, 1983–1995*

The results of the statistical analysis in the previous chapter clearly indicate that changes in patterns of financial globalization have had significant and sizeable effects on IMF lending policies. This link between international capital flows and IMF policies occurs through two channels. First, private debt composition – specifically, the amount and distribution of G-5 commercial bank exposure to IMF borrowing countries – determines the intensity and heterogeneity of preferences among the Fund's major shareholders. Second, private debt composition – specifically, whether capital flows consist of bank lending rather than bond financing, and (to a lesser extent) whether the borrowers are sovereign governments or private actors – also shapes the IMF staff's expectations about the availability of catalytic financing. As the foregoing statistical analysis illustrates, these factors explain a substantial portion of the variation in IMF loan size and conditionality during the last two decades.

Nonetheless, large-sample statistical analysis provides only a partial picture of the political economy of IMF lending. In particular, while quantitative analysis enables us to identify broad cross-national trends in IMF behavior over time, it does not elucidate the causal chain linking changes in financial globalization to IMF lending outcomes, nor does it explain how and to what extent the Fund's G-5 principals and the IMF staff take each of these factors into account in specific cases. In contrast, a case study or "process-tracing" approach offers us an in-depth focus on the *process* of IMF decision-making, and it casts light on the step-by-step chain of events linking various explanatory factors to our dependent variables. Moreover, qualitative analysis helps us to understand the sequencing of, and interaction between, the key variables that ultimately influence IMF lending behavior. Finally, case studies also increase our sensitivity to "equifinality," the possibility that different chains of events or different combinations of independent variables may lead to similar outcomes on the dependent variable.[1] For these reasons, case studies provide a powerful complementary methodological tool that addresses the limitations of the statistical analysis. These advantages are especially relevant when analyzing the politics of IMF lending, since I am not only attempting to explain variation in the Fund's policies but also seeking to understand the process of IMF decision-making. By looking in depth at specific cases – specifically, at IMF lending to both Mexico and South Korea from 1983 to 1997 – the following two chapters shed light on how this process unfolds and how the key actors' preferences are shaped by changes in patterns of financial globalization.

Case selection: Mexico and South Korea, 1983–97

Given the vast economic and political diversity of the IMF's borrowers, it is very difficult to choose any one or two representative country cases on which to focus from the forty-seven countries in the IMF lending data set. Nevertheless, I have chosen to analyze Mexico and South Korea for two key reasons. First, these countries are two of the IMF's largest borrowers over the last two decades: from 1983 to 1997 the Fund provided Mexico with SDR 20.6 billion in financing through four lending arrangements (1983, 1986, 1989, 1995), while it lent South Korea SDR 16.1 billion under three programs (1983, 1985, 1997). Moreover, the Fund's loans to Mexico and South Korea in the 1990s were, at the time of their approval, the largest loans ever provided by the IMF. If we are to understand how and why the Fund makes policy decisions, it is critically important that we explain the IMF's behavior in these significant cases.

Second, Mexico and South Korea each borrowed from the IMF in the 1980s and the 1990s, with a multi-year break between their two episodes of borrowing. As a result, studying these two countries sheds light on the impact of historical changes in the composition of international capital flows to emerging markets on IMF behavior. Indeed, Mexico and South Korea both saw the composition of their private external debt shift significantly from the mid-1980s to the mid-1990s. At the same time, these countries' loans have varied significantly in size

[1] Because statistical methods test the probabilistic relationship between each individual explanatory variable on the dependent variable, they are less well suited for assessing this issue. See George and Bennett (2005).

Table 4.1 *IMF lending arrangements with Mexico, 1983–95*

Date of lending arrangement	Length/type	Loan amount (SDR billions)	Loan amount (percent of quota)	Number of performance criteria	Number of total conditions
January 1, 1983	3 years (EFF)	3.41	2.93	7	7
November 19, 1986	17.5 months (stand-by arrangement)	1.40	1.20	7	7
May 26, 1989	3 years (EFF)	3.71	3.20	7	7
February 1, 1995	18.5 months (stand-by arrangement)	12.07	6.88	7	7

Sources: IMF archives and www.imf.org.

over time. Thus, choosing these cases provides within-country variation in both the independent and dependent variables of my theory, while at the same time controlling for many country-specific factors that complicate interpretation of the large-N statistical results.

Tables 4.1 and 4.2 provide an overview of the IMF's lending arrangements with Mexico and South Korea since 1983. As the tables illustrate, these loans have varied significantly in size during the last two decades, while the number of conditions included in these arrangements has varied relatively little by comparison. This pattern mirrors broader trends of variation in the IMF lending data set: much of the meaningful variation in the number of conditions attached to IMF loans – particularly variation in performance criteria, the "hardest" conditions imposed by the Fund – since 1983 is cross-national, while the size of Fund loans varies significantly both cross-nationally and over time for individual countries.

Testing the argument: observable implications in the case studies

By focusing in detail on the step-by-step process of IMF policymaking, the case studies offer an additional test of my argument that changes in

Table 4.2 *IMF lending arrangements with South Korea, 1983–97*

Date of lending arrangement	Length/type	Loan amount (SDR billions)	Loan amount (percent of quota)	Number of performance criteria	Number of total conditions
July 8, 1983	21 months (stand-by arrangement)	0.58	1.24	3	3
July 12, 1985	20 months (stand-by arrangement)	2.80	0.61	3	3
December 4, 1997	3 years (stand-by arrangement/ SRF)	15.50	19.38	3	10

Sources: IMF archives and www.imf.org.

patterns of financial globalization are a key determinant of variation in Fund lending behavior. Finding confirming evidence of my argument in the case studies requires a clear specification of its observable implications, however. In particular, we must identify unambigous indicators that changes in patterns of financial globalization shaped both G-5 countries' domestic financial interests and IMF staff expectations about catalytic financing in both the Mexican and South Korean cases.

G-5 preference intensity and heterogeneity: the amount and distribution of bank exposure

As argued thus far, G-5 governments' preferences over IMF lending are heavily influenced by their domestic financial interests in particular countries. As two of the largest sovereign debtors throughout the 1980s and 1990s, Mexico and South Korea represent cases in which the G-5 countries have had a significant financial stake over the last two decades. Nonetheless, the intensity and heterogeneity of G-5 bank exposure did vary quite significantly in these two countries during this period, and I expect G-5 governments' preferences over IMF loan size and conditionality to mirror these differences closely. When aggregate G-5 bank exposure is higher, I expect that the IMF will be more likely to set aside moral hazard concerns and support larger loans. At the same time, I expect to see clear divisions between G-5 policymakers and executive directors over the terms of Fund loans to Mexico and South Korea based on the relative extent of their commercial banks' exposure. Those countries whose banks are more highly exposed should favor larger loans, while the remaining G-5 governments should be more skeptical of large-scale bailouts. In the current cases, this suggests that the United States should most fervently support large-scale financing for Mexico, while the European G-5 countries (the United Kingdom, Germany, and France) should be most reluctant to commit Fund resources. Given the norm of consensus policymaking with the executive board, these divisions are not likely to be reflected in the final executive board votes; they should be evident in the board discussions, however. Likewise, we should see executive directors from G-5 countries with more concrete financial interests in Mexico and South Korea (e.g. the United States and Japan) taking a more optimistic stance and expressing greater enthusiasm for the proposed arrangements. In contrast, we should see the G-5 countries with less financially at stake in Mexico and South Korea expressing greater concerns about moral hazard and pushing for more extensive conditionality as the "price" of their support for larger loans. Finally, in addition to finding evidence that G-5 governments' preferences are influenced by their domestic financial interests, we should also observe other countries with less financially at stake expressing greater concerns within the executive board about moral hazard and favoring conservation of the IMF's scarce resources.

Catalytic financing: bank loans versus bonds

The statistical analysis provides strong evidence that IMF loans are larger when a greater share of the borrowing country's debt is owed to bondholders. The logic behind this finding, as argued in chapter 3, is that bondholders are more likely to "cut and run" when a country experiences financial difficulties, whereas commercial banks are generally more willing to provide catalytic financing and reschedule existing debts in the aftermath of an IMF loan, because of their small numbers and longer-term, multi-dimensional ties to borrowing countries. Consequently, it takes more IMF financing to overcome these collective action problems and generate a catalytic effect on private international markets in cases of bond financing. All else equal, I expect to find evidence in the case studies that commercial bank creditors are more likely to lend following each IMF program than bondholders.

Furthermore, I also expect to find documentary evidence that both the IMF staff and the executive board considered the composition of Mexico and South Korea's private international creditors as they designed and approved each lending arrangement. As bond financing becomes a larger share of private external debt in the 1990s, both the Fund's staff and the executive directors should express greater concerns about the availability of sufficient private external financing following the disbursement of Fund credit. In these cases, we should observe the IMF staff proposing – and the executive board approving – larger loans with more extensive conditionality, in an attempt to signal the Fund's commitment to the borrowing country, to signal the borrower's commitment to substantial policy reform aimed at eliminating its balance of payments deficit, and to generate a catalytic effect on private capital flows. Moreover, we should expect these loans to be "front-loaded"; that is, when private creditors are less likely to respond to an IMF loan by providing catalytic financing, the Fund should disburse a larger share of the approved credit immediately, rather than in the later stages of the loan. Once again, the logic here is that a larger amount of IMF financing is necessary to generate a catalytic effect on private capital flows when a country's creditors consist primarily of heterogeneous, disaggregated bondholders rather than a limited number of commercial banks with long-standing ties to the borrowing country and each other through syndicated lending.

In contrast, we should observe both the IMF staff and executive directors supporting smaller IMF loans with less extensive conditionality when private creditors (particularly commercial banks) have explicitly committed to lend new money and/or reschedule existing claims on Mexico or South Korea. In these latter cases, the Fund does not need to fill a country's entire "financing gap" – the discrepancy between its resources and its debt obligations.[2] Rather, a partial bailout from the IMF, combined with a limited amount of conditionality,

[2] Kenen (2001).

is sufficient to trigger new private capital inflows and avert a costly default. Thus, in the Mexican and South Korean cases, the Fund should provide somewhat smaller loans with more modest conditionality when banks and other creditors have formally committed to new lending and/or debt rescheduling – or appear likely to do so in the near future.[3]

Borrower composition: sovereign debt versus private borrowing

As argued in the previous chapters, the composition of borrowers in global financial markets has also changed significantly during the last two decades. In particular, we have seen a shift from "private-public" international capital flows (from private lenders to sovereign governments) to "private–private" lending (lending directly to developing countries' firms and financial institutions) occurring in many developing countries since the early 1980s. As discussed earlier, in chapter 2, the lack of a common borrower in these non-sovereign lending cases creates similar dilemmas of creditor collective action to those arising in cases of bond financing. Indeed, just as sovereign bondholders own a wide array of different instruments of varying interest rates and maturities, non-sovereign lenders hold claims on many different private financial institutions and corporations. Furthermore, most non-sovereign lending consists of short-term interbank lending, whereas syndicated sovereign bank lending and bond financing are generally of longer maturity. As a result, non-sovereign bank lenders can more easily "cut and run" in times of financial crisis.[4] As in cases of international bond lending, large-scale IMF loans are, therefore, a precondition for catalytic financing when non-sovereign capital flows predominate. Likewise, more extensive "structural" conditionality is often required in non-sovereign lending episodes, since governments' macroeconomic policies are generally not the root cause of financial difficulties in these cases.

[3] To be clear, my claim is not that these loans will be small in the *absolute* sense but, rather, that they will be smaller relative to loans made to similar countries with similar economic characteristics that owe more debt to bondholders.

[4] Lipworth and Nystedt (2001).

In the case studies, we should therefore also observe the Fund staff taking the composition of Mexican and South Korean borrowers into account as it designs and proposes IMF loans to the executive board. All else equal, the staff should design and propose larger loans with more extensive conditionality to countries whose external debt consists of larger shares of non-sovereign debt, in the hopes of convincing a less unified group of banks (and in some cases, bondholders) to "roll over" their short-term claims on a wide variety of private borrowers, few of whom have long-standing relationships with their international creditors. Moreover, we should find evidence in the executive board discussions that concerns about capital flight by non-sovereign lenders – particularly by short-term interbank creditors – became a key issue in both Mexico and South Korea in the 1990s lending episodes.

Evidence for alternative explanations

While seeing these observable implications in the Mexican and South Korean cases will bolster my central claim that private debt composition drives the interests of the two key actors – G-5 governments (the "collective principal") and the Fund staff (the "agent") – involved in IMF lending, my argument will be further strengthened if I find comparatively little evidence that other political variables, such as bureaucratic incentives or US geopolitical interests, played a major role in shaping IMF lending to these two countries. Based on the statistical results, I expect to find little or no evidence that bureaucratic rent-seeking was an important factor affecting the IMF's treatment of Mexico and South Korea. In addition, I expect that geopolitical concerns – while arguably important in these cases – should be relative "constants" during the time period that I am examining. As a result, they should not be a key determinant of the variation over time in the characteristics of these countries' IMF loans.

On the other hand, I expect the set of key macroeconomic variables found to be significant in both the statistical analysis above and the existing literature to be key factors affecting the Fund's decision-making calculus in the Mexican and South Korean cases. In short, my claim is not that the IMF staff or its G-5 principals ignore economic factors. These variables clearly play an important role in shaping IMF lending policies, as underlined by the statistical analysis in chapter 3.

Rather, my claim is that "technocratic" macroeconomic variables are necessary but not sufficient determinants of variation in the size and terms of IMF lending in most cases. In order to explain the sizeable variation in the size and terms of the loans the IMF has extended to Mexico and South Korea, we must focus on shifts in the composition of private capital flows to these countries and understand how and why these changes have altered the interests of the IMF staff and the Fund's most powerful member states alike.

Mexico and the IMF, 1983–95

To what extent did changes in patterns of financial globalization – by influencing not only G-5 governments' domestic financial interests but also the IMF staff's expectations about catalytic financing – affect the Fund's treatment of Mexico in the 1980s and 1990s? In the remainder of this chapter, I focus in detail on the IMF's decisions to grant four non-concessional loans to Mexico (1983, 1986, 1989, and 1995) and assess the extent to which the evidence supports my argument. For each IMF lending case, I discuss Mexico's external debt composition, the factors leading Mexico to request IMF assistance, and the roles of G-5 governments and the IMF staff in shaping the Fund's lending behavior. In addition, I assess the response of private creditors to the IMF's lending decisions, as well as the extent to which other political and economic factors influenced the IMF's lending decisions.

The 1983 extended arrangement

Mexico's private international debt composition, 1979–82

At the outset of the 1980s Mexico had just ended a decade of spectacular growth and development. Throughout the late 1970s Mexico had experienced economic growth in excess of 8 percent per year, largely as a result of the rapid increase in world oil prices.[5] To finance this rapid growth and development, the Mexican government borrowed heavily from commercial banks in the industrialized countries. As a result, Mexico's stock of external debt more than quadrupled

[5] Alan Friedman, "A colossal mountain of debt," *Financial Times*, August 20, 1982.

between 1975 ($18.2 billion) and 1982 ($86.1 billion), while its debt to GNP ratio more than doubled, from 21.2 percent to 53.3 percent.[6] Despite Mexico's rising debt and debt service ratios, private creditors continued to view the country, with its strong record of political stability and economic growth, as a model developing country borrower. By the end of 1983, Mexico was the second largest developing country borrower in the world – trailing only Brazil ($98.5 billion) – with total outstanding external debt of $93 billion, two-thirds of which ($62.4 billion) was owed to private international creditors. As with nearly all private international lending at this point, Mexico's creditors consisted overwhelmingly of commercial banks in the advanced industrialized countries providing financing through syndicated loans: 91 percent of Mexico's private external debt was owed to commercial banks, with banks headquartered in the G-5 countries holding the vast majority ($39.8 billion) of these claims.[7] Thus, while Mexico owed an extremely large sum of money to private international creditors, the creditors themselves were quite limited in number: some 500 commercial banks held virtually all of Mexico's private external debt, of which approximately 80 percent was held by about 100 of the largest money-center banks.[8]

Although each of the G-5 countries had large financial ties to Mexico in absolute terms, the United States had a disproportionately large interest in ensuring Mexico's financial stability. Citibank, Chase Manhattan, and other major American commercial banks held $24.9 billion in claims on Mexico, or 62.6 percent of total G-5 bank exposure. Furthermore, Mexican debt equaled 44 percent of the capital of the nine largest United States commercial banks and 35 percent of the reserves of the 15 largest regional banks.[9] Moreover, the two largest American commercial banks, Citibank and Bank of America, had lent so much to Mexico and Brazil combined that a default by either country would threaten their solvency.[10] In contrast, bank lending by the remaining four G-5 countries was significantly smaller: UK banks held $6.4 billion in claims (constituting 16.1 percent of the G-5 total), French banks $4.4 billion (11.1 percent), Japanese banks $2.1

[6] World Bank (2006a).

[7] Unless otherwise cited, all financial and macroeconomic statistics in this chapter are taken from the IMF lending data set described in chapter 3 above and utilized in the statistical analysis.

[8] Boughton (2001, 32). [9] Kraft (1984, 9). [10] Ibid.

billion (5.4 percent) and German banks $1.9 billion (4.8 percent). In comparison to this very large amount of syndicated commercial bank lending, bond debt was a much more limited source of external financing for the Mexican government in the early 1980s: Mexico owed less than $4.5 billion to international bondholders, or 6.1 percent of its private external debt. Roughly one-fifth (19.8 percent) of Mexico's debt was private non-guaranteed debt; 100 percent of this non-sovereign lending was by commercial bank creditors, most of which were the same banks participating in syndicated lending to the Mexican government.

Financial crisis and initial request for IMF financing

Despite its earlier success, Mexico faced a massive external debt crisis by 1982, which forced it to request emergency financing from the IMF. Declining oil prices, coupled with sharply increased US interest rates, led to a doubling of Mexico's external debt from 1979 to 1982.[11] The combination of declining export earnings and rising debt service levels resulting from these shocks seriously undermined the government's fiscal position. By mid-1982 Mexico faced a daunting government budget deficit ($20 billion, equivalent to 14 percent of GDP) and inflation in excess of 60 percent annually.[12] As the peso depreciated rapidly against the dollar, Mexico's ability to meet its $1 billion per month in external debt obligations appeared uncertain at best.[13]

By the end of July, the Mexican government recognized the need for official international assistance in meeting its external obligations. Jesús Silva Herzog, the secretary of finance, requested that William Dale, the IMF's acting managing director, send a mission to Mexico immediately, and negotiations over a Fund lending package began in early August.[14] Matters became even more urgent on August 11,

[11] My focus here is the IMF policymaking process, rather than the background on Mexico's financial crises, which has been extensively documented and analyzed elsewhere. For comprehensive, detailed accounts of the onset and causes of the Mexican debt crisis in the 1980s, see Kraft (1984), James (1996), and Boughton (2001).

[12] Friedman, *Financial Times,* August 20, 1982.

[13] In February 1982 the Mexican government devalued the peso by 30 percent from the prevailing P26 /$1 rate. By July the peso had depreciated to P50/$1. See Friedman, *Financial Times,* August 20, 1982.

[14] Boughton (2001, 289).

when Mexico's commercial bank creditors refused to roll over principal payments due on August 16. Without adequate reserves to make the payments, the Mexican government faced an imminent prospect of default. Silva Herzog flew to Washington to meet with Jacques de Larosière, the newly appointed IMF managing director, on August 13, 1982. De Larosière promised Silva Herzog IMF support, but only on the condition that Mexico find a way to avert a default on its immediate debt payments.[15] Silva Herzog then began intensive discussions with US Treasury officials and Paul Volcker, the chairman of the Federal Reserve, over the terms of short-term "bridge" financing that would enable Mexico to service its external debt while it entered negotiations with the IMF and the commercial banks for a longer-term solution.[16] Ultimately, the United States provided $4 billion in assistance, including $1 billion in advance payments on future Mexican oil exports to the US Strategic Petroleum Reserve, $1 billion in credit guarantees from the US Department of Agriculture, and $1 billion in credit from the Treasury Department's Exchange Stabilization Fund (ESF).[17] With the encouragement of Volcker, the central banks of the United Kingdom, West Germany, Japan, France, and the other G-10 countries also provided $1.85 billion in bridge financing under the auspices of the Bank for International Settlements.[18] With this short-term assistance from the BIS central banks in place, Mexico met its immediate debt payments and avoided default for the time being.

Negotiating with the commercial banks, August 1982

Having secured sufficient official credit from the BIS to avert an immediate default, Silva Herzog and the IMF next sought to convince Mexico's private creditors to reschedule the government's outstanding debt, so that the situation would not be repeated later in the year. To that end, Silva Herzog invited 115 of Mexico's largest commercial bank creditors to a meeting at the Federal Reserve Bank of New York (FRBNY) on August 20, to be hosted by the FRBNY's chairman, Anthony Solomon. Prior to the full meeting, Silva Herzog

[15] Ibid., 291.
[16] See ibid., ch. 7, for a detailed account of these negotiations.
[17] Ibid., 293. [18] BIS (1983, 165).

met with the chairmen of the four largest US commercial banks (Citibank, Chase Manhattan, Manufacturers' Hanover, and Chemical Bank), who agreed to help assemble a creditors' committee that would perform two critical functions. First, the committee would negotiate all future loans with Mexico on behalf of all banks holding syndicated claims. Second, it would organize participation in these new agreements and act as the official liaison between Mexico, its private creditors, and the international financial institutions.[19] The four American bank chairmen coordinated the formation of this Bank Advisory Committee (BAC), which ultimately consisted of representatives of fourteen of the largest commercial bank creditors in eight countries. The BAC, which eventually operated under the management of William Rhodes, a senior vice-president at Citibank, became the key forum for organizing private creditors' responses to financial crises in developing countries for the remainder of the decade.

This direct cooperation between the IMF and Mexico's private creditors soon became a key element of the Fund's strategy for securing private creditors' participation in the management and resolution of financial crises in the 1980s. As this episode illustrates, however, creditor composition played a critical role in facilitating this process. Since commercial banks held the vast majority of Mexico's private external debt, the number of players involved was limited. As noted above, just a few hundred large commercial banks around the world held nearly all of Mexico's sovereign debt. This small number made direct negotiations between Herzog and Mexico's private international creditors feasible and relatively easy to organize quickly. Moreover, Silva Herzog was able to engage Mexico's creditors *prior to* negotiating with the IMF staff over the terms of a Fund loan. As we will see below, changes in the patterns of financial globalization substantially altered the dynamics of this process in later cases; in particular, the shift from bank lending to bond financing led to a substantial disaggregation of Mexico's creditor base during the 1994/95 financial crisis.

With Mexico's major commercial bank creditors on board, Silva Herzog went into the full August 20 meeting with the BAC's full support for his request for a ninety-day rollover of principal on Mexico's

[19] Boughton (2001, 297).

bank loans.[20] After outlining Mexico's plans for macroeconomic adjustment, as well as noting the official financing it had secured (including plans to borrow from the IMF), Silva Herzog received a verbal commitment from the banks to pursue a rollover agreement. Two senior representatives of the IMF staff – Walter Robichek, director of the Western Hemisphere Department, and Manuel Guitian, a senior adviser in the Exchange and Trade Relations Department – attended this meeting (as well as numerous subsequent meetings of the BAC) as observers.[21] Thus, while not yet directly involved in the negotiations, the Fund played an active role in Mexico's interactions with private creditors from the very beginning of the 1980s debt crisis.

Once negotiations on the bank rollover had begun, Mexico intensified its discussions with the IMF on the terms of a three-year arrangement under the Extended Fund Facility. Because the commercial banks had already committed themselves to a rollover, the IMF staff's concerns about catalytic financing were ameliorated, and negotiations with Silva Herzog progressed rapidly. By late August, despite some disagreements about the program's conditionality (specifically, the budget deficit ceiling), Mexico and the IMF negotiating team reached agreement in principle on a program that included a sharp reduction in Mexico's fiscal deficit, from the current level of 15 percent of GDP to a ceiling of 8 percent, and the expectation that commercial banks would respond to the IMF loan with $3.5 billion in credit to the Mexican government.[22]

Just before the program could be finalized, however, the outgoing Mexican president, José López Portillo, undermined Silva Herzog's commitments to the IMF. In his final state of the union address (*informe*) on September 11, López Portillo blamed Mexico's private creditors for the country's economic difficulties and openly rejected the economic reforms proposed by the IMF: "The remedy of the doctors is to deprive the patient of food and subject him to compulsory rest."[23] On August 31 López Portillo imposed exchange controls, nationalized the Mexican banking system, and dismissed Miguel Mancera, the governor of the Banco de México and a close ally of

[20] Silva Herzog initially requested an extension of maturities of one or two years on Mexico's debt, but the four major US bank chairman refused. See Boughton (2001, 297).

[21] Ibid., 298. [22] Ibid., 299. [23] Kraft (1984, 39).

Silva Herzog. The new governor, Carlos Tello, strongly supported López Portillo's rejection of the nearly agreed IMF program terms.[24]

Not surprisingly, López Portillo's speech and subsequent policy shifts created substantial uncertainly about Mexico's future ability (and willingness) to service its external debt, sparking massive capital flight by domestic and international creditors alike. By September 7 Mexico again faced imminent default, as international commercial banks were refusing to roll over interbank credit lines to Mexican banks. Pressure on the banks from Paul Volcker, BIS general manager Fritz Leutwiler, and Brian Quinn of the Bank of England – coupled with rapid disbursement of the previously agreed BIS bridge financing – narrowly averted a disaster.[25] The markets calmed further on September 10, when the Mexican Congress confirmed the results of the July 4 election of pro-reform President-elect Miguel de la Madrid and Silva Herzog agreed to remain as secretary of finance in the new government.

With these changes in the Mexican government in place, the IMF team returned to Mexico City on September 23 for another attempt at concluding negotiations over the terms of the Mexican extended arrangement. The talks soon stagnated again, however, as Silva Herzog faced further domestic opposition to the budget cuts and exchange rate policies proposed by the IMF staff as performance criteria. By November, Silva Herzog and the IMF team agreed to relax the performance criteria on the budget deficit to allow a deficit in excess of 8 percent of GDP, but only if Mexico could secure $5 billion (rather than the previously anticipated $3.5 billion) in new credit from its commercial bank creditors.[26] The IMF staff was particularly concerned that the Fund should not be seen as bailing out Mexico, instead seeking assurances that Mexico's private international creditors would provide sufficient credit, or catalytic financing, in the event that the IMF committed its own resources. The Fund and Mexico reached final agreement on a program on November 10, when Silva Herzog and Tello formally signed a letter of intent requesting a $3.7 billion arrangement under the Extended Fund Facility, equal to 2.9 times quota and containing seven performance criteria, including sharp reductions in the budget deficit, external borrowing, and inflation.[27] In share of quota terms, this loan was the largest IMF package to date.

[24] James (1996, 338). [25] Boughton (2001, 301). [26] Ibid., 304.
[27] Ibid., 306; Kraft (1984, 46).

Securing private creditors' commitments – the rise of "concerted lending"

Prior to the signing of the Mexican letter of intent, IMF officials had participated in the discussions between the Mexican authorities and the commercial banks, but they had done so largely as observers. With the draft program signed and set to come before the Fund's executive board on December 23, however, both the Fund staff and the G-5 countries had strong incentives to ensure the cooperation of private creditors. Having proposed an extremely large commitment of Fund resources, the IMF staff did not want this financing to become a "bailout" for Mexico's commercial bank creditors. Rather, the staff intended the Fund's loan to Mexico to serve as a signal to private markets that the country's authorities were making a good-faith effort to implement the necessary economic reforms – a signal that would ultimately convince the banks to provide fresh lending to Mexico. Similarly, G-5 governments also had a clear interest in securing new commitments from the commercial banks, both because they provided the lion's share of the Fund's quota resources and because they did not want to be accused at home of providing bailouts to wealthy bankers. In short, both the IMF staff and the Fund's member state principals wanted to limit the moral hazard costs of providing Mexico with such a large rescue package, and they were extremely interested in ensuring that the Fund's resources would have a catalytic effect on private capital flows.

In order to accomplish this, de Larosière, the IMF managing director, took the lead in working to convince Mexico's commercial bank creditors to provide new credit once the IMF program went into effect. Once again, the fact that Mexico's creditors consisted almost exclusively of a small group of readily identifiable bankers facilitated this process of direct interaction between Mexico, its private international creditors, and the IMF. At a speech delivered to the International Monetary Conference, a gathering of leading commercial bankers in Philadelphia on November 9, de Larosière assured the bankers that the IMF would condition its own lending to developing countries on policy adjustments that "ensure that economic policies are put on the right track and balance of payments viability is assured over the medium term."[28] Nevertheless, for these Fund programs to

[28] Reginald Dale, "Banks urged to maintain lending to Third World," *Financial Times*, November 10, 1982.

be successful, de Larosière argued, the banks themselves would have to "maintain adequate net financing flows to countries in support of sound adjustment policies, which would involve a very large volume of gross long-term flows in addition to the roll-over of maturing short-term credit."[29]

The following week, at a meeting with members of the Mexican BAC at the FRBNY, de Larosière made it clear that cooperation between the banks and Fund was not simply desirable but rather a *precondition* of IMF assistance to Mexico. He described the size and terms of the proposed Mexican lending arrangement, including the serious fiscal adjustment Mexico would be required to implement in order to receive the IMF credit; in addition, de Larosière stated that official creditors were willing to provide an estimated $2 billion in bilateral lending to supplement the Fund loan.[30] Even with these funds, however, Mexico would still require an additional $5 billion in new financing from the commercial banks in order to continue servicing its international debt over the three-year life of the Fund package. As a result, de Larosière concluded, he would be unable to present the extented arrangement to the IMF executive board for approval unless the banks committed themselves both to rolling over $20 billion in claims coming due between November 1982 and the end of 1984 and to providing the additional $5 billion to the Mexican government over the next three years.[31]

In other words, de Larosière gave Mexico's private international creditors an ultimatum: commit to new lending in conjunction with an IMF loan or face a Mexican default. With the executive board set to consider the Mexican EFF proposal on December 23, de Larosière stated that he would need the banks' commitment in writing by December 15 in order to proceed. At a similar meeting at the Bank of England on November 22, de Larosière met with the chairmen of key commercial banks in Japan, Germany, France, and the United Kingdom, where he reiterated the IMF's demand for a $5 billion private creditor contribution. In a subsequent letter to all Mexico's commercial bank creditors, de Larosière again emphasized that he could not "go to the executive board of the Fund on December 23 ... [with]

[29] Ibid. [30] Boughton (2001, 307).
[31] Clyde H. Farnsworth, "A dramatic change at the IMF," *New York Times*, January 9, 1983.

a program that is not adequately financed."[32] Simply put, the IMF needed explicit assurances that its lending would trigger ("catalyze") private capital inflows; otherwise it would be forced to postpone its own lending decision, and the banks would once again face the threat of a Mexican default.

This direct pressure by the IMF on a borrowing country's private creditors marked a fundamental shift in the IMF's lending policy, and it took the bankers completely by surprise: "When de Larosière said the whole IMF deal was conditional on the banks putting up $5 billion in new money, we were shocked," said a representative of one large United States commercial bank. "When he said we had to have the money by December 15, we were appalled."[33] In addition to being surprised by the IMF's pressure, the banks had two key concerns with the logic of concerted lending. First, the creditor banks faced potentially serious collective action problems: each individual bank had incentives to seek repayment of its loans as soon as possible, leaving others to bear the cost of a potential Mexican default. These incentives to "free-ride" were particularly strong for smaller regional banks in the United States and for banks in Japan, France, and other G-10 countries with far less exposure – both in absolute terms and relative to their size – to Mexico than the United States. While Mexico's twenty-five largest commercial bank creditors, such as Citibank ($2.8 billion), Bank of America ($2.5 billion), and Chase Manhattan ($1.6 billion), had massive exposure to Mexico, many small United States and European banks held only a few million dollars in Mexican debt.[34] For these smaller banks, the logical strategy was to "cut and run," leaving the large money-center banks to deal with Mexico's financial problems. Since the smaller banks accounted for 40 percent of United States bank exposure to Mexico (and a roughly similar percentage of European lending), however, their cooperation was essential for the success of concerted lending. If too many of the small banks declined to provide new loans, the $5 billion target would not be reached, in which case de Larosière would table the IMF program and Mexico would once again face an imminent default.

32 Alan Friedman, "Mexico loan plan brings concerted action by banks," *Financial Times*, December 15, 1982.

33 Kraft (1984, 49).

34 Don Oberdorfer, "Mexico crisis altered US foreign loan views," *Washington Post*, January 30, 1983.

Second, the banks were concerned that they would be penalized by the regulatory authorities for increasing their exposure to such a risky borrower as Mexico. As banks with riskier lending portfolios were required by their central banks and financial regulators to hold more capital on hand, they were understandably reluctant to provide new credit to Mexico at the moment it faced the prospect of a default. To mitigate the banks' regulatory concerns, Solomon, the FRBNY chairman (and nominal host of the meeting), made it clear that bank regulatory requirements related to international lending would be relaxed if the banks complied with de Larosière's request.[35] At a speech that same evening, Volcker reiterated this pledge concerning regulatory forebearance: "When new loans facilitate the adjustment process and enable a country to strengthen its economy and service its international debt in an orderly manner, new credits shouldn't be subject to supervisory criticism."[36]

Despite these concerns about both collective action problems and regulatory punishment, the banks nevertheless moved quickly, and relatively little time elapsed before they agreed to participate in the concerted lending project. Acting under the auspices of the BAC, the largest banks quickly organized and coordinated a new syndicated lending package. The BAC immediately agreed to a ninety-day rollover of Mexico's short-term principal repayments, and it extended this rollover to the end of 1984 on November 30, with the expectation that the Mexican authorities would make full repayment over eight years.[37] That same day, Rhodes and de Larosière met and finalized the terms of the banks' involvement. The BAC would recommend to all banks exposed to Mexico that they provide new loans equal to 7 percent of their existing exposure.[38] Since it was highly unlikely that the BAC could coordinate an agreement among the more than 500 creditor banks in less than four weeks' time, however, Rhodes and de Larosière also agreed on a target of 90 percent participation by the commercial banks. If this "critical mass" of banks committed to the new money package by the time of the December 23 executive

[35] James (1996, 370).

[36] Paul A. Volcker, "Sustainable recovery: setting the stage," text of a speech delivered to the fifty-eighth annual meeting of the New England Council, Boston, Massachusetts, November 16, 1982; quoted in James (1996, 370).

[37] James (1996, 370).

[38] Friedman, *Financial Times*, December 15, 1982.

board meeting, de Larosière would bring the Mexican EFF package to a vote.[39]

Within only a few weeks, thanks to the efforts of Rhodes and the BAC, the overwhelming majority of Mexico's commercial bank creditors had signed on to the concerted lending plan. By December 23 over 500 commercial banks had committed more than $4.3 billion in financing, or roughly 86 percent of de Larosière's request for $5 billion.[40] Although this fell short of the 90 percent target, de Larosière felt sufficiently optimistic that the holdout creditors would eventually capitulate to the IMF's demands that he placed the Mexican loan request on the board agenda. Thus, in slightly more than a month, nearly all Mexico's private international creditors had agreed to provide new lending in the aftermath of the anticipated IMF loan. As we will see below, this coordinated participation by Mexico's commercial bank creditors contrasted sharply with the behavior of its international bondholders during the 1994/5 crisis.

Two key factors facilitated the rapid coordination of commercial bank commitments, and they illustrate the importance of private debt composition in the Mexican case. First, in spite of the banks' collective action problems, the limited number of players involved in syndicated bank lending to sovereign governments facilitated creditor cooperation and mitigated the free-rider problem. Since roughly 50 percent of the Mexican debt was held by the thirty largest money-center banks in the G-5 countries, the BAC quickly secured commitments by these banks to provide one-half ($2.5 billion) of the entire package.[41] Second, the money-center banks then took the lead in organizing the participation of smaller banks in the concerted lending plan. This pressure proved remarkably effective, as all but a handful of the remaining 500 plus banks ultimately participated in the concerted lending plan:

In New York, bankers said last night that the response to Mexico's request for additional loans had been "very positive." One senior banker said that replies had been coming in steadily and that "everything appears to be going remarkably smoothly." In London, an executive at Lloyd's Bank,

[39] Minutes of EBM/82/167 [Executive board meeting] (December 23, 1982), 4.

[40] Boughton (2001, 315).

[41] The 100 largest banks eventually made commitments in excess of $4 billion (Boughton 2001, 313).

which is coordinating responses from 55 British banks, said that more than three-quarters of the responses had arrived and "we haven't had a single negative response."[42]

This self-policing by the largest commercial banks was particularly critical in the United States, where many small regional banks had actively sought to "bail out" of Mexico.[43] In addition, direct intervention by the BIS and the G-10 central banks also played an important role in convincing holdout creditors to participate in the IMF's request. For some creditor banks, the aforementioned promises by Volcker and his G-10 counterparts of regulatory leniency mitigated their concerns about further lending to Mexico. For other banks, the implicit threat of future regulatory punishment proved a stronger motivation to provide new loans to Mexico. As the head of one holdout bank in Florida explained: "The Fed is our main regulator, and in fact we need approval for a merger. The bank examiners came around and started asking questions. That was enough for us."[44] Stanislas Yassukovich, managing director of European Banking Company, a small British bank with ties to Mexico, felt similar pressure from the Bank of England: "We were pretty well told by the deputy governor [of the Bank of England] that if we did not step into line we would be on the carpet. What can you do under those circumstances?"[45]

In the end, despite much grumbling by smaller banks and a good deal of arm-twisting by G-10 governments and the members of the BAC, nearly all Mexico's bank creditors signed up to the concerted lending plan. Nonetheless, since the final $1 billion in concerted lending required the BAC to secure commitments from over 400 smaller banks, negotiations dragged on into February 1983.[46] In the interim,

[42] Alan Friedman and Paul Taylor, "Mexico loan gets backing of US and UK bankers," *Financial Times*, December 16, 1982.

[43] Because their exposure was very small relative to the money-center banks and their own overall lending portfolios, these smaller banks had strong incentives to "cut and run." As one Washington state banker explained, "We could save ourselves without saving the whole system" (Kraft 1984, 52).

[44] Kraft (1984, 53).

[45] William Hall, "The small banks get nervous," *Financial Times*, December 21, 1982.

[46] Ultimately, the main holdouts were the small regional banks in the United States and smaller banks in West Germany and Switzerland. See Peter Montagnon, "Banks ready to commit $4.5 billion funds to Mexico," *Financial Times*, December 23, 1982.

the largest money-center banks provided Mexico with $433 million in bridge financing on February 24, which was intended to allow Mexico to service its debts until the first loans were disbursed in March.[47] Not surprisingly, the largest commitments came from United States banks, which held 62 percent of Mexico's bank debt; American commercial banks provided $1.76 billion, while Japanese banks contributed the next largest amount (approximately $900 million) of new money.[48]

Executive Board approval – December 23, 1982

The composition of Mexico's private international creditors – specifically the fact that Mexico's lenders consisted almost entirely of a limited number of major commercial banks – thus played a key role in shaping negotiations between the IMF staff and the Mexican government in 1982. Through the efforts of the BAC, Mexico's commercial bank creditors were able to organize quickly and make firm, upfront commitments to provide new lending. As a result, the IMF was confident – even before the executive board met – that the Mexican loan would have the desired "catalytic effect" on private capital inflows. With sufficient private commitments of new lending in place, de Larosière brought the Mexican EFF proposal before the executive board on December 23, 1982, where it was unanimously approved.

A close examination of the executive board minutes from the December 23 meeting sheds further light on the process of IMF decision-making and the connections between patterns of financial globalization and the preferences of the key actors involved. In particular, the board discussion highlights several key points that reinforce the theoretical argument and quantitative evidence provided thus far in the book. First, the board discussion provides additional evidence that the anticipated reaction of private international creditors plays a central and critical role in shaping IMF lending decisions. Indeed, the managing director opened the meeting by emphasizing that the proposed IMF loan (coupled with bilateral official commitments of $2 billion from the United States and BIS central banks) would leave Mexico with $5 billion in external debt obligations in 1983 – an

[47] Alan Riding, "Mexico in $5 billion loan pact," *New York Times*, February 25, 1983.

[48] Minutes of EBM/82/167, annex 1, 38.

amount that he had already informed Mexico's commercial bank creditors they had to provide themselves through a combination of "new exposure" and debt rescheduling.[49] De Larosière then provided an updated status report on the extent of private lenders' commitments to date; he noted that, as of 5:00 p.m. on December 22, Mexico's commercial bank creditors had pledged $4.32 billion in lending commitments – a total slightly short of the $4.5 billion (90 percent) target for new syndicated lending that would constitute "critical mass, i.e., an amount large enough to satisfy him [de Larosière] that sufficient momentum had been created in the banking community" to warrant bringing the proposed IMF loan to a vote before the board.[50] De Larosière then thanked those countries – Canada, the United Kingdom, and the Netherlands – whose banks had contributed "amounts in excess of their quotas" to the concerted lending package.[51] He also commented that several major countries' banks – Japan, West Germany, and the United States in particular – were the parties responsible for the shortfall in commitments, though he also noted that these countries had made the largest aggregate commitments to date. Despite the banks' slight shortfall in commitments, de Larosière made it clear that he felt the banks had come close enough to the $4.5 billion target to make clear their strong commitment to provide future financing to Mexico. Consequently, he urged the board to open discussions on the proposed Mexican loan and asked for its "support ... in carrying through the vast international support operations that the Fund had coordinated."[52]

Several executive directors echoed the managing director's optimism about private creditors' willingness to provide new financing to Mexico. For example, Alexandre Kafka (Brazil) "warmly supported" the proposed loan, "despite the shortfall in contributions from commercial banks, which he was sure would be overcome in a short time."[53] Gerhard Laske (West Germany) stated that "he was not worried about the shortfall of some $680 million in new [bank] exposures," and he expressed "reasonable confidence that many of the banks that had not yet responded would fall into line once it

[49] Minutes of EBM/82/167, 3. [50] Ibid., 4.

[51] Ibid. Quotas for individual countries had been established on the basis of the exposure of their commercial banks in Mexico.

[52] Ibid., 3. [53] Ibid., 11.

became known that the executive board of the Fund had agreed to an extended arrangement for Mexico."[54]

This optimism about private creditors' behavior on the part of both the Fund staff and its shareholders was largely the result of the composition of Mexico's private external debt. Since the aforementioned limited number of commercial banks held nearly all of Mexico's private external debt, the Fund's concerted lending strategy had been extremely successful and (the slight shortfall in bank commitments notwithstanding) had been accomplished quite rapidly.[55] In fact, only five weeks had passed since de Larosière's initial meeting with the BAC at the FRBNY. Although a few banks continued to hold out, the commercial banks had organized and collectively reached agreement on participation in the concerted lending scheme in a remarkably short period of time.[56] Had Mexico's private creditors been more numerous and disaggregated, it is highly unlikely that they would have come so close to meeting de Larosière's "critical mass" target, and the board discussion of the Mexican IMF loan would quite probably have been delayed. Furthermore, a larger shortfall of private lending commitments would probably have required a much larger Fund loan that would have covered a greater portion of Mexico's external financing gap. In the event, the Fund was able to stand firm in its commitment to provide only a relatively small portion ($2 billion) of Mexico's external financing needs, while the commercial banks committed themselves to providing the majority.

Christopher Taylor (alternate executive director – United Kingdom) saw the success of concerted lending in the Mexican case as a model to be followed in future lending cases. He emphasized that the IMF could not "meet all of Mexico's financial needs" given its resource constraints, but added that a Fund loan could "give confidence to donors and creditors, particularly commercial banks, and encourage them to continue lending to a country that was having extreme difficulty."[57] In this sense, Taylor stated, "the case of Mexico was a good example of the crucial role that the Fund could play *as a*

[54] Ibid., 23. [55] Ibid., 4.

[56] The primary holdout creditors were small banks in the United States with very small exposure to Mexico, and countries with less overall exposure (e.g. Italy, Belgium, Switzerland). See ibid., 4–5.

[57] Ibid., 34.

catalyst."[58] Similarly, Teruo Hirao (Japan) sought to draw more general lessons about the IMF's role in generating catalytic financing from the Mexican experience:

> The Fund's primary role should be *to restore public confidence* in the economy of a debtor country by formulating a suitable adjustment program, *thereby facilitating the country's access to private credit* ... There might be additional cases like that of Mexico, in which parallel negotiations with private banks would be needed in order to consolidate the basis for implementing the Fund program.[59]

These statements by the British and Japanese executive directors illustrate that the board, like the Fund staff, is also particularly concerned with the expected reaction of international creditors in the aftermath of an IMF loan, as well as the moral hazard consequences of providing a complete bailout to a country and its private lenders.

In addition to highlighting the importance of patterns of financial globalization, the board minutes reinforce the centrality of country-specific macroeconomic criteria in shaping IMF lending decisions. Following de Larosière's introduction and discussion of the status of the concerted lending operation, Miguel A. Senior (Venezuela), the executive director representing Mexico, Spain, and six other Latin American countries, provided a comprehensive overview of the Fund staff's report and the proposed conditionality to be implemented by the Mexican authorities.[60] Senior outlined a series of policy reforms, including reductions in inflation and external borrowing. The "centerpiece of the program" was a "marked reduction of the public sector deficit, from about 16.5 per cent of GDP in 1982 ... to 3.5 per cent in 1985."[61] To reach this target, the Mexican government committed itself both to sharp reductions in spending and to a series of revenue-increasing measures, including "higher taxes, tariffs, and prices."[62]

Once Senior had finished his opening statement, the executive directors each offered their thoughts, comments, and questions on the proposed IMF program. In the course of these discussions, the lion's share of their attention was focused on concerns about the type, content, and scope of these proposed conditions.

[58] Ibid. (emphasis added). [59] Ibid., 33 (emphasis added).
[60] Ibid., 5–11. [61] Ibid., 6. [62] Ibid., 7.

In particular, several executive directors expressed concerns about the specifics – or lack thereof – contained in the Mexican program, including the lack of an overall strategy for Mexico's recovery. While the draft program contained a long list of macro- and microeconomic policy reforms aimed at reducing the public sector deficit (including fiscal policy adjustment, an increase in value added tax, and controlling wage growth), the executive directors were not clear about either the sequencing of these policy reforms or which of these adjustments was expected to have the greatest impact on Mexico's economic situation. For example, Jacques de Groote (Belgium) argued that the draft proposal "was not a program so much as a list of intentions, and of individual decisions taken in some areas of the economic field."[63] Robert Joyce (Canada) shared this concern, noting that "he did not have any clear idea of how the various elements would fit together."[64] Consequently, de Groote emphasized that "frequent reviews would be needed… to ensure that the program was implemented."[65] Similarly, Jacques Polak (the Netherlands) noted the significant degree of uncertainty surrounding the staff's projections of Mexico's performance during the three-year duration of the program.[66] While he praised the staff for submitting a "thorough and detailed" report and draft program to the board, Polak worried that "little was known about what would take place in 1983, let alone in 1985."[67] Polak, Joyce, and others, including A.R.G. Prowse (Australia), worried that the proposed conditionality was neither politically feasible for the Mexican government to implement nor guaranteed to resolve the country's balance of payments problems even if fully implemented.[68]

Nevertheless, despite these concerns, the executive directors gave wide latitude to the IMF staff's proposed program and did not seek to impose their own preferences or modifications. To the contrary, they uniformly praised the staff for their thorough work and analysis, and they strongly supported the proposed program. Taylor's remarks are illustrative: he "joined the other speakers who had paid tribute to the staff for the amount of work that it put into the Mexican request, under considerable pressure," and he "warmly endorsed the staff appraisal and the proposed decisions."[69] Similarly, Kafka "thanked

[63] Minutes of EBM/82/168 (December 23, 1982), 4.
[64] Ibid., 8. [65] Ibid., 4. [66] Ibid., 4–5. [67] Ibid., 5.
[68] Ibid. See discussion at pp. 4–17. [69] Ibid., 34.

the staff for the special efforts that it had made to keep executive directors up to date about measures taken recently by the Mexican authorities," while Laske, Richard Erb (United States), and Bruno de Maulde (France) commended both the managing director and the staff for their handling of the Mexican crisis.[70] Joyce and Polak acknowledged the staff's exceptional efforts under serious time constraints and in light of the magnitude of Mexico's problems; although they had raised a variety of detailed concerns about the feasibility and effectiveness of the proposed conditions, they nevertheless expressed full support for the proposed program.[71] The executive directors' focus on the content and details of conditionality in the Mexican EFF arrangement, as well as their willingness to accept the proposed conditions without alterations, illustrates the significant amount of autonomy and influence exercised by the IMF staff in the Fund lending process. Moreover, it reinforces the idea that IMF lending, while unquestionably influenced by the domestic interests of the Fund's large shareholders, is, to some extent, a technocratic process driven largely by the economic and financial characteristics of the particular borrowing country in question.

Nonetheless, although the December 23 board meeting illustrates the key role and substantial autonomy of IMF bureaucrats, it also highlights the central role played by the Fund's largest shareholders in IMF policymaking. Despite the concerns noted above about the content of conditionality, the G-5 executive directors praised de Larosière for his efforts at securing the banks' cooperation and uniformly supported the package, on the grounds that global financial stability depended on an immediate and effective response by the Fund. As Erb stated, "It was difficult to overstate the significance of the program's successful implementation, not only for Mexico but also for the Fund and for the system."[72] Erb's only concern was a preference for more frequent program reviews given the many uncertainties about Mexico's situation. Laske also offered his support for the program and noted that he "was not worried about" the fact that the commercial banks had not met de Larosière's target.[73] The banks' commitments were sufficient, he concluded, "that the Fund could have reasonable confidence that many of the banks that had not yet

[70] Ibid., 11, 18, 21. [71] Ibid., 5–11.
[72] Minutes of EBM/82/167, 18. [73] Ibid., 23.

responded would fall into line once it became known that the executive board of the Fund had agreed to an extended arrangement."[74] Hirao stated that the Japanese government was "fully prepared" to support the IMF program, while Taylor "warmly endorsed the staff appraisal and the proposed decisions."[75]

Among the G-5 executive directors, only de Maulde expressed any skepticism about the program. He raised concerns about both debtor and creditor moral hazard, noting that Mexico "was a clear case of an adjustment unduly delayed with the support of misguided borrowing, on an ever-shorter-term basis, from unwise commercial banks."[76] This relative lack of enthusiasm is somewhat surprising, given that French commercial banks, with $4.4 billion of lending, were more highly exposed to Mexico than either Japanese or German banks ($2.1 billion and $1.9 billion, respectively). Nevertheless, while de Maulde was more concerned about moral hazard than his G-5 colleagues, his concerns were tempered by equally significant worries about the systemic consequences of a Mexican financial crisis: "The size of Mexico's external problem," he noted, "was such that the consequences of letting it escalate could well have been severe for the entire international monetary system."[77] Ultimately, de Maulde concluded that France "could fully support the objectives of the program" in light of the Mexican crisis's implications for international financial stability.[78]

Thus, the Fund's largest shareholders, including the G-5 countries that exercise de facto control over the executive board, uniformly supported approval of the proposed Mexican EFF arrangement. G-5 support was broadly matched by the remaining executive directors, who also expressed their enthusiasm for the proposed program.[79] This unanimity among the Fund's largest shareholders, coupled with the sizeable upfront lending commitments of the commercial banks, led the board to approve unanimously the Mexican request for a three-year EFF arrangement totaling SDR 3.41 billion (2.93 times quota). although the G-5 countries strongly supported approval of the large-scale loan, however, they also supported the staff's proposed conditionality (seven performance criteria). Indeed, despite their governments' strong domestic and international interests in

[74] Ibid. [75] Ibid., 33–4. [76] Ibid., 12. [77] Ibid. [78] Ibid.
[79] Ibid., 11–18, and minutes of EBM/82/168, 3–19.

assisting Mexico, the G-5 executive directors emphasized that it was the Mexican government that bore primary responsibility for the onset of the current crisis. For example, Erb noted that Mexico's debt problems clearly "showed what could happen when a country's decision makers failed to make prompt adjustments in economic policies as conditions changed."[80] Laske echoed Erb's concerns about the severity of the crisis and noted that the Mexican government's policy choices in 1981 and 1982 had "proved to be too timid to prevent a further aggravation of the internal and external imbalances, and they had failed to prevent a grave economic crisis."[81] Although he acknowledged that the loan's conditionality would harm both economic growth and employment in Mexico, Laske concluded that "there was ... no workable alternative to such strong austerity measures, which were being imposed not for austerity's sake, but rather to restore national and international confidence" in Mexico.[82] He was "particularly impressed by the combination of various performance criteria, which went beyond what was usually incorporated into Fund programs with member countries. Considering the extremely difficult economic situation confronting Mexico," he concluded, "the somewhat more elaborate network of criteria was certainly justified."[83]

Therefore, while G-5 governments strongly supported the large-scale Mexican loan on account of the country's importance to both their domestic financial interests and global financial stability, they also supported the staff's proposed conditionality in order to limit moral hazard and ensure that Mexico undertook the policy reforms necessary to ensure its long-term solvency. This stance reflects the way in which the G-5 collectively wrestle, on a case-by-case basis, with the liquidity/moral hazard trade-off inherent in IMF lending. While a large Fund loan clearly served the domestic financial interests of G-5 governments in the 1983 Mexican case, it also placed substantial IMF resources at risk – resources provided largely by the G-5 themselves through their quota contributions.

Ultimately, the combination of substantial financing with relatively extensive conditionality was an outcome consistent with G-5 governments' dual interests in the Mexican case. At the same time, this outcome reflected the Fund staff's influence over lending decisions, as well as its concerns about catalytic financing. Indeed, while

[80] Minutes of EBM/82/167, 18. [81] Ibid., 22. [82] Ibid. [83] Ibid.

the G-5 had strong domestic financial interests in Mexico, the staff's primary goal was to signal Mexico's firm commitment to sustainable macroeconomic policies – thereby convincing the commercial banks to continue lending to Mexico in the future. In part, this required a substantial financial commitment by the Fund. Nevertheless, it also required significant policy adjustment by the Mexican government to alleviate the country's balance of payments problems. In short, the interests of both key actors in IMF policymaking came together to yield the final outcome in the 1983 Mexican lending episode. G-5 governments and the IMF staff both exercised partial, but incomplete, authority, and each group's preferences were strongly influenced by the composition of private international capital flows to Mexico.

Short-term success and recovery, 1983–5

In the short term, the 1983 EFF arrangement proved to be a great success. By March 1983 Mexico appeared to be back on the track to financial recovery. On March 23 the BAC announced that the $5 billion "critical mass" target had been reached, with 526 bank creditors participating.[84] By August Mexico had fully repaid the $1.85 billion BIS bridge loan; by December it had retired all $864 million in arrears on its private debt that had accumulated during the 1982 crisis.[85] One year after the approval of Mexico's IMF package, de Larosière contacted the BAC and informed the banks that Mexico had met all the performance criteria for 1983 by "substantial margins."[86] He then asked for a second round of concerted lending on the order of $3.8 billion, which would supplement the Fund's disbursements during 1984. With the successes of 1983 serving as a catalyst, the BAC secured commitments from more than 500 banks for the full amount by April 1984. Once again, the composition of Mexico's private international creditors played a key role: the banks' ability to organize rapidly and cooperate under the auspices of the BAC, coupled with their long-term interests in Mexico, enabled the IMF to secure new financing commitments that further mitigated its concerns about moral hazard resulting from the very large Mexican loan.

[84] A handful of small creditors never participated, but the major money-center banks made additional commitments to cover the difference in funds (Kraft 1984, 54; James 1996, 371).

[85] Kraft (1984, 55). [86] Boughton (2001, 364).

With the second concerted lending agreement finalized, the IMF and the commercial banks began to explore a longer-term solution to Mexico's financing needs. Although the BAC had managed once again to assemble a critical mass of participants in the new $3.8 billion loan, it now recommended that de Larosière encourage the banks to commit to a multi-year rescheduling package that would allow Mexico to reschedule some of the debt it owed in the coming months.[87] At the International Monetary Conference in Philadelphia in May 1984, de Larosière met with the chairmen of the BAC member banks (along with Volcker, Leutwiler of the BIS, and several IMF senior staff members) and made the case for a multi-year rescheduling agreement (MYRA): "It is ... in everyone's interest that Mexico's [adjustment] efforts be complemented by a change in its external debt profile in a way that would enhance stability."[88] The members of the BAC governing board, including William Rhodes, Walter Wriston (the chief executive of Citibank), and Wilfried Guth (chairman of Deutsche Bank) all reacted favorably to de Larosière's proposal. The following day Rhodes announced the banks' intention to negotiate with Mexico over the rescheduling of some $40 billion of the country's $90 billion in private international debt.[89] On September 8, after two months of negotiations, the BAC and the Mexican authorities reached agreement on the rescheduling of approximately $48 billion of Mexico's sovereign debt that fell due between 1985 and 1990. Under the terms of the agreement, the commercial banks agreed to lengthen the maturity of their syndicated loans from eight to fourteen years, to smooth principal and interest repayments, and to reduce Mexico's interest rate spreads over LIBOR.[90] The MYRA lowered Mexico's debt payments by $487 million per year in 1985 and 1986, by $379 million per year from 1987 to 1991, and by $325 million from 1991 to 1998.[91]

With these further commitments from the banks in place, Mexico was able to meet its debt obligations and implement the conditionality included in the extented arrangement. Between 1983 and 1985, as Mexico continued to meet its performance criteria targets, the IMF

[87] Ibid., 365.

[88] IMF/RD Managing Director file "Philadelphia meeting, 1984" (accession 85/231, box 3, section 177), quoted in Boughton (2001, 366).

[89] James L. Rowe, Jr., "Loan terms to be eased for Mexico," *Washington Post*, June 5, 1984.

[90] Boughton (2001, 368).

[91] Richard J. Meislin, "Mexico reports accord to ease debt payments," *New York Times*, September 8, 1984.

staff provided favorable reviews in its staff reports and expressed clear support for continued disbursement of the SDR 3.41 billion package. Overall, the staff viewed the 1983 extended arrangement as a clear success, given Mexico's return to financial stability and good standing in global markets. In its third-year review, the staff expressed a favorable view of Mexico's prospects and performance under the program:

> In summary, in the last few years Mexico has made remarkable advances in its efforts to recover from the economic crisis of 1981–82 ... [T]he authorities have implemented policies which have led to a substantial gains [*sic*] in Mexico's economic situation and an improvement in the structure of the economy. The authorities have also shown the capacity to correct economic policies when deviations from the programmed path have occurred, and they have reiterated their willingness to adopt further adjustment measures, as needed, to ensure the success of the adjustment program ... [I]n the view of the staff, the program presented for 1985 is consistent with the attainment of the aims established under the extended arrangement.[92]

As a result of their apparent success, the IMF's policies toward Mexico from 1982 to 1984 soon became a blueprint for its overall approach to developing country lending in the mid-1980s. In April 1983 the executive board formally adopted concerted lending as its policy for providing financing to borrowing countries: "The executive board would need sufficient safeguards [i.e. private funding commitments] to ensure that the Fund's resources would be used to support a viable and financeable adjustment program."[93] Within this framework, the IMF would condition its lending to Mexico and other developing country borrowers on the provision of new (catalytic) financing by the borrower country's private international creditors.

The 1986 stand-by arrangement

Renewed difficulties, 1985–6

Despite the emergence of concerted lending and multi-year rescheduling as the normal mode of IMF lending, it became increasingly

[92] See "Mexico – staff report for the 1985 Article IV consultation and use of fund resources under the extended arrangement – program for the third year," EBS/85/123 (May 13, 1985).

[93] Minutes of EBM/83/58 (April 6, 1983), 36–7; published in IMF (1983, 162–3).

evident that this approach did not offer a long-term solution to Mexico's debt problems. Although debt rescheduling had lengthened the maturity profile of Mexico's external debt, it had not reduced its overall debt burden. Thus, while Mexico had managed to avoid the immediate threat of a default in 1984/5, it still faced serious questions about the long-term sustainability of its external financing situation. Furthermore, by the end of 1985 Mexico also faced new macroeconomic difficulties. After solid current account surpluses in 1983 and 1984, Mexico saw a marked reversal in its trade balance in 1985, largely as a result of another round of sharp declines in oil prices. With wage policy and fiscal adjustment policies weakening, inflation rose to 53.7 percent year-on-year by August, and the peso depreciated sharply against the dollar.[94] In addition, the Mexican government had missed its targets for several of the extended arrangement's performance criteria for the end of 1984. When the IMF staff team visited Mexico City to conduct its program review in mid-August it found that Mexico fell short on several key performance criteria (including the targets for foreign exchange reserves, domestic credit growth, and the fiscal deficit), and the Fund had no choice but to suspend disbursement of the remaining $900 million of the 1983 program.[95]

Mexico's debt problems worsened in mid-September, when two massive earthquakes – an 8.1 quake on the Richter scale on September 19 and a 7.5 quake the following day – further destabilized its financial position. The earthquakes killed thousands of people in and around Mexico City, and the economic damage eventually totaled the equivalent of 3.5 percent of annual GDP.[96] Although the 1983 extended arrangement remained suspended, the IMF did offer SDR 290 million in emergency financing, which the executive board approved, and disbursed immediately, on January 10, 1986.[97] In April, the World Bank provided $400 million in additional disaster relief aid, and Silva Herzog simultaneously began talks with de Larosière and the IMF staff over the terms of a new Fund program to replace the cancelled loan under the EFF.

[94] David Gardner, "Mexico may need further pact to reschedule debt," *Financial Times*, August 8, 1985.

[95] Boughton (2001, 371). [96] Ibid.

[97] Despite this emergency assistance, the Fund came under severe criticism for "cutting off" Mexico in the wake of the earthquakes. See James L. Rowe, "IMF cuts off lending to Mexico," *New York Times*, September 20, 1985.

Mexico's debt composition, 1985–6

At the beginning of 1986, therefore Mexico found itself once more facing a potential external debt crisis. Despite three years of adjustment under the 1983 extended arrangement, the country's overall private external debt had continued to grow, rising from $62.4 billion in 1982 to $73.4 billion by the end of 1985. The vast majority of this debt (95.1 percent) was still held by commercial banks, with G-5 commercial banks holding $51.6 billion in Mexican debt. At only $3.6 billion in outstanding issues, bonds continued to play only a limited role in Mexico's external debt situation. Private non-guaranteed debt, which remained entirely in the form of interbank lending, had risen slightly ($15.1 billion), but remained stable as a share (19.7 percent) of Mexico's private external debt.

Despite this continuity in Mexico's financial ties to global markets, two major changes in Mexico's external debt composition had occurred since 1982. First, as a result of the 1984 MYRA, Mexico's annual amortization payments on its private external debt had declined sharply, from $9.6 billion per year from 1986 to 1989 to $1.1 billion per year thereafter.[98] Thus, while Mexico's overall debt burden remained substantial, its short-term obligations had fallen markedly. Second, the distribution of debt among G-5 commercial banks had shifted. Although US commercial banks continued to hold the largest share of Mexican debt, their exposure had declined in both absolute and relative terms, from $24.9 billion and 62 percent of G-5 bank lending to Mexico in 1982 to $23.1 billion and 44.8 percent in 1985. Similarly, while UK banks remained Mexico's second largest creditors, they also had reduced their exposure slightly, from $6.4 billion in 1982 to $6.3 billion in 1985. By contrast, commercial banks in the other G-5 countries had significantly increased their Mexican exposure in the three years following the IMF's approval of the 1983 extended arrangement. French banks now held $5 billion in Mexican debt (compared to $4.4 billion in 1982), while German banks had nearly doubled their lending to Mexico from $1.9 billion (5 percent of the G-5 total) to $3.5 billion (7 percent). More importantly, Japanese banks had increased their lending to Mexico sharply; by 1985 they held $13.1 billion in claims on Mexico (25 percent of the G-5 total),

[98] Boughton (2001, 415).

or nearly seven times the amount they had held in 1982 ($2.1 billion; 5 percent). As a result, US and Japanese commercial banks now held almost a half (49.3 percent, $36.2 billion) of Mexico's entire stock of private international debt and over two-thirds of G-5 bank claims (69 percent). In contrast, European G-5 banks held only 20.2 percent ($14.8 billion) of Mexico's debt, and their combined share of G-5 bank exposure was only 21 percent. This significant difference in exposure would directly influence how each of the G-5 countries viewed IMF lending to Mexico throughout the remainder of the 1980s.

Negotiating the stand-by arrangement, March–August 1986

By early 1986 Mexico found itself once again at the edge of an imminent financial crisis: the government owed $950 million in principal to international bank lenders on March 21. Although the commercial banks still had extensive, long-term ties to Mexico, they had now endured three years of concerted lending and debt rescheduling and were becoming increasingly reluctant to continue providing Mexico with new credit. Consequently, the banks refused to roll over this payment unless and until Mexico signed a new letter of intent with the Fund.[99] Faced with few alternatives, Silva Herzog began formal negotiations with the IMF, and the banks subsequently agreed to a six-month rollover of the March 21 payment. Negotiations continued to drag on through May 1986, as Mexico and the IMF staff clashed over how much fiscal restraint would be required to rein in inflation and resolve the government's balance of payments problems.

By June Mexico still had not reached an agreement with the IMF on the terms of a new lending program, and private creditors began to pull out of the country. The Banco de México announced on June 3 that it had lost $500 million in reserves during May, leaving it with less than $3.2 billion on hand (compared to $7.3 billion at the end of 1984).[100] Silva Herzog resigned on June 17, after which Gustavo Petricioli, the new Mexican secretary of finance, traveled immediately to Washington and resumed negotiations with de Larosière and the

[99] Ibid., 438.
[100] "Mexico – staff report for the 1986 Article IV consultation and request for stand-by arrangement," EBS/86/161, Suppl. 1 (August 15, 1986), 11.

IMF staff. With Mexico rapidly running out of reserves and again facing default, the two sides finally reached agreement on the terms of a new letter of intent, which Petricioli signed on July 22. The proposed IMF program was an eighteen-month stand-by arrangement for SDR 1.4 billion (about $1.7 billion, equivalent to 1.2 times quota). As in 1983, it included seven performance criteria, with emphasis on the standard macroeconomic targets such as budget deficits and foreign exchange reserve levels. The program also contained a contingency clause under which the IMF would provide an additional SDR 800 million if the world price of oil – Mexico's chief export – fell below $9 per barrel.[101] Although the proposed SBA was smaller than the IMF's previous commitment to Mexico, its duration was shorter: the new loan was to last only half the time of the previous extended arrangement (eighteen months as against three years), and it was less than half the size (41 percent) of the 1983 package. Extrapolated out to thirty-six months, however (the length of the 1983 extended arrangement), the new loan would have equaled 2.4 times Mexico's quota – a level comparable to the 2.93 times quota ratio of the 1983 loan. The new loan thus represented another sizeable commitment of IMF resources to Mexico.

The IMF staff report, August 15, 1986

In its proposal to the executive board, the IMF staff acknowledged Mexico's substantial progress in addressing the debt crisis of 1982/3: "Four years ago the Government of Mexico was faced with a difficult economic situation. The economy was moving into recession, the country's foreign exchange reserves were under serious pressure, and inflation was accelerating rapidly."[102] The staff noted that the "Mexican economy [had] made substantial gains in 1983 and 1984," through "a major strengthening of the fiscal position, a tightening of credit, and a large initial adjustment of the currency, followed by frequent adjustments based on projected inflation."[103] The staff also emphasized the banks' willingness to participate in debt rescheduling

[101] Ibid., app. 5. Conversely, the IMF loan would decrease in size if oil prices rose above $14 per barrel, which would enable Mexico to service its external debts with less official assistance.

[102] Ibid., Suppl. 1. [103] Ibid., 5.

and to provide new lending as a key factors contributing to the success of the 1983 stand-by arrangement.[104]

Mexico's renewed financial difficulties, the staff stated, were the result of two key factors: (1) rising inflation, coupled with insufficient changes in government spending and the exchange rate level; and (2) "fiscal slippages ... compounded by the weakening of the international petroleum market and by the impact of the September 1985 earthquakes on economic activity in general and on the public finances in particular."[105] These factors had, in turn, undermined international creditors' confidence in Mexico and once again triggered capital flight. Despite a series of additional policy adjustments (including devaluation, public spending cuts, and the liberalization of import permits), the staff noted that "the [1983 IMF] program could not be brought back on track and by the end of 1985 five of the seven performance criteria under the extended arrangement were not met."[106]

The proposed new loan aimed to address these problems through a "combination of fiscal and monetary measures with structural policies to restore balance of payments viability" and "break the inflationary trend" while "setting the basis for reestablishing economic growth."[107] The seven performance criteria included a series of quarterly limits on government spending, the net foreign assets of the Banco de México, and external borrowing by the Mexican government.[108] Since, as noted above, declining oil prices had caused a substantial portion of Mexico's new financial difficulties, the staff tied both the proposed loan amount and conditionality "to the evolution of oil prices."[109] Thus, the staff's calculations of Mexico's external financing requirements, as well as the specific numerical targets for the performance criteria, would change depending on future movements in the world price of petroleum.[110]

As with the 1982–5 extended arrangement, the staff made it clear that the new program "calls for substantial recourse to new external financing."[111] Indeed, the report emphasized that policy adjustment alone – while necessary – would not fully address Mexico's external

[104] Ibid. [105] Ibid., 7. [106] Ibid.; see also table 3 (p. 8).
[107] Ibid., 10. [108] Ibid., 30–2.
[109] Ibid., 12. See appendix 5 (p. 57) for specific details of this "oil contingency mechanism."
[110] EBS/86/161, app. 5. [111] Ibid., 26.

debt problems: "Since full and immediate adjustment due to the drop in oil export earnings would be both politically very difficult and damaging to capital formation, the program calls for sizeable external support from all creditors that have been involved in financing Mexico's development in the past."[112] As a result, the staff emphasized, the proposed program would be successful only if it generated a catalytic effect on private capital flows over the 1986–7 period. The staff calculated the Mexican government's financing need from private international creditors to be "$6 billion over the two-year [1986–7] period," an increase of about 5.5 percent a year from current levels.[113] Although it acknowledged the sizeable commitment this involved on the banks' part, the staff believed that this "external financing proposal that has been advanced strikes a reasonable balance between financing and adjustment and deserves the support of the country's creditors."[114]

The program negotiated and designed by the IMF staff therefore combined substantial policy adjustment (conditionality) by the Mexican government with a sizeable amount of IMF financing. This combination reflected the staff's dual goals: inducing lasting change in the Mexican government's economic policies and convincing private international creditors to renew their commitment to Mexico. Nevertheless, the staff's closing statement in its report clearly illustrated that the Fund was now less certain of the new loan's success than it had been three years previously:

> The [Mexican] authorities have presented an economic program that *should* produce a substantial improvement in the country's general economic performance, and *should* facilitate changes in economic structures that are needed if Mexico is to achieve sustained economic growth. The efforts of the authorities need to be complemented by external cooperation if the program is to be implemented successfully, with the maintenance of orderly payments arrangements. *It has to be recognized, nevertheless, that the program is subject to considerable risk, particularly in view of the recent shocks which the economy has experienced.* Thus, the authorities will need to keep developments in the economy under closer scrutiny, and *should be ready to adjust policies promptly if circumstances should indicate that additional measures are required.*[115]

[112] Ibid., 44. [113] Ibid., 35. [114] Ibid., 46.
[115] Ibid., 47 (emphasis added).

The staff was also less optimistic that the proposed IMF program would have the desired catalytic effect on private international capital flows. Given Mexico's ongoing economic difficulties, it believed that a sizeable amount of the IMF's own financing would be necessary to convince private international creditors to continue lending to Mexico: "This [large loan] reflects the magnitude of the problem being experienced by the Mexican economy and the response of the authorities to the problem, as well as the need to signal to the creditors that the Fund will continue to have an important role in the country's adjustment process."[116] Therefore, despite its belief that the new IMF program should include substantial conditionality, the staff also supported a renewal of the Fund's large financing commitment to Mexico.

Concerted lending returns

With a new IMF loan proposal on the table, de Larosière and Petricioli once again sought to secure new lending commitments from Mexico's private international creditors in advance of the executive board meeting. Accordingly, they pursued the same strategy of direct negotiations with the major commercial banks that had proven so effective in 1982–4. On July 23–24, 1986, they met with representatives of eighty major commercial banks at the Pierre Hotel in New York, including William Rhodes and the board members of the BAC. De Larosière again proposed a sizeable concerted lending package consisting of an immediate contribution of $500 million plus a commitment by the BAC to assemble an additional $6 billion in syndicated bank lending covering the remainder of 1986 and 1987.[117] The $500 million contribution by the banks was intended to be part of a larger $1.6 billion package of bridge financing – a package that also included $545 million from the US Exchange Stabilization Fund and $550 million from the BIS and its component central banks.[118]

Although the BAC agreed to provide the $500 million in immediate bridge financing, negotiations with Mexico over the longer-term package proved significantly more difficult than in 1982.[119] Once again,

[116] Ibid., 46. [117] Boughton (2001, 443).
[118] See Peter Montagnon, "Mexico finalizes $1.6 billion bridging loan arrangement," *Financial Times*, August 28, 1986.
[119] It is worth noting that disagreements also arose within the BAC over whether or not to extend the $1.6 billion in immediate financing, with Swiss

changes in the composition of private international capital flows to Mexico played a central role. In particular, many G-5 commercial banks were far less vulnerable to a Mexican default than three years earlier, as they had now strengthened their capital reserves to insulate themselves against future losses incurred through sovereign lending to Mexico and other developing countries. By 1986 the largest banks in each of the G-5 countries had made reserve provisions averaging more than 20 percent of the value of their loans to developing countries. These provisions made new lending more expensive for the banks; while they maintained their existing exposure to Mexico through concerted lending and the MYRAs, they therefore began to reduce their voluntary new lending to Mexico and other less developed countries (LDCs): "Any new voluntary extensions of short-term trade credit have been more than offset by net repayments of existing loans. Banks have curtailed net new lending, even to developing countries that have avoided debt problems."[120] Mexico's lackluster economic performance over the previous three years also played an important role in fueling the banks' skepticism about new concerted lending. Having already rescheduled nearly $50 billion in outstanding debt and committed more than $5 billion in new loans under the 1983 extended arrangement, the banks were increasingly reluctant to commit further resources to a country whose future prospects were uncertain at best.

Since negotiations between the Mexican authorities and the BAC did not begin in earnest until September, BAC chairman William Rhodes informed de Larosière on September 4, 1986, that an agreement on the terms of a new concerted lending package – let alone participation by a "critical mass" of Mexico's commercial bank creditors – could not be secured prior to September 8, when the IMF executive board was to consider the proposed Mexican lending arrangement. Rather than postponing the meeting, de Larosière sought and received the support of several executive directors for taking the "exceptional" step of approving the Mexican loan "in principle" on the condition that Mexico reach a subsequent deal with its private and official creditors alike.[121]

Bank Corporation agreeing to participate only after direct pressure by de Larosière. See Alexander Nicoll, "Mexican creditors close to loan deal," *Financial Times*, August 14, 1986.

120 Morgan Guaranty, "World financial markets"; quoted in Montagnon, *Financial Times*, August 28, 1986.

121 Boughton (2001, 443).

Executive board approval – September 8, 1986

When the executive board met on September 8, several executive directors expressed serious reservations about the likelihood of the Mexican program succeeding.[122] The country's rising debt levels, coupled with its failure to meet the performance criteria under the 1983–5 extended arrangement and the commercial banks' growing reluctance to provide new financing, raised concerns about moral hazard problems resulting from another injection of IMF liquidity. Nonetheless, the board ultimately believed that the new IMF loan was essential, since a Mexican default would have severe negative effects on the stability of the global financial system. As Michael Foot, the United Kingdom's alternate executive director, argued, IMF support was warranted on systemic grounds, because of "the importance of its [Mexico's] orderly adjustment to the [stability of the] international monetary system."[123] Likewise, Jacques Polak (the Netherlands) noted "the crucial role of Mexico in the development of the international debt situation."[124] Put simply, Mexico was "too big to fail" in the eyes of the Fund and its major shareholders: a new Mexican financial crisis or default would have serious adverse consequences, both for global financial stability and for the domestic financial interests of the Fund's largest shareholders.

Although consensus emerged concerning approval of the loan package, so, too, did clear divisions within the executive board over the amount of IMF financing. Specifically, several board members – particularly the European directors – opposed the inclusion of the oil price contingency supplement, the SDR 800 million to be provided should world oil prices fall further.[125] In contrast, both Charles Dallara (United States), and Hirotake Fujino (Japan) strongly supported the oil price contingency plan.[126] These divisions over whether or not to grant extra IMF resources mirrored the relative differences in G-5 debt exposure to Mexico: with roughly one-half of Mexico's private external debt held by their commercial banks, the United States and Japan strongly favored the contingency clause, which would ensure that Mexico had sufficient resources to service its debts even if its export earnings continued to decline. The European directors, whose

[122] Minutes of EBM/86/148 (September 8, 1986), 23; cited in Boughton (2001, 444).

[123] Ibid., 445. [124] Ibid., 444. [125] Ibid. [126] Ibid.

governments (and banks) had less at stake in ensuring a Mexican bailout, were far less enthusiastic about including the oil supplement.[127]

In spite of these concerns, only one director, Charles Rye of Australia, abstained from approving the arrangement, on the grounds that Mexico's problems pre-dated the 1985 earthquakes and the prospects for program success were very slim.[128] In the end, Dallara and the rest of the G-5 directors threw their weight behind the staff's proposed program, despite Mexico's repeated failure to meet its performance criteria targets under the 1983–5 extended arrangement.[129] The executive board approved the loan, but only on the condition that Mexico reach agreement on new financing from both the commercial banks and its Paris Club creditors by September 29:

> This stand-by arrangement ... shall become effective on the date on which the Fund finds that satisfactory arrangements have been made with respect to the financing of the estimated balance of payments deficits for the period of the stand-by arrangement, but provided that such finding shall be made not later than September 29, 1986.[130]

This conditional approval by the board illustrates the degree to which the Fund's member state principals, like the IMF staff, were notably more concerned with moral hazard in 1986 than they had been in 1982/3, and far less optimistic about the prospects for successful catalytic financing. Thus, while the G-5 still had a strong domestic financial interest in providing Mexico with large-scale IMF financing, they were becoming increasingly concerned that the Fund's scarce resources were being used to "bail out" Mexico's private creditors. Quite simply, the Fund's largest shareholders found themselves increasingly torn between the liquidity/moral hazard trade-off and their dual goals of protecting their domestic financial interests and conserving the Fund's quota resources. In this situation, the IMF's

[127] Polak, in particular, thought that the oil contingency should be addressed through the Fund's Compensatory Financing Facility (CFF), rather than as part of the current proposal. Minutes of EBM/86/148; quoted in Boughton (2001, 444). The CFF was created in 1963 to assist countries experiencing export shortfalls as a result of fluctuating world commodity prices (www.imf.org/external/np/exr/facts/howlend.htm).

[128] Boughton (2001, 445). [129] Ibid.

[130] Executive board decision no. 8385 (86/149), adopted September 8, 1986.

ultimate decision was a contingent one: the full amount of financing approved by the board would become available only if and when Mexico's private and official creditors carried through with their pledges to reschedule existing debt and provide catalytic financing.

Securing the banks' participation, September–November 1986

With only three weeks to go to the executive board's imposed deadline, de Larosière – with the assistance of US Federal Reserve chairman Volcker – pressured both the BAC and the Mexican authorities to reach an agreement on the terms of the $6 billion in new bank loans for the remainder of 1986 and 1987. On September 15 Mexico's Paris Club creditors agreed to reschedule $1.8 billion in official sovereign debt, which the IMF hoped would provide further impetus for the banks to reach agreement on new loans to Mexico.[131] Nonetheless, no agreement had been reached by September 30, when the IMF/World Bank annual meetings began in Washington. At the meetings, Volcker, de Larosière, and Barber Conable (president of the World Bank) met together with the BAC chairman and finally hammered out an agreement between Mexico and the banks. Under the terms of the arrangement, the banks agreed to provide $7.7 billion in new lending (increased from $6 billion as it included money for the period beyond 1987) and to reschedule $54 billion in Mexico's outstanding debt at twenty years' maturity and an interest rate of 13/16 of a point over LIBOR.[132]

Since the executive board's conditional approval of Mexico's stand-by arrangement had expired on September 29, a new vote was required to reapprove the program. De Larosière tentatively scheduled this meeting for October 31, in order to give the BAC additional time to secure a "critical mass" (90 percent) of participation by Mexico's private creditors. Given the board's skepticism about the program's prospects in September, he did not want to call another vote without explicit assurances of sufficient private financing. In the interim, a combined team consisting of representatives from the BAC, the IMF,

[131] Peter Montagnon, "Mexico may miss IMF deadline," *Financial Times*, September 29, 1986.

[132] Alexander Nicoll, "Latin American debt crisis: chronology of events," *Financial Times*, July 30, 1992.

the World Bank, the Mexican government, and the BIS central banks conducted an intensive "road show" aimed at convincing as many holdout banks as possible to participate in the package.[133] Fewer than 40 percent of the banks had committed by the end of October, however, and the board meeting was put off again, to November 19. The 90 percent of "critical mass" level banks committing themselves to participate in the new concerted lending scheme was finally reached in mid-November, and the executive board approved the Mexican stand-by arrangement unanimously at its November 19 meeting. The first two tranches, of SDR 225 million each, were disbursed immediately.[134]

Ultimately, despite the postponement of the board decision and many banks' reluctance to provide new financing for Mexico, the concerted lending process occurred relatively rapidly and painlessly. Once again, the composition of private international capital flows to Mexico was central to this success: the relatively small number of commercial bank creditors, combined with the BAC's role as coordinator, facilitated broad agreement on new syndicated lending to Mexico. With these private commitments in place, the IMF felt secure in approving its own large-scale loan, confident that the necessary catalytic financing would be in place to secure Mexico's future financial stability. In short, a concrete commitment from private lenders to respond to the Fund's policies with their own financing played a critical role in shaping the IMF's own lending decision. Nevertheless, assembling these private lending commitments had taken more time than in 1983, and the banks were becoming increasingly reluctant to continue participating in concerted lending operations. In addition, clear divisions between the Fund's principals over the liquidity/moral hazard trade-off had begun to emerge; these differences over the merits of continued IMF lending to Mexico would only become starker in the coming years.

[133] "Mexico – request for stand-by arrangement," EBS/86/161, Suppl. 5 (October 29, 1986). To secure the banks' cooperation, the package was reduced to $5 billion but supplemented by $1 billion in World Bank co-financing and an additional $1.7 billion in potential World Bank lending linked to growth and oil price targets for Mexico.

[134] The first tranche had originally been slated for disbursement in September as part of the board's conditional approval of the stand-by arrangement on September 8, 1986. Minutes of EBM/86/185 (November 19, 1986).

Performance under the stand-by arrangement, November 1986–March 1988

As in 1983, Mexico initially fared quite well under the 1986 SBA, meeting all the arrangement's performance criteria for December. When a handful of holdout creditor banks delayed disbursement of the initial $3.5 billion of the $6 billion loan until late April 1987, however, Mexico missed several PC targets for the first quarter.[135] The IMF staff subsequently revised these targets, which had originally been designed on the assumption that bank financing would be available to Mexico much earlier. Mexico met the revised PCs for the June program review, though, and the executive board approved disbursement of the next tranche, for SDR 600 million.[136]

By October, however, Mexico once again faced serious problems. Following the "Black Monday" collapse of the US stock market on October 19, 1987, the Mexican market fell by 75 percent through the end of November. Faced with rising inflation (of some 150 percent annually) and large-scale capital outflows, Mexico implemented a new set of policies, the *Pacto de Solidaridad Económica* (Pacto), aimed at stabilizing the economy and keeping it in line with the IMF program. The Pacto involved four key elements: a 3 percent increase in the fiscal surplus, through a combination of spending cuts and increases in domestic energy prices; a sharp reduction in tariffs and non-tariff barriers; an 18 percent devaluation of the peso to stimulate exports; and the institutionalization of centralized wage bargaining to control inflation.[137] The Pacto succeeded in stabilizing Mexico's financial situation, and the Fund approved – with some modifications, including the waiver of the end-1987 PC targets – disbursement of the final two tranches of the 1986 stand-by arrangement on March 10, 1988. The completion of the 1986 loan brought Mexico's outstanding IMF debt to a then record SDR 4 billion (3.35 times quota).

The 1989 extended arrangement

Mexico's international debt, 1988–9

At the end of 1988 Mexico remained the second largest developing country borrower in global financial markets. Five years of IMF

135 Boughton (2001, 448).

136 Minutes of EBM/87/81/R-1 (June 3, 1987). 137 Lustig (1992).

programs, debt rescheduling, and new lending by its commercial bank creditors had not reduced the country's debt burden: Mexico still owed $63.4 billion to private international creditors. Overwhelmingly, these creditors remained commercial banks (94 percent of its long-term debt), with G-5 banks holding the vast majority ($46.5 billion) of this debt. Bond debt remained a very small portion (6 percent) of Mexico's overall private external debt, although the country faced the prospect of significant new payments coming due in 1990, as a consequence of the 1984 MYRA. In addition, private non-guaranteed debt had declined from 19.7 percent to 8.4 percent of the total, as the commercial banks reduced their interbank exposure to Mexico in the wake of six years of rescheduling and new money commitments on the syndicated sovereign lending side.

Although sovereign bank lending remained the dominant form of international capital flow into Mexico, G-5 bank exposure declined further from 1986 to 1989. As Mexico's debt problems persisted into the late 1980s, private lenders became less and less willing to extend new loans to the troubled borrower. In May 1987 Citibank had announced plans to add $3 billion to its reserves as a provision against potential losses on LDC lending, as well as long-term plans to close down its sovereign lending portfolio.[138] Other major US banks followed, and, by the end of 1988, American banks' exposure to Mexico had declined from $23.1 billion to $15.9 billion. As a share of total G-5 bank lending, US commitments had also declined, from 44 percent in 1986 to 36 percent in 1989. European banks had also reduced their exposure, albeit from far lower existing levels: UK banks held $5.8 billion in Mexican debt (13 percent of the G-5 total), French banks $4.6 billion (10 percent), and German banks $2.9 billion (7 percent). Japanese banks, in contrast, had slightly increased their Mexican lending from $13.1 billion in 1986 to $13.3 billion at the end of 1988, thereby raising their share of G-5 bank lending to 30 percent.

Thus, while the overall distribution of bank claims among G-5 countries had declined substantially as a result of the decline in US bank exposure – the coefficient of variation of G-5 bank exposure fell from 121.4 in 1983 to 67.6 in 1989 – American and Japanese creditors still held over two-thirds of Mexico's private external debt.

[138] Milt Freudenheim, James F. Clarity, and Katherine Roberts, "Citicorp allots $3 billion to cover Third World debts," *New York Times*, May 24, 1987.

This stark division in G-5 domestic financial exposure would be reflected in the subsequent IMF debates about the size and terms of the new Fund program, as the preferences of the European G-5 governments increasingly diverged from those of the United States and Japan.

The Brady Plan and the Mexican extended arrangement, April–May 1989

Although the completion of the 1986 stand-by arrangement had restored short-term stability, Mexico still faced longer-term external debt problems. Five years of IMF programs, concerted lending, and debt rescheduling might have averted a Mexican default but they had done little to alleviate the country's overall debt burden. If the banks were no longer willing to provide new financing, however, Mexico would be unable to continue meeting its debt service payments. By 1987, therefore, it had become clear to both the Mexican authorities and the IMF that a longer-term strategy to reduce Mexico's debt was needed. At first, the Mexican government itself sought to negotiate debt reduction directly with its private international creditors. On December 29, 1987, Mexico and Morgan Guaranty Bank announced a deal to swap $20 billion in outstanding bank loans for bonds, with the principal guaranteed by the US Treasury.[139] As Morgan had negotiated this deal outside the standard Bank Advisory Committee framework, however, few other commercial banks participated; ultimately, fewer than 100 of Mexico's 500 plus bank creditors exchanged $3.67 billion in loans for $2.56 billion in bonds – a 30 percent reduction in principal.[140]

Despite this limited success, the Morgan deal set the table for debt/equity swaps and debt reduction as a long-term solution to Mexico's external debt problems. While various debt reduction plans had been debated within the IMF and G-10 countries as early as 1983, the IMF's key officials strongly embraced debt/equity swaps and debt reduction in 1987–9. In his farewell address to the executive board

[139] Robert A. Bennett, "Morgan Bank outlines its Mexican debt plan," *New York Times*, December 31, 1987.

[140] Citibank, Mexico's largest creditor, was particularly angry that the BAC had not been consulted, and it refused to participate in the deal. See Boughton (2001, 491).

in January 1987, de Larosière recognized that securing the commercial banks' participation in future concerted lending packages would probably prove very difficult, as many had "strengthened their positions" by building up loss reserves and decreasing their developing country debt exposure.[141] As a result, he concluded, "the banks may have to make more options available" to Mexico and other developing country borrowers, including the possibility of significant debt reduction.[142] Incoming managing director Michel Camdessus echoed these sentiments in May 1987, when he called for "additions to the menu of [debtor countries'] options that in effect work to reduce the existing stock of debt."[143]

These endorsements of a strategy for facilitating external debt reduction began a process that ultimately yielded the Brady Plan in May 1989.[144] The Brady Plan (named for US Treasury secretary Nicholas Brady, its key proponent) envisioned the development of a menu of debt reduction options from which private creditors could choose, all of which would involve swapping bank loans for bonds with some reduction in principal. Under the guidelines of the plan, the IMF would earmark a portion of its loans to borrowing countries such as Mexico specifically for debt reduction. In addition to offering these "set-asides," the Fund would simultaneously offer additional credit ("augmentation") over and above its normal lending levels to finance interest payments on borrowers' commercial bank debt and to facilitate debt/equity swaps. The plan also called for the IMF to modify its policy of concerted lending – the strategy of lending to countries only after they had already secured private creditors' commitments of new financing. Rather, the IMF staff now recommended that the Fund "should be prepared to approve outright an arrangement with a member *before agreement on a suitable financing package has been agreed with creditors in cases where negotiations with creditors proved to*

141 Minutes of EBM/87/9 (January 14, 1987), 34.

142 Ibid.

143 Michel Camdessus, remarks to the seminar on "Latin America and the world economy," Aspen Institute Italia and SELA (Sistema Economico Latinoamencano y del Caribe), Caracas, Verezuela (May 2, 1988); quoted in Boughton (2001, 482).

144 For a detailed account of the formulation of the Brady Plan, its details, and the debates within the IMF and G-10 countries over its implementation, see Cline (1995) and Boughton (2001, ch. 11).

be prolonged."[145] In other words, rather than withholding credit until the commercial banks finalized a new money package, the IMF would now "lend into arrears" so long as the borrowing country and the banks had begun good-faith negotiations on new financing.

Taken together, these principles constituted a new debt strategy aimed at finding a long-term resolution to the now decade-long external debt problems of Mexico and other developing country borrowers. More importantly, the Brady principles illustrated the IMF staff's recognition that Fund lending might be required *ex ante* to convince a more skeptical group of private international creditors once again to provide new financing to Mexico and other developing country borrowers. In other words, the Fund's lending strategy would need to evolve in response to changes in the composition of international capital flows to Mexico and other developing countries.

The development of the Brady Plan coincided with Mexico's negotiations with the IMF over the terms of a new three-year arrangement under the EFF. In February 1989, following his re-election, Mexican president Carlos Salinas de Gortari decided to seek new financing from the IMF. In negotiations with the Fund staff, Mexico's central bank chief, Miguel Mancera, argued that incorporation of the Brady principles – specifically, debt reduction and lending into arrears – into the lending arrangement was essential if Mexico was to meet its external debt payments in 1989.[146] On April 3 Camdessus agreed to these terms, and Mexico signed the letter of intent on April 11. The proposed extended arrangement would provide Mexico with SDR 2.8 billion (2.4 times quota) and included seven performance criteria.[147] Camdessus also agreed to bring the program before the board as quickly as possible once it had approved the Brady Plan guidelines.

The IMF staff report, May 9, 1989

On May 9 the IMF staff delivered its report and draft program to the executive board. On the whole, the staff remained optimistic about

[145] "The Fund's policy on financing assurances," EBS/89/79 (April 20, 1989), 13 (emphasis added).

[146] Boughton (2001, 512).

[147] The board later approved two 40 percent augmentations of SDR 466.2 million each (in January 1990 and May 1992), along with a one-year program extension, bringing the total loan amount to SDR 3.71 billion (3.2 times quota) and the program length to four years (1989–93).

Mexico's prospects and encouraged continued IMF support: "In sum, the Mexican authorities have embarked on, and are strongly committed to, a major medium-term growth-oriented program. These efforts deserve the early support of the Fund in the form of an extended arrangement."[148] As in 1986, the staff proposed a loan with an "annual access rate" equal to 80 percent of Mexico's quota, although the new loan was to be of three years' duration rather than the previous program's two years.[149] Likewise, the level of conditionality was similar to the 1983 and 1986 programs: the new loan included the same seven performance criteria, including quarterly limits on public sector borrowing, government spending, and the Banco de México's net domestic and foreign assets. Thus, in many ways, the proposed loan under the EFF envisioned an extension of the Fund's current level of support for Mexico for an additional three years.

The staff report provided a comprehensive overview of Mexico's economic performance from 1987 to 1989, noting the success of the Pacto in reducing inflation to moderate rates and increasing the government's primary budget surplus, although the overall budget remained in deficit because of foreign debt payments.[150] In spite of these successes, however, the staff cited Mexico's ongoing external debt problems and the capital account deficit, which was rising as "net inflows from commercial banks in 1987 of $4.4 billion gave way to net outflows of $1.5 billion in the following year."[151] These substantial private capital outflows, which were driven both by Mexico's increasingly large debt service payments and the banks' reluctance to provide new financing, posed an ever more serious barrier to new investment and economic growth.[152]

Therefore, the anticipated response of private international creditors once again strongly influenced the IMF staff's views of the current EFF program. While the staff continued to hope that the new IMF loan would "help catalyze financing from other [private] sources," however, it no longer believed that the banks – having already rescheduled approximately $52.5 billion of Mexican debt over the last five years – would provide sufficient financing to resolve Mexico's debt problems.[153] Indeed, the staff emphasized that, "[u]nder

[148] "Mexico – staff report for the 1989 Article IV consultation and request for extended fund arrangement," EBS/89/91 (May 9, 1989), 34.

[149] Ibid., 1. [150] Ibid., 5–7.

[151] Ibid., 12. [152] Ibid., 13. [153] Ibid., 25, 34.

the assumption that the external financing being sought would be obtained entirely through the traditional new money approach [concerted lending]," Mexico would see little if any improvement in its external balance or its growth rate.[154]

As a result, the staff now envisioned that private creditors' contributions would include not only new financing and debt rescheduling but also – in line with the newly adopted Brady Plan – a menu of options including "reduction of principal, reduction of interest rates, interest recycling, and 'new money' loans."[155] Negotiations over such a debt reduction plan had already begun between the Mexican government and its commercial bank creditors, the staff noted, although no agreement had yet been reached. Nevertheless, the staff urged full and rapid approval of the extended arrangement, in the belief that it would reassure the banks and generate the desired catalytic effect on private capital flows:

> Although the financing arrangements for Mexico are not fully in place, the extended arrangement is being proposed for approval so as to provide an endorsement of the [Mexican] authorities' economic program by the international community. This will help strengthen the authorities' ability to implement the program; in addition, approval of the extended arrangement *will provide a clear signal of the Fund's support for Mexico's efforts to obtain external financing, and would help catalyze other resources.*[156]

In addition, the staff argued, immediate approval of the IMF loan in advance of the debt reduction agreement would tide Mexico over until a longer-term solution to its payments imbalance could be reached: "[w]ithout Fund approval at this stage, the cash flow position of Mexico would be even tighter than is envisaged at present."[157]

Although the Brady Plan was not yet official IMF policy – the executive board was slated to debate the proposals on May 19 – the IMF staff designed the arrangement on the assumption that the Brady principles would be a central element of the Mexican program. On May 25, following the board's approval of the Brady Plan, the staff issued a supplement to its May 9 report that provided an update on the status of the debt negotiations between Mexico and the commercial banks

[154] Ibid., 15. [155] Ibid., Suppl. 1 (May 25, 1989), 4.
[156] Ibid., 27 (emphasis added). [157] Ibid.

and clarified the role of debt reduction in the proposed program. The report noted that Mexico had started negotiations with the BAC on April 19 over a new financing package on the order of $4.5 billion per year.[158] According to the staff, the banks had agreed in principle to including debt reduction options in the package, on the condition that Mexico enter a new multi-year IMF program.[159] To facilitate this agreement between Mexico and its private international creditors, the staff proposed that "30 percent of each purchase [disbursement of IMF credit under the extended arrangement] would be set aside for debt reduction operations," and would be available "subject to observance of performance criteria under the arrangement."[160]

The staff's supplementary report also noted the Mexican government's stated intention to request an additional 40 percent "augmentation" of the extended arrangement (SDR 466.2 million) once it had finalized a debt reduction agreement with the banks.[161] The staff's initial reaction to this idea was favorable, even though the augmentation would require lending to Mexico in excess of its IMF quota limits.[162] Although it supported the augmentation in theory, however, the staff did not advocate for immediate approval of the 40 percent increase in loan size. Rather, the staff simply indicated its belief that Mexico would qualify for such an augmentation "upon an appropriate review by the Executive Board" and "in the event that the arrangements for financing Mexico's program provide for appropriate debt service reduction."[163] This position, which was contrary to the Mexican government's desire for immediate access to the additional IMF credit, reflected the staff's underlying concerns about moral hazard and the fact that it might take months for the banks and the Mexican authorities to finalize an agreement. If the IMF pre-committed extraordinary resources in the interim, the staff feared, Mexico's private creditors might use the opportunity to "bail out" before a proper debt reduction program could be implemented.

In sum, facilitating the resumption of a long-term, sustainable relationship between Mexico and its private international creditors was the centerpiece of the staff's EFF proposal in May 1989. To that end,

[158] Ibid., 4.
[159] See ibid., 2–4, for details of the proposed agreement and the various debt reduction options.
[160] Ibid., 4–5. [161] Ibid., 4. [162] Ibid. [163] Ibid., 6.

the staff favored a third loan similar to those previously approved in 1983 and 1986, with additional IMF resources to be considered only if and when the banks and Mexico agreed on a debt reduction scheme. The program was submitted to the board and placed on the docket for discussion at the May 26 meeting.

The executive board debate, May 26, 1989

As with the staff's report, the executive board debate centered on the impact of the proposed IMF loan on Mexico's debt sustainability and its ability to access international capital markets in the future. Leonor Filardo (Venezuela), the executive director representing Mexico, opened the meeting with a comprehensive discussion of Mexico's economic situation and the proposed program. She noted that "the structural and macroeconomic policies implemented during the past six years" under the 1983 and 1986 IMF programs "have created an adequate economic environment conducive to the resumption of growth."[164] Nonetheless, Filardo continued, Mexico's external debt levels remained extremely high and were preventing a full economic recovery: "the level of external resource transfers facing the economy is incompatible with restoring growth, since it implies that an important portion of domestic savings is being used to service debt instead of financing investment."[165] Eliminating this "debt overhang," she argued, was essential to reducing "macroeconomic uncertainty and capital flight" and facilitating Mexico's "renewed access to voluntary markets."[166] The proposed IMF program, in conjunction with the ongoing debt reduction negotiations between Mexico and its commercial bank creditors, was a critical step "in helping Mexico traverse from stagnation to self-sustained growth."[167]

After providing details of Mexico's debt reduction offer to the commercial banks, Filardo presented the Mexican government's request for a modification of the staff's proposed program. Specifically, she submitted a "formal request for outright approval of a full 40 percent augmentation of the extended arrangement," rather than (as the staff had proposed) a postponement of a final decision on the augmentation until Mexico concluded debt reduction negotiations with the

[164] Minutes of EBM/89/64 (May 26, 1989), 7.
[165] Ibid. [166] Ibid., 13. [167] Ibid., 13–14.

banks.[168] While Filardo acknowledged that this request "contrasted with the proposed decision," she argued that immediate and "full augmentation would provide an incentive to the banks to participate promptly in the most cost-effective debt reduction operation possible for both themselves and Mexico."[169] In short, Filardo and the Mexican government argued that a larger, upfront IMF financing commitment was necessary to convince Mexico's private international creditors to agree to provide further financing in the form of debt reduction. Filardo concluded by noting that this request for the full 40 percent augmentation "was closely in accordance with the recently adopted guidelines" on debt reduction under the Brady proposals.[170]

Following Filardo's statement, the board engaged in its customary "tour of the table," with each executive director offering his or her comments, questions, and concerns about the proposed program. On the whole, the directors took a favorable view of the proposed Mexican arrangement. Speaking first, as the longest-serving executive director, Alexandre Kafka (Brazil) noted that the proposed loan "continues a major macroeconomic and structural adjustment that, with lapses, has been going on for seven years, and that has already achieved major results in terms of inflation, the balance of payments, and economic efficiency."[171] Kafka praised the staff proposal for continuing Mexico's "major efforts at structural reform," as well as its "equally impressive" set of macroeconomic improvements, including reductions in the budget deficit and government borrowing.[172] Although he had some concerns about the assumptions underlying the program (e.g. the assumed GDP growth rate and the narrow projections for the current account deficit at only 2 percent of GDP), Kafka strongly supported the staff proposal. Ultimately, he stated, "we would be prepared to join a consensus in favor of outright approval of the 40 percent augmentation sought by Mexico, on the grounds just stated by Ms. Filardo."[173]

Kafka's enthusiastic support of the program was matched by several other non-G-5 executive directors, including Ernesto Feldman

[168] Ibid., 15. [169] Ibid.

[170] Ibid. See minutes of EBM/89/61 (May 23, 1989) for details of the Fund's proposed role in debt reduction.

[171] Minutes of EBM/89/64, 17.

[172] Ibid. [173] Ibid., 19.

(Argentina) and Yusuf Nimitallah (Saudi Arabia).[174] Likewise, Marcel Masse (Canada) favored approving the 40 percent augmentation immediately "without a critical financing mass in place."[175] Other directors expressed growing concerns about Mexico's continued debt problems, however. Several European directors, in particular, worried that the proposed conditions would not be sufficient to resolve Mexico's balance of payments difficulties, and they remained unsure about private international creditors' response to the IMF program. Markus Fogelholm (alternate executive director – Finland), the director representing the Nordic countries, noted Mexico's substantial progress since 1983, including its "high primary surplus in the fiscal accounts," and "a major liberalization of the trade system."[176] Nevertheless, he cautioned that "all is not well, as evidenced by the persistent deficits in the external accounts" and the continuation of high real interest rates driven by Mexico's extensive public sector borrowing.[177] Moreover, Fogelholm worried, he could not foresee any improvement in Mexico's debt situation in the near future: "the most significant cause for concern in the economic situation is that there is no sign of a medium-term viability in the external accounts. And it is difficult to see how circumstances could easily change for the better," given the high level of international interest rates and the low probability that Mexico's exports would increase substantially in the coming months.[178]

In light of these concerns, Fogelholm expressed "some hesitation" about Mexico's request for immediate approval of the 40 percent augmentation in loan size; instead, he supported the staff's proposed delay of a final decision on the augmented loan until more information about Mexico's negotiations with its commercial bank creditors became available.[179] Johann Prader (Austria), the alternate executive director representing Austria, Belgium, Luxembourg, Hungary, and Turkey, adopted a similar wait-and-see position on the additional IMF credit, as did Gert-Jan Hogeweg (alternate executive director – the Netherlands), representing Cyprus, Israel, Romania, and Yugoslavia.[180] Likewise, Renato Filosa (Italy) favored a postponement of the augmentation decision, on the grounds that private international creditors' reaction remained unclear:

[174] Ibid., 19–24. [175] Ibid., 35.
[176] Minutes of EBM/89/65 (May 26, 1989), 3.
[177] Ibid., 3. [178] Ibid., 4. [179] Ibid., 5. [180] Ibid., 10.

> [T]here were great uncertainties about whether the commercial banks would participate in the strengthened strategy [i.e. the Brady debt reduction plan]. Moreover, there was some distance between the proposals made by Mexico to the banks and the banks' response to them. Before deciding on the appropriateness of the augmentation, and especially in view of the wide financing gap, more information was needed on the size, composition, and terms of debt and debt service reduction that the banks and Mexico were prepared to accept, including the contribution that Mexico itself would make.[181]

As these remarks indicate, several board members shared serious concerns about the moral hazard consequences of providing immediate, large-scale IMF financing. If the Fund approved the full augmentation before Mexico concluded its debt negotiations with its commercial bank creditors, they worried, the loan might not have the desired catalytic effect on private capital inflows. Rather, the banks might have less incentive to agree to both a debt reduction plan and the provision of new lending to Mexico.

This executive board debate over the benefits of greater IMF liquidity (i.e. the immediate augmentation of the proposed loan) relative to the moral hazard costs reflected clear divisions between the Fund's largest shareholders: the G-5 governments. In offering his authorities' support for "outright approval" of the 40 percent augmentation, Gunther Grosche (West Germany) illustrated the factors influencing the executive directors' views of this trade-off. On the one hand, he stated, West Germany "could fully endorse the proposed decisions, including the proposed level of access [i.e. the augmentation], on account of Mexico's "good track record" with the IMF and the strength of the program.[182] Moreover, Grosche continued, he was encouraged by "the seriousness with which both parties [Mexico and the banks] were negotiating and by their obvious willingness to come to an agreement within a reasonable time."[183] On the other hand, Grosche made it clear that West Germany also had concerns about moral hazard, noting that his government supported such a large loan – and the immediate disbursement of the augmentation – only "in view of Mexico being a special case" and because West Germany was willing to "trust the staff and management's judgment."[184] Grosche also made it clear that

181 Minutes of EBM/89/64, 28.

182 Ibid., 31. 183 Ibid. 184 Ibid., 29, 31.

he had doubts about whether the proposed conditionality was sufficiently stringent to ensure adequate balance of payments adjustment. Specifically, he expressed concern that the staff had not proposed any new conditions in the loan; rather, the new program contained the same seven performance criteria as the 1983 and 1986 programs. While he "had no difficulty supporting a program that did not propose many new measures ... provided that those measures were strong in relation to the access requested and that there was a need for temporary balance of payments support," Grosche stressed West Germany's belief that "prompt corrective actions" of both the macroeconomic (fiscal and monetary) and structural (liberalization and privatization) conditionality might be warranted if Mexico's difficulties continued. In short, Grosche concluded, West Germany would support approval of the proposed loan and the immediate augmentation, but not without some concerns about both the amount of financing and the relative modesty of the loan's conditionality in relation to its size.

The strongest opposition to Mexico's request came from the United Kingdom, which did not want to pre-commit to the loan size augmentation before Mexico had reached an agreement with the banks. "His authorities," warned Frank Cassell (United Kingdom), "were concerned that the share of the external financing burden falling on the official sector could be disproportionately high" if the Fund made lending commitments to Mexico before private creditors did the same.[185] This comment indicated a clear concern about the moral hazard implications of such a large Fund loan: if the Fund provided an immediate bailout, the banks might become less willing to provide their own contributions to debt reduction, and the Mexican government would have less incentive to implement the necessary economic reforms. Cassell also worried that further "exceptional" lending to Mexico would place the Fund at significant risk of becoming too heavily exposed to a single country: "Granting up to 40 percent of quota for interest support might well be justified by the exceptional circumstances of Mexico's case, but Directors would need to consider it carefully, especially as outstanding lending to Mexico would amount to almost one-fifth of the Fund's total lending, a massive commitment to any one country."[186]

[185] Minutes of EBM/89/65, 12. [186] Ibid., 11.

Finally, Cassell expressed concern about having the IMF lending "into a financing gap" – that is, lending in the absence of clear amounts of new financing to be provided either by Mexico itself or by its commercial bank creditors.[187] Although he was not opposed, in principle, to the 40 percent augmentation, Cassell was "not in favor of precommitting Fund resources, just as Mexico was not prepared to do the same with its own resources."[188] In sum, the British government was worried that an immediate and large-scale IMF loan would become a bailout, enabling Mexico and its private international creditors to escape without making their own contributions to the resolution of the crisis. For these reasons, Cassell and the UK government favored approval of the extended arrangement but could "not support [Filardo's] outright approval of a 40 percent augmentation at present."[189] Instead, the British favored the staff position of waiting until Mexico had finalized an agreement with the banks before approving the increase in the size of the loan under the EFF.

In contrast to West Germany's measured support and the United Kingdom's strong opposition, the United States enthusiastically endorsed Mexico's demands, just as it had in 1983 and 1986. Charles Warner (alternate executive director – United States) offered his "definitive approval today of the 40 percent additional access sought by the Mexican authorities to facilitate a successful financing package with the commercial banks."[190] Whereas the British and West Germans worried about the moral hazard risk of an immediate augmentation, Warner did not share their concerns about extending Fund resources prior to securing new financing commitments from the banks. Indeed, his endorsement of the proposed extended arrangement, as well as the upfront disbursement of the 40 percent augmentation, was unqualified:

> We are persuaded that the case has been made in the staff report and in Ms. Filardo's opening statement for a first disbursement of the extended

187 Ibid., 12. 188 Ibid., 13.

189 Ibid., 13. Cassell's position was not surprising, as the United Kingdom had argued firmly in favor of a more limited augmentation rule (25 percent rather than 40 percent) during the May 19–23 debates over the Brady principles. In addition, Britain and West Germany had proposed that the augmentation funds be separated from the main portion of future IMF loans and placed in escrow accounts at the BIS in Basel. See minutes of EBM/89/58 (May 19, 1989), 8–12.

190 Minutes of EBM/89/64, 36.

arrangement *in the absence of full financing assurances* ... The criteria which need to be met, and in my opinion have been met, are, that approval is essential for program implementation, that negotiations with the banks have begun, and a financing package consistent with external viability can be expected within a reasonable period of time.[191]

Given Mexico's substantial private external debt and its past good behavior as a Fund borrower, Warner argued, the country was "eminently eligible for application of our strengthened debt strategy."[192] As a result, he offered the US government's "definitive approval" of the 40 percent augmentation, as well as support for its immediate disbursement.[193]

Along with Warner, Dominique Marcel (alternate executive director – France) strongly supported the proposal for an immediate 40 percent augmentation and emphasized the importance of sending a "clear signal to the international financial community" that the IMF was serious about implementing the Brady Plan.[194] Marcel explicitly noted the Fund's goal "in catalyzing the needed [private] financial flows" to ensure Mexico's future growth and debt sustainability.[195] Although he too remained concerned about the likelihood of new private lending, Marcel emphasized the French government's strong support for the program, including the 40 percent augmentation: "Considerable uncertainties remain over the prospects for Mexico's negotiations with the banks at a time when the financing gap is substantial. My authorities, however, are of the view that Mexico merits prompt Fund support."[196] In fact, Marcel argued that the upfront augmentation of the proposed IMF loan was necessary to reassure private creditors of the Fund's commitment to Mexico, lest they changed their mind and refused to provide new financing:

In the current relatively delicate context of the negotiations, it is critical to make it perfectly clear that the Fund fully supports Mexico in its efforts to adjust and to reduce its debt burden. The Board has to convey such support unambiguously to the international financial community. This is also important in making the Fund's strategy credible.[197]

Summing up, Marcel stated that France would support the 40 percent augmentation, so long as the additional credit was disbursed after the completion of an interim program review.

[191] Ibid. (emphasis in original). [192] Ibid. [193] Ibid. [194] Ibid., 44.
[195] Ibid., 42. [196] Ibid., 43. [197] Ibid., 44.

Following Warner and Marcel, Koji Yamazaki (Japan) also offered his "welcome and support" for Mexico's request, citing the Mexican government's "significant efforts" since 1982, and the need to ensure that Mexico's ongoing debt problems did not "undo the past successes achieved by the [Mexican] authorities in collaboration with the international financial community."[198] Yamazaki supported the proposed 40 percent augmentation of the IMF loan, and he reiterated Japan's willingness – first stated during the May 19 board discussion of the Brady Plan – to provide "parallel" bilateral financing once the IMF program and the private debt reduction plan had been finalized.[199]

These divisions illustrate clearly how disagreements between the G-5 governments over the financial importance of a borrowing country affect Fund decision-making. In this case, the G-5 countries with stronger domestic financial ties to Mexico supported the augmentation, while those with less at stake favored postponing any decision on the larger package until a Brady deal had been struck with private creditors. Cassell's skepticism marked a notable departure for the British, who had strongly supported each of the two previous IMF loans to Mexico. As UK banks had steadily reduced their Mexican exposure (from \$6.9 billion in 1982 to \$5.8 billion in 1989), however, the British had become less enthusiastic about another Mexican bailout and more concerned about the moral hazard costs of another oversized IMF loan. The British government's view of the liquidity/moral hazard trade-off therefore shifted notably in line with changes in its domestic financial interest in Mexico. In contrast, the Japanese government offered notably stronger support for Mexico in 1989, including its willingness to provide bilateral supplementary financing in conjunction with the IMF loan. For Japan, whose bank exposure to Mexico had risen significantly since the early 1980s (from \$2.1 billion in 1982 to \$13.3 billion in 1988), continued IMF support of Mexico had important implications for both international and domestic financial stability. West Germany and France also supported the loan and the augmentation proposal, but their support was more measured, as was their domestic financial exposure to Mexico.

Thus, preference heterogeneity among the G-5 countries over the 1989 Mexican loan correlated strongly with variation in domestic financial exposure to Mexico. In spite of these divisions between the Fund's largest shareholders, however, a solid majority of the overall

[198] Ibid., 48. [199] Ibid., 50–1.

votes in the executive board favored immediate approval of the 40 percent augmentation.[200] As Camdessus noted in his concluding statement, "A majority of the Directors supported the suggestion of Ms. Filardo to amend the proposed decision to allow for an outright and full 40 percent augmentation of the extended arrangement."[201] Although the augmentation proposal ultimately succeeded, G-5 preference heterogeneity did influence the meeting's outcome. Rather than force a decision over the British government's strong objections, Camdessus suggested a compromise: the board would approve the staff's original proposal without the immediate 40 percent augmentation but would also agree by consensus to support the "eventual augmentation of the extended arrangement by up to 40 percent" pending an agreement between Mexico and the banks and a subsequent review by the IMF staff.[202] Ultimately, Camdessus's proposal carried the day:

> The Fund notes the intention of the authorities to request augmentation of the amount of the extended arrangement ... by an amount up to the equivalent of forty (40) percent of Mexico's quota of SDR 1,165.5 million. *The Fund will be prepared to consider an augmentation of the amount of the extended arrangement in the event that the arrangements for the financing of Mexico's program provide for appropriate debt service reduction* and upon determination by the Fund that such arrangements are consistent with the objectives of the program, and with the guidelines on Fund involvement in the debt strategy, adopted May 23, 1989.[203]

This outcome is notable for two reasons. First, it clearly illustrates the effects of preference heterogeneity among the IMF's de facto political principals – the G-5 governments – on Fund lending decisions. Specifically, the compromise solution approved here demonstrated an attempt to reconcile the divergent preferences of the United States, Japan and France, on the one hand, and West Germany and the United Kingdom, on the other, over the timing and requirements for the 40 percent augmentation of Mexico's new Fund program. Although

[200] Boughton (2001, 514) estimates that the British-led opposition contingent represented only 37 percent of the votes, whereas the American-led bloc in favor of the augmentation held a clear majority of board votes.
[201] Minutes of EBM/89/65, 31.
[202] Ibid., 34. [203] Ibid., 34 (emphasis added).

other executive directors and countries made their preferences known within the board, the crux of the debate – as well as the eventual board decision – centered on the differences between the Fund's largest shareholders.

Second, the postponement of the final decision on the 40 percent augmentation also illustrates the constraints on US power within the IMF. Contrary to both popular perception and many scholarly arguments, the United States did not unilaterally impose its will upon the board in this case, nor does the documentary evidence even suggest that it sought to do so. While the Fund's decision largely reflected American preferences, the outcome ultimately reflected the composite preferences of the G-5 countries, rather than simply the will of the United States alone. Thus, the 1989 Mexican loan illustrates the extent to which Fund policymaking is a collective enterprise in which a small group of powerful states exercises disproportionate influence, but no single country enjoys complete control of the process. In short, this episode casts further doubt on the commonly held view that the IMF is simply the servant of the United States government.

Private creditors' response: the Brady deal

In the days following the IMF's approval of the Mexican extended arrangement, other official international creditors added their contributions to the package. The Paris Club agreed on May 30, 1989, to grant Mexico \$2.5 billion in debt relief from 1989 to 1992, and the World Bank approved three loans totaling \$1.5 billion on June 13.[204] In November the Japanese Export-Import Bank provided \$1 billion in "parallel financing," as promised by Yamazaki during the May 26 board meeting.[205] With the IMF program and this additional official financing in place, Mexico and the banks pressed forward with the negotiations for debt reduction. On July 23 the parties reached an agreement, the first completed in accordance with the new Brady Plan. Under the terms of the deal, the banks were presented with a menu of debt reduction options, including loan/bond swaps and new money, each representing an approximately 55 percent discount ("haircut")

[204] Boughton (2001, 514).

[205] See "Past commitments of JEXIM to parallel financing with the IMF" (www.jbic.go.jp/english/base/release/exim/1997-e/A15/nr97–11.php).

on Mexico's existing bank debt. The first option allowed the banks to swap outstanding loan claims for thirty-year bonds at 65 percent of the original face value, at an interest rate spread of 13/16 over LIBOR. Alternatively, banks could exchange loans for bonds at par value with a reduced fixed interest rate of 6.25 percent. Finally, creditors not interested in bank/bond swaps could opt for the traditional concerted lending approach; under this option, the banks would provide new money equal to 7 percent of outstanding claims in 1989, and 6 percent in each of the subsequent three years at LIBOR plus 13/16.[206] In the event, nearly all Mexico's commercial bank creditors opted for the swap: 49 percent exchanged $22 billion in loans for the lower interest, fixed-rate bonds of the same face value, while 41 percent exchanged $20 billion for the floating rate bonds at a 35 percent discount.[207]

The 1989 extended arrangement and the Brady deal marked the effective end of Mexico's 1980s debt crisis. With the Brady deal finalized, concerns about Mexico's access to private capital were alleviated, and the IMF executive board subsequently approved the 40 percent augmentation of the EFF package in January 1990, which granted the Mexican authorities access to an additional SDR 466.2 million.[208] Over the course of the extended arrangement program, Mexico stabilized its fiscal situation, brought inflation down to single-digit rates, and once again became a darling of international financial markets. The economy grew rapidly: GDP nearly doubled between 1989 and 1994, rising from $223 billion to $421 billion, with an average growth rate of 3.4 percent. In 1993 the Mexican government managed to overturn a decade of persistent budget deficits and run a small surplus (equivalent to 1.4 percent of GDP). Although Mexico still had outstanding IMF loans in excess of three times its quota and owed private creditors nearly $70 billion in accumulated debts, the country was widely considered to have successfully regained its good standing in global financial markets.

The 1995 stand-by arrangement

In spite of this successful conclusion to the 1980s debt crisis, Mexico's stabilization and success proved to be relatively short-lived. In 1994

[206] "Mexico – commercial bank financing package," EBM/89/171 (August 23, 1989).

[207] Nicoll, *Financial Times*, July 30, 1992.

[208] Boughton (2001, 515).

the country once again found itself in severe financial crisis and in need of IMF financing. As in the 1980s, both the G-5 countries and the IMF staff played central roles in shaping the Fund's policy responses to the Mexican crisis. As the events of 1994–5 illustrate, however, the interests and expectations of these actors had changed significantly as a result of shifts in the composition of Mexico's private external debt. In particular, the shift from bank lending to bond financing altered the IMF staff's expectations about private creditors' willingness to provide new financing to Mexico in the aftermath of the 1995 Fund program. At the same time, changes in the relative bank exposure of the G-5 countries created even greater friction between the United States and its European G-5 counterparts over the amount of IMF and bilateral assistance to Mexico. As a result, the Fund's treatment of Mexico in 1994–5 differed significantly from its handling of the country's financial difficulties in 1983–9.

Mexico's debt composition, 1993–4

Despite the 1989 Brady deal and the subsequent economic recovery, Mexico's external debt burden continued to rise during the early 1990s. To some extent, Mexico proved to be a victim of its (and the IMF's) success: as fears of a Mexican default waned and the country met its payments on its outstanding debt, private international creditors eagerly returned to Mexico – primarily through purchases of new sovereign bonds issued by the Mexican government. By 1994 Mexico owed $140 billion in external debt, and its external debt to GDP ratio had risen slightly, to 45.9 percent. A key shift had transformed the composition of Mexico's private external debt by 1994, however, as bonds had almost entirely replaced bank loans as the government's primary long-term source of external financing. In 1989 Mexico still owed 94.4 percent of its long-term private external debt to commercial banks; by 1994 it owed 83.5 percent to bondholders rather than bank lenders.

This shift from bank lending to bond financing marked a clear departure from Mexico's international borrowing in the 1980s, and several key factors contributed to this change in the country's pattern of integration into global financial markets. Without a doubt, the Brady Plan played a major role, as it enabled Mexico's bank creditors to swap their outstanding bank loans *en masse* for sovereign bonds in

1989/90. In addition to converting their outstanding claims on Mexico, however, the major G-5 international banks also reduced their new lending to all LDCs in the early 1990s. For example, BankAmerica sold or swapped $1.7 billion in sovereign bank loans and pulled out of seven developing countries entirely in 1989/90, with a long-term goal of reducing its LDC exposure from $6.9 billion to $3.2 billion.[209] Having endured defaults, pressure from the IMF to participate in concerted lending, and multiple types of debt restructuring throughout the 1980s, the banks were understandably reluctant to engage in new medium-term syndicated lending. Finally, domestic policy changes by the Mexican government also contributed to the shift from bank lending to bond financing. In particular, the government removed restrictions on foreign creditors' ability to hold government bonds in 1990, a change that led directly to an increase in foreign creditors' share of cetes holdings (twenty-eight-day government bonds), from 23 percent in 1991 to 66 percent at the end of 1993.[210]

In spite of the rising prominence of bond financing, however, G-5 commercial banks remained an important source of external financing for Mexico throughout the early 1990s. At the end of 1993 they held $41.6 billion in claims on Mexico, although this was a decline from $46.5 billion in 1989 (and a peak of $51.6 billion in 1986). The distribution of this bank lending had changed significantly between 1989 and 1994, however, with United States banks once again holding nearly one-half (47 percent, $23.0 billion) of G-5 commercial bank claims (up from 36 percent in 1989). The primary factor driving this change in G-5 bank exposure heterogeneity was the sharp drop in Japanese bank exposure, from $13.3 billion in 1989 to $4.1 billion in 1994. British bank exposure continued to decline, from $5.8 billion in 1989 to $4.5 billion in 1994, while French and German exposure increased only slightly, to $5.5 billion and $4.2 billion, respectively. As discussed further below, this growing disparity in G-5 exposure to Mexico would have significant implications for the positions assumed by G-5 governments

209 Steven Mufson, "Banks retreat from Third World: one of the biggest lenders, BankAmerica, pulls out of seven nations," *Washington Post*, September 27, 1990.

210 Banco de México (1996). Cetes, or Certificados de Tesorería de Federacíon a 28 días, are one-month, peso-denominated Treasury bills issued by the Mexican government.

within the IMF executive board over the proposed Mexican loan in February 1995.

Moreover, while bondholders became increasingly important sources of external financing for Mexico in the early 1990s, their composition also changed in both type and maturity. In 1991 the majority of Mexico's outstanding sovereign bonds were one-month, peso-denominated bonds (cetes) held domestically. By 1994, with creditors concerned about rising inflation and a potential devaluation of the peso, the Mexican government found it increasingly expensive to issue peso-denominated debt. In order to continue attracting foreign capital, it therefore began rolling over its stock of cetes into short-term, dollar-indexed bonds (tesobonos). This shift accelerated throughout 1994: in January 95 percent of Mexico's bonds were peso-denominated bonds; by December, when the crisis hit, tesobonos comprised 85 percent of Mexico's outstanding international bond debt.[211]

The 1994 crisis

These significant changes in Mexico's private debt composition played a critical role in determining the nature of its financial crisis in 1994. In the 1980s Mexico's international debt problems had resulted from long-term macroeconomic imbalances that created both short- and long-term debt problems.[212] Quite simply, Mexico went bankrupt in 1982, due to a combination of poor national economic policies (e.g. persistent budget deficits, excessive international borrowing) and international shocks (e.g. a global recession triggered by sharp increases in United States interest rates).[213] By contrast, Mexico's macroeconomic fundamentals were fairly strong in the 1990s. Although its external debt to GDP ratio had risen to 45.9 percent from roughly 40 percent in the 1980s, Mexico's debt service level had fallen significantly as a result of the MYRAs and the Brady Plan. Whereas in 1982 Mexico's ratio of debt service to exports equaled 51 percent, by 1994 it had fallen to 25.8 percent. Moreover, Mexico's long-term debt levels were moderate by global standards: with a ratio of public debt to GDP of

211 General Accounting Office [GAO] (1996).

212 Sachs, Tornell, and Velasco (1996).

213 Chang (1999); Sachs, Tornell, and Velasco (1996); Lustig (1992); Kraft (1984).

50.7 percent, Mexico's debt sustainability position exceeded that of many OECD countries, which had an average public debt/GDP ratio of 70.6 percent.[214]

Instead, Mexico's financial difficulties in 1994 were largely the result of a series of unexpected shocks that led international investors to flee Mexico despite its relatively stable macroeconomic position. In March 1994 the presidential candidate of Mexico's ruling party (the Institutional Revolutionary Party – PRI), Luis Donaldo Colosio, was assassinated. In the aftermath the peso depreciated by 10 percent against the dollar and the Banco de México raised interest rates on cetes to 7 percent in order to stem capital flight.[215] Investors' demand for cetes continued to lag, however, and the Banco de México continued to raise interest rates, which reached 18 percent in mid-April.[216] Mexico faced further pressure to raise interest rates throughout the remainder of 1994, as the US Federal Reserve raised its own rates six times between January and November, from 3 percent to 5.45 percent.[217] As capital flight continued into the spring and summer, the Mexican government faced a choice between several equally unattractive options. It could continue raising interest rates on cetes to meet its short-term financing needs, but at the expense of growth and the solvency of its domestic banking system. Alternatively, the government could slash spending to reduce demand, decrease imports, and alleviate the downward pressure on the peso. Finally, the government could devalue the peso in an attempt to reverse its balance of payments problems.[218]

Ultimately, the Mexican government postponed this choice by converting its stock of short-term bonds from peso-denominated cetes into dollar-indexed tesobonos. This shift allowed the Mexican authorities to access external financing at lower interest rates while alleviating international creditors' concerns about a potential devaluation.[219] In the short term, this new debt strategy worked effectively. Foreign investors eagerly purchased tesobonos – the stock of outstanding bonds rose from $3.1 billion in March 1994 to $29.2 billion

[214] Sachs, Tornell, and Velasco (1996, 23). [215] Ibid., 16.

[216] GAO 1996, 10. [217] Ibid., 56. [218] Ibid., 10.

[219] Because tesobonos were indexed to the dollar, foreign investors incurred no currency risk and were willing to buy them at lower yields than cetes. Yields on tesobonos were, on average, six to eight percentage points lower than those on cetes in 1993–4. See ibid.

in December – and the Banco de México's reserves stabilized at $17 billion from May through August.[220] By mid-November, however, it became clear that an increasing dependence on tesobonos had created a severe short-term financing problem for Mexico, as the country was now dependent on the willingness of these short-term bondholders to continually roll over their claims and reinvest in Mexican debt on a monthly basis. Unfortunately, this willingness did not last long, as international investors began selling off tesobonos following another assassination, of the PRI Secretary General, Francisco Ruiz Massieu, in September, and a three-quarter basis point hike in US interest rates in November. On December 9, when the newly installed Mexican president, Ernesto Zedillo, announced that Mexico's expected current account deficit in 1995 would be higher than previously anticipated, the tesobono sell-off intensified and Mexico's foreign exchange reserves dwindled to $10 billion.[221] With almost $30 billion in additional tesobonos coming due in the first quarter of 1995, the country once again faced the prospect of defaulting on its international debt.

The US bilateral package

Prior to requesting IMF financing, Mexico sought bilateral assistance from the major creditor countries. As Mexico's largest trading partner and the G-5 country with the most at stake financially in Mexico, the United States took the lead in providing this financial support. For the United States, whose commercial banks held $23 billion in Mexican debt, avoiding a Mexican default was a key domestic interest. On January 5 1995, under the auspices of the North American Framework Agreement (NAFA) – a previously existing swap arrangement between the US, Canadian, and Mexican central banks the United States announced plans to provide Mexico with an additional $3 billion in credit, while the Canadian government increased its swap line by $1.1 billion.[222] Acting through the BIS, other G-10 central banks pledged an additional $5 billion in credit. Although they eventually assented to the arrangement, the major European central

[220] Ibid., 11. [221] Ibid., 10.

[222] Lustig (1996, 25). The Federal Reserve and the US Treasury had jointly established the existing swap line in March 1994, following the Colosio assassination. Under the terms of this arrangement, the Banco de México could draw up to $6 billion. See ibid., 18–19.

banks were initially opposed to the BIS assistance, which they hoped would serve only as a "bridge" to a full IMF lending arrangement.[223]

On January 6, following the announcement of the short-term bilateral/BIS package, the Mexican government formally requested IMF assistance. Once negotiations over the IMF program had begun, however, it quickly became clear that neither the announcement of a Fund program nor the initial bilateral package had convinced market actors to cease their flight from Mexican markets. Accordingly, on January 12, the US administration of President Bill Clinton announced plans to supplement the IMF and BIS loans to Mexico with $40 billion in loan guarantees, which would allow the Mexican government to borrow the additional private credit necessary to continue servicing its tesobono debt. The United States also asked the BIS central banks to increase their "bridge" package to $10 billion, but the German Bundesbank, the Bank of England, and De Nederlandsche Bank (the Dutch central bank) strongly opposed the larger commitment.[224]

Two key factors contributed to the Europeans' skepticism about providing IMF and bilateral financing to Mexico. First, they had little domestic interest in bailing out Mexico, since their own banking systems had relatively few ties to the country: the total bank exposure of the three European G-5 countries (the United Kingdom, Germany, and France) in 1994 was only $14.2 billion, compared to $23 billion for the United States. Second, European officials questioned whether Mexico's difficulties really constituted a systemic financial crisis warranting IMF/BIS support. Since the vast majority of Mexico's private international creditors were bondholders rather than banks, there seemed to be little risk that a Mexican default would have destabilizing effects on financial stability in the developed countries, even if individual investors incurred substantial losses. Moreover, with few long-term ties to Mexico, tesobono bondholders were very likely to utilize IMF/BIS lending as an opportunity to "bail out" of Mexico entirely. Thus, European officials were especially concerned with the moral hazard costs of large-scale financing to Mexico. UK officials, in particular, felt strongly that Mexico was not a systemic problem

[223] George Graham, Peter Norman, Stephen Fiedler, and Ted Baracks, "Mexican rescue: bitter legacy of the battle to bail out Mexico," *Financial Times*, February 16, 1995.

[224] Ibid.

for the global financial system and that the IMF, BIS, and G-10 central banks were "being roped into bailing out United States pension and mutual funds which had invested imprudently in high-yielding Mexican paper."[225]

For the US government, however, ensuring Mexico's financial stability remained a key domestic economic and political objective. Over the next two weeks, therefore, the Clinton administration worked to secure the support of Congress, whose assent was required before the $40 billion in loan guarantees could be finalized. On January 26 the IMF announced plans to conclude a $7.8 billion lending arrangement with Mexico. As congressional opposition to the United States loan guarantees solidified, however, Mexico's private creditors continued to bail out of the country. Without the American loan guarantees, even the very large IMF loan would not spare Mexico from defaulting on its short-term debt. With a Mexican default imminent, the Clinton administration switched courses and pursued what it called "plan B," a new rescue package funded with $20 billion from the Treasury Department's Exchange Stabilization Fund, which President Clinton could utilize without congressional approval.[226]

US officials also sought increased IMF and bilateral support for Mexico in conjunction with "plan B," despite the Europeans' lack of enthusiasm. On January 30 Clinton administration officials informed Camdessus and Stanley Fischer, the IMF's first deputy managing director, of the United States' new plans and indicated their hope that the IMF would also increase its support for Mexico.[227] On January 31, shortly before publicly announcing the ESF loan, administration officials also spoke with Andrew Crockett, general manager of the BIS, and requested his assistance in securing additional funds from the BIS's member banks; Crockett advised the United States that Clinton could announce "that discussions were under way" for a doubling of the previously committed $5 billion, but he made it clear that he first had to consult with the other BIS members' central bank officials before any concrete decision could be reached.[228]

[225] Ibid.

[226] Ibid. On the ESF, see Henning (1999) and GAO (1996). For detailed analyses of the United States decision to switch to "plan B," see Graham *et al.*, *Financial Times*, February 16, 1995, and Rubin and Weisberg (2003).

[227] Graham *et al.*, *Financial Times*, February 16, 1995.

[228] Ibid.

Fearing that the Europeans' opposition to large-scale IMF/BIS lending would slow the process down, US Treasury officials subsequently engaged in direct and intensive discussions with IMF officials – including Camdessus and Fischer – over the terms of the joint IMF/ESF rescue package. At 7:00 a.m. on January 31 Camdessus informed Robert Rubin, the US Treasury secretary, and his deputy, Lawrence Summers, that the IMF had decided to increase the size of its forthcoming loan to Mexico from $7.76 billion to $17.8 billion, three and a half times more than it had lent to any single country in its history.[229] Camdessus did not inform the executive board of the Fund staff's change in plans until 9:00 a.m., however, when he also informed the directors that the new Mexican program would be discussed and voted upon at the next day's board meeting.[230]

Not surprisingly, several European governments with seats on the executive board were extremely upset at not having been fully consulted by Camdessus and the US Treasury. They were further angered later in the day, when President Clinton announced the new IMF/ESF package at a White House speech to the National Governors' Association, even though the executive board had not yet met to discuss the proposed IMF program. As outlined by Clinton, the proposed IMF package totaled SDR 12.07 billion (6.88 times quota, $17.8 billion). In both absolute and relative terms, this was the single largest Fund loan ever – fully three and a half times larger in size (in amount per quota terms) than any previous IMF lending arrangement.[231] Over and above the IMF's own financing, the proposed package included an additional $25 billion in bilateral and multilateral commitments. The United States would provide $20 billion, including $6 billion in swap lines from the Federal Reserve. The Canadian government would contribute $1 billion, while other BIS central banks would add a further $10 billion.[232] As outlined by Clinton, the package also included $3 billion in commitments from an American–British–Japanese consortium of commercial banks, although the money ultimately did not materialize.[233]

[229] Ibid. [230] Ibid.

[231] "Mexico – first review under the stand-by arrangement," EBS/95/47 (March 22, 1995).

[232] See GAO (1996, 109–10).

[233] Graham *et al.*, *Financial Times*, February 16, 1995.

For many European financial officials, this was the first they had heard of "plan B" and the enhanced BIS commitments.[234] Since the board had not yet voted on the new Fund program, nor had the BIS financing been formally agreed upon, European governments felt that the United States had overstepped its bounds. As one senior European official stated: "President Clinton goes to the press and says the IMF will do this and that. It was just not acceptable. We are not banana republics."[235] Clearly, the United States' G-5 counterparts were dissatisfied, not only with the content of the IMF package but also with the way that United States officials had sidestepped standard IMF and BIS procedures to pursue its own domestic financial interests.

The executive board meeting, February 1, 1995

The board meeting of February 1, 1995, brought to the fore the tensions between the G-5 governments. It was only earlier that morning that the proposed program had been finalized and circulated by the Fund staff, leaving the executive directors little, if any, time to analyze its contents.[236] The package consisted of an eighteen-month stand-by arrangement of SDR 12.07 billion, with seven performance criteria. As in the previous cases of lending to Mexico the 1980s, these conditions included targets for government spending, targets for domestic credit and reserves for the Banco de México, and private external debt ceilings for the Mexican government.[237]

Given the unusual circumstances and timing, Camdessus opened the meeting with a background statement of explanation. He noted the systemic importance of dealing quickly with the Mexican crisis, and he emphasized the "potential for serious contagion effects" if the Fund did not address the crisis rapidly and decisively.[238] Camdessus announced the Clinton administration's decision to "mobilize $20 billion [from the ESF] immediately in support of the Mexican program."[239] He also

[234] Ibid. [235] Ibid.

[236] See EBS/95/14 (January 26, 1995) for the initial draft and EBS/95/14, Suppl. 1 (January 30, 1995) and Suppl. 2 (February 1, 1995), for the updated and final versions.

[237] EBS/95/14 and EBS/95/47, 19.

[238] Minutes of EBM/95/11 (10:00 a.m., February 1, 1995), 42.

[239] Ibid.

noted, "I have also been informed by Mr Crockett, General Manager of the Bank for International Settlements (BIS), and by Mr Tietmayer, Chairman of the G-10, that, in the framework of the BIS, a group of G-10 central banks intends to increase their support to Mexico from $5 billion to $10 billion."[240] With these resources secured, Camdessus urged that the board approve the SDR 12.07 billion IMF loan, with SDR 5.26 billion to be disbursed immediately.[241] In addition, Camdessus noted that the proposed IMF program also included "an augmentation, on contingency basis, by July 1, 1995, equal to SDR 6.81 billion less contributions from a group of central banks willing to contribute to Mexico's exchange stabilization fund."[242] The Fund staff was proposing this augmentation, he stated, "in order to assure that there will be no shortfall in the resources available to Mexico."[243] The board would make the final decision about the amount, timing, and terms of this augmentation, Camdessus concluded, either during the June review of the proposed stand-by arrangement or "in the context ... of an extended arrangement [i.e. a new Fund program]."[244]

Despite this substantial front-loading and augmentation of the loan, Camdessus expressed his firm belief that moral hazard was not a serious concern, given that the standard review process would remain in place and that Mexico's compliance with the program's conditionality was necessary in order to receive the ongoing financing from the BIS central banks: "I have concluded that this will not weaken either the conditionality of the program agreed with the Mexican authorities or the incentive for full compliance with that conditionality."[245] Camdessus also emphasized that Mexico's access to the BIS financing would be linked to the April review of the proposed IMF program, and recommended that the board grant him direct control over disbursement of these supplementary funds.[246]

Javier Guzmán-Calafell, the Mexican executive director, followed Camdessus's introduction with the customary presentation of the proposed program. He emphasized that "the circumstances under which this [IMF] support has been negotiated are extraordinary, and have indeed found a fast, professional, and constructive response on the part of both management and the staff."[247] Acknowledging that the board had not been given the usual amount of time to consider the

[240] Ibid. [241] Ibid. [242] Ibid. [243] Ibid., 43. [244] Ibid.
[245] Ibid., 42. [246] Ibid., 43. [247] Ibid., 44.

proposed stand-by arrangement, Guzmán-Calafell thanked the executive directors "for agreeing to take a decision on the issue under such a severe time constraint."[248] He then quickly zeroed in on the central problem facing Mexico: the "sharp curtailment in the flow of foreign capital into Mexico" from a net inflow of $30.9 billion in 1993 to "only $14.1 billion in the first 11 months of 1994."[249] Despite a number of measures, including depletion of its foreign exchange reserves, allowing the peso to depreciate, and issuing an ever larger amount of short-term bond debt (tesobonos), the Mexican government had been unable to stem the capital outflows and now faced severe "short-run liquidity problems resulting mainly from maturing Tesobonos."[250]

In this context, Guzmán-Calafell continued, the Mexican government sought IMF financing in support of "the adoption of painful adjustment measures" aimed at resolving the crisis. These included a reduction in the current account deficit, tighter monetary policy, and "a commitment to wage and price moderation."[251] In conjunction with these policy adjustments, he noted, Mexico had also secured the financial assistance package outlined by Camdessus, which included commitments from the United States ($20 billion), Canada ($1.5 billion), the BIS central banks ($10 billion), and Mexico's commercial bank creditors ($3 billion).[252]

Finally, Guzmán-Calafell informed the board that Mexico was "working with leading investment banks to offer investors market-oriented and voluntary mechanisms to swap Tesobonos for [longer-term] securities denominated and payable in US dollars."[253] This debt swap, if successful, would further alleviate Mexico's liquidity problems and ensure a future stream of private capital inflows. Taken together, these measures and the proposed IMF program, he believed, contained "an adequate mix of adjustment and financing, which will allow the restoration of orderly conditions in the financial and foreign exchange markets."[254] Guzmán-Calafell ended by thanking, once again, the Fund staff, the board, and those countries that had made bilateral financing commitments to Mexico for their prompt action in response to Mexico's "exceptional circumstances."[255]

In the ensuing board discussion, sharp cleavages quickly emerged among the G-5 countries over both the proposed program and the

[248] Ibid. [249] Ibid., 43. [250] Ibid., 49. [251] Ibid. [252] Ibid., 51.
[253] Ibid., 52. [254] Ibid. [255] Ibid., 53.

hastiness of the decision-making process. Speaking first, Karin Lissakers (United States) made it clear that the United States government firmly supported the proposed loan. Her comments clearly reflected the Clinton administration's strong domestic and international interests in providing substantial and rapid aid to Mexico: "I do believe we have acted responsibly and with dispatch to meet not only an important neighbor and partner's needs, but indeed the needs of the international financial community."[256] While Lissakers acknowledged that the "unprecedented" and "ad hoc" nature of the current loan decision "makes all of us uneasy," she firmly believed that the proposed program was in accordance with the IMF's "principles" and its shareholders' "obligations of the Articles of Agreement."[257]

The US government's firm support for Mexico and the proposed IMF program, Lissakers argued, arose out of its belief that the current crisis was unprecedented:

> I think we have to understand what we are facing here. I think it is not overdramatizing the situation to say that we may in fact be facing, grappling now with the first financial crisis of the 21st century. That is why it is so difficult, because it is not only quantitatively but qualitatively different from anything this institution has tried to address before. The size of the crisis is indeed unprecedented and the potential for spillover – an extremely quick spillover – enormous.[258]

The reason for this, Lissakers continued, was the fundamental shift in the composition of international capital flows to developing countries, from commercial bank lending to bond financing. This structural change in patterns of financial globalization, she argued, rendered the long-standing IMF strategy – a combination of relatively limited Fund financing and 1980s-style concerted lending by commercial bank creditors – obsolete:

> The growing reliance on securitized international private financial flows [i.e. bond debt] means that the number of creditors has grown enormously. The days when Managing Director de Larosière and Federal Reserve Chairman Volcker could call together in one room six central bankers and 12 commercial bankers to solve a large problem are over ... We [now] have

[256] Ibid. [257] Ibid. [258] Ibid.

to speak to an unidentifiable collection of thousands, if not millions of investors – investors who can move with the flick of a button and transfer amounts of money that swamp this institution and potentially could swamp the resources of individual governments that stand behind this institution [i.e. the United States].[259]

In response to these changes in global financial markets, Lissakers stated, the Fund and board "will have to adapt the institution to the new realities of the financial markets, and we will have to do so quickly."[260]

Given its belief that the current crisis was unprecedented in severity and scale, the US government had committed, Lissakers reiterated, an unprecedented amount of its own resources ($20 billion) from the Exchange Stabilization Fund, and she urged "the rest of the international community ... to step up very quickly" with additional, matching resources.[261] Lissakers also recognized that Mexico would need to undertake substantial policy adjustment in order to resolve the crisis, including tighter monetary policy and a reduction in the current account deficit. She therefore expressed support both for the proposed early program review (to be conducted in March) and for the proposed performance criteria.[262] Nevertheless, in spite of the extremely large size of the proposed IMF loan, Lissakers also made it clear that the United States did not believe moral hazard to be a serious concern. Rather, she emphasized that Mexico's crisis was one of liquidity rather than solvency: "We should be clear about – not exaggerate – the underlying policy weaknesses. The fact is that we are not dealing with a country that has a runaway budget deficit. We are not dealing with a country that has an unmanageable current account deficit ... Mexico has a severe liquidity problem."[263] Consequently, she concluded, the United States did not see the need for overly stringent conditionality to match the unprecedented amount of IMF financing.

Several executive directors from the Western hemisphere shared the US government's firm enthusiasm for the proposed loan, including Alexandre Kafka (Brazil) and Ian Clark (Canada).[264] Kafka supported immediate disbursement of the full $7.8 billion that Camdessus had requested. Furthermore, he informed the board that

[259] Ibid., 53–4. [260] Ibid., 53. [261] Ibid., 54.
[262] Ibid., 55–6. [263] Ibid., 55. [264] Ibid., 58, 74.

his Latin American constituents had committed to "a joint $1 billion [bilateral financing] fund" as part of the BIS-coordinated aid package "as an act of extraordinary faith and cooperation with a friend and neighbor."[265] A number of other directors also expressed clear support, although they raised concerns about the Fund's liquidity, the dangers of committing too many resources to a single Fund borrower, and the moral hazard implications of such large-scale lending.[266] Echoing Lissakers' recognition of new realities in global financial markets, Shaalan noted the "increasingly dominant role" of private capital flows "in shaping economic and financial developments around the globe."[267] In this environment, he supported the "unprecedented scale" of IMF lending to Mexico.[268] Shaalan worried, however, that the Fund was ill-equipped to provide such large-scale loans in the future to all borrowers: "I am not too sanguine about our capacity to ... rise to the challenge in the case of Mexico, while upholding our sacrosanct principle of uniformity of treatment. What if another crisis erupts elsewhere? Do we have the resources to be financially involved to the extent proposed in the case before us?"[269] If such large-scale lending was now in order, Shaalan concluded, the IMF would require a new round of quota increases in order to ensure it had sufficient resources to deal with future financial crises.[270]

Although Shaalan and other non-G-5 executive directors generally supported the American position, the other major shareholders' views of the proposed loan ranged from cautious support to outright hostility. Hachiro Mesaki (Japan) stated that the Japanese government could "basically support the proposal" on the grounds that Mexico's stability was critical for the global financial system as a whole, and because Japan believed that Mexico's creditors would accelerate their capital flight in the absence of IMF support: "We cannot afford to let the market receive the wrong signal, that the

[265] Ibid., 59.
[266] Ibid. See, for example, the comments of Ming Zhang (China), Abdel Shaalan (Egypt), Giulio Lanciotti (Italy), and K. P. Geethakrishnan (India).
[267] Ibid., 57. [268] Ibid.
[269] Ibid. Kafka shared these concerns about equal treatment in the future and urged the development of more institutionalized rules and mechanisms "that would enable the Fund to confront similar situations in a more orderly manner" (59). Likewise, Lanciotti warned that the current decision would set an important precedent for future cases of a similar magnitude (68).
[270] Ibid. Zhang echoed Shaalan's views on quotas (65).

international community has forsaken Mexico."[271] His authorities had serious concerns about the moral hazard implications of the proposed package, however, Mesaki continued. In particular, he was afraid that the markets would view the unprecedented IMF loan as a bailout, which would undermine the Fund's ability to generate catalytic effects in the future: "I basically understand that a large-scale financing scheme ... is needed to address the current emergency. Nonetheless, the appropriateness of such unprecedented support may be debatable from the viewpoint of the catalytic role of the Fund."[272] If the Fund provided such large-scale financing in all future cases, he cautioned, private creditors would have little incentive to reverse their capital flight during financial crises.

In order to mitigate these moral hazard concerns, Mesaki urged several steps. First, he warned that "the board and management should make clear their view that this stand-by arrangement is an extremely exceptional measure, which takes fully into account the importance of this case for the international financial markets and for the global economy."[273] Second, Mesaki urged that the Board postpone its decision on the approval of Camdessus's proposed $10 billion in "contingent additional financing" until further economic developments could be observed.[274] Third, he emphasized that Mexico had to implement the program's conditionality "steadfastedly."[275] Fourth, Mesaki urged that the Fund shift its research focus toward crisis prevention, in order to limit the occurrence of future Mexican-style liquidity crises. Finally, he raised the question of whether Mexico's predicament – and that of potential future borrowers – had arisen out of an ill-advised adherence to fixed exchange rates and short-term debt instruments in the emerging world of highly volatile private international capital flows.[276]

In sum, the Japanese government supported the current proposal, but with some serious reservations about its future implications and about the size of the Fund's upfront commitment to Mexico. Michel Sirat (alternate executive director – France) adopted a similarly qualified position. While he acknowledged Lissakers' point about the importance of changes in the structure of global financial markets,

[271] Ibid., 61. [272] Ibid. [273] Ibid. [274] Ibid. [275] Ibid., 62.

[276] Ibid. This comment, in retrospect, was a prescient foreshadowing of the problems that would emerge in Thailand, South Korea, and elsewhere during the 1997–9 Asian financial crisis.

Sirat also reminded the board not to forget that Mexican policy errors had played a key role in the current crisis. In particular, the Mexican government's heavy reliance on short-term debt (tesobonos) and its failure to raise interest rates in the face of capital flight "was inappropriate and has in effect led to the development of a debt crisis."[277] This response to the markets' loss of confidence in Mexico was an ill-advised policy choice by the Mexican government, Sirat emphasized, and "one should not overrationalize ex post" by concluding that the magnitude of Mexico's crisis was inevitable.[278]

Nevertheless, Sirat continued, the crisis was now sufficiently severe – and the "systemic risk" sufficiently real – that the French government viewed the proposed program as appropriate: "At this stage of the crisis, the amounts [of IMF financing] involved, the difficulties in defining a market-based and voluntary restructuring package, and the past sharp reduction in Mexico's reserves certainly call for large external financing in conjunction with an appropriate economic program."[279] On the whole, Sirat found the proposed conditionality to be sufficient, although he viewed it as "a sort of best case scenario in the present circumstances."[280] Indeed, he expressed a good deal of skepticism about the program's success if projections about Mexico's trade flows, capital inflows, and inflation proved less optimistic than the staff were currently calculating.[281] In such a scenario, he noted, additional fiscal adjustment would be necessary in order to ensure a full recovery from the financial crisis.[282]

Ultimately, Sirat announced France's intent to support the proposed IMF program, although he did so with two clear reservations. First, he emphasized that "my authorities are uncomfortable with the idea of a 100 percent upfront financing of the initial $7.8 billion," and would prefer "keeping a second tranche, even rather small, linked to a review of the initial performance of the program."[283] This two-phase lending process, he argued, would "reinforce markets' confidence in the Fund conditionality" while also limiting moral hazard on the part of both the Mexican government and its private international creditors.[284] Second, Sirat also expressed France's preference for having the $10 billion in additional IMF financing kept as "a second line of defense" that would be approved by the board in July 1995, rather

[277] Ibid., 77. [278] Ibid. [279] Ibid., 78. [280] Ibid., 79. [281] Ibid.
[282] Ibid., 79–80. [283] Ibid., 80. [284] Ibid.

than as part of the current stand-by arrangement.[285] This approval, he suggested, should be subject to two conditions: the completion of the appropriate review of the current program, and assurance that the use of the $10 billion in additional IMF credit "could be made only after a prior use of the US Exchange Stabilization Fund."[286] In short, the French government wanted the US government, given its clear position as the most enthusiastic champion of the current proposal, to commit its own bilateral resources fully before the IMF contributed additional credit.

The qualified support for the proposed IMF program offered by the Japanese and French governments contrasted sharply with the clear displeasure of other European executive directors, including the three remaining G-5 directors. Stefan Schönberg (Germany) expressed particular unhappiness with the terms of the loan and the hastiness of the decision-making process. He began by stressing the German government's "dissatisfaction" with the bypassing of standard IMF procedures – specifically, the standard time lag between the circulation of the staff report and the board meeting – "which did not allow for the orderly assessment of the proposals."[287] "The staff paper," he noted, "had been distributed only earlier in the day, which had made it very difficult for him to consult properly with his authorities."[288] Schönberg derided this violation of IMF protocol as particularly "deplorable," given that the proposed loan "might involve a violation of long-standing, proven principles of the Fund, particularly with respect to the amount of lending [on a per quota basis], its phasing [the substantially front-loaded disbursement of the loan], and the risks to the Fund" in terms of the magnitude of its exposure to Mexico.[289]

In a sharp rebuke to the American position, Schönberg stated his preference for a short delay in the board discussion, in order to allow the EDs to "assess all aspects of the proposal," to "forge a consensus among the membership" on the terms of the IMF loan, and to allow the "high-level discussions [that] were currently in progress among European and other G-7 officials [over additional bilateral aid to Mexico]" to reach a conclusion.[290] Going further, Schönberg directly objected to Lissakers' argument that immediate approval of the IMF loan was required as a clear signal to Mexico's private international creditors. Indeed, he "remained unconvinced that a further delay of

[285] Ibid., 81. [286] Ibid. [287] Ibid., 65. [288] Ibid. [289] Ibid. [290] Ibid.

one or two days might derail the financial markets, given that it had taken the US authorities several weeks of public discussion to come to a conclusion about the best approach to dealing with the Mexican crisis."[291] The impact of an additional day or two of delay seemed unclear at best, he concluded.

In terms of the program itself, Schönberg found the conditionality to be "adequate," although he wondered why it "was being presented unchanged," in light of the recent changes in bilateral financing commitments (i.e. the move to "plan B" by the United States).[292] Given the loan's unprecedented size, however, Schönberg asserted that "there would need to be at least some tranching [phasing] of the $7.8 billion that was to be made available immediately."[293] Specifically, he proposed that the Fund's immediate commitment be limited to $3.9 billion, with the additional $3.9 billion coming from the US ESF, given the Americans' strong interest in immediate approval. Similarly, Schönberg noted that Germany also preferred "some tranching" of the "so-called contingency element," and he believed this disbursement should be contingent on a mid-1995 review of Mexico's progress under the proposed stand-by arrangement.[294] This questioning of both the relatively modest conditionality and upfront disbursement of the loan highlighted the German government's clear moral hazard concerns. Moreover, Schönberg's suggestion that the Fund's immediate commitment be halved (from $7.8 billion to $3.9 billion) and replaced by US bilateral funding reflected the Germans' strong belief that the Clinton administration should match its rhetoric about the urgency and severity of the Mexican crisis by pledging its own financing first, rather than advocating use of the IMF's scarce resources. Simply put, the German government was unconvinced of the need for a full-scale IMF bailout, and it had serious concerns about the moral hazard consequences of the proposed loan.

Huw Evans (United Kingdom) echoed the German government's concerns about the proposed program. He joined Schönberg and others in noting the "extraordinary request" of the Mexican government, and he pointed out that the current loan represented a "five or ten times higher" level of lending to a single country than the largest loan (68 percent of quota) extended in 1994.[295] Moreover, Evans noted that the current proposal of more than SDR 12 billion represented

[291] Ibid. [292] Ibid., 66. [293] Ibid. [294] Ibid. [295] Ibid., 72.

more than twice the IMF's entire lending commitments in the previous year and would now constitute nearly half the Fund's total credit outstanding (SDR 30 billion).[296] Thus, Evans worried that approval of the Mexican proposal would leave the IMF overly committed to a single borrower and without sufficient resources to respond to additional crises should the need arise.

Like Schönberg, Evans was also "very unhappy about the way the Mexican operation had been handled."[297] "It had been wrong," he stated, "to expect the Board to take such an important decision on the basis of papers circulated only one hour before the original starting time of the meeting."[298] He emphasized that the Fund "was a rules-based institution, which relied heavily on precedent," and he worried about the future implications of such a hasty decision in the current case.[299] Even more so than Schönberg, Evans also made clear his objection to the US government's view of the severity of Mexico's crisis and its systemic importance. While he acknowledged the strength of the proposed conditionality and Mexico's strong track record with the IMF, Evans was skeptical that Mexico warranted such exceptional support: "[I]t was difficult to argue that Mexico's program was five or ten times stronger than that of Turkey."[300] In a thinly veiled swipe at the American position, Evans stated that he "did not find convincing some of the more alarming views about the systemic threat posed by the Mexican crisis, though clearly there were some risks of contagion."[301] Rather, he "was worried for reasons of moral hazard that the international community would be seen to be underwriting all of Mexico's risks."[302] Furthermore, Evans argued, the sizeable front-loading of disbursement violated the Fund's long-standing view that the promise of future financing was essential to "keeping a program on track" and ensuring that a borrowing country implemented conditionality.[303] "That principle," he noted, "had been accepted for many years for all other countries and he did not think that Mexico should be an exception."[304] Indeed, Evans found it troubling that:

> within a period of 24 hours it had been proposed to make more financing available to Mexico, much of it upfront, but no additional adjustment

[296] Ibid. [297] Ibid., 73. [298] Ibid. [299] Ibid., 73–4.
[300] Ibid., 72. Turkey was the largest IMF borrower at the time.
[301] Ibid. [302] Ibid. [303] Ibid. [304] Ibid.

[conditionality] had been contemplated. Moreover, there was conspicuous vacuousness about what would happen in July 1995 and beyond under the proposed arrangement. In his view, it was hard to escape the conclusion that there was overall less conditionality, which was why some chairs [including his own] had difficulty with the proposed decision.[305]

In sum, the British, like the Germans, worried that the proposed program – with its combination of large-scale, immediate IMF financing and relatively limited conditionality – would be seen by Mexico's private international creditors as a bailout and would create serious moral hazard problems in the future. For these reasons, Evans stated the British government's preference for a complete separation of board decisions about the $7.8 billion "initial request" for IMF financing and the "additional $10 billion," the latter of which should "be drawn only as a last resort."[306] To that end, he opposed Camdessus's suggestion that the managing director have final decision-making authority over the disbursement of the $10 billion contingency financing; rather, Evans argued, the "determination of any augmentation should be made by the Board ... [I]t should be made clear in the proposed decision that all decisions about purchasing, phasing, and terms and conditions should be decisions of the Board."[307] Finally, in a further sign of the United Kingdom's concerns over moral hazard, Evans stated that "he would like to see very frequent monitoring of Mexico's performance under the stand-by arrangement, with perhaps a weekly or monthly report to the Board," as well as the establishment of "a resident representative in Mexico City to ensure constant and high-level contacts with the authorities."[308] Such "exceptional monitoring," he concluded, was a necessary corollary of the "exceptional access" to IMF credit requested by the Mexican government.[309]

The German and British dissatisfaction with both the content and the process of the Mexican proposal was echoed by the remaining non-G5 European executive directors. For example, Johann Prader (alternate executive director – Austria), representing Austria, Belgium, Hungary, Luxembourg, and Turkey, stated that "our chair very strongly shares the views expressed by Mr. Schönberg, Mr. Evans, and Mr. Sirat" about both the tranching of the $10 billion contingency portion of the loan and the need for the full US bilateral commitment to

[305] Ibid., 87. [306] Ibid., 73. [307] Ibid. [308] Ibid. [309] Ibid.

be spent before additional IMF financing was put at risk.[310] Likewise, Prader reiterated the board's anger at the violation of the standard decision-making timetable: "While there is no disputing that the Fund had to act swiftly, the way this demand for additional access to Fund resources was handled has left bitter feelings."[311] Thus, as a group, the Europeans felt strongly that Camdessus and the Clinton administration had unnecessarily and inappropriately bypassed standard norms of IMF decision-making in order to push through an extraordinarily large rescue package for Mexico.[312]

In a final attempt to register the magnitude of their authorities' dissatisfaction, both Evans (United Kingdom) and Sirat (France) proposed amendments to the text of the proposed stand-by arrangement. In direct contradiction to Camdessus's proposal, Evans proposed that the board – rather than the managing director – have the final say over all disbursements of the bilateral financing to be made available by BIS central banks.[313] Similarly, Sirat sought the inclusion of specific language making clear that the augmented IMF financing (i.e. the $10 billion over and above the initial $7.8 billion) would be drawn by Mexico only "after prior use of other, first-line resources," including the full $20 billion from the US ESF.[314] To that end, he proposed that the program include a phrase noting that "full account will be taken of the availability and use of other sources of [bilateral/official] finance for Mexico."[315] Together, these amendments addressed the Europeans' two primary concerns about the proposed loan: the violation of the Fund's standard decision-making procedures, which gave final and complete authority to the executive board over all lending decisions; and the concern that the US government was pushing for an immediate and unprecedented commitment of IMF resources without clear and immediate assurances that its own bilateral financing would be utilized first.

Although he acknowledged these concerns, Camdessus declined to include Evans' amendments in the text, noting that his proposal was redundant, given that the calculation of bilateral financing was

310 Ibid., 90. 311 Ibid.

312 Ibid. See also similar concerns from the Netherlands, as expressed by Oleg Havrylyshyn (alternate – Ukraine) at page 95, Jarle Bergo (Norway) at pages 99 to 100, and Krzysztof Link (Poland) at page 102.

313 Ibid., 112. See page 43 for Camdessus's proposal.

314 Ibid., 113. 315 Ibid.

a "purely arithmetic" exercise rather than a "judgmental" one.[316] Similarly, he deemed Sirat's proposal unnecessary, as the text already indicated that the availability of outside financing (both private and official) was specified as a key criterion of the Fund's reviews under the proposed stand-by arrangement.[317] Instead, Camdessus called for a final board decision on the current text, on the grounds that time was of the essence and further delay would only exacerbate Mexico's crisis. In line with its decision-making norms, the board approved the package by a consensus resolution.[318] Following the meeting, however, Schönberg and Evans both approached Camdessus and asked to have their votes retroactively recorded as abstentions.[319] In the coming days, all the non-appointed European directors (Switzerland, Norway, Belgium, the Netherlands), representing thirty-six countries in central and eastern Europe and central Asia, followed suit.[320] These steps represented a stark and nearly unprecedented departure from the board's norm of consensus decision-making, and they clearly indicated the European countries' deep dissatisfaction not just with the content of the rescue package but also with the process by which it had been developed.

Thus, although the United States' position ultimately carried the day within the executive board, the approval of the 1995 Mexican program was highly controversial and reflected sharp divisions between the members of the Fund's collective principal. Publicly, these differences were smoothed over at the G-7 finance ministers' meeting held in Toronto on Friday, February 3, 1995.[321] After the meeting, the US Treasury secretary, Robert Rubin, remarked, "There is no question that every member of the G-7 supports the package fully. I really

[316] Ibid., 112. [317] Ibid., 113.

[318] Recall that IMF lending decisions are made "on a consensus basis with respect given to the relative voting power of the states" (Mussa and Savastano 1999; van Houtven 2002). Approval of the Mexican loan therefore indicates that executive directors holding a majority of votes within the board supported approval of the lending proposal.

[319] Graham *et al. Financial Times*, February 16, 1995.

[320] Minutes of EBM/95/11 (10:00 a.m., February 1, 1995), 114. Belgium later revoked its abstention. The recorded abstentions were: Bergo (Norway), Havrylyshyn (Ukraine), Link (Poland), Evans (UK), and Schönberg (Germany).

[321] Clyde H. Farnsworth, "US allies mute discord over Mexico," *New York Times*, February 5, 1995.

don't think we left with ill will."[322] Likewise, the Canadian finance minister, Paul Martin, agreed that "the G-7 ministers ... expressed their total satisfaction with the international efforts to assist Mexico, which have helped ease its financial crisis."[323] Nonetheless, it was clear that the Europeans were extremely upset and perceived the decision as an "end run" around standard IMF decision-making procedures engineered by Camdessus and the Americans. "It is in nobody's interest to see the package collapse," said a senior German official, "but it had to be made clear that this must not happen again."[324]

As with the 1989 Mexican program, this lending episode once again vividly illustrates the importance of preference heterogeneity among G-5 governments in shaping Fund lending decisions. Moreover, it provides further evidence that domestic financial interests play a central role in shaping G-5 governments' views of IMF policies. Indeed, the positions adopted by G-5 executive directors – strong support for the proposed program by Lissakers (United States), qualified support by Mesaki (Japan) and Sirat (France), and sharp opposition by Evans (United Kingdom) and Schönberg (Germany) – correlated directly with the relative amount of financial exposure each G-5 country had to Mexico in 1995. The United States held 47 percent ($23 billion) of Mexico's commercial bank debt, while the British and Germans held relatively little Mexican debt ($4.6 billion and $4.7 billion, respectively). Japanese bank exposure was the lowest among the G-5 in 1995 ($4.4 billion, 10 percent of G-5 exposure), but this was a recent development and did not fully reflect Japan's long-standing financial ties to Mexico; indeed, as late as 1990 Japan's share of G-5 bank exposure had been 20 percent, and, at the height of the 1980s debt crisis, Japanese banks had held approximately 30 percent of Mexico's private external debt. Similarly, while French exposure was only slightly higher than that of Germany and the United Kingdom ($4.7 billion), its lending to Mexico had almost doubled since 1992, while British and German lending had remained stagnant since the implementation of the Brady Plan. Therefore, although their support for the proposed IMF program was less enthusiastic than that of the United States, neither Japan nor France shared the serious concerns of the British and the Germans about moral hazard.

322 Ibid.
323 Greg Ip, "Crisis had perfect timing," *Financial Post*, February 7, 1995.
324 Graham *et al.*, *Financial Times*, February 16, 1995.

Performance under the 1995 program

In the weeks following the approval of the IMF program, the skepticism and moral hazard concerns expressed by Evans, Schönberg, and the non-G-5 European executive directors proved to be justified. Quite simply, Mexico's international creditors "bailed out" completely in the wake of the Fund loan. By August 1995 90 percent of Mexico's tesobono holders in December 1994 had "cut and run."[325] As a result, the IMF package effectively constituted a direct transfer of official resources to Mexico's private international creditors. By the end of 1995 Mexico had borrowed $13.5 billion from the United States and drawn $13 billion from the IMF. Over the same period, the country had paid off almost all the $25 billion in tesobonos outstanding in January 1995. This "rush to the exits" by Mexico's bondholders clearly illustrates how changes in debt composition affect the response of private international creditors to the IMF's lending programs. In the 1980s Mexico's private creditors consisted of a limited number of commercial banks with long-term ties to the country, common interests as a result of syndicated lending, and a history of cooperation among themselves in lending during good times and bad. Consequently, the banks were both willing and able to negotiate with each other and the IMF to reach agreement on debt rescheduling and concerted lending. In January 1995, however, the vast majority of Mexico's private creditors were short-term bondholders with few long-term ties either to each other or to Mexico. When the crisis hit, these bondholders simply liquidated their holdings and fled; at no point did they seek to cooperate with each other (as the banks had in the 1980s), nor did they interact with Mexico, the IMF, or the G-5 governments to explore the possibility of debt rescheduling or coordinated rollovers. In this environment, the Fund was left to fill Mexico's entire financing gap itself, through an extraordinarily large and front-loaded loan, in an attempt to convince Mexico's creditors to reverse their capital flight.

Ultimately, despite the bondholders' initial response, the IMF program proved quite successful in this goal of catalyzing new private capital flows. Indeed, over the course of several months, the IMF/ESF package helped to restore market actors' confidence in Mexico's

[325] GAO (1996, fig. 5.1, 137).

financial stability and enabled the Mexican government to successfully re-access private international capital markets. On May 4, 1995, Mexico's state-owned National Development Bank issued $110.3 million in bonds, with a maturity of one year at an interest rate of LIBOR plus 3.5 percent.[326] Two weeks later Mexico's export development bank issued $30 million in bonds with a maturity of one year at LIBOR plus 5.8 percent.[327] As the year progressed and the specter of default faded, private international creditors accelerated their return to the Mexican market. Between July and November, the Mexican government issued $4 billion in new international bonds, including a $1 billion issue of two-year bonds at LIBOR plus 5.375 percent underwritten by Citibank, Credit Suisse, and the Bank of Tokyo.[328]

These renewed capital inflows replenished Mexico's foreign exchange reserves – which rose from $4 billion in December 1994 to $13.4 billion in August 1995 – and enabled the government to continue servicing both the interest and the principal of its private external debt. More importantly, the IMF package, coupled with the new long-term bond issues, lengthened the maturity profile of Mexico's external debt, thereby freeing the government from further reliance on short-term tesobonos. By 1997 the average maturity of Mexico's private external debt had increased from 3.4 to 7.7 years.[329] With its economy stabilized, Mexico managed to repay all the money it had borrowed from the US Treasury by January 1997, and it had made SDR 2.6 billion in early repayments to the IMF by August 1997.[330] Thus, despite the initial concerns about moral hazard, the 1995 IMF program did successfully trigger new capital inflows and return Mexico to good standing in global financial markets.

Assessment: global finance and the politics of Mexican IMF lending

These four cases of IMF lending to Mexico during the 1980s and 1990s provide further evidence in support of the common agency theory of Fund policymaking. Furthermore, they offer additional confirmation of my core argument that changes in the composition of private international capital flows are the key determinant of variation in IMF

326 GAO (1996, 21). 327 Ibid. 328 Ibid.
329 Banco de México (1997). 330 GAO (1996, 21).

loan characteristics. Throughout the Mexican lending episodes, G-5 governments and the Fund staff both played important roles in shaping decisions about the size and terms of IMF programs, yet neither entirely controlled the process. On the one hand, the Fund's largest shareholders exercised enormous authority within the executive board, and the heterogeneity of G-5 preferences was a key factor shaping the board's debates and decisions. G-5 influence was particularly visible in 1989 and 1995, when debates between these governments about the size and phasing of IMF lending dominated the board discussions and shaped the ultimate outcomes. On the other hand, the IMF staff's influence within the Fund decision-making process cannot be discounted. In negotiating directly with the Mexican authorities and the commercial banks, and in setting the agenda for the executive board with its proposals, the staff significantly influenced each lending decision. This influence was particularly strong over conditionality: while many board members raised questions or voiced concerns about the content of specific conditions proposed by the staff in each episode, there is little evidence that the G-5 countries (or other board members) sought to overturn or reject these proposals.[331]

This set of findings from the Mexican case – substantial G-5 influence over loan size decisions, coupled with significant staff autonomy in designing conditionality – closely mirrors the results of the statistical analysis in chapter 3. Thus, the quantitative and the qualitative analyses both shed light on the important roles of the key actors in the IMF lending process, as well as the limits of each group's ability to control Fund decision-making. In addition, the Mexican cases strongly support the hypothesized link between changes in patterns of financial globalization and variation in G-5 and IMF staff preferences over IMF loan size and conditionality. The preferences of G-5 governments throughout the four episodes correlated strongly with their domestic financial interests, and preference heterogeneity among these countries clearly shaped the executive board discussions. Similarly, the IMF staff's expectations about catalytic financing varied substantially over time; in particular, the shift from commercial bank lending in the

[331] Of course, the absence of visible G-5 or board pressure on the staff vis-à-vis conditionality is not, by itself, evidence of an absence of influence. Nonetheless, the lack of overt pressure on the staff strongly suggests that it enjoyed substantial autonomy over the design of the conditionality in Mexico's IMF programs during the 1980s and 1990s.

1980s to bond financing in the 1990s played a central role in shaping the Fund's response to the 1994/5 Mexican crisis.

G-5 preference heterogeneity and intensity: the importance of commercial bank exposure

As expected, Mexico's sizeable financial ties to the G-5 countries profoundly influenced the Fund's lending decisions in the 1980s and 1990s alike. As the first or second largest sovereign borrower from private commercial banks throughout this period, Mexico clearly received more favorable treatment from the Fund than other large developing countries with smaller financial ties to the major creditor countries. Without these direct and extensive ties to the industrial countries and private markets, neither the G-5 countries nor the Fund staff would have considered Mexico's financial difficulties to be a systemic threat to global financial stability. Indeed, the Fund provided far less credit to other large developing countries with smaller ties to the major creditor countries. A brief comparison between Mexico and South Korea (discussed in further detail in the next chapter) illustrates the point. In 1983 Mexico owed $39.8 billion to G-5 commercial banks, while South Korea owed half that amount ($20.8 billion); South Korea's loan of 1.24 times quota (SDR 0.58 billion) was less than half the size of Mexico's in quota terms (SDR 3.41 billion, 2.93 times quota). By contrast, G-5 commercial banks had extensive ties to both Mexico ($41.6 billion, 1995) and South Korea ($68.5 billion, 1997) in the 1990s, when the IMF provided these countries with the two largest Fund loans in its history (6.88 times quota and 19.39 times quota, respectively).[332]

Although the strong G-5 banking ties to Mexico were a key reason why it received larger IMF loans than similar countries, changes over time in the amount and distribution of G-5 commercial bank exposure help to explain important variation within the Mexican cases. As the four IMF lending episodes illustrate, the intensity and cohesiveness of the G-5 countries' interests shifted significantly over time as the composition of Mexico's debt changed. As G-5 aggregate commercial bank exposure declined in the later 1980s, clear rifts emerged

[332] I discuss the similarities and differences between the Mexican and South Korean cases further in chapter 6.

between the United States, the United Kingdom, West Germany, Japan, and France over the size and terms of IMF loans to Mexico. In 1983, despite the large difference in American banks' exposure to Mexico relative to that of banks from the other G-5 countries, support for the IMF rescue package was strong and uniform. Given its substantially higher bank exposure to Mexico, the United States took a significantly more active role in managing the crisis: the Treasury and the Federal Reserve committed significant bilateral financing because of the risk a Mexican default posed for its commercial banks, and the Federal Reserve chairman, Paul Volcker, and other senior American financial officials actively intervened to facilitate the cooperation of Mexico's commercial bank creditors. Nevertheless, the remaining G-5 countries also had very substantial banking ties to Mexico, and they expressed clear support for the 1983 stand-by arrangement. Indeed, as noted above, only France expressed some concern about the size of the 1983 program in the December 23, 1982, executive board meeting.

In the subsequent Mexican lending episodes, however, clear disagreements arose with the board among the G-5 governments, with their preferences for and against larger loans closely mirroring the growing differences in the degree to which each country's commercial banks were exposed to Mexico. In 1986 and 1989 the United States and Japan, the two G-5 countries whose banks remained heavily invested in Mexico, strongly supported the proposed IMF loans to Mexico. In contrast, the major European countries (especially West Germany and the United Kingdom), whose banks were far less vulnerable to a Mexican crisis, expressed significantly less enthusiasm for the Fund's continued large-scale support of Mexico. The 1989 board meeting illustrates this cleavage especially clearly: while Frank Cassell (United Kingdom) and Günther Grosche (Germany) opposed both the 40 percent augmentation of the Mexican loan and the disbursement of Fund resources before private creditors committed themselves to providing new money, Charles Warner (alternate executive director – United States) and Koji Yamazaki (Japan) strongly supported these proposals. Although the board ultimately approved the 1989 lending arrangement, the British and West Germans did succeed in postponing both the augmentation and the early disbursement.

By 1995, these differences between the G-5 countries had become even sharper. Although aggregate G-5 bank exposure remained at roughly the same levels as in 1983 ($41.6 billion), only American banks remained heavily exposed ($23.0 billion). As evidenced by their initial bilateral efforts and subsequent contribution of $20 billion to the IMF-led rescue package, US officials remained strongly in favor of assisting Mexico. In contrast, with their weaker commercial banking ties to Mexico, the Europeans – especially the British and Germans – hardened their opposition to a large-scale IMF rescue. While they chose not to block approval of the 1995 IMF bailout, the European directors did register their dissent by abstaining *ex post* from the board vote. Japan, whose banks had reduced their exposure from $13.3 billion 1989 to $4.1 billion in 1994, also no longer expressed the strong support for Mexican IMF lending that it had in 1986 and 1989, although it did not actively oppose the loan. Moreover, in sharp contrast to its actions in Mexico in 1989 and South Korea in 1997, Japan did not offer substantial bilateral aid of its own as a supplement to the IMF package.

IMF staff preferences: banks, bonds, and catalytic financing

In addition to G-5 commercial bank exposure, variation in the composition of Mexico's international creditors – in particular, the shift from commercial bank lenders to bondholders – also had a clear impact on the IMF's lending decisions, primarily by virtue of its impact on the staff's assessments about the "catalytic effect" of Fund lending on private capital inflows. Indeed, throughout the 1980s and 1990s the issue of whether Mexico's creditors were banks or bondholders directly affected the expectations of the Fund staff over the likely availability of private financing in the aftermath of an IMF loan. In the 1980s, when nearly all Mexico's private creditors were commercial banks, the Fund and Mexico were able to engage in direct negotiations with the Bank Advisory Committee to secure explicit "new money" commitments and to coordinate the rescheduling of outstanding Mexican debt. With private financing explicitly pledged in advance of the Fund program, the IMF was willing to commit significant resources to Mexico without serious concerns that Fund lending would constitute a "bailout" to private creditors. As William Dale, first deputy managing director of the Fund, said in the aftermath of the 1983 Mexican rescue package, "The IMF is not bailing out the banks, it's really bailing them in."[333] Unlike Mexico's bondholders in 1994/5, Mexico's commercial bank creditors in the 1980s were willing to increase their lending exposure, for several reasons. First, the commercial banks – especially the large money-center banks in the G-5 countries – had long-standing ties to Mexico and were loath to sever these relationships entirely once a financial crisis occurred. Second, the relatively small number of commercial banks (approximately 500 in Mexico's case, with fewer than 100 banks holding over a half of Mexico's external debt in the 1980s), coupled with the coordinating role of the BAC, facilitated private creditor cooperation and mitigated the collective action problems associated with international lending.[334] Third, the commercial banks were susceptible to pressure from G-5 governments and central banks to participate in concerted lending. As the 1983 episode illustrates, US Federal Reserve officials and Bank of England representatives used their oversight authority as both carrot and stick to secure the participation of holdout banks in concerted lending. Finally the IMF itself played a critical role in directly seeking private creditors' involvement and resolving the banks' collective action problems. As Walter Wriston, chairman of Citicorp, acknowledged, "It was clear that somebody had to step in and play a leadership role."[335] Through their numerous direct meetings with William Rhodes and other BAC representatives, de Larosière and other IMF officials played a critical role in securing the banks' participation in both concerted lending and the Brady Plan in the 1980s.

The commercial banks' willingness and ability to cooperate with the Fund had clearly waned by 1989, however. As the major money-center banks in the G-5 countries reduced their exposure to Mexico, they became less and less amenable to participate in the quasi-voluntary process of concerted lending. Although Rhodes and the BAC still managed to secure the banks' participation in the Brady Plan, this process took much longer in 1989 than it had in either 1986 or 1983. This growing reluctance of private creditors to continue lending to Mexico only increased following the 1989 Brady Plan, when the vast majority of Mexico's bank debt was transformed into bonds. By 1994, when Mexico once again sought IMF assistance, its private

[333] Clyde H. Farnsworth, "A dramatic change at the IMF," *New York Times*, January 9, 1983.

[334] Lipson (1986). [335] Farnsworth, *New York Times*, January 9, 1983.

creditors consisted of tens of thousands of heterogeneous bondholders rather than a few hundred commercial banks lending through syndicates. In this environment, no group of major creditors emerged to assume the two key roles played by the money-center banks and the BAC in the 1980s: negotiating with the IMF over the terms of new money and debt rescheduling; and securing the participation of smaller, holdout creditors. Faced with serious collective action problems and fearing a default, nearly all Mexico's creditors during the 1994 crisis chose to "cut and run" rather than provide new financing.

The IMF thus faced a completely different situation in 1994 from what it had from 1983 to 1989, due in large part to the shift in the composition of Mexico's private international creditors. In the 1980s, knowing that it could depend on the banks to continue lending to Mexico, the IMF staff proposed loans that were smaller than the country's overall financing needs. Therefore, while the 1983, 1986, and 1989 lending arrangements were large in both absolute and per quota terms, they represented only a portion of the money Mexico needed to service its outstanding external debt. The commercial banks, through the contribution of new loans and the rescheduling of existing debts, provided the rest. By the 1990s, however, the banks were of only secondary importance to Mexico as a source of external financing: bondholders held 83.5 percent of Mexico's long-term debt and 67 percent of its short-term debt.[336] Even if the IMF had convinced the G-5 commercial banks to roll over all $41.6 billion of their Mexican debt in 1995, Mexico would still have faced a probable default as a result of bondholder-driven capital flight.

This shift from long-term bank lending to short-term bond financing had important implications for the Fund's lending strategy to Mexico in 1995. Faced with the unsavory choice between a Mexican default and a full "bailout" – a lending package that fully financed Mexico's external debt service with no private creditor contributions – the IMF chose the latter. With G-5 (especially US) creditors heavily exposed, the Fund provided Mexico with enough money to pay off its bondholders completely, even as they "bailed out" of the country by selling off their tesobonos. In this case, the G-5 countries' concerns about both systemic stability and the stability of their own domestic

[336] Institute for International Finance (1998).

financial systems outweighed the moral hazard concerns of providing large-scale IMF financing without any assurances by private creditors that they would also continue lending to Mexico.

While the shift in the composition of international creditors from banks to bondholders played a critical role in shaping Mexico's experience with the IMF in the 1990s, the Mexican case was not one in which the identity of the borrowers shifted. Even in the 1990s, the vast majority of Mexico's debt was sovereign borrowing: private non-guaranteed debt ("private–private" flows) totaled only 24.5 percent of total Mexican external debt in 1995. As we will see below, this contrasted sharply with South Korea, where the shift from sovereign debt to private–private capital flows played a central role in the country's experience with the IMF during the height of the Asian financial crisis.

Evidence for alternative explanations of IMF behavior

Macroeconomic conditions

In addition to lending strong support for both the common agency framework and the hypotheses linking variation in IMF lending to patterns of financial globalization, the Mexican cases also illustrate the continued importance of country-specific macroeconomic criteria (e.g. budget deficits, external debt levels, foreign exchange reserves) as determinants of Fund loan characteristics. In each of the programs discussed above, both the IMF staff and the executive board spent a substantial portion of their time analyzing Mexico's macroeconomic fundamentals, and these variables played a central role in shaping decisions about the size and terms of each of the four IMF loans in the 1980s and 1990s. As a result, although G-5 domestic financial interests and IMF staff concerns about catalytic financing were both extremely important determinants of Fund lending behavior in the Mexican cases, so, too, were the views of the staff and the executive directors about Mexico's past and future growth prospects, its debt sustainability, and the structural adjustment policies it would pursue in order to restore external balance.

That said, economic variables alone do not explain the variations in the amount of money Mexico received in each episode in relation to its Fund quota. Indeed, if country size or straightforward financial need (based on external debt indicators) was the primary determinant of the Fund's financing decisions, then Mexico's IMF loans between 1983 and 1995 should not have varied so widely in size. In fact, the case for viewing the IMF as a purely "technocratic" international institution is significantly weakened by the absence of a clear correlation between Mexico's key external debt indicators and the size of its IMF loans. From 1983 to 1994 Mexico's external debt/GDP ratio remained nearly constant at 40 to 45 percent of GDP, while its debt service burden (debt service/exports) dropped sharply from 45 percent in 1983 to a range of 20 to 35 percent from 1989 to 1994.[337] Although Mexico actually faced a smaller debt service burden in 1995 than in the 1980s, it received a significantly larger loan (6.9 times quota). This is not to say that the Fund believes macroeconomic indicators are unimportant; indeed, Mexico's severe shortage of foreign exchange reserves during the 1994 crisis (a sharp decline from the equivalent of 3.3 months of imports in December 1993 to 0.7 in December 1994) was a key factor behind the massive scale of the 1995 IMF package. The Mexican authorities' reserve level was actually lower (0.6 months of imports) in January 1983, however, when it received a loan of 2.9 times quota, than in February 1995 (0.7 months of imports).[338] In order to account for this variation in loan size, it is necessary to consider not only macroeconomic variables but also variation in patterns of financial globalization and the ways in which they affected the interests of the IMF's key decision-makers.

While macroeconomic factors and country-specific external debt indicators do not seem to have played a primary role in shaping IMF decisions about the *size* of Mexican loans, however, they clearly had a strong influence on IMF staff and executive board views of *conditionality*. In each episode of Mexican lending, the IMF staff report shows the staff assessing the likelihood that Mexico will meet the specified targets for reserves, budget deficits, current account balances, and other performance criteria. Similarly, the executive board minutes demonstrate that directors paid significant attention to the specific targets proposed by the Fund staff and often disagreed with the staff's predictions about Mexico's future performance under the lending arrangements. For example, in the board discussions over the 1989 Mexican extended arrangement, Charles Warner (alternate executive director – United States), E. A. Evans (Australia), and Frank

[337] World Bank (2006a). [338] Ibid.

Table 4.3 *Key data: IMF lending to Mexico, 1983–95*

Date of IMF lending arrangement	1/1/83	11/19/86	5/26/89	2/1/95
G-5 bank exposure ($ billions)	39.8	51.6	46.5	41.6
Coefficient of variation, G-5 bank exposure	121.4	79.1	67.6	87.8
US share, G-5 bank exposure	0.62	0.44	0.36	0.51
UK share, G-5 bank exposure	0.16	0.12	0.13	0.11
Japanese share, G-5 bank exposure	0.05	0.25	0.30	0.10
German share, G-5 bank exposure	0.05	0.07	0.07	0.11
French share, G-5 bank exposure	0.11	0.10	0.10	0.13
Percent bond debt	6.1	4.6	6.0	78.6
Percent private non-guaranteed debt	19.8	19.7	8.4	24.5
GDP ($ billions)	173.7	184.5	223	420.8
External debt/GDP (%)	35.9	39.8	41	45.9
Short-term debt/reserves	14.75	0.96	1.25	6.10
IMF loan size (SDR billions)	3.41	1.40	3.73	12.07
IMF loan size (amount/quota)	2.93	1.20	3.20	6.88
IMF loan size (amount/GDP)	0.02	0.008	0.017	0.029
Number of performance criteria	7	7	7	7
Number of prior actions	0	0	0	0
Number of benchmarks/targets	0	0	0	0
Outstanding IMF debt (amount/quota)	0	1.04	3.06	1.51
G-5 UN voting affinity (mean "S" score)	−0.07	−0.11	−0.11	0.12
Coefficient of variation, G-5 "S" scores	27.8	26.7	31.4	23.4
IMF liquidity ratio	0.36	0.42	0.29	0.21
Quota review in progress?	No	No	Yes	Yes
Mexican IMF quota (SDR millions)	1,165.5	1,165.5	1,165.5	1,753.3

Note: Data are lagged one year.

Cassell (United Kingdom) all offered extensive comments and questions on specific elements of the staff's proposal. Cassell, in particular, thought that the staff's assumptions concerning Mexico's fiscal deficit, its ability to reduce the inflation rate, and the profitability of

Mexico's public sector enterprises – all factors contributing directly to the country's ability to attract private external financing in the future – were overly optimistic.[339]

Rather than dismissing the importance of economic factors, the Mexican case therefore provides useful insights into the scope and limits of their influence on the IMF's lending behavior. Clearly, the Fund staff focuses heavily on country-specific macroeconomic and external debt indicators as it tailors the general framework and structure of IMF programs to the particular balance of payments and external debt problems facing individual borrowing countries. These criteria alone, however, are necessary but not sufficient determinants of variation in the size and terms of IMF loans. Ultimately, we must also focus on political economy factors – most importantly, private international debt composition – in order to explain both why the interests of the key actors involved in Fund decision-making shift over time and across cases and how these changes in the preferences of the Fund's principal and agent lead to variation in IMF loan size and conditionality.

US geopolitical interests

Although the Mexican case study strongly supports both the common agency framework and its hypotheses linking patterns of financial globalization to variation in IMF lending, it offers little evidence in favor of either geopolitical theories of Fund behavior or those that treat the United States as the IMF's sole political principal. The United States played the leading role among the G-5 countries in shaping IMF policies toward Mexico from 1983 to 1995, yet it seems clear from the evidence that financial and economic concerns, rather than security interests or geopolitical calculations, were the primary determinant of American interests in Mexico. Indeed, in the one Mexican episode in which "the high politics of IMF lending" has most often been cited – the 1995 stand-by arrangement – non-economic strategic concerns appear to have been used only as a tool to mobilize congressional support for the original US bilateral plan to offer loan guarantees to Mexico.[340] To the extent that the US government overstated

[339] See minutes of EBM/89/64 and EBM/89/65, especially EBM/89/65, pages 10 to 13.

[340] Thacker (1999).

Mexico's economic need for IMF assistance, it did so primarily on the grounds that a Mexican financial crisis constituted a threat to the international financial system rather than a threat to American or global security.[341]

It is possible, of course, that American officials used Mexico's importance for domestic financial institutions instrumentally – that is, as "cover" for underlying geopolitical interests. If this were the case, though, we should have at least observed the relevant officials within the US government (e.g. the secretary of state, the national security advisor) taking an active role in advocating IMF assistance. Instead, the key American and G-5 officials involved with Mexico and the IMF were those from finance ministries and central banks. In the United States, for example, the planning of the ESF rescue package and the negotiations with the IMF over the 1995 stand-by arrangement were conducted by the secretary of the Treasury, Robert Rubin, his chief deputy, Lawrence Summers, and other lower-level officials from the Treasury Department and the Federal Reserve. Moreover, accounts of this period from these officials – particularly Rubin himself – cast further doubt on this geopolitical explanation, noting the lack of involvement of national security officials in the handling of Mexico's financial crises.[342] Thus, while the US government may have viewed Mexico's financial crises through the broader lenses of regional security and political stability, it does not appear that these non-financial factors played a central role in the Fund's decision-making process.

Two additional factors in the Mexican case also cast doubt on geopolitical explanations of IMF behavior. First, in contrast to several major IMF borrowers (e.g. Turkey) in the 1980s and 1990s, Mexico received very little military aid from the United States at any point during this period: US military assistance to Mexico never exceeded $1 million per year between 1983 and 2003, and it reached its lowest level ($0.2 million) in 1995. If geopolitics really were driving IMF lending, militarily important countries should have received larger loans than Mexico. Second, there is no mention of any concrete indicators of US geopolitical interests in Mexico – for instance, concerns about regional political instability stemming from a Mexican

341 Broz (2005); Henning (1999); GAO (1996).

342 See, for example, Rubin and Weisberg (2003).

financial crisis, or concerns about large inflows of illegal immigrants into the United States – at any point in the actual policy discussions concerning the Fund's four loans to Mexico over the 1983–95 period. In sum, the absence of concrete, observable indicators that American geopolitical and/or foreign policy goals are the primary determinant of IMF lending behavior lends little support to this theory.

In addition to casting doubt on geopolitical theories of IMF lending, the Mexican case calls into question the related view that the United States exercises unilateral power as the Fund's sole political principal. To be sure, the direct and pre-emptive involvement of the US Treasury and the Clinton administration in the 1995 episode does illustrate that the United States is "first among equals" among the G-5 countries. Moreover, the fact that the IMF approved the 1995 Mexican program despite the Europeans' harsh opposition to both the contents of the loan and the extraordinary nature of the decision-making timetable lends support to the commonly held view that the IMF is primarily the servant of the US government. Nonetheless, there are several reasons to be cautious in drawing overly broad implications about the importance of American influence and geopolitical interests from the 1995 Mexican case. First, given its geographical location and long-standing financial and geopolitical importance to the United States, Mexico represents a "most likely" case for US-centric theories of IMF policymaking – one in which the evidence should be incontrovertible if this viewpoint is to be accepted as a general theory of IMF decision-making. If we are to accept this explanation of IMF lending behavior, the four Mexican loans discussed above should provide clear and unqualified support for this theory. As this chapter has illustrated, however, this was clearly not the case; rather, as the board debates and G-5 actions during the 1980s lending arrangements document in great detail, the remaining G-5 countries exercised substantial influence over Fund policy decisions vis-à-vis Mexico, and disagreements between G-5 governments had tangible effects on IMF lending outcomes (most notably in the discussions about the 40 percent augmentation of the 1989 program). Second, the European executive directors' deep dissatisfaction with the way in which the 1995 stand-by arrangement was approved suggests that such episodes – in which the US government seeks to bypass standard IMF decision-making norms and pre-emptively announces the terms of a Fund program – are exceedingly rare events. If such procedures were commonplace, it is highly unlikely that the events of February 1995 would have triggered such anger and displeasure among the British, German, and other European governments. Consequently, we should be cautious about inferring a generalizable causal relationship from the single episode of Mexico's 1995 IMF loan.

Finally, as the quantitative analysis in chapter 3 illustrated, there is robust evidence that G-5 preference heterogeneity has a significant and substantively large effect on Fund lending outcomes. Therefore, the fact that US influence appeared to be extremely strong in one episode (Mexico 1995) is not sufficient cause to reject the common agency theory of IMF policymaking and simultaneously embrace the conventional wisdom of American dominance of the Fund. In short, while the 1995 Mexican episode highlights the importance of US influence and interests within the Fund, it does not falsify the competing alternatives. Instead, the balance of evidence presented in this chapter suggests that the 1995 Mexican loan was an extraordinary, isolated episode rather than a broadly representative case of IMF decision-making. In the end, the evidence from the Mexican case suggests that – like country-specific macroeconomic conditions – American interests are a necessary, but not sufficient, factor explaining variation in IMF lending. Clearly, one must consider the US government's views of the liquidity/moral hazard trade-off in order to explain why the IMF's lending policies vary over time and across cases. As the four episodes described above illustrate, however, accounting for American interests without also considering those of the Fund's other large shareholders yields an incomplete and often inaccurate picture of the politics of IMF decision-making.

Bureaucratic rent-seeking

Similarly, the Mexican case offers little support for the public choice literature's view that the self-interested rent-seeking of Fund bureaucrats drives IMF lending behavior. At no point do we observe the board seeking to rein in a "runaway" staff interested in maximizing its autonomy and/or budgets. In fact, there is scant evidence that such concerns even crossed the minds of executive directors as they considered the staff's lending proposals. On the contrary, the directors repeatedly praised the staff for its diligence and efforts in seeking to design IMF programs for Mexico grounded in sound macroeconomic policies that would restore the country to long-term debt sustainability.[343] This praise may, of course, simply be diplomatic "boilerplate" – kind words offered by the executive directors in all board discussions. That said, given many directors' willingness to express their views frankly (both positive and less so) about the staff's proposed conditionality in the Mexican lending cases, one would expect to see equally frank comments – if not direct efforts to change the conditions themselves – if the board felt that the staff was overstepping its bounds and engaging in bureaucratic rent-seeking.

In the end, bureaucratic politics does not seem to be a major factor explaining variation in IMF decision-making. Although the Fund staff does not appear to exploit agency slack maliciously for its own benefit, however, it may have a tendency to be more lenient with Fund borrowers than its political principals in some cases. Compared to the executive board, the staff often seemed to grant Mexico the benefit of the doubt in its calculations and projections. This tendency suggests that the IMF staff may be guilty of being "too close" to the countries with which it is negotiating, as several recent accounts of IMF policymaking in the 1990s have contended.[344] The evidence does support this perspective to some extent: at several points during the four Mexican lending episodes, the board questioned the assumptions of the Fund staff or found their projections overly optimistic. For instance, as noted above, several executive directors believed that the staff's assumptions behind the quantitative performance criteria included in the 1989 extended arrangement were less than entirely realistic given the severity of Mexico's financial difficulties. Thus, while the data do not support the argument that the IMF staff systematically engages

343 See, for example, minutes of EBM/82/168 (December 23, 1982), 7.

344 Mussa (2002); Blustein (2001). Woods (2006) finds that this closeness is most likely to occur when the Fund finds "sympathetic interlocutors" within borrowing country governments, as in Mexico in the 1990s (90). These situations, she argues, are most likely to result in successful economic reform, since the borrower and the IMF share common policy reforms. Chwieroth (2008) similarly argues that the Fund frequently plays the role of "cheerleader" in support of a government's pre-existing desire to implement politically sensitive economic reforms. The archival evidence presented above, however, suggests that this mutually agreeable relationship may also lead the staff to be overly optimistic in its forecasts of a borrower's economic prospects – and, therefore, in its proposals concerning loan size and conditionality.

in rent-seeking, they do suggest that Fund staff members – in their eagerness to assist their borrowing country clients – may sometimes propose loans that are more generous and lenient than the circumstances warrant based purely on macroeconomic and external debt criteria.

Furthermore, just as we should be cautious in drawing overly broad implications about the validity of US-centric theories of the IMF from the Mexican case studies, we should also exercise caution in completely rejecting public choice theories as a result of the foregoing analysis. Indeed, if Mexico represents a "most likely" case for theories of IMF lending emphasizing US geopolitical interests, it constitutes a "least likely" case for public choice theories. Given Mexico's clear economic and political importance to the Fund's largest shareholders, there is little reason to believe that the staff would have the opportunity to exploit agency slack and engage in bureaucratic rent-seeking. Rather, this type of behavior is most likely to be observed in "less important" countries – i.e. those in which G-5 governments have fewer direct financial interests and no long-term geopolitical ties. As predicted by the common agency theory, IMF staff autonomy, or agency slack, should be greatest in these cases, rather than in larger countries such as Mexico (and South Korea), which are of substantial domestic financial importance to the Fund's political principals and of greater importance for the stability of the global financial system. In short, although the Mexican case studies lend little support to bureaucratic views of IMF decision-making, they do not constitute a general test of these theories.

Conclusions

In this chapter, I have analyzed IMF lending to Mexico from 1983 to 1995 as a further test of the observable implications of my argument that changes in the composition of private international capital flows are the key factor explaining variation in the Fund's lending decisions. As this analysis of Mexico's four IMF loans between 1983 and 1995 has illustrated, variation in the amount and distribution of G-5 commercial bank exposure directly affected the interests of the most powerful member states within the IMF's executive board, while the shift in the identity of Mexico's private international creditors – from commercial banks to bondholders – strongly influenced the staff's expectations about market actors' response to the Fund's policies. Taken together, these factors explain how and why the Fund reached different decisions about the level of resources it should provide Mexico during this period, as well as the scope of conditionality attached to these loans. Although other explanatory factors (most notably macroeconomic criteria) did come into play, the balance of evidence clearly points to variation in the composition of private international capital flows to Mexico as the key factor driving its treatment by the IMF over the last two decades.

The Mexican cases do not fully address two important issues, however. First, although focusing on Mexico on its own allows us to isolate important "within-country" changes over time in the political economy of IMF lending, this analysis, on its own, tells us little about how IMF decision-making varies from country to country. Second, while the Mexican cases illustrate the effects of two of the three key changes in patterns of financial globalization outlined in chapter 2 – changes in the amount and distribution of G-5 commercial bank exposure and the shift from bank lending to bond financing – on IMF lending decisions, they do not illustrate the effects of the third shift: the move from sovereign borrowing to "private–private" capital flows. As we will see in the following chapter, this change in the composition of international capital flows played an important role in shaping the IMF's lending policies to South Korea during the Asian financial crisis in the late 1990s. The following chapter, which pairs the Mexican case studies with a similar analysis of IMF lending to South Korea in the 1980s and 1990s, sheds light on these important issues and enables us to draw further conclusions about the determinants of cross-country variation in the political economy of IMF lending.

5 *Global finance and IMF lending to South Korea, 1983–1997*

Thus far, both the statistical evidence and the Mexican case studies lend strong support to both the common agency theory and my core argument linking changes in patterns of financial globalization to variation in IMF lending policies. In this chapter, I conduct a final empirical test by focusing on IMF lending to South Korea from 1983 to 1997. As with the Mexican loans in the 1980s and 1990s, the IMF's three loans to South Korea in this period varied significantly in both size and conditionality. To what extent do changes in the composition of international capital flows – through their impact on G-5 countries' domestic financial interests and the IMF staff's expectations about catalytic financing – explain this variation? In order to answer this question, I once again follow the strategy adopted in the previous chapter. For each South Korean loan, I consider the factors leading the country to request IMF assistance, and I then explore the roles of G-5 governments, the IMF staff, and changing patterns of financial globalization in shaping the Fund's lending decisions. In addition, I assess the extent to which alternative political and economic factors influenced the IMF's decisions in these cases.

South Korea's international debt composition, 1983–97

Although it ranked behind only Mexico and Brazil as the largest sovereign borrower in the 1980s, South Korea was a markedly smaller player in world financial markets. Whereas Mexico owed a total of \$93 billion in external debt (\$39.8 billion to commercial banks) in 1983, South Korea owed less than half that amount (\$40.4 billion) even though the countries were roughly the same size (South Korea's GDP was \$188 billion in 1983, Mexico's \$230 billion). GDP per capita was roughly equivalent in the two countries (\$4,953 in Mexico, \$3,886 in South Korea), although South Korea went on to surpass

Mexico in per capita wealth by the late 1980s.[1] Total external debt was equivalent to 21.5 percent of South Korea's GDP, compared to 40.4 percent for Mexico. Likewise, international bank lending to South Korea was significantly less than to Mexico: G-5 commercial banks held $20.8 billion in claims on South Korea, nearly all in the form of medium-term syndicated loans. US banks held the majority of these claims ($11.7 billion, or 55 percent), with Japan ($4.2 billion) and the United Kingdom ($2.5 billion) also relatively highly exposed.[2] By contrast, banks from West Germany ($0.8 billion) and France ($1.6 billion) had smaller stakes in South Korea. As in Mexico, bond financing remained a very small source of external financing for South Korea in the 1980s, comprising only 2.1 percent of the country's private external debt. Similarly, non-sovereign borrowing comprised a relatively small portion of South Korea's international debt: private non-guaranteed debt totaled 26.9 percent of the country's private external debt. Figures 5.1 to 5.4 illustrate South Korea's private debt composition from 1983 to 1997 along each of these key dimensions, as well as how these compare with the equivalent metrics for Mexico over the same time period.

These charts illustrate two key differences in patterns of financial globalization for South Korea and Mexico. First, G-5 countries' domestic financial interests in these countries shifted markedly over time. In the 1980s G-5 bank exposure to Mexico was more than twice what it was to South Korea, and (after 1984) more evenly distributed (figures 5.1 and 5.2). As a result, G-5 preferences in favor of IMF lending to Mexico were both more intense and less heterogeneous. By the mid-1990s, however, the situation had dramatically reversed. G-5 banks were now substantially more exposed to South Korea than Mexico overall, and this bank exposure was far more evenly distributed. These differences, as discussed in further detail below, help to explain the substantial changes in IMF lending policies to both countries.

Second, as figure 5.3 illustrates, bond financing played a much larger role in both Mexico and South Korea in the 1990s. Nearly all Mexico's private external debt shifted from bank lending to bond

[1] Constant 2000 dollars. Data taken from World Bank (2006b).

[2] By comparison, as noted above, US banks held 62 percent of G-5 claims on Mexico in 1983.

Figure 5.1 Total G-5 commercial bank exposure to South Korea and Mexico, 1983–97
Source: BIS, consolidated international banking statistics, 2006.

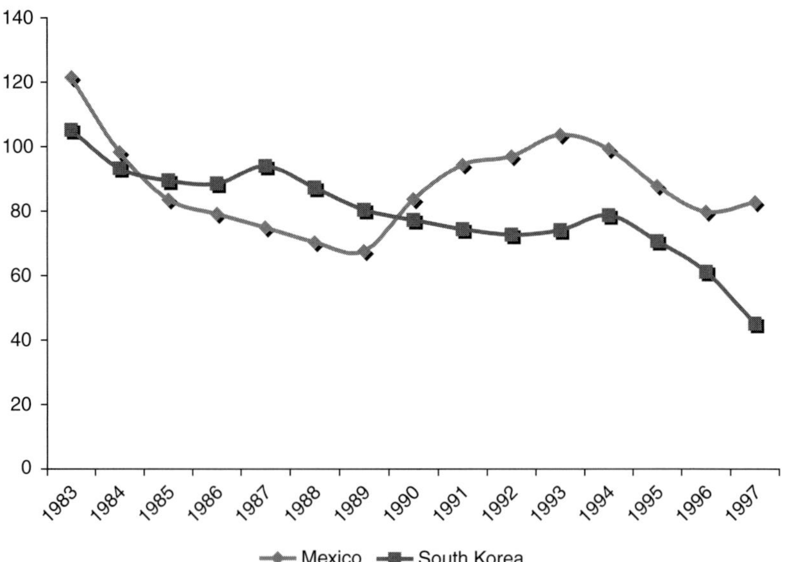

Figure 5.2 Coefficient of variation, G-5 commercial bank exposure to South Korea and Mexico, 1983–97
Source: BIS, consolidated international banking statistics, 2006.

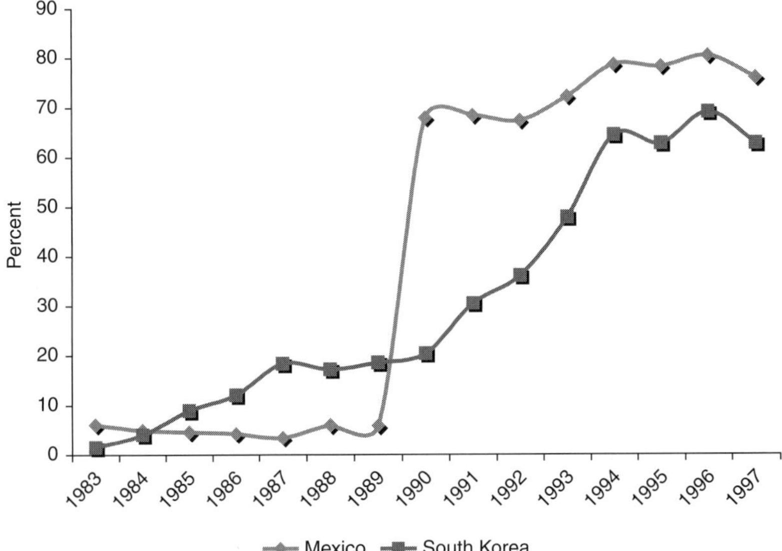

Figure 5.3 Bond debt (as percentage of total long-term private external debt), South Korea and Mexico, 1983–97
Source: BIS, consolidated international banking statistics, 2006.

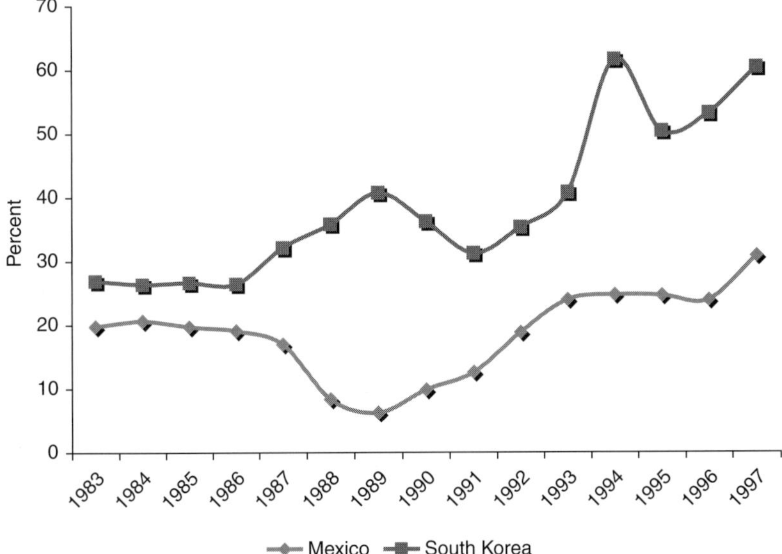

Figure 5.4 Private non-guaranteed debt (as percentage of total private external debt), South Korea and Mexico, 1983–97
Source: BIS, consolidated international banking statistics, 2006.

financing in the aftermath of the Brady Plan: by 1995 nearly all Mexico's external borrowing consisted of sovereign bonds. A similar shift also occurred in South Korea, as the government shifted nearly all its borrowing from bank lending to bond financing and major South Korean multinationals (e.g. Samsung, Hyundai) began issuing their own international bonds.[3] That said, as figure 5.4 demonstrates, commercial bank lending remained critically important to South Korea, even as banking flows to Mexico fell dramatically. Indeed, more than a half of South Korea's private external debt in the mid-1990s consisted of private–private capital flows, the vast majority of which was short-term, interbank financing from G-5 commercial banks to South Korean private financial institutions. In contrast to the 1994/5 Mexican crisis, which was overwhelmingly driven by the behavior of Mexico's sovereign bondholders, this new form of non-sovereign bank lending occupied center stage during the 1997/8 financial crisis in South Korea.

The 1983 stand-by arrangement

From 1963 to 1979 South Korea's GDP grew at over 10 percent per year, real per capita GDP tripled, and the country transformed itself from an agrarian to an industrial society through a successful strategy of export-led development.[4] As part of this strategy, South Korea entered into a series of fourteen one-year stand-by arrangements with the Fund between 1965 and 1982. These programs were largely precautionary: the South Korean government's primary goal was to obtain a seal of approval for its macroeconomic policies that would enable it to borrow more extensively on private international capital markets. In 1979/80 South Korea faced a balance of payments crisis, resulting from high inflation, a decline in export competitiveness due to exchange rate appreciation, and a series of domestic political crises.[5] To manage these problems, South Korea continued to borrow from the IMF under two one-year SBAs (March 1980–February 1982). With

[3] By 1997 46.8 percent ($18.6 billion) of South Korea's bond debt was private non-guaranteed bond debt, while the remainder ($21.2 billion) was South Korean sovereign debt.

[4] "South Korea – staff report for the 1983 Article IV consultation and request for stand-by arrangement," EBS/83/119 (June 8, 1983), 1.

[5] Ibid., 3.

the help of IMF financing, the country boosted exports, cut its fiscal deficit, and successfully reduced inflation to less than 5 percent per year. In addition, the South Korean government managed to reduce the current account deficit in half, to the equivalent of 3.9 percent of GDP, and increased the GDP growth rate to 5.4 percent per year.[6]

In spite of these impressive gains, South Korea still faced the prospect of further adjustment to ensure future growth and long-term debt sustainability. As a result, it entered into negotiations with the Fund over the terms of a new, two-year stand-by arrangement in March 1983. An IMF team headed by Bijan Aghevli visited Seoul during April 15–30, 1983, and negotiated an economic program with the South Korean government.[7] The authorities formally signed and submitted a letter of intent to the IMF on June 3, 1983, with a request for a stand-by arrangement of SDR 575.8 million (2.25 times quota) running to March 31, 1985.[8] The proposed program contained only three performance criteria: a ceiling on the net domestic assets of the banking system, a ceiling on net public sector borrowing from the banking system, and a ceiling on South Korea's outstanding (disbursed) external debt, along with a related sub-ceiling on outstanding short-term external debt.[9]

The IMF staff report, June 8, 1983

The IMF staff's views of South Korea in 1983 clearly illustrate how expectations about private international creditors' future behavior influence the Fund's preferences over the size and terms of its lending arrangements. Since the South Korean government had a strong track record in meeting the conditions of its previous IMF programs and in servicing its external debt, the IMF staff took a very favorable

[6] Ibid., 6. [7] Ibid., 1.

[8] Ibid., attachment 3, 30. Under the terms of the IMF's eighth quota review, completed in March 1983, South Korea's quota was to increase by 80.9 percent to SDR 462.8 billion on November 30, 1983 – a fact noted by both the IMF staff and the executive board during the decision-making process. This quota increase took into account the substantial increase in South Korea's GDP, thereby more accurately reflecting its relative size in the global economy. As a result, by the time South Korea received its first disbursement from the 1983 stand-by arrangement, the program equaled only 1.24 times its new quota.

[9] Ibid., 17.

view of the proposed 1983 program. In the June 8 staff report accompanying its proposal to the executive board, the staff noted South Korea's adjustment efforts and strong performance under the 1980–2 stand-by arrangements. Given its prior record, the staff argued, South Korea fully warranted the Fund's support:

> The staff believes that the program targets and associated policies represent a comprehensive adjustment effort worthy of Fund support. Notwithstanding Korea's ability to borrow in international capital markets, the large balance of payments need of Korea relative to its quota justifies access to Fund resources on the scale proposed. The authorities' record of economic management testifies to their commitment to effectively implement the required policies and attain the objectives of the program.[10]

As expected, the staff's favorable stance toward South Korea was influenced by its expectation that IMF financing would have the desired catalytic effect on private capital inflows: the staff confidently anticipated that South Korea's commercial bank creditors would continue lending to the government over the course of the new Fund program. Since nearly all of South Korea's external financing was provided by G-5 commercial banks with long-term ties to the country, the Fund staff was not especially concerned about moral hazard. Rather, it fully expected that implementation of the policies outlined in the proposed stand-by arrangement by the South Korean government would "bolster Korea's standing in financial markets and enhance its ability to raise the required medium- and long-term loans" to ensure debt sustainability in the future.[11] The staff did express concern, however, about recent increases in South Korea's level of short-term debt (almost 30 percent of the country's total external debt in 1982/3), which had increased the country's "vulnerability to potential disruptions in international capital markets."[12] As part of the new program, the staff therefore insisted that the South Korean government freeze any further short-term borrowing. Its large amount of short-term debt notwithstanding, the staff felt that South Korea's overall external debt situation was sustainable in the long-term: "The level of South Korea's outstanding external debt is consistent with its debt servicing capacity."[13]

[10] Ibid., 19. [11] Ibid. [12] Ibid. [13] Ibid.

Executive board meeting, July 8, 1983

Like the staff, the Fund's member states also took a favorable view of South Korea's request for a new lending arrangement. When the executive board met a month later to consider the proposed stand-by arrangement, A. R. G. Prowse (Australia), the executive director representing ten east Asian/Pacific countries, spoke on behalf of the South Korean government. Echoing the staff's praise of South Korea's past performance, Prowse hailed the country as "one of the most successful economies among Fund members in terms of current and prospective performance."[14] Prowse argued that South Korea had "pursued strong adjustment policies since 1980," and he ascribed the country's need for IMF assistance to "unfavorable external economic conditions ... including recession in important markets, high interest rates, and growing protectionism."[15] Noting South Korea's "outstanding" record of cooperation with the Fund, as well as its rising importance in the world economy, Prowse concluded that the board should approve the country's loan request "without reservation."[16]

In the ensuing discussion, the directors expressed uniform support for the South Korean program. Teruo Hirao (Japan) praised the South Korean government's "wide-ranging adjustment" in 1981–3 that had curbed inflation, reduced the public sector deficit, and liberalized trade.[17] Thomas A. Connors (alternate executive director – United States) remarked that "the Korean authorities had managed the economy exceptionally well." Gerhard Laske (West Germany) noted that South Korea's external debt level was already high (its outstanding debt was the fourth largest among developing countries), but, "given the country's record and the prudent policies adopted by the authorities, he had no reason to seriously question South Korea's ability to manage the debt burden."[18] Although several directors, including Laske, Christopher Taylor (alternate executive director – United Kingdom) and Hirao worried that South Korea's relatively high level of short-term debt left it vulnerable to the volatility of global capital markets, each offered his clear support for approval of the stand-by arrangement.[19] Thus, the G-5 executive directors broadly shared the

[14] Minutes of EBM/83/99 (July 8, 1983), 3.
[15] Ibid., 6. [16] Ibid., 7. [17] Ibid., 9. [18] Ibid., 11. [19] Ibid., 10–12.

Fund staff's confidence in South Korea's economic prospects and enthusiasm for the proposed stand-by arrangement.

Despite this broad general support for the staff's proposal, the board debated whether South Korea's debt and macroeconomic situation was actually *too strong* to warrant continued Fund support. Both Laske and Michael Casey (Ireland) wondered whether South Korea in fact needed all the financing it had requested, given its good standing in private international capital markets. Casey noted that South Korea "had relatively sizeable access to medium-term and long-term commercial bank credit," which should allow it to continue servicing its external debts and accumulating reserves. In other words, the need for IMF financing to generate a catalytic effect on private capital markets was unclear, given that South Korea already seemed to be a private borrower in good standing. As a result, Casey "was not fully convinced that South Korea really needed to make such a significant drawing under the stand-by arrangement."[20]

Taylor raised similar concerns about the wisdom of committing the IMF's scarce resources to a country that could access private international capital markets even without the benefit of IMF catalytic financing. In his view, South Korea's excellent track record with the IMF, its strong macroeconomic policy program, and its ongoing "ability to raise finances on the international capital markets" suggested that "perhaps their need of Fund resources was not as great as that of potential other candidates."[21] In addition, Taylor wondered whether the IMF's extended support of South Korea – the country had entered fourteen arrangements over the previous eighteen years – remained justified given "the heavy pressures being exerted on the Fund's liquidity position at the present time."[22] Although he stopped short of recommending that the Fund refuse the loan, Taylor hoped that South Korea would not need to draw on the finances fully, so that they might be directed to "countries whose need might be greater," such as the crisis countries in Latin America.[23]

Speaking on behalf of the IMF staff, D. K. Palmer, the associate director of the Exchange and Trade Relations Department, downplayed the directors' concerns. Responding to Taylor's concerns about lending scarce IMF resources to a country currently able to borrow on private markets, Palmer noted that IMF lending would cover only a very

[20] Ibid., 11. [21] Ibid., 14. [22] Ibid. [23] Ibid.

small portion (one-tenth) of South Korea's balance of payments deficit during the two years of the stand-by arrangement. Citing inconclusive discussions between the Fund staff and commercial banks about new syndicated lending to the country, Palmer also cautioned the directors not to overestimate South Korea's ability to access sufficient private financing to continue servicing its debts.[24] Ultimately, he argued, "it was uncertain whether Korea could obtain the financing, and it was important for the Fund to support the proposed program in order to give confidence to the international capital markets."[25] From the staff's perspective, continued IMF liquidity was necessary as a signal to private creditors that would catalyze new bank lending and guarantee South Korea's future access to international capital markets.

In the end, the board unanimously approved the 1983 South Korean stand-by arrangement. The executive directors' concerns about South Korea's financial need notwithstanding, the Fund's member states ultimately expressed little opposition to the new program. Given South Korea's strong record under its previous IMF programs, private international creditors' ongoing willingness to lend to the country, and the relatively small size of the proposed new Fund loan, the directors were not particularly concerned about moral hazard. They had few qualms about the loan, therefore, and they did not question the fact that the proposed program contained quite limited conditionality. In addition, since the G-5 countries had relatively weak financial ties to South Korea – at least compared to their commercial banks' extremely sizable exposure to Mexico and the other Latin American countries during the ongoing debt crisis – they had little reason to press the staff and other member states for a larger lending package. In short, the liquidity/moral hazard trade-off was mitigated by South Korea's strong economic performance and the relative lack of intense G-5 domestic financial interests. Ultimately, the combination of South Korea's relatively solid economic position and its somewhat lesser importance for the G-5 resulted in the approval of a modest IMF loan with limited conditionality.

South Korea's subsequent performance under the 1983 program justified the Fund's continued support. As the Fund staff reported in its 1985 review of the 1983–5 program, the South Korean government fully implemented the loan's conditions: "All performance criteria were

[24] Ibid., 20. [25] Ibid.

observed and policy measures were taken as planned; South Korea made all purchases envisaged under the stand-by arrangement."[26] As a result of its successful adjustment, South Korea enjoyed sustained GDP growth of 5 to 10 percent per year from 1981 to 1985, while reducing inflation from over 30 percent to under 10 percent. Furthermore, the government reduced its budget deficit from the equivalent of 4.5 percent of GDP in 1981 to under 1.5 percent in 1984, and the country's overall balance of payments deficit fell from $2.7 billion in 1981 to less than $1.5 billion in 1984.[27] Commenting on these achievements, the Fund staff praised the South Korean government and described the 1983–5 stand-by arrangement as "a classic adjustment program."[28] Indeed, for the IMF staff, the 1983 loan illustrated the best-case scenario: the Fund's liquidity and conditionality reassured market actors of South Korea's future stability and ensured the continued flow of private financing to the country.

The 1985 stand-by arrangement

Despite the success of the 1983 IMF loan, South Korea's external debt levels remained largely unchanged in 1985: the country's ratio of external debt to GDP declined only from 23.7 percent to 20.6 percent, its ratio of debt service to exports fell only slightly from 22.8 percent to 21.6 percent, and its reserve levels remained essentially unchanged from 1983. Although South Korea continued to attract private international lending from commercial banks, it remained vulnerable to potential debt servicing problems. Therefore, when the 1983 stand-by arrangement expired on March 31, 1985, the government requested a new twenty-month stand-by for SDR 280 million (0.61 times quota). The accompanying economic program included the same three performance criteria as in the 1983 program: a ceiling on net credit to the public sector from the banking system, a ceiling on the net domestic assets of the banking system, and a ceiling on outstanding external debt (with a related sub-ceiling on outstanding short-term external debt).[29] In its background report to the executive board, the Fund staff once again endorsed South Korea's adjustment

[26] "South Korea – staff report for the 1985 Article IV consultation and request for stand-by arrangement," EBS/85/151 (June 14, 1985), 3.

[27] Ibid., 4–5. [28] Ibid., 17. [29] Ibid., 23.

policies and expressed continued optimism about the country's prospects for medium-term debt sustainability: "The external service burden remains manageable, and adherence to the policies underlying the adjustment effort should ensure that ... Korea enjoys continued adequate access to international financial markets."[30]

As in 1983, the IMF staff paid close attention to the expected behavior of South Korea's private creditors as it designed the new program. Although the proposed stand-by arrangement was modest in size, the staff believed that it would "convey to the international financial markets a clear and objective signal" to private creditors of South Korea's creditworthiness; indeed, the staff designed the program on the assumption that the IMF's resources would be coupled with "sizeable external borrowing (some $10 billion)" from private creditors over the course of the twenty-month SBA.[31] As two years ealier, the staff's confidence that a relatively small IMF loan would have a catalytic effect on private markets was bolstered by the composition of South Korea's international creditors: 95.2 percent of the country's debt was owed to commercial banks, with banks from the G-5 countries holding 77 percent of this debt. Since the commercial banks were few in number and held extensive long-term ties to South Korea, the staff did not expect the government to face serious difficulties in negotiating new syndicated bank loans, nor did the staff fear that the banks would "cut and run" once the new IMF loan had been disbursed. Thus, given South Korea's relatively strong macroeconomic situation and its continued good standing with both the IMF and private creditors, the staff favorably recommended the new stand-by arrangement for approval by the executive board.

Executive board meeting, July 12, 1985

As in 1983, the executive board also broadly supported South Korea's request for a new lending arrangement. Overall, the executive directors "commended the Korean authorities for their decisive economic management, which had yielded impressive results in the economy."[32]

[30] Ibid., 30. [31] Ibid., 13.

[32] Minutes of EBM/85/105 (July 12, 1985); quoted in minutes of EBM/85/187 (December 27, 1985).

The G-5 directors, in particular, favorably endorsed the proposed program. Hirotake Fujino (Japan) "expressed his deep appreciation of the [South Korean] authorities' efforts to implement successfully their far-reaching adjustment policy."[33] Likewise, Charles Dallara (United States) praised South Korea's "impressive adjustment effort" and enthusiastically supported approval of the stand-by arrangement, although he did express concern about the prolonged use of resources by countries (such as South Korea) that still enjoyed adequate access to private international financing.[34]

For the G-5 countries, the 1985 South Korean loan – like its 1983 predecessor – did not present much of a conflict between protecting their own domestic financial interests and achieving the Fund's twin institutional goals of maintaining international financial stability and assisting its member states. Since the two South Korean loans were relatively small in size (in both absolute and per quota terms), G-5 governments were less worried about the moral hazard risk from IMF lending. In addition, since G-5 commercial banks were far less exposed to South Korea than to Mexico, the Fund's principals had less incentive to push for the use of additional IMF liquidity. Finally, since the South Korean economy (with a GDP of $93.2 billion) was less than half the size of Mexico ($184.3 billion), IMF and G-5 concerns about systemic instability were diminished. That said, these concerns were not entirely eliminated, since G-5 banks had lent more only to Mexico ($46.2 billion) and Brazil ($46.7 billion), and only Mexico, Brazil, Iran, and China exceeded South Korea's size (in GDP terms) among developing countries in 1985.

In short, the combination of South Korea's limited financial need, the smaller size of its economy, and the commercial banks' reduced exposure once again mitigated the liquidity/moral hazard trade-off for the G-5 countries, just as the clear availability of private financing had alleviated the IMF staff's worries about providing new financing to South Korea. Whereas IMF lending to Mexico had been very controversial and the G-5 countries had exerted their influence to ensure that the Fund provided oversized rescue packages to the Mexican government, the Fund's loans to South Korea in 1983 and 1985 were very much "business as usual," with the board approving the IMF staff's proposal with few objections. Ultimately, the 1983 and 1985 IMF programs helped South Korea to manage its balance of payments difficulties and resume its successful economic development. After running current

[33] Ibid., 6. [34] Ibid., 17.

account deficits from 1978 to 1985, South Korea ran a significant current account surplus from 1986 to 1988.[35] Economic growth, which had fallen into single digits in 1984 and 1985, surged once again to 10.6 percent in 1986 and 11.1 percent in 1987.[36] As rapid growth resumed, South Korea's external debt level fell sharply, from the equivalent of 21.7 percent of GDP in 1985 to 10.5 percent by 1989, even though the country continued to borrow extensively from commercial banks on world markets. In December 1989 South Korea repaid the final installment of its outstanding IMF debt, and it would not seek financing from the Fund again until the 1997/8 Asian financial crisis.[37]

In contrast to the IMF's loans to Mexico during the height of the 1980s Latin American debt crisis, the South Korean programs in 1983 and 1985 represent cases of IMF lending under more "normal" macroeconomic circumstances to a country facing more modest balance of payments problems with less serious implications for the overall stability of the global financial system. As a result, both the amount of IMF credit and the accompanying conditionality were more modest in comparison to the 1980s Mexican programs. Accordingly, the South Korean loans generated far less debate and concern within the executive board – and, in particular, among the G-5 directors – than the much larger Mexican loans in 1983, 1986, and 1989. In summary, the political and economic tensions that had been central in the debates about IMF lending to Mexico were far more muted in the 1983 and 1985 South Korean episodes, and the Fund's decision-making process was far less politicized in these latter cases. As we will see below, however, this would change significantly by the 1990s, when the Asian financial crisis threatened both the international financial system as a whole and the domestic financial stability of the Fund's principals.

The 1997 IMF package

South Korea's debt composition, 1996/7

Following its balance of payments problems in the 1980s, the South Korean economy resumed its rapid upward trajectory in economic

[35] World Bank (2005). South Korea's current account deficit in 1983 had been equivalent to –1.8 percent of GDP; in 1988 its surplus was 7.7 percent of GDP.

[36] Ibid.

[37] Maggie Ford, "South Korea emerges as fully fledged economic power," *Financial Times*, January 11, 1989.

growth and development. South Korea's impressive economic performance continued into the 1990s, as GDP and GDP per capita growth remained in the high single digits from 1989 to 1997. By the mid-1990s South Korea's external debt had risen to $137 billion, the third largest among emerging market countries behind Mexico ($149 billion) and Brazil ($198 billion). As in the 1980s, though, South Korea's debt levels were modest in relation to the overall size of its economy: external debt totaled the equivalent of only 25 percent of GDP, while the country's ratio of debt service to exports had declined from 21.6 percent in 1985 to 8.2 percent in 1997. The Bank of Korea's foreign exchange reserves levels had also strengthened since the 1980s, rising from one month of imports in 1985 to 1.4 in 1997. These debt levels, which were quite modest compared to Mexico's in 1995, were largely the result of the continued massive growth in the South Korean economy. From 1985 to 1997 GDP rose from $93.7 billion to $557.6 billion, while GDP per capita more than doubled from $4,388 to $10,069.[38]

As with Mexico, changes in the composition of private international capital flows had significantly altered South Korea's external debt composition by the mid-1990s (table 5.1). Sovereign bonds had largely replaced bank lending as the South Korean government's primary source of private external financing. By 1997 bondholders held 69.1 percent of South Korea's private external debt, compared to 4.1 percent in 1985, and sovereign bond issues had effectively replaced medium-term syndicated lending as the government's primary source of new external financing. Despite this shift toward bond financing, the commercial banks had not severed their ties to South Korea. Rather, they had shifted away from long-term sovereign lending and become a key source of short-term external financing for private financial institutions and firms in the country. In 1997 this private non-guaranteed debt accounted for a majority (53.2 percent) of South Korea's overall private external debt, more than double the 26.4 percent it had been in 1985. Thus, in marked contrast to Mexico, where the country's private external debt in the mid-1990s consisted largely of sovereign bonds, both sovereign bond financing and non-sovereign bank lending now constituted important types of international capital flows to South Korea.

[38] Constant 2000 dollars. World Bank (2005).

Table 5.1 *Key data: IMF lending to South Korea, 1983–97*

Date of IMF lending arrangement	7/8/83	7/12/85	12/4/97
G-5 bank exposure ($ billions)	20.8	22	68.5
Coefficient of variation, G-5 bank exposure	105.2	89.5	45.1
US share, G-5 bank exposure	0.55	0.40	0.22
UK share, G-5 bank exposure	0.12	0.09	0.10
Japanese share, G-5 bank exposure	0.20	0.37	0.33
German share, G-5 bank exposure	0.04	0.03	0.15
French share, G-5 bank exposure	0.08	0.09	0.16
Percent bond debt	1.5	4.1	69.1
Percent private non-guaranteed debt	26.9	26.4	53.2
GDP ($ billions)	76.9	93.7	557.6
External debt/GDP (%)	23.7	20.6	25.0
Short-term debt/reserves	1.8	1.2	5.7
IMF loan size (SDR billions)	0.58	0.28	15.5
IMF loan size (amount/quota)	1.24	0.61	19.38
IMF loan size (amount/GDP)	0.008	0.003	0.028
Number of performance criteria	3	3	3
Number of prior actions	0	0	0
Number of benchmarks/targets	0	1	7
Outstanding IMF debt (amount/quota)	3.01	3.45	0
G-5 UN voting affinity (mean "S" score)[1]	N/A	N/A	0.43
Coefficient of variation, G-5 "S" scores[1]	N/A	N/A	18.0
IMF liquidity ratio (%)	0.36	0.42	0.29
Quota review in progress?	No	Yes	Yes
Country's IMF quota (SDR millions)	462.8	462.8	799.6

Notes: Data for 1983 and 1985 are lagged one year; data for the 1997 loan are not lagged, since the loan was extended in late December.

[1] South Korea joined the United Nations in 1991.

This surge in private–private lending to South Korean financial institutions significantly increased the commercial banks' exposure to South Korea, even though they no longer engaged in medium-term syndicated lending to the government. Indeed, G-5 commercial banks' claims on South Korea tripled from $22 billion in 1985 to $68.5 billion in 1997, even as bank lending declined as a proportion of South Korea's total external debt. By contrast, G-5 bank exposure to Mexico declined from $51.6 billion in 1986 to $39.9 billion in 1997. In comparison to Mexico, G-5 bank exposure to South Korea was also far more evenly distributed in the mid-1990s; the coefficient of variation on G-5 bank exposure in Mexico in 1995 was 87.8, while it was only 45.1 in South Korea in 1997. Nonetheless, substantial differences remained in individual G-5 exposure. Whereas US banks had been the primary G-5 lenders to South Korea in the 1980s, Japanese banks were now the most highly exposed ($23.2 billion); four major Japanese commercial banks were South Korea's largest private international creditors, while two more ranked in the top ten most highly exposed institutions. Nevertheless, banks in the United States ($16.0 billion), France ($11.6 billion), and Germany ($10.4 billion) had also lent sizeable amounts to South Korean financial institutions. British banks, with only $7.2 billion in claims, were relatively under exposed to South Korea compared to their European counterparts, although their exposure in absolute terms was much larger than it had been to Mexico in 1994 ($4.5 billion). All told, roughly 200 international banks held claims on South Korea, although thirteen of the world's largest money-center banks held nearly 40 percent of the total short-term interbank debt.[39] In sum, by the mid-1990s G-5 domestic financial interests in South Korea were both more intense and more homogeneous than in Mexico.

The Asian financial crisis hits South Korea

From a macroeconomic perspective, South Korea's economy appeared robust in 1997. GDP growth had exceeded 7 percent in each of the three previous years, inflation stood at only 4 percent through the third quarter of the year, and the current account deficit was projected to be equivalent to only 3 percent of GDP. This strong aggregate performance masked serious structural problems in South Korea's

[39] Peter Lee, "Korea stares into the abyss," *Euromoney*, March 1998. These banks were Citibank, Bank of America, Chase Manhattan, J. P. Morgan, Bank of Nova Scotia, Bank of Tokyo-Mitsubishi, Sanwa Bank, Deutsche Bank, Commerzbank, Westdeutsche Landesbank, Société Générale, HSBC, and SBC Warburg Dillon Read (Kim and Byeon 2001).

financial system, however. Many of South Korea's industrial conglomerates (chaebol) had accumulated large amounts of short-term debt by borrowing extensively from South Korea's banks, which had in turn borrowed massive amounts on the international interbank markets following the liberalization of short-term capital flows in the mid-1990s. Fueled by these large-scale capital inflows from international commercial banks, the chaebol had leveraged themselves heavily in continued pursuit of growth: by the mid-1990s the average publicly traded South Korean company owed debts in excess of 400 percent of shareholder equity.[40] Thus, despite South Korea's impressive macroeconomic performance, the country's financial system rested on extremely shaky foundations.

In mid-1997 a combination of domestic and international shocks triggered South Korea's crisis. Domestically, several major private institutions faced severe financial difficulties. In June Kia Group sought emergency loans from the South Korean Development Bank to avert bankruptcy, while Seoul Bank applied to the Bank of Korea for special loans when it faced problems borrowing abroad.[41] In August, after several more South Korean banks had revealed major financial problems, the Korean government announced that it would ensure the payment of all foreign debt liabilities by South Korean private financial institutions.[42] As a result of this policy change, which transformed the interbank debt of South Korean firms into de facto short-term sovereign debt, the South Korean government's immediate debt service obligations increased substantially.

These domestic financial difficulties were exacerbated by the spread of international financial instability throughout east Asia beginning in mid-1997. Speculative attacks on the Thai currency, the baht, forced Thailand to seek IMF financing, which was approved in August. In October the Hong Kong stock market crashed, and both Hong Kong and Taiwan suffered speculative attacks on their currencies. South Korea's international investors, already concerned about the stability of the country's banks and corporations, to which they had lent substantially, feared that South Korea might be the next east Asian country to be hit by financial

[40] Blustein (2001). [41] Independent Evaluation Office [IEO] (2003, 118).
[42] Ibid.

contagion. These concerns triggered substantial capital flight by South Korea's international investors in the fall of 1997. Capital outflows intensified in October and November, after Moody's had downgraded the credit ratings of several South Korean banks and Standard and Poor's had downgraded the South Korean government's sovereign rating.[43] On November 7 South Korean newspapers reported that the government faced foreign exchange shortages and had begun discussions with the IMF about a rescue package. After initial denials, Kang Kyung-shik, the minister of finance and economy, announced South Korea's intention to seek an IMF loan on November 21.[44]

Negotiating the IMF package, November–December 1997

Despite its denials of the media reports, the South Korean government had already begun discussions with the IMF prior to the November 21 announcement. The IMF managing director, Michel Camdessus, had traveled secretly to South Korea on November 16 to meet with Kang Kyung-shik and Lee Kyung-shik, the central bank governor.[45] These talks yielded an agreement in principle that South Korea would seek IMF assistance on the order of approximately $30 billion.[46] On November 26 Hubert Neiss, director of the IMF's Asia and Pacific Department, arrived with his team to begin the formal negotiations over the terms of the Fund program.[47] As the negotiations progressed, however, it soon became clear that South Korea's problems were worse than the IMF had initially anticipated. On paper, South Korea held $30 billion in foreign exchange reserves – more than enough to cover the country's short-term debt payments for several months until a Fund program could be arranged. $19 billion of these reserves were already deposited at overseas bank branches, however, to cover the repayments on the short-term interbank debt that the South Korean government had

[43] Ibid.

[44] Nicholas Kristof, "Seoul plans to ask the IMF for a minimum of $20 million," *New York Times*, November 22, 1997, A1.

[45] Blustein (2001); Zhang (2001).

[46] Blustein (2001, 129).

[47] Nicholas Reynolds, "South Korea faces more pain, say analysts," *South China Morning Post* (Hong Kong), November 27, 1997, 14.

assumed in August.[48] In addition to these repayments, South Korea also required approximately $12 billion per month in reserves to pay for its imports. South Korea's need for IMF financing was, therefore, both extremely large and immediate. On December 3, after tense negotiations, the IMF and South Korea agreed to a $55 billion rescue package.[49] With South Korea continuing to face large-scale capital outflows, Camdessus scheduled an emergency board meeting the next day to secure immediate approval and disbursement of the Korean stand-by arrangement.[50]

Under the terms of the proposed program, the IMF would provide SDR 15.5 billion ($21 billion) under a stand-by arrangement over the course of three years. The loan, at 19.38 times South Korea's Fund quota, would be, by far, the largest ever as a percentage of a country's quota in the history of the IMF. South Korea's quota in 1997 was inordinately small relative to the size of its economy, however; as a share of the borrower's GDP, the program was actually slightly smaller than the 1995 Mexican package (4.0 percent of GDP for South Korea, compared to 4.6 percent of GDP for Mexico).[51] In comparison to the 1983 and 1985 South Korean IMF loans, the 1997 package also contained more extensive conditionality: the program's letter of intent specified three performance criteria, but also included seven additional benchmarks and indicative targets. The first two PCs set a ceiling on net domestic assets for the Bank of Korea, and a floor for its international reserves.[52] The third PC set a floor for the interest rate at which the Bank of Korea could lend to South Korean commercial banks.[53] The additional benchmarks consisted of a series of measures

[48] IEO (2003, 113).

[49] Ibid., 118. See Blustein (2001) for an account of the negotiations.

[50] "Camdessus welcomes conclusions of talks with South Korea on IMF program," *News Brief* 97/27, International Monetary Fund, December 3, 1997 (www.imf.org/external/np/sec/nb/1997/nb9727.htm).

[51] Roubini and Setser (2004, 125). This discrepancy between South Korea's IMF quota and its GDP was the result of the country's very rapid growth from 1985 to 1997. During the 1998 quota review the problem was partially rectified, as South Korea's quota was raised from SDR 799.6 million to SDR 1,633.6. As a share of this larger, more accurate quota, the 1997 South Korean package equaled 9.49 times quota. It was therefore still the largest IMF loan as a percentage of quota in the Fund's history.

[52] "Korea – memorandum on the economic program," December 3, 1997 (www.imf.org/external/np/loi/120397.htm).

[53] Ibid., annex D.

aimed at reforming South Korea's monetary and financial supervisory policies, in order to avoid the excessive international borrowing by private financial institutions that was the root cause of the current crisis. These reforms included granting greater independence to the central bank, consolidating bank supervision, the publishing of foreign exchange reserve data, and passing new legislation mandating that South Korean firms provide consolidated financial statements certified by external auditors (as in the advanced industrial economies).[54]

In addition to the IMF's resources and the proposed conditionality, the South Korean rescue package also included substantial tandem financing from the multilateral development banks: the World Bank contributed $10 billion in aid, while the Asian Development Bank (ADB) provided $4 billion. The package also included $20 billion in bilateral funding, which would be provided by bilateral credits should South Korea require additional assistance; Japan pledged $10 billion to this "second line of defense," while the United States promised $5 billion and the United Kingdom pledged $1.25 billion.[55] The magnitude of this bilateral financing correlated closely with the extent of G-5 financial exposure to South Korea. Thus, the Japanese and the Americans contributed markedly larger amounts than their less exposed European counterparts.

The IMF staff report and executive board approval, December 3–4, 1997

The inclusion of this "second line of defense" financing as part of the $55 billion IMF-led rescue package was a major point of contention between the Fund staff and the G-5 governments. Initially, Neiss's team in South Korea had designed the IMF program with two key assumptions: (1) that the "second line of defense" bilateral financing commitments were firmly in place and would be fully drawn by South Korea; and (2) that nearly all (80 percent) of South Korea's short-term creditors would "cut and run" in the immediate aftermath of the loan's disbursement.[56] As the staff team in Seoul worked through the night of December 3 to prepare the staff report for the

[54] Ibid., annex E.
[55] John Burton, "South Korea gets $55 billion rescue package," *Financial Times*, December 4, 1997.
[56] IEO (2003, 113).

next day's emergency executive board meeting, however, it was informed by Bijan Aghevli, deputy director of the Asia and Pacific Department, that the G-5 countries would not approve a Fund program that explicitly committed them to provide $20 billion in bilateral financing.[57] In particular, the US Treasury, still facing criticism by and opposition from Congress over the Mexican bailout in 1995, was reluctant to utilize its Exchange Stabilization Fund a second time for international lender of last resort purposes. Although Treasury officials insisted that the United States would provide the resources if necessary, they hoped that the IMF/World Bank financing, on its own, would be sufficient to resolve the South Korean crisis and would provide them political cover. As one key aide to Robert Rubin, the US Treasury secretary, later admitted: "It [the "second line of defense"] was an experiment in trying to make something look as real as possible without ultimately having to spend the money. It had a sort of Catch-22 quality to it: if you don't need the money, you don't get it. And if you do need it, then you probably haven't met the conditions for disbursal."[58]

The G-5 countries' reluctance to provide the "second line of defense" financing clearly illustrates how the Fund's largest shareholders wrestle with competing domestic pressures when making decisions about IMF lending policies. On the one hand, G-5 governments – especially the United States and Japan, whose commercial banks were most highly exposed, with 55 percent of total G-5 bank exposure to South Korea – had strong incentives to support the IMF loan and the "second line of defense" bilateral financing. With their commercial banks highly vulnerable to further instability in Korea, a default could have had severe negative effects on G-5 domestic financial stability, perhaps even threatening the solvency of one or more major financial institutions. On the other hand, the United States and other G-5 governments wanted to avoid the criticism of voters and their representatives at home, who would surely view yet another major IMF bailout as "welfare for banks" at the expense of taxpayers' domestic interests.[59] Faced with two equally unpalatable choices – refusing to provide the "second line of defense" needed to avert a South Korean default, or supporting the IMF rescue package

[57] Blustein (2001, 178–9). [58] Quoted in ibid., 179.
[59] Broz (2005, 2002).

and confronting political opposition at home – the United States and its G-5 counterparts pressured the IMF staff to design a new program that would convince the markets of South Korea's solvency while eliminating the need for the "second line of defense" financing.

Faced with this direct last-minute pressure from the Fund's largest shareholders, Aghevli and the Seoul negotiating team had little choice but to redesign the program. Under the rules of the IMF, the board would not be allowed to approve a program that was not "fully financed" – i.e. that showed a country would lack sufficient resources to service its external debt even after the IMF provided assistance. Therefore, if the $20 billion in bilateral financing could not be included in the overall package, South Korea would need to find the money somewhere else. With only hours left before the executive board meeting, the IMF staff reached a makeshift "solution": they changed the staff report's assumption of a 20 percent rollover rate by Korea's short-term creditors to 80 percent.[60] As the Fund's own Independent Evaluation Office later reported in its post-crisis review of the IMF's role in South Korea, this change in the expected rollover rate was "arbitrary," reflecting not the staff's actual expectations but, rather, the need to present the board with a program the next day that was fully financed.[61]

This episode clearly illustrates both the influence of G-5 governments and the limits of staff autonomy in high-profile IMF lending cases. Ultimately, the South Korean staff team had little choice but to bend to this pressure from the Fund's major shareholders and modify the program's assumptions. That said, the staff made clear its skepticism about the program's prospects in its report to the board: "It is difficult to estimate with any certainty the likely development in capital flows over the program period, given the uncertainty surrounding the rolling over of private sector short-term debt."[62] In effect, this was a polite way for the staff to articulate its pessimism about the catalytic effect of the proposed lending package, as well as its serious concerns about the dangers of moral hazard associated with large-scale IMF lending to South Korea in the absence of financing commitments from either official or private creditors. As noted, the staff expected the majority of South Korea's short-term creditors to "cut and run" in

[60] IEO (2003, 113); Blustein (2001, 180). [61] IEO (2003, 113).
[62] Quoted in Blustein (2001, 180).

the immediate aftermath of the Fund loan, as evidenced by its initial assumption of a 20 percent rollover rate. Under severe pressure from the G-5 countries and Camdessus to send a proposal to the board in time for the next day's meeting, however, Aghevli and his team in Seoul had no alternative but to present a "financing scenario" in which South Korea could fully service its external debt under an IMF program without the "second line of defense."[63]

The next day the executive board approved the proposed stand-by arrangement, and the Fund immediately disbursed SDR 4.1 billion ($5.56 billion) to the South Korean government. Although the "second line of defense" had not been formally included in the program, the IMF press release announced that a package of $55 billion – including the additional bilateral money – had been approved:

> [A] number of countries (Australia, Belgium, Canada, France, Germany, Italy, Japan, the Netherlands, Sweden, Switzerland, the United Kingdom, and the United States) have informed the IMF that *they are prepared*, in the event that unanticipated adverse external circumstances create the need for additional resources to supplement Korea's reserves and resources made available by the IMF and other international institutions, *to consider* – while Korea remains in compliance with the IMF credit arrangement – *making available supplemental financing* in support of Korea's program with the IMF. This second line of defense *is expected to be* in excess of US$20 billion.[64]

This ambiguous statement provided the G-5 governments and the other advanced industrialized countries with the necessary cover to satisfy their competing domestic political interests. To South Korea's commercial bank creditors, G-5 officials could claim that the IMF was offering the country $55 billion in resources – an amount that would ensure its external debt sustainability and avert a default. To voters at home, however, these same officials could announce that they had avoided spending taxpayer dollars on a costly bailout for another emerging market country. Of course, this tenuous balance between liquidity and moral hazard could be achieved only if the Fund program worked – that is,

[63] IEO (2003, 113).
[64] "IMF approves SDR 15.5 billion stand-by credit for Korea," *Press Release* 97/55, International Monetary Fund, December 4, 1997 (www.imf.org/external/np/sec/pr/1997/pr9755.htm) (emphasis added).

if the logic of catalytic financing held and South Korea's private international creditors did indeed roll over their existing claims and continue to provide financing in the weeks and months ahead.

Not surprisingly, the markets were less than convinced by the IMF's announcement, and the Fund staff's skepticism about international creditors' willingness to roll over their short-term claims on South Korea was quickly vindicated. Initially, the markets responded positively to the IMF program announcement: the South Korean won appreciated 2.5 percent and the South Korean stock market rose by 15 percent in the week following the loan's approval. When *Chosun Ilbo*, a major South Korean newspaper, leaked a copy of the December 3 IMF staff report on December 8, however – the report containing the staff's initial 20 percent rollover assumption – South Korea's international investors began to grasp the full severity of the country's liquidity problems.[65] Specifically, they recognized that South Korea would not be able to meets its short-term external debt obligations unless the "second line of defense" financing was truly available to supplement the IMF and World Bank's commitments. Fearing a default, the country's interbank creditors called in their claims and sought to flee the country as quickly as possible. Within a day, the Bank of Korea was flooded with requests from South Korean banks needing reserves to pay international creditors who had refused to roll over their short-term claims. Over the next two weeks the won went into free fall, losing 10 percent per day from December 8–12, and the central bank's foreign exchange reserves dwindled rapidly.[66] Market actors clearly had not bought into the elaborate fiction of the "second line of defense," and South Korea would soon have to default on its remaining external debt unless private capital outflows could be reversed.[67]

Concerted lending revived: the commercial banks' rollover agreement

With a South Korean default imminent and the "second line of defense" still not explicitly available, officials within the IMF and the

[65] Blustein (2001, 181).

[66] Ibid., 183. "Korean won hits new low," *Toronto Star*, December 9, 1997, D10.

[67] According to Blustein's account, the Bank of Korea calculated that its reserves would be exhausted by December 31, unless Korea received additional assistance. See Blustein (2001, 192).

G-5 governments began debating possible alternatives. Essentially, the Fund and its major shareholders had three options: (1) allow South Korea to default, with potentially massive negative consequences for the global financial system, including the potential failure of one or more G-5 commercial banks; (2) increase the size of the IMF-led rescue package, in the hope that private creditors would cease selling off South Korean debt, while risking the wrath of voters and legislators at home; (3) find a way to explicitly "bail in" South Korea's private creditors by securing their commitment to roll over existing debts and contribute new money along the lines of the concerted lending packages of the 1980s. Both Camdessus and the IMF first managing director, Stanley Fischer, favored the "bail-in" option, and they were supported by several major officials within the G-5 countries, most notably Hans Tietmayer (chairman of the German Bundesbank), Lawrence Summers (deputy US Treasury secretary), and Edwin Truman (director of the US Treasury's International Finance Division), who had been one of Federal Reserve chairman Paul Volcker's chief deputies during the 1980s debt crisis in Latin America.[68]

Noting the similarities of South Korea's debt composition to that of Mexico and other countries in the 1980s – the majority of its short-term debt was held by a limited number of commercial banks located primarily in the G-5 countries – the IMF and G-5 officials argued that a new attempt at concerted lending offered the best chance of averting a South Korean default.[69] Their hope was that the commercial banks would ultimately find it in their long-term interests to roll over their existing claims on South Korea and provide new financing that would enable the country to make its way through the crisis without defaulting. In addition, the IMF executives and their G-5 counterparts, having already committed unprecedented resources to South Korea, desperately wanted to avoid the real and moral hazard costs associated with the "bailout" scenario, in which South Korea's private international creditors escaped without losses while the Fund and its member states were left with the bill.

[68] Blustein (2001, 187–90).

[69] In South Korea's case, this was true of short-term debt, but not debt overall, since a substantial portion of South Korea's debt included long-term, sovereign bond financing. Private non-guaranteed interbank lending comprised a majority of debt coming due immediately, however, as well as the majority of the capital flight.

By December 20, after a week of intensive discussions between the IMF staff and G-5 government officials – and between the IMF, US Treasury and Federal Reserve officials, and representatives of the South Korean government – a consensus emerged in support of pursuing a new round of concerted lending, based largely on the model employed during the Latin American debt crisis in the 1980s.[70] On December 22 William McDonough, the chairman of the Federal Reserve Bank of New York, summoned the top executives of six of the largest US commercial banks to a meeting at the Fed's Wall Street offices.[71] He informed the bankers that South Korea was losing $1 billion in reserves each day and had only $6 billion in reserves left on hand. McDonough then urged the banks to maintain their credit lines to South Korea.[72] Although he made it clear to the banks that the US government would not force them to participate in concerted lending, he also warned them that failure to cooperate would rapidly trigger a South Korean default:

> This is not an official position of the US government. But, let me tell you what my view is, and what I'm advising my colleagues in Washington, which is ... there should be no additional public-sector money for Korea unless you guys reschedule the debt. That's my position. It doesn't mean it will be followed, because it is not yet US policy. But I wanted you to know that, because the flow of funds is such that we're talking about a South Korean default next week if this matter is not resolved.[73]

Later that day Summers informed his G-7 counterparts of McDonough's meeting and urged them to schedule similar meetings with their domestic commercial banks. Over the course of the week such meetings were indeed held, in London at the Bank of England and in Frankfurt at Deutsche Bank headquarters, with the major British and German commercial banks involved in South Korean lending.[74]

On December 23 Fischer and the G-7 deputies held a conference call meeting, at which they agreed on the wording of a statement to

[70] For a complete account of these discussions, see Blustein (2001).

[71] The six banks were J. P. Morgan, Chase Manhattan, Citibank, Bank of America, Bankers Trust, and the Bank of New York. Lee, *Euromoney*, March 1998.

[72] Ibid.

[73] Quoted in Blustein (2001, 196). For a detailed step-by-step account of the banks' negotiations and agreement on debt rescheduling, see Kim and Byeon (2001).

[74] Lee, *Euromoney*, March 1998.

be issued the following day.[75] In the statement, the IMF committed itself to accelerate the disbursement of an additional SDR 1.5 billion ($2 billion) to South Korea, on December 30, while the World Bank and the ADB would do the same with $5 billion of the resources they had originally committed to the December 4 package.[76] In addition, the United States and other major creditor countries that had promised "second line of defense" financing would now pledge to "be prepared to support the disbursement of a substantial portion, $8 billion," of these resources in exchange for South Korea's signature on a revised, more stringent IMF program, which the IMF staff team had already begun to negotiate in Seoul.[77] Nevertheless, the *News Brief* release emphasized that this new bilateral financing would be made available only "in the context of a significant voluntary increase in rollovers or extensions of the maturities of existing claims by international bank creditors on Korean financial institutions."[78]

Before the IMF statement could be released, however, the Fund and its major shareholders needed to secure the banks' participation. To that end, McDonough held a second meeting with the major US bank executives on December 24, at which they formally agreed to negotiate a rescheduling agreement with South Korea. At the Bank of England that same day, the major British banks agreed to roll over their claims up to March 31, 1998, so long as other G-5 commercial banks did the same.[79] With the American and British banks' commitments in hand, the IMF published its press release, even though commitments from major banks in Germany, Japan, and France took several more days to secure. Despite having the largest stake in South Korea among the G-5 countries, the Japanese banks were very reluctant to roll over their claims. These concerns stemmed from worries about their own domestic bad debts and the falling Nikkei index, however, rather than from a lack of interest in South Korea: the Japanese recession of the 1990s and its associated financial problems had already eroded Japanese banks' capital, and their position was that they would roll over their claims only if all other G-5 banks did the same.[80] At the same time, the American and European banks were unlikely to keep

[75] Blustein (2001, 199).

[76] "Korea strengthens economic program; IMF to activate additional financial support," *News Brief* 97/32, International Monetary Fund, December 24, 1997 (www.imf.org/external/np/sec/nb/1997/nb9732.htm).

[77] Ibid. [78] Ibid. [79] Lee, *Euromoney*, March 1998. [80] Ibid.

their pledges if they found out that the Japanese banks would not participate in concerted lending. Thus, both G-5 domestic financial interests and collective action problems among private international creditors played a key role in shaping the dynamics of the rollover negotiations.

Ultimately, it was the intervention of William Rhodes, the same Citibank vice-chairman who had spearheaded the successful concerted lending plans of the 1980s, that succeeded in resolving the banks' collective action problems. Using his long-standing contacts with the major Japanese banks, as well as his relationship with the Japanese vice-minister of finance, Eisuke Sakakibara, Rhodes persuaded the Japanese banks to roll over their claims for two weeks and to send a representative bank to a meeting of South Korea's major creditors at J. P. Morgan's headquarters on December 29.[81] Once the Japanese had agreed to participate, the rest of South Korea's major creditors fell into line. At the December 29 meeting, Rhodes – who acted as chairman – announced that the major banks in each of the G-7 countries had agreed to the rollover plan, although for differing periods.[82] To buy time until a longer-term deal could be reached, Rhodes suggested that the banks extend their rollovers to March 1998: "Based on my experience, that was the minimum amount of time needed to roll out the 1998 maturities to some sort of medium-term deal."[83] The banks agreed and subsequently divided the tasks – much like the Bank Advisory Committee had during the 1980s – of negotiating with the South Korean government and securing cooperation among all of the country's bank creditors once an agreement had been reached.

What followed in the ensuing month looked very much like the process of concerted lending during Mexico's crisis from 1983 to 1989. With Rhodes serving as the key coordinator, the major G-5 money-center banks secured the participation of nearly all South Korea's short-term creditors in the rollover agreement by January 16. After two weeks of intensive negotiations with the South Korean government, the banks agreed to reschedule $22 billion of short-term interbank debt on January 28, 1998. Under the terms of the agreement, the banks exchanged their short-term claims for an equal amount of long-term bonds, fully guaranteed by the government at rates 2.25 to 2.75 percentage points over LIBOR.[84] To facilitate the banks' cooperation,

[81] Ibid. [82] Ibid. [83] Ibid. [84] Kim and Byeon (2001, 48).

the IMF and G-10 central banks established a monitoring system – managed by Edwin Truman of the US Federal Reserve and Matthew Fisher of the Fund – to track how many banks had signed up to the rescheduling agreement.[85] By March 4, 134 banks in thirty-two countries had submitted letters of acceptance amounting to $21.84 billion, or 96.4 percent of the eligible interbank debt coming due on March 16.[86]

Recovery and performance under the 1997 stand-by arrangement

With both the IMF package and new private lending commitments firmly in place, the South Korean crisis soon came to a close. On March 31, 1998, the government formally signed the swap agreement with the banks in Seoul. With the signing of the short-term bank debt rescheduling agreement, South Korea's immediate liquidity problems subsided. With the rollover agreement finalized, the government was able to float a new sovereign bond issue, consisting of $1 billion in five-year bonds and $3 billion in ten-year bonds.[87] After a sharp decline in economic performance in 1998 (GDP fell by 6.7 percent and the unemployment rate nearly tripled to 6.8 percent), South Korean GDP grew by 10.7 percent in 1999, and its foreign exchange reserves increased to $74 billion as private capital inflows resumed. In addition, the won stabilized on foreign exchange markets and the country's current account moved back into surplus. By April 2001 South Korea had made all the scheduled repayments on the commercial bank loans it had exchanged in 1998, and it fully repaid the 1997 IMF package by the end of 2001, well ahead of schedule.

Assessment: global finance and the politics of South Korean IMF lending

As with the IMF's loans to Mexico between 1983 and 1995, the three South Korean lending episodes from 1983 to 1997 provide further evidence in support of the common agency theory of IMF decision-making. Indeed, each of the South Korean cases demonstrates once again that the Fund's behavior is shaped by the intensity and heterogeneity

[85] Blustein (2001, 202). [86] Kim and Byeon (2001, 48).
[87] IEO (2003, 119).

of the domestic financial interests of the G-5 countries, as well as by the IMF staff's expectations about the catalytic effect of Fund lending. In addition, the cases illustrate how G-5 and IMF staff interests have both changed over time in line with shifts in the composition of international capital flows. Each of the components of private debt composition – the amount and distribution of G-5 bank exposure, the identity of the lenders (banks versus bondholders), and the identity of the borrowers (sovereign versus private) – played an important role in shaping the IMF's treatment of South Korea in 1983, 1985, and 1997. In contrast, the evidence in support of other economic and political factors affecting IMF lending decisions is less convincing.

G-5 preference intensity and heterogeneity: the importance of commercial bank exposure

As in the Mexican case and the statistical analysis, South Korea's experience with the Fund during the 1980s and 1990s clearly illustrates that the intensity and heterogeneity of interests among the IMF's principals heavily influences its lending decisions. Specifically, changes in the level and distribution of G-5 commercial bank exposure played a key role in determining the size and terms of South Korea's IMF programs. Although South Korea was the third largest commercial bank borrower among emerging market countries in the mid-1980s ($22 billion in G-5 bank loans in 1985), G-5 commercial banks were significantly more exposed to the crises in Mexico ($51.5 billion in loans) and Brazil ($46.7 billion). This discrepancy in aggregate G-5 financial exposure helps to explain the notable lack of urgency in the G-5 executive directors' statements about the South Korean programs of 1983–5, as compared with their view of the Mexican loans of 1983–9. It also helps to explain why both the 1983 and 1985 South Korean SBAs were only one-half the size of Mexico's 1983 and 1986 arrangements, in percentage of quota terms. With their domestic financial stability less at risk, the G-5 countries were less inclined to support large-scale IMF lending than they had been in the Mexican case.

As with Mexico, G-5 bank lending to South Korea in the 1980s was heavily weighted toward the United States and Japan (40 percent and 37 percent of total G-5 lending in 1985, respectively), with European banks far less exposed. Unlike in Mexico, however, these differences did not lead to sharp cleavages within the executive board over the size of South Korea's loans; rather, support for both the 1983 and the 1985 programs was clear and uniform among the G-5 executive directors. This lack of G-5 conflict, despite a fairly high degree of bank exposure heterogeneity, is probably due to the aforementioned fact that South Korea was financially less important than Mexico for the Fund's largest shareholders. That said, the available evidence does suggest that G-5 governments' intensity of support for the South Korean arrangements reflected their relative differences in commercial bank exposure: the Japanese and American directors lavished praise on the South Korean authorities and enthusiastically commended the staff's proposals in 1983, whereas British and German officials worried about South Korea's high levels of short-term debt and wondered whether other countries were more worthy of IMF assistance. A similar pattern emerged in the 1985 decision-making process. By the mid-1990s, however, South Korea had become significantly more important as a debtor to G-5 commercial banks, which held $68.5 billion in outstanding claims on the South Korean government and South Korean private sector institutions. Indeed, only Brazil ($75.2 billion) had borrowed more from G-5 commercial banks by the mid-1990s, while the banks' exposure to Mexico ($41.6 billion) lagged significantly behind. At the same time, the distribution of G-5 commercial bank lending had become much more evenly distributed between the five countries: Japanese and American lending now totaled only 55 percent of total G-5 lending to South Korea (compared to 77 percent in 1983), while each of the three European G-5 countries now provided more than 10 percent of G-5 bank loans.

With the G-5 countries all significantly invested in South Korea's financial stability in 1997, none of the Fund's principals questioned whether the country warranted the IMF's support; its importance for both G-5 domestic financial interests and global financial stability was unquestioned. Therefore, the IMF's approval of such an abnormally large loan for South Korea is not particularly surprising, nor is it surprising that the G-5 governments, along with a select group of additional countries, pledged $20 billion in "second line of defense" financing as a supplement to the IMF loan. Instead, what is noteworthy about the 1997 South Korean case is the direct pressure by G-5 governments on the IMF staff to modify the terms of the loan – specifically, to alter the anticipated rollover rate of South

Korea's short-term creditors. Had South Korea been of less importance to the major creditor countries, it is likely that the negotiations between Bijan Aghevli's IMF staff team and the Korean authorities in Seoul would have continued – and the December 4 executive board vote been postponed – once it had become clear that the South Korean program was not fully financed. In the event, the Fund staff changed their projections of the country's future financing situation in order to secure immediate approval of the loan. This episode clearly emphasizes the degree to which IMF staff members operate "in the shadow" of the executive board as they negotiate and design lending arrangements. In particular, it suggests that the Fund staff, in certain cases, faces pressure to deviate from purely economic calculations in order to meet the political and economic demands of the IMF's largest shareholders. Thus, the South Korean case further illustrates the dynamics of the principal–agent relationship between G-5 governments and the IMF staff that lies at the heart of Fund policymaking.

IMF staff preferences: the importance of borrower and lender composition

While G-5 preference intensity and heterogeneity strongly influenced the IMF's lending behavior in the South Korean cases, changes in the composition of South Korea's international borrowers and lenders played an even more prominent role. First, the question of whether South Korea's creditors were banks or bondholders directly affected the expectations of the Fund staff and executive board over the likely availability of private financing in the aftermath of an IMF loan. As with Mexico, South Korea in the 1980s borrowed internationally almost exclusively from G-5 commercial banks: over 95 percent of its private external debt in 1983–5 consisted of syndicated medium-term bank loans. With sizeable long-term ties to South Korea and each other, the commercial banks were not likely to "cut and run" if South Korea faced future financial difficulties, nor were they likely to face serious collective action problems in negotiating debt rescheduling agreements if they were needed. As a result, South Korea could count on continued access to new private international financing to ensure both the success of its IMF programs and its continued growth and development. Knowing that South Korea would have little difficulty in accessing future private financing, both the Fund staff and G-5 executive directors expressed an interest in limiting the size of the country's IMF loans. From the standpoint of the IMF and its key decision-makers, South Korea required less Fund assistance in order to ensure its short-term and long-term stability than Mexico and many other emerging market countries in more serious financial straits. Likewise, South Korea's loans did not require extensive conditionality, given the country's relatively modest balance of payments problems and its ongoing access to private capital; consequently, the two South Korean IMF loans in the 1980s each included only three performance criteria.

By the 1990s, however, South Korea's private external debt had undergone the two key shifts outlined in chapter 2. First, sovereign bond issues had largely replaced bank loans as the government's primary source of long-term external debt. Second, in spite of this shift in South Korea's sovereign borrowing, the country as a whole remained heavily dependent on bank lending, as South Korean financial institutions and corporations amassed large amounts of private non-guaranteed debt in the form of interbank loans. In fact, more than a half (53.2 percent) of South Korea's overall external debt consisted of private non-guaranteed debt in December 1996. When the South Korean government publicly guaranteed these private sector debts in August 1997, the country's external debt profile began to look remarkably similar to that of the Latin American debtor countries in the 1980s, with sovereign debtors owing most of their debt to a very small number of international commercial banks. South Korea's debt composition in 1997 contrasted sharply with Mexico's during the 1994/5 crisis, therefore, in which the Mexican government owed the vast majority of its external debt to tens of thousands of bondholders widely distributed throughout the world.

These differences in the composition of international capital flows to South Korea and Mexico had important implications for market actors' behavior during the two crises, which in turn affected the IMF's lending decisions. By and large, Mexico's tesobono bondholders had few long-term ties to the country, and they quickly responded to the 1995 IMF program by "bailing out" completely from Mexican markets. Although private capital did return to Mexico within six months, private creditors played no role in the immediate resolution of the Mexican crisis, nor did they attempt to coordinate new lending or debt rescheduling among themselves. For South Korea, by contrast, the majority of the commercial banks had extensive long-term interests in the country, even though much of their lending consisted of short-term interbank financing. Although the banks – like Mexico's bondholders – rapidly pulled their short-term interbank credits in the immediate aftermath of the December 4 IMF loan, they very quickly agreed to participate in the revived concerted lending process, which functioned quite similarly to the events in the 1983–9 Mexican case. Thus, within three weeks of the IMF program's approval, South Korea's bank creditors had assembled an updated Bank Advisory Committee and engaged directly in negotiations among themselves and with the South Korean government over the terms of a rollover and debt rescheduling. In effect, while Mexico's bondholders "bailed out" in response to the IMF's financing, South Korea's commercial bank creditors "bailed in" and participated directly in the resolution of the country's financial crisis.

These very different reactions of Mexico's bondholders and South Korea's bank creditors to the IMF rescue packages clearly factored into the Fund staff's decision about the amount of money it needed to commit to each borrower. As a share of short-term debt, both the overall Mexican package and the IMF lending component were significantly larger (approximately 150 percent and 50 percent, respectively) than those offered to South Korea (about 45.5 percent and 20 percent, respectively) – differences that reflect a more pessimistic assessment by the IMF staff about the likely response of private international creditors to a Fund program. With no expectation that Mexico could avoid a default by quickly accessing new private financing, the Fund saw the need to fill the country's "financing gap" with a very large rescue package. In South Korea, by contrast, the Fund was confident that the commercial banks – despite closing out their short-term interbank lending positions – would resume lending to the South Korean government in the medium term. Within a few weeks of the December 1997 loan the Fund's optimism was vindicated, as the banks reversed their capital flight through the aforementioned rollover and debt–equity swap agreements. By March 1998 the banks had agreed to "bail in" for the long term through debt rescheduling and the provision of new money, and South Korea's recovery from the crisis had begun.

Evidence for alternative explanations of IMF lending

Macroeconomic conditions

As with Mexico, the majority of the IMF staff's attention, as well as the dominant share of the executive board's concerns, focused on South Korea's economic performance and external financing needs. Clearly, one reason South Korea's IMF loans in the 1980s were smaller than Mexico's was the stark difference in the countries' economic situations: South Korea's external debt to GDP and debt to exports ratios were significantly lower than Mexico's, and the South Korean government held twice the level of foreign exchange reserves (see tables 4.3 and 5.1). Simply put, South Korea needed less money from the Fund in the 1980s because its debt problems were less severe than those of Mexico. Likewise, the IMF prescribed less extensive conditionality, since South Korea required less extensive policy adjustment in order to redress its balance of payments problems.

While macroeconomic conditions may explain much of the variation in IMF lending to Mexico and South Korea in the 1980s, however, they cannot explain the massive change in the size of South Korea's loans between 1983–5 and 1997. For example, in 1997 South Korea's ratio of external debt to GDP was 25 percent, only slightly higher than in 1983–5 (20.6/23.7 percent), and its ratio of debt service to exports had actually fallen sharply from 21.6/22.8 percent to 8.2 percent.[88] If the IMF was making its decisions based purely on macroeconomic criteria, such as external debt levels and budget deficits, then we should have observed South Korea receiving a similarly modest loan in 1997 (as it did in the 1980s), rather than a massive package equal to 19.4 times quota. Thus, although macroeconomic considerations undoubtedly factored into the IMF's decision-making calculus in the South Korean cases, other variables – including patterns of financial globalization – must also be taken into account in order to understand and explain variation in the size and terms of these loans.

US geopolitical interests

Even more so than Mexico, South Korea represents a critical or "most likely" case for geopolitical theories of IMF lending, which emphasize

[88] World Bank (2006a).

the United States' strategic interests as the primary determinant of Fund policies. To the extent that American strategic concerns do affect IMF behavior, they should have played a major role in the South Korean context, given the extensive US military presence in the country and the ongoing division of the Korean peninsula. Once again, however, the balance of evidence does not support this theory, even though it remains prominent in both the academic and policy literatures. Despite the continued presence of large American troop placements in South Korea in the 1990s, direct US military aid to the South Korean government had ceased by 1994. In fact, the relationship between US geopolitical interests and the size of South Korea's IMF loans is exactly the opposite of that anticipated by the geopolitical explanation: in 1983–5, when South Korea received loans of "normal" size, the United States provided roughly $200 million per year in military assistance; by 1997 this aid had declined to zero. Although some sources describe US foreign policy officials (e.g. the Secretary of State, Madeleine Albright, and members of the National Security Council) stressing the need to support South Korea for geopolitical reasons, there is no evidence that any of the major G-5 or IMF financial policymakers took these concerns seriously.[89] In his press conference following the December 4 program announcement, the IMF first deputy managing director, Stanley Fischer, dismissed the importance of US–South Korean strategic ties. Asked whether he thought the Americans should provide more bilateral money because of the United States' geopolitical ties to South Korea, he demurred: "Perhaps, but I don't have any sense that that's a major factor in this crisis."[90] Likewise, Robert Rubin downplayed the importance of geopolitics in the United States' or the IMF's handling of Korea: "South Korea was a crucial military ally ... [O]ne fear was that instability would create an opportunity for North Korea to do something provocative. But what I think troubled us most was a different kind of unknown, namely the potential risk to the world's financial system."[91] Once again, this lack of public statements about the importance of geopolitics in IMF decision-making may simply be a mask concealing the underlying preferences of the

[89] Rubin and Weisberg (2003).
[90] Press conference of Stanley Fischer, first deputy managing director, International Monetary Fund, December 5, 1997, 8:35 a.m., IMF Meeting Hall B, Washington, DC (www.imf.org/external/np/tr/1997/tr971205.htm).
[91] Rubin and Weisberg (2003, 230); Blustein (2001, 138).

key actors involved. The failure to find clear, definitive support for this view in either the available primary or secondary resources casts significant doubt on its merits as a generalizable explanation of IMF lending, however.

Ultimately, as in the Mexican cases, geopolitical theories of IMF behavior perform poorly in explaining variation in the size and terms of South Korea's IMF loans in the 1980s and 1990s. The case studies highlight two reasons why this may be the case. First, the geopolitical approach lacks clear micro-foundations linking the interests of the key actors involved in Fund decision-making to IMF lending policies. Moreover, it requires us to believe that the extensive archival and secondary evidence showing IMF policymaking to be driven largely by economic and financial factors is merely a "cover" or smokescreen for underlying US strategic interests. Although this interpretation of events may be plausible, it seems improbable given that neither the IMF staff nor the key G-5 governmental officials involved in Fund policymaking (e.g. finance ministry and central bank officials, executive directors) appear to have taken these geopolitical concerns seriously in either the Mexican or South Korean cases. Rather, the focus of these decision-makers remained firmly directed toward the domestic and international financial implications of the two countries' balance of payments problems. Second, this view of IMF lending is further weakened by the fact that American strategic interests in Mexico, South Korea, and other countries deemed geopolitically important (e.g. Turkey, Russia) have not varied significantly over the last twenty years. Instead, the United States' strategic interests in Mexican and South Korean political stability have remained fixed, constant goals of all American presidential administrations since the early 1980s, even in the aftermath of the Cold War. Even if geopolitical interests did factor into the IMF's decision-making calculus in South Korea and Mexico, therefore, these concerns cannot really explain the substantial variation in Fund lending to the two countries over time.

Finally, in addition to weakening the case for a geopolitical view of the IMF, the South Korean case provides further evidence that the United States does not exercise unilateral control over Fund decision-making. As in the Mexican cases, all G-5 governments, as well as the IMF staff, had extensive input in the Fund lending process. Once again, South Korea's experience with the IMF illustrates that Fund policymaking is a collective enterprise, in which a select group of states exercises disproportionate influence over outcomes but no single actor enjoys complete control over the process. Although the US government clearly played a central role in formulating the Fund's response to South Korea's financial crisis in 1997, so, too, did the Japanese and British authorities. Moreover, the IMF staff exercised broad autonomy in both 1983 and 1985, as the executive board quickly endorsed the two lending arrangements with relatively little discussion and few objections to the staff's proposals. In the end, these cases, like the Mexican loans, strongly suggest that scholars and policymakers need to discard the persistent stereotypes of the IMF – both those that treat the Fund as the United States' "lapdog" and those that portray its staff as "runaway bureaucrats" – in favor of a more complex but ultimately more accurate view of the Fund as an institution whose policies are determined by the common agency relationship at the heart of IMF policymaking.

Bureaucratic rent-seeking

Similarly, the balance of evidence in the South Korean cases offers little support for public choice theories that emphasize the rent-seeking incentives of IMF staff members. While the Fund staff did take primary responsibility for negotiating and designing each of the South Korean programs, their proposals were subject to thorough analysis and discussion in each of the executive board meetings. In these discussions, we do find directors periodically questioning the staff's assumptions or expressing skepticism about the likelihood of South Korea actually meeting the projected targets of the program. This may suggest that the staff's close relationships with its client countries drive it toward leniency in program design. Neither the primary source documents nor the available secondary accounts of the IMF's involvement in South Korea suggest that the staff's behavior was influenced by more selfish ulterior motives, however, such as budget maximization or increasing autonomy. Moreover, there is no evidence that the types of variables cited as evidence of bureaucratic rent-seeking – e.g. Fund quota reviews, higher liquidity ratios, and/or faster growth in the size of the staff – had any impact whatsoever on the IMF's treatment of South Korea during the last two decades. Instead, the staff appears to have based its calculations and decisions primarily on South Korea's private debt composition and macroeconomic characteristics rather than its own self-interested career objectives. As noted above, the main exception to this "technocratic" behavior in the South Korean case was the recalculation of the country's financing gap in 1997, in response to pressure from G-5 governments and the executive board. Although this episode illustrates the influence of politics on staff behavior, it does not support the public choice logic.

Conclusions

Ultimately, the evidence from both the Mexican and South Korean case studies firmly corroborates the key findings of the earlier statistical analysis, and it lends further support for the book's core argument and hypotheses. Specifically, the data confirm the critical influence of changes in patterns of financial globalization on IMF lending decisions. By shaping the preferences of both the "collective principal" (G-5 governments) and the "agent" (the IMF staff) involved in Fund decision-making, changes in the composition of borrowing countries' private international debt explain a substantial portion of the observed variation in IMF loan size and conditionality. Although other economic and political variables also influence Fund behavior, one cannot explain how and why the IMF makes lending decisions without taking into account the diverse ways in which developing countries are connected to the global financial system.

Nevertheless, the case studies should be viewed as complements to the statistical analysis, and we should be careful in drawing too many definitive conclusions about the political economy of IMF lending from a close analysis of only two country cases. To assess fully the role of private debt composition (and other variables) on specific Fund lending decisions, additional case studies are clearly necessary. In particular, one might imagine that geopolitical factors play a more prominent role in some cases, such as Russia and Turkey, in which political instability and ongoing military conflicts are key issues, or in smaller countries of particular historical importance to certain G-5 members (e.g. north Africa and France, the United Kingdom and its former colonies). Similarly, the Fund's behavior may have been less influenced by G-5 governments in less "systemically important" countries, such as Ecuador and the Philippines, that also borrowed from the IMF at the same time as Mexico and South Korea; in these cases, we might find stronger evidence in support of the public choice theory of IMF lending. Nonetheless, the empirical evidence presented in this book clearly indicates that variation in IMF lending in the contemporary world economy has been driven primarily by two key factors: the intensity and heterogeneity of G-5 domestic financial interests and the Fund staff's expectations about market actors' future behavior. Each of these factors is, in turn, influenced by changes in the composition of international capital flows. The quantitative evidence and the qualitative evidence thus both lend strong support to the book's core argument and hypotheses.

6 Conclusions

Global finance and the political economy of IMF lending

How and why does the IMF make lending decisions, and why do its policies vary so widely over time and across cases? In this book, I have challenged existing explanations of the political economy of IMF lending and developed a new analytical framework for understanding and explaining variation in Fund lending policies. Drawing on principal–agent theories of international institutions, I developed a "common agency" theory of IMF policymaking, in which two key actors – the Fund's largest member states (the "collective principal") and the IMF staff (the "agent") – jointly determine lending decisions. This framework emphasizes that states and Fund bureaucrats both exercise partial, but incomplete, authority over IMF decision-making. Therefore, we must account for variation in both actors' preferences in order to explain differences in the size and terms of IMF loans. Furthermore, the common agency approach highlights the importance of preference heterogeneity among the Fund's largest shareholders, the "G-5" countries (the United States, the United Kingdom, Germany, Japan, and France), which collectively exercise de facto political control over the IMF.

Drawing on this common agency framework, chapter 2 developed the core logic underlying the book's central claim: that changes in patterns of financial globalization are the key determinant of variation in the IMF's lending policies. By shaping the preferences of G-5 governments and the IMF staff alike, shifts in the composition of private international capital flows have led to substantial variation in Fund loan size and conditionality. In particular, three critical types of variation in private international debt composition influence IMF lending behavior: (1) the amount and distribution of lending by commercial banks in the G-5 countries; (2) whether international lenders to a particular developing country are commercial banks or bondholders; and (3) whether developing country borrowers are sovereign governments or private firms. These variables enable us to specify the intensity and heterogeneity of G-5 governments' preferences over IMF lending, as well as the Fund staff's expectations about the potential catalytic effect of a Fund loan on future private capital flows.

In chapters 3 to 5, I subjected this theory and its hypotheses to intensive empirical testing using a combination of quantitative and qualitative analysis. In both the statistical analysis and the case studies, I found clear evidence that the intensity and heterogeneity of G-5 domestic financial interests are key determinants of IMF lending policies. Specifically, variation in the amount and distribution of G-5 commercial bank exposure has had significant effects on both IMF loan size and conditionality during the last two decades. Moreover, the relationship between these variables is conditional and interactive: G-5 preference heterogeneity matters most in cases in which the preferences of the Fund's principals, as a group, are most intense. In contrast, in countries of less financial importance to the G-5, the IMF staff exercises greater autonomy ("agency slack"), and its own preferences carry greater weight in the Fund decision-making process. These results suggest, as I have argued, that the IMF's lending decisions are strongly influenced by the domestic financial interests of its most powerful member states. When the G-5 countries' commercial banks are highly exposed to a given borrowing country, their governments will be more willing to tolerate the moral hazard costs of large-scale IMF lending in order to protect their own domestic financial interests. Conversely, when the G-5 countries have few financial ties to a borrowing country, they will be more reluctant to commit IMF resources. Moreover, when they do support IMF loans within the executive board in these latter cases, the G-5 countries will demand more extensive conditionality in order to limit the moral hazard costs associated with Fund lending.

These findings are evident not only in the time-series cross-sectional data but also in the case studies. Indeed, in both the Mexican and the South Korean cases, relative differences in G-5 bank exposure translated into disagreements between G-5 executive directors over the size and terms of these countries' IMF loans. While the Fund did approve large-scale loans in each instance for Mexico and South Korea, the less enthusiastic G-5 governments succeeded in delaying some financing (e.g. the 1989 augmentation for Mexico) rather than disbursing credit immediately. Moreover, both the Mexican loans and the 1997 South Korean package contained substantial conditionality, much of which was aimed at alleviating the moral hazard concerns of the less sympathetic G-5 governments.

In addition, the data also support my hypotheses linking variation in the identity of borrower countries' private international lenders (banks versus bondholders) and borrowers (governments versus private firms) to IMF lending decisions. These variables, as discussed above, primarily shape the Fund staff's expectations about market actors' responses to an IMF program. Specifically, they determine the extent of private creditors' collective action problems, and, therefore, the likelihood that these lenders will respond to an IMF loan by providing new (catalytic) financing of their own to a borrowing country. As discussed thoroughly in chapter 2, collective action problems among private international creditors are greater in cases of bond financing and non-sovereign lending than in episodes of sovereign bank lending. In these cases, the Fund staff will therefore propose larger loans with more extensive conditionality, in an attempt to alleviate international creditors' concerns about a country's future ability to service its debt, and to convince them to "bail in" rather than "bail out" in response to an IMF loan. Furthermore, conditionality in bond financing and non-sovereign lending cases is more likely to be "front-loaded" in the form of prior actions (rather than imposed *ex post* as performance criteria), in order to send as strong a signal as possible to international creditors of a country's future creditworthiness. The statistical analysis in chapter 3 provides clear support for this connection between staff expectations about catalytic financing and variation in private international debt composition. In particular, there is robust evidence that the extent to which a country depends on international bond financing as opposed to commercial bank lending is a major determinant of both IMF loan size and conditionality. This finding is supported further by the strong evidence in chapter 4 linking the shift in Mexico's international lenders (from commercial banks to tesobono bondholders) to the extraordinary size of its IMF loan in 1995.

Although the evidence linking the shift from sovereign lending to non-sovereign (i.e. private non-guaranteed) capital flows is more limited, the South Korean case study in chapter 5 highlights the importance of non-sovereign lending in some IMF lending cases. Indeed, had South Korea's bank lending in 1997 consisted only of medium-term syndicated commercial bank lending to the South Korean government, it is unlikely that the banks would have pulled out of the country to the extent that they did in December 1997. In the event, the banks' exposure consisted nearly entirely of short-term lending to the South Korean chaebol and private financial institutions, and they continued to call in their loans and leave the country even after the IMF approved the stand-by arrangement on December 4. In the absence of the coordinating mechanisms and longer time horizons that existed in syndicated sovereign lending, South Korea's private non-guaranteed bank creditors behaved much like Mexico's tesobono bondholders: they "cut and run" at the first opportunity. Ultimately, the banks reversed course, in late December and early January, only once three events had occurred: (1) the IMF had increased its commitment to South Korea, and G-5 governments had replaced the vague "second line of defense" pledge with firmer bilateral commitments; (2) G-5 officials had enlisted William McDonough and pressured the largest commercial banks into assembling an ad hoc creditors' committee; and (3) the South Korean government had offered to swap the private non-guaranteed debt for new sovereign bonds. In other words, the 1997 South Korean crisis was not resolved until the IMF had provided more extensive financing and the country's private external debt had been transformed from short-term, private–private debt into 1980s-style long-term sovereign lending. Thus, while the large-N statistical evidence linking variation in IMF lending to the shift from sovereign lending to private–private capital flows is mixed, this change in patterns of financial globalization has played a critical role, as expected, in some recent and important cases – most notably in South Korea and other countries affected by the Asian financial crisis (e.g. Thailand, Indonesia).

Assessing the alternatives

In the empirical analysis, I not only tested my hypotheses about the relationship between patterns of financial globalization and IMF lending but also sought to gauge the relative explanatory power of this argument against competing explanations of IMF behavior. Not surprisingly, the analysis reinforced the findings of past studies that a borrowing country's macroeconomic and external debt characteristics are important factors determining the nature of the "deal" it receives from the IMF. Indeed, both the statistical analysis and the case studies highlight the importance of country-specific economic variables in shaping the views of G-5 governments and the IMF staff over the liquidity/moral hazard trade-off facing the Fund as it makes lending decisions. The data suggest at least two reasons, however, why these factors (e.g. country size, external debt ratios, economic growth, reserve levels) are necessary but not sufficient determinants of IMF lending variation. First, it is very difficult to ascertain whether a country faces problems of solvency or liquidity just by looking at broad macroeconomic indicators. Quite simply, there is no clear cut-off point along any macroeconomic or external debt metric at which a country can be deemed insolvent. Rather, in weighing the liquidity/moral hazard trade-off, the IMF staff also needs to consider how a loan will affect market actors' behavior, which in turn depends on the composition of a borrower's external debt. Thus, two countries with identical ratios of external debt to GDP and debt service to exports may not be equally "solvent" if the composition of their private international creditors – and therefore the likelihood that those creditors will provide new financing in the aftermath of an IMF loan – differs as a result of changes in patterns of financial globalization.

Second, country-specific macroeconomic and external debt indicators tell us little about the politics of the IMF decision-making process. In particular, they do not shed much light on the relative importance of a given borrowing country for the Fund's G-5 political principals. As my research illustrates, these countries' domestic financial interests play a critical role in shaping the IMF's lending policies. Therefore, while country-specific economic indicators give us a sense of the severity of a country's financial difficulties, they tell us very little about whether or not the IMF's key member states will find it in their domestic interests to support an IMF loan to alleviate these problems. In short, purely economic indicators, by themselves, cannot explain the outcome of an inherently political process such as IMF lending.

In addition to highlighting the limits of wholly economic views of IMF lending, this book also casts doubt on alternative political theories of the Fund. As noted above in chapters 4 and 5, I find scant evidence that US geopolitical interests systematically affect IMF policymaking. Neither the quantitative analysis nor the case studies in this book suggest that countries are more likely to receive IMF bailouts (larger loans on more lenient terms) because of geostrategic ties to the United States. Given that Mexico and South Korea are both critical geopolitical allies of the United States, the absence of evidence that geopolitical and/or foreign policy concerns played a key role in shaping Fund lending decisions in these cases casts serious doubt on the merits of such views of IMF policymaking. Although realist scholars of international relations continue to assert that the IMF is simply another avenue through which the United States pursues its global strategic interests, the balance of evidence points far more convincingly toward a political economy view of Fund lending that emphasizes financial interests. In fact, it is only when American "strategic" or "geopolitical" interests are construed in the broadest possible terms – terms that subsume economic or financial ties between the United States and a given country under the umbrella of geopolitics – that one can infer a systematic relationship between these factors and IMF policies. In contrast, once the concept of geopolitical ties is translated into concrete empirical measures (e.g. bilateral military and economic aid, UN voting affinity), one finds very little evidence that these factors play an important role in shaping IMF decision-making.[1]

Similarly, the analysis offers only limited support for public choice theories that emphasize the rent-seeking behavior of Fund staff members as the key determinant of IMF lending policies. The statistical results suggest that the variables identified by these theories as important factors influencing Fund lending decisions (e.g. IMF quota reviews, the Fund's liquidity ratio) have little or no substantive effect on the size and terms of Fund loans. Moreover, the case studies of South Korea and Mexico offer little evidence in support of the public choice view of IMF policymaking. To some extent, this lack of empirical support is not surprising: uncovering concrete proof of "agency slack" in principal–agent relationships is notoriously difficult, as the agent is unlikely to admit publicly to such behavior even if he or she is engaging in it.[2] Nevertheless, the fact that the variables identified by public choice scholars as key indicators of bureaucratic rent-seeking were rarely cited in the IMF staff reports, the executive

[1] The statistical analysis does suggest that the heterogeneity of G-5 UN voting affinity is a determinant of some IMF loan characteristics. This measure lends further credence to the common agency model, however, rather than theories privileging the United States as the Fund's sole political principal.

[2] Hawkins *et al.* (2006).

board minutes, or the reliable secondary sources suggests that other economic and political factors play a far more significant role in shaping IMF lending decisions.

Ultimately, the notable lack of support for these alternative political economy explanations of IMF lending may be the result of their attempts to identify a single actor or group (e.g. the United States, the IMF staff) as the sole key player in IMF policymaking. As I have argued repeatedly in this book, such an approach has severe limitations, since it fails to take into account the complex principal–agent relationship between the Fund's member states and the IMF staff. This relationship, which is best characterized by a collective principal or common agency model, gives both powerful states and the IMF staff partial influence – but not total control – over Fund lending policies. Consequently, the IMF is neither the servant of the United States (or other G-5 governments) nor the autonomous master of its own destiny. In other words, neither the "lapdog" nor the "runaway bureaucrat" view of the IMF accurately portrays the dynamics of Fund policymaking. By attempting to specify the extent to which each of these actors influences IMF decision-making, as well as how this varies over time and across cases, this book has attempted to provide a more complex, but ultimately more accurate, framework for explaining the behavior of the IMF in the contemporary global economy.

Applicability to additional cases

Although the statistical analysis provides strong evidence that the book's argument holds across the full range of IMF lending cases covering the last two decades, the case studies focus on only two of many recent financial crises in which the IMF has been involved. Furthermore, since most IMF archival documents become available only when a ten-year period has elapsed, the Mexican and South Korean case studies necessarily end in the late 1990s. This raises the important empirical question of whether the argument presented in this book helps us to understand and explain specific IMF lending decisions in additional, more recent cases. Although more detailed research is essential to answer this question fully, an initial plausibility probe seems promising.

For example, the book's argument helps to explain the IMF's treatment of Argentina and Brazil during their last period of financial crises from 1998 to 2003. Over this period Argentina received four IMF loans, ranging in size from 1.36 times quota (1998) to 5.26 times quota (2003). These loans included a relatively modest number of performance criteria (four to six), but they also included a substantial number of additional conditions (four to nineteen).[3] Similarly, Brazil received three loans during this period, ranging in size from four times quota (2001) to 7.52 times quota (2002). As in the case of Argentina, these loans contained a fairly standard number of performance criteria (five to seven), but also included a large number of additional conditions (six to fourteen). In both cases, these IMF loans were substantially larger and contained more conditions than those the two countries received during the Latin American debt crisis of the 1980s.

As expected, this outcome appears to reflect changes in the composition of international capital flows. In both Argentina and Brazil, shifts in the 1990s from sovereign bank lending to bond financing and private non-guaranteed debt exacerbated international creditors' collective action problems, thereby increasing the IMF's concerns about the availability of catalytic financing. In the 1980s Brazil and Argentina's external debt consisted almost exclusively of sovereign bank lending; bond financing and private non-guaranteed flows were extremely small in both cases. As in South Korea and Mexico, the G-5 countries had significant and relatively evenly distributed exposure to both countries in this period, although Brazil was of substantially greater importance.[4] Although G-5 bank exposure remained high in both cases during the 1998–2003 period, these countries also owed extremely large amounts of both bond debt and private non-guaranteed debt: bondholders held 83.2 percent of Argentina's private external debt in 2001, and 38.6 percent of Brazil's debt, while private non-guaranteed flows – once again, largely in the form of interbank lending – comprised 28.2 percent of Argentina's private external debt and 63.8 percent of Brazil's. In light of these changes in the composition of capital flows to Argentina and Brazil, we can make sense of the substantial increase in the size of these countries' IMF loans, as well as the increase in the number of conditions they

[3] See appendix 1.

[4] G-5 bank exposure to Argentina in 1987 ($22.1 billion), for example, was similar to that of South Korea in 1985 ($22 billion), while exposure to Brazil in 1988 ($55.9 billion) closely mirrored that of Mexico in 1986 ($51.6 billion).

included from 1998 to 2003. Rather than providing more modest IMF loans with a relatively limited number of conditions, as in the 1980s, the Fund now engaged in extremely large-scale lending and imposed more substantial conditionality in an effort to persuade a more heterogeneous, disaggregated group of creditors to provide new lending to Brazil and Argentina.

This growing concern about the availability of catalytic financing stemming from changes in the composition of international capital flows also sheds light on a number of other recent high-profile IMF lending decisions. For example, a focus on patterns of financial globalization helps to explain the magnitude of Thailand's 1997 loan during the Asian financial crisis (5.05 times quota). With 23.1 percent of Thailand's debt held by bondholders and 88.4 percent held by private non-guaranteed lenders (primarily interbank creditors), the prospects for catalytic financing were limited, thereby necessitating large-scale IMF lending. Similarly, the Fund's very large loan (6.9 times quota) in 2002 to Uruguay – a small country of relatively little importance to either the global financial system or the Fund's G-5 principals – can be understood as a further attempt to trigger a catalytic effect on private capital flows. Since the vast majority of Uruguay's private external debt (81.7 percent) was held by heterogeneous, disaggregated bondholders, the outlook for catalytic financing was bleak, and the Fund's large loan and extensive conditionality (twenty-two conditions, including eleven performance criteria and three prior actions) are best understood as a signal to private creditors of Uruguay's future stability and creditworthiness.

Finally, exploring additional cases also highlights the continued importance of preference heterogeneity among G-5 governments. In particular, it helps us to understand the lack of sizeable loans in cases in which we might not otherwise expect this outcome. For example, the relatively modest loans provided to Russia and most central and eastern European countries (CEECs) throughout the post-Cold-War period can be interpreted as a result of the substantial unevenness of G-5 domestic financial interests. In these countries, German banks generally held between 60 and 90 percent of total G-5 bank exposure, while the remaining G-5 countries held very little CEEC debt during the 1990s and 2000s. Consequently, the German government had strong, vested interest in these countries' financial stability, while its G-5 counterparts were more concerned with the moral hazard consequences of IMF lending.

In sum, although we must be cautious about inferring too much from this brief perusal of additional specific lending cases, there is good reason to believe that the theory developed in this book holds substantial explanatory power. Future research – particularly studies that take full advantage of the archival evidence soon to be available for the IMF's loans over the last decade – will allow more complete and rigorous tests of the common agency framework and its hypotheses in these more recent cases of IMF lending.

Future research: the IMF and the politics of international finance

While the data do provide very strong support for my argument, this book has also identified several unanswered questions that suggest the need for future research on both the political economy of IMF lending and, more broadly, on the politics of international finance. First, more work analyzing the substantive content of IMF conditionality is clearly warranted. The results here identify factors influencing Fund conditionality in broad terms, but additional research is needed to understand fully how and why specific policy targets – rather than the number of conditions – are included in IMF loans. In particular, future research needs to focus on explaining the conditions under which the IMF imposes "structural" (microeconomic) conditionality on its borrowers rather than simply including the standard macroeconomic performance criteria that most often appear in its programs. In addition, future work should also seek to identify the extent to which different types of conditionality (e.g. prior actions versus performance criteria) are more (or less) successful in generating catalytic effects on private capital inflows.

Second, a potential implication of my argument linking patterns of financial globalization to IMF lending behavior is that private creditors will, over time, shift their international lending toward the types of debt most likely to be "bailed out" by the IMF, whether because of G-5 domestic financial interests or staff concerns about catalytic financing. This logic would suggest a further shift away from bank lending and toward bond financing, as well as a shift from sovereign to non-sovereign debt. To some extent, this is exactly what we have seen in international capital markets, as bond issues and short-term interbank lending from G-5 commercial banks to emerging market private financial institutions have grown markedly in recent years.[5] Whether or not IMF lending has played a causal role in this new change in private international debt composition is an open empirical question worthy of future research.

Third, and more broadly, this book also points to the need for further research on the dynamics of public–private interaction in global governance. As the politics of IMF lending illustrate, tensions between states, international institutions, and global markets are a hallmark of the modern international political economy. This increase in public–private interaction in the global economy is not an IMF-specific phenomenon, however. Rather, public authorities and market actors are increasingly cooperating with each other to set, implement, and enforce the rules of global governance. For example, one important area in which public–private interaction has advanced significantly is international financial regulation.[6] Both at the regional (e.g. European Union) and international levels (e.g. the Basel Committee on Banking Supervision), supranational and national authorities have increasingly sought the active involvement of private actors in the establishment and implementation of rules and standards governing international capital flows. Nevertheless, the extent to which private actors have a seat at the international policymaking table varies widely across issue areas. In some cases international cooperation remains entirely the domain of states and supranational bureaucrats, whereas in others private actors themselves cooperate completely independently of political authorities. Understanding private actors' changing roles in global financial governance – and what effects these have on policy outcomes – is a critical next step toward a more comprehensive understanding of contemporary international relations.

At the same time, this book reminds us that, in many ways, nation-states remain the most critical and powerful players in global financial governance.[7] In addition, it highlights the fact that the distribution of power in the international system continues to matter

[5] Dobson and Hufbauer (2001). [6] Mosley (2005); Singer (2007).

[7] On the central role of states in managing the development of the international financial system in the post-Bretton-Woods era, see Helleiner (1994). See Eichengreen and Kenen (1994) for a similar discussion of the Bretton Woods period. For a more forward-looking analysis focused on United States policies, see Steil and Litan (2006).

in the international political economy.[8] Indeed, a core finding of this book is that a small group of powerful states, the G-5 countries, continues to enjoy a privileged position within the IMF, and Fund loans have clearly reflected the intensity and heterogeneity of these states' preferences. This finding raises the question of whether or not these countries' influence is the same within other international financial institutions, and why this might vary over time and across cases. A detailed analysis of policymaking within the World Bank, the Bank for International Settlements, and other institutions (e.g. the European Central Bank) would shed valuable light on this important empirical question.

Finally, although the analysis presented in this book focuses on IMF policymaking in the last twenty years, my findings also suggest the need for further research on the historical political economy of international finance. Financial crises and policies to manage and resolve them have been a staple of the world economy for centuries, and the central dilemma facing the key actors involved in IMF policymaking since the 1980s – the trade-off between liquidity and moral hazard – is no different from that confronting states and private actors in global markets during earlier eras, including the nineteenth century, the interwar years, and the Bretton Woods era. Although the IMF has existed only since 1944, major creditor countries cooperated to provide emergency financing to countries during financial crises and to seek private creditor participation in debt rescheduling in each of these eras. Moreover, the composition of capital flows to sovereign borrowers varied widely during each of these periods as well. By highlighting the importance of changes in the amount, instruments, and maturity of private international capital flows for the management of financial crises, this book points the way toward a strategy for understanding the politics of global financial governance in previous historical eras.

Broader implications: international political economy and international cooperation

Beyond its importance for our understanding of the IMF and global financial governance, this book has important implications for

[8] Kirshner (1997); Andrews (2006).

our theoretical understanding of international political economy and international organizations. First, it demonstrates that international relations scholars need to consider the political and economic interests of multiple actors in order to understand the dynamics of contemporary international cooperation. Theories of international institutions, in general, have too often identified a single factor (e.g. interstate strategic interaction, domestic politics within powerful states, the behavior of supranational bureaucrats) as "the" critical determinant of international relations behavior. While these one-dimensional theories are parsimonious, they simply do not reflect the complexities of the contemporary international political economy, in which states, private actors, and supranational bureaucrats all play important roles in shaping patterns of global governance. As this study illustrates, the IMF is not simply an unaccountable international institution controlled by its staff, nor is it completely beholden to the interests of its most powerful member state(s). Rather, both states and the IMF staff directly influence Fund decision-making and policy outcomes. At the same time, we cannot understand these actors' interests and the IMF's decisions without also taking into account how these policies affect the subsequent behavior of private actors in world financial markets. Ultimately, the essential task facing international political economy scholars today is to identify the *conditions under* and the *extent to which* each of these actors and interests affects policymaking within international organizations, rather than arguing over whether they matter at all.

Second, my research also sheds light on the complex relationship between domestic politics and international cooperation. Specifically, it illustrates how institutional design choices within international organizations are an important mediating factor between member states' domestic interests and the actions of international institutions. The rules and structures of policymaking within international organizations – particularly, those having to do with voting and permanent membership of an institution's key internal decision-making bodies – play a critical role in "locking in" representation of certain states' domestic interests at the international level. In the case of the IMF, the weighted voting rules of the executive board privilege the domestic political economy interests of the G-5 countries over those of other Fund member states. By contrast, in international organizations in which other decision rules prevail (e.g. "one state, one vote") or in which member-state oversight of international secretariats is limited, powerful states' domestic economic and political interests are less likely to shape policy outcomes. In short, the extent to which domestic politics affects international cooperation should vary between different international organizations based on the unique design characteristics of these institutions. Thus, rather than simply assuming the influence of the United States and other powerful states in global governance, international relations scholars would do well to consider how the design of specific international organizations filters these countries' domestic interests and mediates their influence over world politics.

Third, my research suggests that we can substantially enhance our understanding of international institutions by studying the actual *policies* made by international organizations, rather than restricting our focus to the questions of cooperation and institutional design that have dominated the political science literature for the last thirty years. Without a doubt, understanding why and how states cooperate, why they choose to delegate authority to international organizations, and why these institutions vary in design are critically important questions – particularly when we are studying newly established institutions or issue areas in which international cooperation remains in the nascent stages. In the case of long-standing international organizations such as the IMF, however, the most important empirical and theoretical puzzles have to do with *what* these institutions do – how the "rules of the game" are implemented and why this varies – rather than why they exist in the first place. Despite three decades' worth of research, contemporary scholars of international institutions have made surprisingly little progress toward resolving these puzzles and explaining how institutionalized politics and policymaking actually operates, on a day-to-day basis, at the international level. As an increasing number of international relations scholars move beyond questions of cooperation and institutional design to analyze the decision-making process of specific international institutions, however, the approach followed here – specifying the actors involved in international policymaking and focusing on the variables that affect those interests over time and across cases – could prove fruitful. In particular, applying this approach to other international institutions across a range of issue areas could further our understanding of the roles played by states, international bureaucrats, and private actors in global governance.

Fourth, this book highlights the utility of common agency models of delegation for analyzing policymaking within a variety of institutions. For instance, this framework might be applied usefully in the domestic context to analyze the extent to which central banks and regulatory agencies act independently of their legislative or executive principals. Likewise, we might explain variation in the policies of the World Bank, the World Trade Organization, and other formal international organizations (e.g. non-economic institutions such as the UN Security Council) by focusing more closely on preference heterogeneity among these institutions' member states. By treating preference heterogeneity as an important explanatory variable, we can generate clear, testable hypotheses about the relative influence of principals and agents in a wide variety of domestic and international institutions.

Finally, and perhaps most importantly, this book speaks to one of the enduring core issues in international political economy: the relationship between markets and politics. By exploring the substantial variation in countries' financial ties to the world economy and its implications for IMF policymaking, this book builds on and contributes to the extensive international political economy literature on the politics of globalization. This literature seeks to understand the ways in which international capital mobility – the free flow of finance across national borders – influences both domestic politics and international relations. At the domestic level, scholars have focused primarily on identifying the extent to which financial globalization constrains national governments' economic policy autonomy.[9] At the global level, research has focused on the role of the international financial institutions and the connection between financial globalization and efforts to harmonize national financial regulations.[10] Despite its many contributions, this literature is beset by a critical weakness: with few exceptions, international political economy scholars have treated "capital mobility" or "international financial integration" largely as an abstract, monolithic force.[11] From this perspective, international investors are a nameless, faceless group acting collectively (and uniformly) as a constraint on the policies of national governments and the international financial institutions alike.

[9] Mosley (2003); Rodrik (1997).

[10] Singer (2007), Roubini and Setser (2004); Vreeland (2003); Simmons (2001).

[11] See Cohen (2002) for an overview of the foundational literature in international political economy on the political causes and consequences of capital mobility. For a notable recent exception, see Mosley and Singer (2008).

As this book illustrates, this traditional approach to understanding the political economy of international finance paints a misleading and overly simplistic picture of today's global financial markets. Indeed, it overlooks the complex variation in countries' financial ties to the world economy, as well as the substantial differences between cases in the identity of international creditors. My goal throughout this book has been to move beyond these existing theories, in order to develop and test clear hypotheses about the relationship between private international creditors, states, and international organizations. Rather than seeking evidence for or against broad-brush claims about globalization (e.g. "capital mobility undermines national governments' economic policy autonomy"), this study has searched for a more sophisticated – and ultimately more accurate – understanding of the influence of financial globalization on international politics, as well as the ways in which this influence varies over time and across cases. In the case of the IMF, at least, this approach has substantial explanatory power and significantly enhances our understanding of the political economy of international finance.

Policy implications: IMF reform and global financial stability

While my primary goal in this book is to enhance our scholarly understanding of both the IMF and international political economy, my research also speaks to the ongoing policy debate about the role of the Fund in contemporary global financial governance. As noted at the outset of this book, the IMF has been the object of vociferous criticism in recent years in the industrialized countries and the developing world alike.[12] In the developed world, the Fund's critics have assailed both the institution and its policies as misguided and ineffective. These critics, including such prominent figures as Joseph Stiglitz, point the finger of blame at the Fund's largest shareholders for politicizing IMF lending, and at the Fund staff for misdiagnosing the causes of financial crises and imposing "cookie-cutter" programs on all borrowers.[13] Developing countries, in contrast, complain that

[12] See Vines and Gilbert (2004) for an extensive treatment of these critiques.

[13] Stiglitz (2002). Stiglitz goes further and disparages the IMF staff as a group of "third rank economists from first rate universities," implying that the

the Fund's conditionality is too onerous, and they point to their lack of voice within the IMF's decision-making process as evidence that the Fund is nothing more than a tool of Western imperialism. Quite simply, governments throughout the developing world view the IMF as both ineffective and illegitimate, and they are increasingly reluctant to seek its financing. In fact, in the decade since the Asian financial crisis in the late 1990s, many emerging market economies, including South Korea, Taiwan, and India, have sought to "self-insure" themselves against future crises by building up large "war chests" of foreign exchange reserves – reserves that will not just discourage international investors from engaging in speculative attacks but also preclude the need for IMF financing if a crisis does occur.[14]

The findings of this book help us both to understand the sources of this widespread dissatisfaction with the IMF and to assess the merits of these critiques. On the one hand, they suggest that there is substantial validity in the charge that IMF policies are heavily biased toward the preferences of the United States and other advanced industrialized countries. As the statistical analysis and the case studies both demonstrate, the G-5 countries exercise disproportionate – if not overwhelming – influence within the Fund's executive board, and their preferences have been one of the most substantial determinants of variation in IMF loan size and conditionality over the last two decades. Thus, to the extent that these countries' preferences reflect domestic financial interests rather than the interests of borrowing countries or the international financial system as a whole, the developing countries' charges of unfairness and illegitimacy ring true.

On the other hand, I find scant evidence in my research to support Stiglitz's critique of the IMF staff as a group of mediocre

Fund's policy mistakes are due, in part, to a lack of sufficient brainpower within the IMF. See Joseph Stiglitz, "What I learned at the world economic crisis," *New Republic*, April 17, 2000, and Kenneth Rogoff, "An open letter to Joseph Stiglitz" (http://imf.org/external/np/vc/2002/070202.htm).

14 See, for example, Charles Wyplosz, "The fuss about foreign exchange reserve accumulation" (www.voxeu.org/index.php?q=node/182) and Lawrence Summers, "Reflections on global account imbalances and emerging markets reserve accumulation," L. K. Jha memorial lecture, Reserve Bank of India, Mumbai, March 24, 2006 (www.president.harvard.edu/speeches/2006/0324). Whether these reserves will prove sufficient in the current global crisis – or whether the east Asian countries will once again seek IMF assistance – remains an open question.

economists blindly imposing identical policies on all countries. First, as the Mexican and South Korean case studies document in extensive detail, the staff's recommendations have varied substantially between lending cases. Second, this line of criticism is further undermined by the wealth of archival evidence documenting the executive board's repeated and universal praise of the IMF staff for its diligence, thorough analysis, and sincere efforts in assisting borrowing countries and implementing sound economic policy reforms. Third, the new IMF lending data set that is presented and analyzed in this book documents the extensive variation in the Fund's choices of loan size and conditionality during the last two decades. The charges of Stiglitz and other similar critics simply do not stand up to the balance of evidence presented in this book, therefore. Although the Fund may, indeed, be excessively influenced by the domestic interests of G-5 governments, it simply has not pursued a "one-size-fits-all" lending strategy over the last twenty years, nor do the IMF's failures seem to be the result of a lack of brainpower, diligence, or training among the Fund staff.

The relative merits of these critiques of the IMF notwithstanding, there is widespread consensus in developed and developing countries alike that some degree of reform of the Fund, as well as the broader "international financial architecture," is necessary in order to better manage and prevent global financial crises in the future. Indeed, in the decade since the Asian financial crisis, policymakers and academics have advanced a welter of such reform proposals.[15] These proposals, many of which remain on the global agenda today as part of the discussion concerning international responses to the global credit crisis, fall broadly into three camps: (1) those aimed at "lending reform," or changes in the size, terms, or frequency of IMF loans; (2) those seeking "governance reform," or changes in the Fund's rules and decision-making processes; and (3) those seeking to increase "burden sharing" – i.e. to address private creditors' collective action problems and increase the likelihood that market-driven solutions to financial crises might be identified and implemented without extensive IMF lending. I briefly assess both the prospects for and merits of several of these proposals in light of this book's analysis and findings.[16]

[15] Eichengreen (1999); Kenen (2001); Sturzenegger and Zettelmeyer (2006).

[16] For a comprehensive treatment of the IMF reform debate, see Truman (2006).

Lending reform: increasing or restricting IMF lending

Although proposals to reform IMF lending policies differ in their specifics, they can be split into two broad groups based on the proponents' views of the liquidity/moral hazard trade-off. On the one hand, many have argued that the IMF, as currently constituted, lacks sufficient resources (liquidity) to stave off financial crises in emerging markets. Those who adopt this viewpoint downplay concerns about moral hazard, arguing instead that more, rather than less, IMF lending is necessary to enhance international financial stability. A key proponent of this view is Stanley Fischer, the former first managing director of the IMF, who has argued in favor of transforming the Fund into a true lender of last resort.[17] On the other hand, many observers have argued that the moral hazard caused by IMF lending exacerbates rather than enhances global financial stability.[18] In this view, current IMF lending resolves today's crises at the expense of even greater instability in the future caused by the subsequent risky behavior of both private creditors and emerging market borrowers. Scholars and policymakers in this camp advocate the curtailment of large-scale IMF lending and/or the imposition of stricter rules for accessing IMF financing. The Meltzer Commission report issued in the wake of the Asian financial crisis, which recommended explicit "pre-qualification" rules for IMF borrowers and the imposition of stricter limits on the length and size of Fund loans, is one prominent example of this alternative view.[19]

My research offers some perspectives on how we should assess the relative merits of these various proposals. Above all, it suggests that a "one-size-fits-all" solution for the IMF simply does not exist. In today's complex international financial system, in which private capital flows to emerging markets vary extensively in size, and in which the identity of borrowers (sovereigns versus private actors) and lenders (banks versus bondholders) differs substantially across countries, it is not at all clear that global financial stability would be enhanced if the IMF always stood ready to provide unlimited LOLR financing for all countries. In fact, if private creditors and emerging market countries knew, without a doubt, that unlimited IMF financing would

[17] See Fischer (1999). Proposals to increase the size of IMF quotas dramatically and to create additional multilateral lending agencies, such as the Asian Monetary Fund, also fall into this camp.

[18] See, for example, Calomiris (1998).

[19] Meltzer (2000).

be available during a crisis, their incentives to pursue responsible macroeconomic and lending policies would diminish significantly. At the same time, placing strict limits on all countries' access to IMF lending – or requiring all borrowers to meet stringent pre-qualification criteria – is likely to result in a sharp increase in the incidence of sovereign defaults and a subsequent rise in global financial instability.[20] Indeed, it is difficult to imagine that international financial stability would have been enhanced if the IMF had simply ceased lending to South Korea, Thailand, and Mexico in the mid-1990s, even if these loans raised serious moral hazard concerns.

In the end, despite the desire of many policymakers and scholars to find a single "magic bullet" strategy for reforming IMF lending policies, such proposals misunderstand the very nature of the problems the Fund exists to address. Each case of IMF lending involves a difficult trade-off for the Fund and its major shareholders: the choice between reducing the risk of a default and exacerbating moral hazard. Since an IMF loan invariably has both effects, the dilemma confronting policymakers is determining the extent to which the moral hazard costs of IMF lending outweigh the benefits of liquidity in a specific country case. This is rarely, if ever, simply an economic choice that can be adjudicated on the basis of a few macroeconomic or external debt indicators. On the contrary, as I have argued throughout this book, it is a highly political decision influenced by the interests of both the Fund and its member states, and these interests vary systematically in accordance with changes in patterns of financial globalization.

Furthermore, even if optimal or more efficient IMF lending policies could be devised, it is highly unlikely that they would be implemented in the case of major international financial crises. Quite simply, the political interests of the actors involved in IMF policymaking are too great: given the strong desire of the G-5 countries to ensure international financial stability and the stability of their own domestic financial systems, it is difficult to believe that any commitments to curtail IMF lending would be credible in the event of future large-scale financial crises. Rather, it is far more likely that these countries would change their minds and push for exceptions to the new rules within the IMF executive board, or, alternatively, that they would cooperate on

[20] On pre-qualification, as well as the logic behind sharp reductions in IMF lending, see Meltzer (2000) and Calomiris (1998).

an ad hoc basis to provide bilateral financing through other channels, such as the BIS. At the same time, it is also unlikely that the G-5 countries, for domestic political reasons (i.e. voters do not want to "bail out the banks" with taxpayers' money), would vote in favor of the massive quota increases necessary to transform the IMF into something more akin to a true international lender of last resort.

Finally, many proposals to reform IMF lending overlook a larger, more urgent dilemma facing the Fund. Given the explosive growth in the size of international capital flows and world trade, it is increasingly apparent that the IMF lacks the resources necessary to do its job. Indeed, the Fund's quota resources relative to world trade have fallen by more than a factor of ten since its creation in 1944.[21] Likewise, the IMF's roughly $250 billion in usable resources are now dwarfed by the sheer magnitude of private international capital flows: global holdings of international debt securities now total $20.7 *trillion*, while new debt issues in 2007 alone reached almost $400 billion.[22] Thus, under even the most optimistic scenario – one in which broad political consensus has emerged in favor of continued large-scale IMF lending, risk-averse developing countries once again eagerly borrow from the Fund, and the IMF staff manages to "get the economics right" as it designs lending programs – the IMF may no longer have sufficient resources to play the role of crisis lender in global markets that it fulfilled in the 1980s and 1990s. Ultimately, then, an increase in the IMF's lending resources is a critical prerequisite to any discussion of when, under what conditions, and to what extent the Fund should engage in large-scale lending operations in the future. In light of this problem, the recently announced plans to triple the Fund's resources, from approximately $250 billion to $750 billion, represent an important step toward ensuring that the IMF continues to play a central role in efforts to maintain global financial stability in the next decade.[23] Nevertheless, some economists estimate that the Fund would require an additional $750 billion to $1.75 trillion in order to be fully equipped to handle "a systemic emerging market crisis" in the coming years.[24]

[21] Buira (2004). [22] IMF (2008, table 2, statistical appendix, 146).
[23] "G-20 reaffirms IMF's central role in combating crises," *IMF Survey*, April 3, 2009 (www.imf.org/external/pubs/ft/survey/so/2009/NEW040309A.htm).
[24] Buiter (2008).

Governance reform: voting rules and modifying the IMF executive board

In addition to proposals to alter IMF lending practices and augment the Fund's resources, many observers have proposed changes to the Fund's internal decision-making rules as a way to change its policy behavior.[25] These proposals generally begin with the assumption that G-5 government pressure is the main factor leading the IMF to provide bailouts to some countries but not others, whether or not their financial needs warrant such loans. Therefore, they argue, changing the quota allocations and voting weights in the Fund's executive board to give other states – particularly the major emerging market borrowers, such as Mexico, Brazil, Turkey, and South Korea – a larger say in IMF decisions would lead to more efficient and equitable policy outcomes. In this view, relaxing the major creditor countries' control over the executive board would relieve pressure on the IMF staff to treat some countries more generously than others simply because they are financially or politically important to the G-5 countries. In short, advocates of voting reform see it as a way to both democratize and depoliticize IMF decision-making.

Recently these governance reform proposals have led to concrete changes, as the IMF executive board approved a redistribution of voting rights and quotas within the Fund in April 2008.[26] Under the terms of these reforms, IMF quotas (and, therefore, executive board votes) will be modestly reallocated in order to amplify the voice of developing countries within Fund decision-making.[27] Unfortunately, my research casts doubt on the likelihood that this limited reform of "chairs and shares" will substantially alter IMF lending outcomes.[28] First, as several observers have already noted, the current reforms do not change the fundamental dynamics of IMF policymaking: G-5 governments will retain enough voting power to exercise de facto control of the executive board, so we are unlikely to see substantial

[25] For an overview of the various non-governmental organizations that have criticized the IMF and other international financial institutions, see Elliott, Kar, and Richardson (2002).

[26] "IMF Executive Board recommends reforms to overhaul quotas and voice," Press Release no. 08/64, International Monetary Fund, March 28, 2008.

[27] For a detailed analysis of these reforms, see Linn, Bryant, and Bradford (2008).

[28] Truman (2006).

changes in the politics of IMF lending.[29] Second, even if the Fund were eventually to approve a more extensive reallocation of executive board seats and voting shares, there is little reason to believe that such reforms will actually depoliticize IMF lending in practice and lead to policy outcomes driven solely by economic efficiency. In fact, reducing G-5 governments' influence over IMF policymaking would not eliminate member states' individual financial interests from the Fund's decision-making calculus; rather, it would simply replace G-5 interests and influence with the domestic political and economic concerns of other executive board member states. For example, just as Mexico and South Korea received favorable treatment from the IMF in the 1990s, due in part to G-5 governments' strong financial stakes in these countries, they might continue to receive bailouts in the future if the voting weight of the major emerging market countries increased at the expense of the G-5. One can think of this outcome as a further manifestation of the moral hazard problem: emerging market borrowers, wielding their newly acquired influence within the IMF, might secure larger loans with less stringent conditionality than they currently could obtain under the existing voting structures.

Ultimately, while these voting reform proposals are undoubtedly well intentioned, they fundamentally misunderstand the inherently political nature of IMF decision-making. Implicitly, they make the assumption that reducing G-5 influence will remove "politics" from IMF lending and enhance the Fund's independence. So long as the Fund's member states have the final say over IMF policies, however, their domestic political economy interests will invariably shape the Fund's lending behavior. Although these domestic interests may change in content as non-G-5 countries gain more seats at the table, they will never be entirely eliminated as long as the basic decision-making rules of the IMF remain in place. Simply put, no amount of voting reform will completely purge politics from IMF lending, since the Fund is ultimately responsible to its member state shareholders and will remain so regardless of changes in its internal decision-making procedures.

In addition, spreading voting power more evenly among a broader group of states is also likely to increase the scope for agency slack, by exacerbating the problem of preference heterogeneity within the executive board. Thus, reducing the influence of G-5 domestic

[29] Bryant (2008).

politics through voting reform might have the unintended side effect of increasing the prevalence of bureaucratic "rent-seeking" in IMF lending. Ironically, the real effect of voting reform might then be an increase in the power and autonomy of the Fund staff, rather than a larger voice for developing country borrowers. With the power of the IMF's largest shareholders reduced, a reformed executive board may be less successful in monitoring the IMF staff, and therefore less influential over lending decisions.

In the end, much like the proposals to reform Fund lending policies, changes in the Fund's voting rules will not transform the inherently political process of IMF policymaking into a purely technocratic exercise. That said, it may be possible to minimize the degree to which Fund policies are skewed by the domestic political interests of a limited number of states. The recent proposal to require IMF lending decisions to be approved by "double majorities" (i.e. a majority of board votes, plus a majority of board members) may achieve this goal.[30] Under this system, the G-5 countries would retain their disproportionate influence as a result of their quota contributions, but they would require the support of at least eight other board members in order to approve a Fund lending arrangement. As Ngaire Woods argues, "This reform would immediately create an incentive for the powerful members of the board to forge alliances with a larger number of borrowing countries – large and small. Equally, it would give borrowing members an incentive to participate more actively, more constructively, and with greater input into the strategic decisions made [in the IMF]."[31] Thus, while an IMF completely devoid of politics is highly unlikely to emerge from these proposed governance reforms, the double majority system may enhance both the Fund's legitimacy and its effectiveness.

Burden-sharing: "bailing in" the private sector

If the ultimate goal of reforming the rules of global financial governance is to reduce the frequency and severity of financial crises – and,

[30] Woods (2006) Strand and Rapkin (2005).

[31] Woods (2006, 210). Former IMF economist Eswar Prasad has put forward an alternative proposal that also holds promise. Under the Prasad proposal, existing IMF quotas would be reduced by 20 percent across the board, and these newly available quotas would be auctioned, with an upper limit on any country's share. This would give more voice, effectively, to those countries most willing to contribute more resources to the IMF. See *The Economist*, "The IMF: mission: possible," April 8, 2009.

therefore, to limit the corresponding need and demand for large-scale IMF lending – neither abolishing the Fund nor seeking to eliminate the domestic interests of powerful countries through voting reform is likely to be truly effective. Instead, the most promising proposals for reforming the international financial architecture are those that focus on how to "bail in" or "involve" the private sector in managing and resolving financial crises.[32] Rather than seeking to augment or restrict IMF lending by changing the Fund's own rules or resources, these proposals seek to enhance the ability and willingness of private creditors to cooperate during crises in the orderly provision of new financing, debt rescheduling, and debt reduction. The logic underlying these proposals is simple: if mechanisms can be devised to increase the likelihood that private creditors will provide new financing and/or reschedule existing debts during a financial crisis, international financial stability can be maintained without the need for large-scale IMF bailouts.

Since the Mexican crisis in 1994/5, several varieties of proposals to improve private sector involvement have been advanced. These proposals gained further prominence in the wake of Argentina's 2001 default on its private external debt and the protracted struggle between the Argentine government and its global bondholders over the terms of a subsequent debt restructuring.[33] The first proposal, known within the IMF as a "sovereign debt restructuring mechanism" (SDRM), essentially calls for the creation of a sovereign bankruptcy court along the lines of the "chapter 11" rules for bankrupt firms in the United States.[34] A similar but less formal proposal advocates the use of IMF-imposed "standstills," or temporary suspensions of a country's debt payments coupled with stays on private creditor litigation, as a way of buying time until orderly debt rescheduling agreements can be concluded.[35] A third set of proposals calls for the mandatory inclusion of "collective action clauses" in all sovereign bond issues.[36] These clauses

[32] For extensive discussions of these proposals, see Eichengreen and Portes (1995), Cline (2002), Rieffel (2003), and Roubini and Setser (2004). See also Sturzenegger and Zettelmeyer (2006, chs. 1–3).

[33] Gelpern (2005).

[34] Krueger (2001). For an extensive overview of sovereign debt restructuring initiatives over time, see Rogoff and Zettelmeyer (2002). For a discussion of the theoretical and practical difficulties of implementing such mechanisms, see Sturzenegger and Zettelmeyer (2006, esp. chs. 3 & 12).

[35] Kenen (2001).

[36] Eichengreen and Portes (1995); Eichengreen and Mody (2000).

allow a specified supermajority of bondholders to approve a rescheduling or debt reduction in the event of a sovereign crisis or default.[37] By minimizing the collective action problems among private creditors, these institutions may serve as effective substitutes for the private committees (e.g. the Bank Advisory Committee in the 1980s, bondholders' committees in the 1930s) and small numbers that facilitated creditors' active participation in the management and resolution of financial crises in previous eras. In effect, these institutions seek to transform a large number of heterogeneous and disaggregated creditors, such as sovereign bondholders or interbank lenders, into a group with shared interests, akin to the limited number of commercial banks that participated in syndicated loans and concerted lending arrangements in the 1980s.

As others have noted, there are a variety of potential economic and political difficulties with the establishment and implementation of these proposals.[38] Nonetheless, these types of policies have a number of important benefits. First, by specifying the "rules of the game" in international finance more clearly, these proposals may reduce the incidence of financial crises. Indeed, if private lenders do not fear being left holding the bag while others "bail out" during a crisis, large-scale capital flight might never occur and many major financial crises may be averted. Second, in the event that matters escalate to the point that a country does require IMF assistance, these institutions may allow the Fund to generate a catalytic effect on market financing with smaller loans and less extensive conditionality. Since individual private creditors would know that others are less likely to "cut and run" with such institutions in place, they might be more willing to recommit to the borrowing country even if the IMF provides only limited financing. Finally, although the need for large-scale IMF lending may never be eliminated entirely, enhanced mechanisms for "bailing in" the private sector can mitigate the moral hazard problems associated with these programs by ensuring that private creditors share the burden of managing and resolving financial crises more equitably with the IMF.

[37] In the absence of such clauses, changes to existing bond contracts generally require unanimity. This leads to the "holdout creditor" problem, in which even a single bondholder can delay the workout of debt problems and pursue litigation. See Roubini and Setser (2004).

[38] Roubini and Setser (2004). See, in particular, the authors' analysis in chapter 8.

In summary, these "burden-sharing" reforms hold substantial promise for actually enhancing global financial stability and for increasing the effectiveness of crisis management and resolution. While the use of collective action clauses in new international bond issues has become increasingly commonplace, however, substantial questions exist about formal sovereign bankruptcy measures, and these roadblocks have thus far prevented further reform. First, there are significant moral hazard concerns. On the borrower side, countries facing an imminent financial crisis might "rush to default" if they know that a formal workout mechanism exists for restructuring defaulted debt.[39] On the lender side, we might see either a "rush to the exit," as creditors seek to get paid before a country declares default, or a "rush to the courthouse," in which creditors pursue litigation in response to countries' non-payment of sovereign bonds.[40] For these reasons, the existence of clear, institutionalized procedures for restructuring sovereign debt might, paradoxically, actually *increase* the probability of debt crises and defaults.

Second, it is not clear that a formal sovereign bankruptcy institution would actually prevent more financial crises, let alone leave developing countries better off in welfare terms. Indeed, most recent financial crises have been caused by the sharp reversal of short-term capital flows – whether interbank lending, as in the 1997 South Korean crisis, or bond financing, as in the 1995 Mexican crisis – rather than by movements in long-term bond financing. Therefore, an improved mechanism for restructuring long-term sovereign bonds, such as the IMF's proposed SDRM, would not necessarily leave developing countries less prone to crises, since the most problematic varieties of debt would not be covered by the new institution. Moreover, because a formal sovereign bankruptcy mechanism could encourage governments to engage in opportunistic default, such an institution might discourage international creditors from lending to developing countries, leading to a renewed shortage of capital and investment in many emerging markets.

Finally, progress toward more extensive "burden-sharing" arrangements has been stymied by the resolution of Argentina's external debt

[39] See Roubini and Setser (2004, ch. 8), and Sturzenegger and Zettelmeyer (2006, ch. 3). This problem lies at the root of private creditors' substantial opposition to an SDRM.

[40] Roubini and Setser (2004, 294–6).

problems in 2005. After defaulting on $82 billion in private external debt in 2001, Argentina found itself mired in protracted negotiations with its hundreds of thousands of international bondholders over the terms of a debt restructuring. As these negotiations dragged on, debates within the IMF and elsewhere about the need for a formal SDRM accelerated. In June 2005, however, Argentina succeeded in convincing the vast majority of its creditors (76 percent) to accept a massive "haircut": these bondholders exchanged $62 billion in defaulted debt for $35 billion in new bonds.[41] Although this deal left Argentina with substantial foreign debt obligations, it was generally seen as a victory for the Argentine government, and it cast doubt on the need for more formal, institutionalized debt restructuring mechanisms. Whether or not this view holds for all countries – or whether Argentina is a one-time outlier – remains to be seen in the future. At least for the time being, however, the move toward a formal international institution for resolving sovereign debt problems has stalled.

Conclusions

As stated at the outset, this book has sought to understand and explain the connections between financial globalization and global governance. In studying the politics of IMF lending, and the ways in which Fund decisions have been influenced and altered by changes in the composition of international capital flows, I have attempted to enhance our understanding of one of the most prominent and oft-criticized international organizations. Moving beyond common stereotypes and generalizations about the IMF, I have sought a more rigorous and more accurate explanation of how and why the Fund does what it does, and why this varies over time and across cases. At the same time, this book demonstrates that the IMF is a dynamic institution whose role continues to evolve in response to changes in the composition of global financial markets. Indeed, maintaining global financial stability is very much like shooting at a moving target: markets continue to become increasingly complex, the causes and consequences of financial crises continue to change, and the already unprecedented magnitude of private international capital flows continues to grow.

[41] See Gelpern (2005) for a detailed discussion of the negotiations and process by which this outcome was reached.

Despite its critics, the IMF will continue to play a critical role in this environment, although the interests of and pressures on its staff and its principals will invariably shift over time and across cases. Nouriel Roubini and Brad Setser, two of the foremost authorities on policies for managing international financial crises, perhaps summarize matters best: "Different countries, different crises, different solutions."[42] The argument and evidence presented in this book illustrate that this is true not only because countries borrowing from the IMF face different economic and financial problems, but also for political reasons: changes in the composition of private international capital flows directly affect the preferences of those actors involved in IMF decision-making over the size and terms of Fund lending. In highlighting this intersection between global finance and IMF policies, this book hopes to encourage further study of the complex and evolving relationship between international economics and international politics.

[42] Roubini and Setser (2004, 16).

Appendices

Appendix 1
Non-concessional IMF Loans, 1984–2003

Table A1.1 *Non-concessional IMF loans, 1984–2003*

Country	*Program date*	*Program length (months)*	*Amount (SDR millions)*	*Amount (share of IMF quota)*	*Performance criteria*	*Total conditions*
Algeria	5/31/89	12	155.70	0.25	0	0
Algeria	6/3/91	10	300.00	0.48	n/a	n/a
Algeria	5/27/94	12	457.20	0.50	n/a	n/a
Algeria	5/22/95	36	1,169.28	1.28	7	27
Argentina	12/28/84	15	1,182.50	1.06	10	10
Argentina	7/23/87	14.25	947.50	0.85	8	8
Argentina	11/10/89	16	736.00	0.66	7	7
Argentina	7/29/91	11	780.00	0.70	7	11
Argentina	3/31/92	48	4,020.25	2.62	8	8
Argentina	4/12/96	21	720.00	0.47	6	6
Argentina	2/4/98	36	2,080.00	1.35	4	8
Argentina	3/10/00	36	10,850.14	5.13	6	7
Argentina	1/12/01	12	6,086.66	2.87	6	25
Argentina	1/24/03	8.25	11,155.50	5.27	6	11
Belize	12/3/84	16	7.13	0.75	4	4
Bosnia and Herzegovina	3/29/98	36	94.42	0.78	n/a	n/a
Bosnia and Herzegovina	8/2/02	15	67.60	0.40	5	22

Brazil	1/29/92	19	1,500.00	0.69	6	6
Brazil	12/2/98	36	13,024.80	6.00	5	11
Brazil	9/14/01	15	12,144.40	4.00	7	15
Brazil	9/6/02	12	22,821.12	7.52	7	21
Bulgaria	3/15/91	12	279.00	0.90	5	14
Bulgaria	4/17/92	12	155.00	0.33	5	8
Bulgaria	4/11/94	11.5	139.48	0.30	5	5
Bulgaria	7/19/96	11	400.00	0.86	7	21
Bulgaria	4/11/97	14	371.90	0.80	10	40
Bulgaria	9/25/98	36	627.62	1.35	15	44
Bulgaria	2/27/02	24	240.00	0.37	7	21
Chile	8/15/85	36	750.00	1.70	8	8
Chile	11/8/89	12	64.00	0.15	0	5
China	11/12/86	12	597.73	0.25	0	5
Colombia	12/20/99	36	1,957.00	2.53	5	16
Colombia	1/15/03	24	1,548.00	2.00	6	13
Costa Rica	3/13/85	13	54.00	0.64	6	6
Costa Rica	10/28/87	17	40.00	0.48	6	6
Costa Rica	5/23/89	12	42.00	0.50	5	6
Costa Rica	4/8/91	12	33.64	0.40	5	12
Costa Rica	4/19/93	10	21.04	0.18	6	8
Costa Rica	11/29/95	15	52.00	0.44	6	18
Croatia	10/14/94	18	65.40	0.25	9	n/a

Table A1.1 *(cont.)*

Country	*Program date*	*Program length (months)*	*Amount (SDR millions)*	*Amount (share of IMF quota)*	*Performance criteria*	*Total conditions*
Croatia	3/12/97	36	353.16	1.35	6	n/a
Croatia	3/19/01	14	200.00	0.55	7	13
Croatia	2/3/03	14	105.88	0.29	7	18
Czech Republic	3/17/93	12	177.00	0.30	4	4
Dominican Republic	4/15/85	12	78.50	0.70	5	5
Dominican Republic	8/28/91	19	39.24	0.35	6	6
Dominican Republic	7/9/93	9	31.80	0.20	5	5
Dominican Republic	8/29/03	24	437.80	2.00	10	29
Ecuador	3/11/85	12	105.50	0.70	4	4
Ecuador	8/15/86	12	75.40	0.50	5	5
Ecuador	1/4/88	14	75.35	0.50	8	8
Ecuador	9/15/89	17.5	109.90	0.73	8	9
Ecuador	12/11/91	12	75.00	0.50	6	6
Ecuador	5/11/94	18	173.90	0.79	5	5
Ecuador	4/19/00	20	226.73	0.75	13	36
Ecuador	3/12/03	13	151.00	0.50	16	30
Egypt	5/15/87	18.5	250.00	0.54	10	13

Egypt	5/17/91	24	234.40	0.51	9	12
Egypt	9/20/93	36	400.00	0.59	7	27
Egypt	10/11/96	23.5	271.40	0.40	7	31
El Salvador	8/27/90	12	35.60	0.40	6	6
El Salvador	1/6/92	14	41.50	0.33	5	5
El Salvador	5/10/93	19	47.11	0.38	6	6
El Salvador	7/21/95	14	37.68	0.30	5	5
El Salvador	2/28/97	15	37.68	0.30	6	6
El Salvador	9/23/98	17	37.68	0.30	6	6
Estonia	9/16/92	12	27.90	0.60	6	17
Estonia	10/27/93	17	11.63	0.25	6	6
Estonia	4/11/95	17	13.95	0.30	6	7
Estonia	7/29/96	13	13.95	0.30	5	24
Estonia	12/17/97	15	16.10	0.35	5	15
Estonia	3/1/00	18	29.34	0.45	5	18
Gabon	12/22/86	24.25	98.69	1.35	4	7
Gabon	9/15/89	16	43.00	0.59	7	10
Gabon	9/30/91	18	28.00	0.38	7	10
Gabon	3/30/94	12	38.60	0.35	5	7
Gabon	11/8/95	36	110.30	1.00	13	17
Gabon	10/23/00	18	92.58	0.60	11	44
Guatemala	10/26/88	16	54.00	0.50	5	5
Guatemala	12/18/92	15	54.00	0.35	6	6
Guatemala	4/1/02	12	84.00	0.40	6	13

Table A1.1 *(cont.)*

Country	*Program date*	*Program length (months)*	*Amount (SDR millions)*	*Amount (share of IMF quota)*	*Performance criteria*	*Total conditions*
Guatemala	6/18/03	12	84.00	0.40	n/a	n/a
Hungary	1/13/84	12	425.00	0.80	6	6
Hungary	5/16/88	12	265.35	0.50	5	7
Hungary	3/14/90	13.5	159.21	0.30	5	8
Hungary	2/20/91	36	1,114.00	2.10	5	14
Hungary	9/15/93	15	340.00	0.45	4	4
Hungary	3/15/96	23	264.18	0.35	4	15
Indonesia	11/5/97	36	8,338.24	5.57	10	14
Indonesia	8/25/98	26.5	5,383.10	3.59	9	21
Indonesia	2/4/00	46	3,638.00	1.75	8	12
Jamaica	6/22/84	12	64.00	0.44	5	5
Jamaica	7/15/85	22.5	115.00	0.79	7	8
Jamaica	3/2/87	15	85.00	0.58	7	9
Jamaica	9/19/88	18	82.00	0.56	5	5
Jamaica	3/23/90	20.5	82.00	0.56	6	6
Jamaica	6/28/91	15	43.65	0.30	5	5
Jamaica	12/11/92	36	109.13	0.54	5	5

Jordan	7/14/89	18	60.00	0.81	3	3
Jordan	2/26/92	18	44.40	0.36	4	7
Jordan	3/25/94	24	189.30	1.56	4	6
Jordan	2/9/96	36	238.04	1.96	5	9
Jordan	4/15/99	37	127.88	0.75	8	17
Jordan	7/3/02	24	85.28	0.50	7	13
Kazakhstan	1/26/94	16	123.75	0.50	6	30
Kazakhstan	6/5/95	12	185.60	0.75	6	23
Kazakhstan	6/17/96	36	309.40	1.25	6	21
Kazakhstan	12/13/99	36	329.10	0.90	7	26
Latvia	9/14/92	12	54.90	0.60	5	17
Latvia	12/15/93	15	22.88	0.25	6	8
Latvia	4/21/95	15	27.45	0.30	6	8
Latvia	3/24/96	13	30.00	0.33	7	14
Latvia	10/10/97	15	33.00	0.36	7	14
Latvia	10/10/99	16	33.00	0.26	5	28
Latvia	4/20/01	20	33.00	0.26	6	15
Lithuania	10/21/92	11	56.93	0.55	5	24
Lithuania	10/22/93	17	25.88	0.25	6	7
Lithuania	10/24/94	36	134.55	1.30	9	20
Lithuania	3/8/00	15	61.80	0.43	10	18
Lithuania	8/30/01	19	86.52	0.60	8	17
Macedonia FYR	5/5/95	13	22.30	0.45	5	19
Macedonia FYR	11/29/00	36	24.12	0.35	8	16

Table A1.1 *(cont.)*

Country	*Program date*	*Program length (months)*	*Amount (SDR millions)*	*Amount (share of IMF quota)*	*Performance criteria*	*Total conditions*
Macedonia FYR	4/30/03	13.5	20.00	0.29	10	17
Mauritius	3/1/85	18	49.00	0.91	4	4
Mexico	11/19/86	17.5	1,400.00	1.20	7	7
Mexico	5/26/89	48	3,729.60	3.20	7	7
Mexico	2/1/95	18.5	12,070.20	6.88	7	7
Mexico	7/7/99	17	3,103.00	1.20	4	5
Morocco	9/12/85	17.5	200.00	0.65	6	7
Morocco	12/16/86	15.5	230.00	0.75	6	11
Morocco	8/30/88	16	210.00	0.68	6	9
Morocco	7/20/90	18	100.00	0.33	8	11
Morocco	1/31/92	14	91.98	0.22	7	15
Panama	7/15/85	19.5	90.00	0.88	5	5
Panama	2/24/92	31	74.17	0.50	5	5
Panama	11/29/95	16	84.30	0.56	4	4
Panama	12/10/97	36	120.00	0.80	4	4
Panama	6/30/00	21	64.00	0.31	7	14
Paraguay	12/15/03	15.5	50.00	0.50	16	30

Peru	4/26/84	15	250.00	0.76	5	5
Peru	3/18/93	36	1,018.10	2.18	6	6
Peru	7/1/96	33	300.20	0.64	6	6
Peru	6/24/99	35	383.00	0.60	6	18
Peru	3/12/01	12	128.00	0.20	6	6
Peru	2/1/02	25	255.00	0.40	8	20
Philippines	12/14/84	18	615.00	1.40	14	16
Philippines	10/24/86	18	198.00	0.45	7	7
Philippines	5/23/89	36	660.60	1.50	10	17
Philippines	2/20/91	18	334.20	0.76	6	6
Philippines	6/24/94	42	791.20	1.25	6	6
Philippines	4/1/98	24	1,020.79	1.61	6	6
Poland	2/5/90	12	545.00	0.80	6	6
Poland	4/18/91	13	1,224.00	1.80	6	6
Poland	3/8/93	12	476.00	0.48	5	5
Poland	8/5/94	18	333.30	0.34	5	10
Romania	4/11/91	12	380.50	0.73	5	16
Romania	5/29/92	12	314.04	0.42	5	7
Romania	5/11/94	19	320.50	0.43	9	20
Romania	4/22/97	13	301.50	0.40	8	38
Romania	8/5/99	10	400.00	0.39	9	28
Romania	10/31/01	18	300.00	0.29	12	30
Russia	8/5/92	17	719.00	0.17	0	0
Russia	4/11/95	12	4,313.10	1.00	10	22

Table A1.1 *(cont.)*

Country	*Program date*	*Program length (months)*	*Amount (SDR millions)*	*Amount (share of IMF quota)*	*Performance criteria*	*Total conditions*
Russia	3/26/96	36	9,214.13	2.14	10	17
Russia	7/20/98	20	3,992.47	0.93	11	11
Russia	7/28/99	17	3,300.00	0.56	8	44
Serbia and Montenegro	6/11/01	11.5	200.00	0.43	8	32
Serbia and Montenegro	5/14/02	36	650.00	1.39	9	26
Slovakia	7/22/94	20	115.80	0.45	6	8
South Korea	7/12/85	20	280.00	0.61	3	4
South Korea	12/4/97	36	15,500.00	19.38	3	10
Thailand	6/14/85	21.5	400.00	1.03	6	6
Thailand	8/20/97	34	2,900.00	5.05	6	9
Trinidad and Tobago	1/13/89	13.5	99.00	0.58	7	7
Trinidad and Tobago	4/20/90	13.5	85.00	0.50	6	6
Tunisia	11/4/86	18	103.65	0.75	4	8
Tunisia	7/25/88	36	207.30	1.50	5	10
Turkey	4/4/84	12	225.00	0.52	5	5
Turkey	7/8/94	20	610.50	0.95	6	6
Turkey	12/22/99	36	9,254.40	9.60	8	28
Turkey	12/22/00	36	5,784.00	6.00	5	22

Turkey	2/4/02	35	12,821.20	13.30	8	46
Ukraine	4/7/95	12	997.30	1.00	5	40
Ukraine	5/10/96	9.5	598.20	0.60	4	14
Ukraine	8/25/97	12	398.92	0.40	6	58
Ukraine	9/4/98	36	1,919.95	1.93	6	53
Uruguay	9/27/85	17	122.85	0.75	5	5
Uruguay	12/12/90	15	94.80	0.58	6	6
Uruguay	7/1/92	15	50.00	0.22	6	7
Uruguay	3/1/96	13	100.00	0.44	5	7
Uruguay	6/20/97	21	125.00	0.55	5	9
Uruguay	3/29/99	12	70.00	0.23	0	10
Uruguay	5/31/00	22	150.00	0.49	5	17
Uruguay	4/1/02	24	2,128.30	6.94	11	22
Venezuela	6/23/89	36	3,857.10	2.81	6	6
Venezuela	7/12/96	12	975.65	0.50	7	25
Average	–	**20.02**	**1,222.78**	**1.21**	**6.40**	**13.40**

Notes: Non-concessional loans are stand-by arrangements, extended arrangements, and borrowings under the Supplemental Reserve Facility. The countries listed in this table include all IMF borrowers not eligible for concessional loans, as of August 2005 (www.imf.org/external/np/exr/facts/prgf.htm). n/a = documents unavailable.

Sources: IMF archives (letters of intent, memoranda of economic policies, staff reports) and www.imf.org.

Appendix 2
IMF lending: background and overview

The IMF's main non-concessional lending instruments are the stand-by arrangement and the extended arrangement (the name given to loans made under the EFF). The SBA is designed to assist countries facing short-term (one- to two-year) balance of payments problems, while the extended arrangement is designed to assist countries facing slightly longer-term difficulties (around three years) whose resolution requires more extensive structural reforms. In addition to its short-term lending, the IMF also provides long-term loans to very low-income countries under the Poverty Reduction and Growth Facility, which replaced the Structural Adjustment Facility and the Enhanced Structural Adjustment Facility in 1999. These loans are extended at a very low (concessional) interest rate of 0.5 percent and are based on a "poverty reduction strategy" prepared jointly by the country, the IMF, the World Bank, and various private sector partners. These latter facilities are longer-term (five- to ten-year) loans more akin to development lending than the shorter-term IMF arrangements. The Fund also provides emergency assistance to countries facing natural disasters or recovering from military conflict (www.imf.org/external/np/exr/facts/conflict.htm).

Over the last ten years the Fund has modified its non-concessional lending arrangements several times. In response to the Asian financial crisis, the IMF established an additional short-term lending facility, the Supplemental Reserve Facility. Loans under the SRF, which were available in the form of additional resources under a stand-by or an extended arrangement, were intended for countries facing "severe balance of payments difficulties arising from a sudden loss of market confidence accompanied by capital flight and a sharp drain in international reserves"; the loans were made for one year and carried an additional penalty rate over and above the market rate for stand-by and extended arrangements. The Fund also established the Contingent Credit Lines in 1999, as a crisis prevention measure. The

CCL was intended to assist countries with strong fundamentals that might nonetheless be vulnerable to contagion effects from other countries. From 1999 to 2003, however, no member borrowed from the Fund under this new lending facility, because of concerns that such borrowing would trigger (rather than stem) private capital outflows by signaling a country's potential debt problems. The IMF abolished the CCL facility in November 2003.

In 2008 the Fund made several further modifications to its lending policies, in response to the global credit crisis. First, it doubled countries' access to stand-by and extended arrangements, from 100 percent of a country's quota on an annual basis, and 300 percent cumulatively, to 200 percent and 600 percent, respectively (www.imf.org/external/np/exr/facts/howlend.htm). Second, the IMF introduced a new loan type, the Short-term Liquidity Facility (www.imf.org/external/pubs/ft/survey/so/2008/POL102908A.htm), which it further modified and renamed the Flexible Credit Line in March 2009. Like both the CCL and SLF, the FCL is intended explicitly for crisis prevention: it is designed "for countries with very strong fundamentals, policies, and track records of policy implementation and is particularly useful for crisis prevention purposes. FCL arrangements are approved for countries meeting pre-set qualification criteria." Finally, with the FCL in place, the IMF eliminated the SRF (http://www.imf.org/external/np/pp/eng/2009/040909.pdf).

Table A2.1 *Terms of IMF lending facilities*

Lending facility	Charges[1]	Lending period	Repayment schedule (expected)	Limit on size of loan
Stand-by arrangement	Basic rate + 100–200 basis points	1 – 2 years	3¼ – 5 years	200% of quota annually, 600% cumulatively
Extended arrangement (EFF)	Basic rate + 100–200 basis points	3 years	4½ –7 years	200% of quota annually, 600% cumulatively

Table A2.1 *(cont.)*

Lending facility	Charges[1]	Lending period	Repayment schedule (expected)	Limit on size of loan
Flexible Credit Line	Basic rate + 100–200 basis points	6 months – 1 year	3¼ – 5 years	No set limit; lending determined on a case-by-case basis
Poverty Reduction and Growth Facility	0.5%	5½ – 10 years	n/a	n/a

Note: [1] The SDR basic interest rate, as of December 29, 2009, was 0.23 percent (www.imf.org/external/fin.htm).
Source: www.imf.org/external/np/exr/facts/howlend.htm.

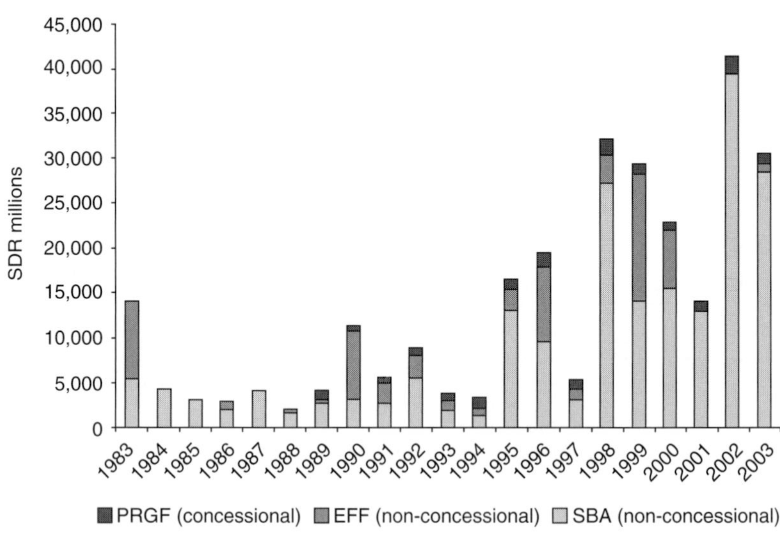

Figure A2.1 Total amount pledged under IMF lending arrangements, 1983–2003
Source: IMF, annual reports.

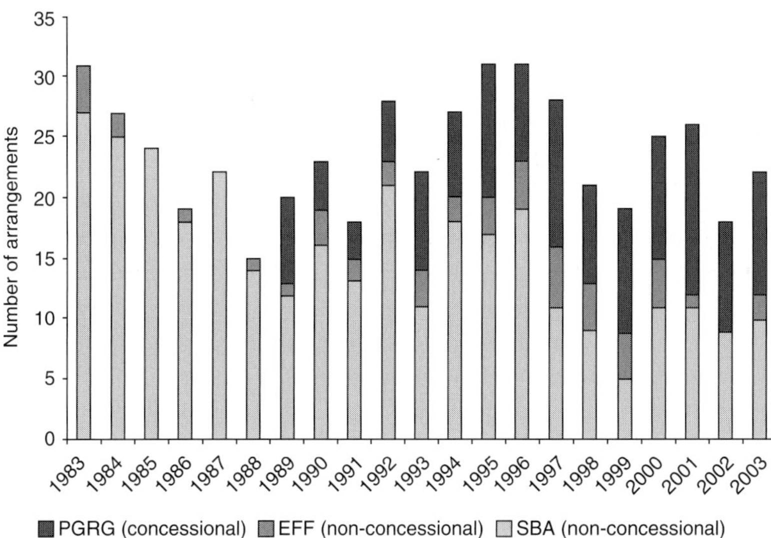

Figure A2.2 Total number of IMF lending arrangements, 1983–2003
Source: IMF, annual reports.

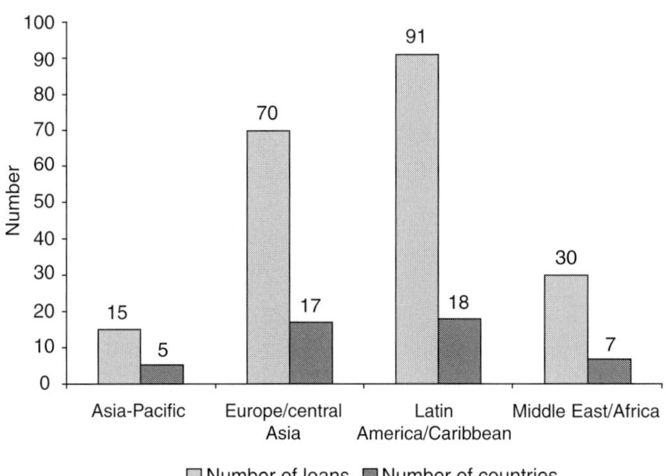

Figure A2.3 Non-concessional IMF lending arrangements by region, 1983–2003
Note: Forty-seven IMF borrowing countries not eligible for long-term (PRGF) concessional loans.
Source: IMF, annual reports.

Appendix 3
Statistical analysis

Table A3.1 *Propensity score matching, post-estimation bias analysis*

Variable	*Sample*	*Mean*		*Pre-matching bias (%)*	*Reduction in bias (%)*	*t*	*P* > |*t*|
		Treated	*Control*				
G5BANK	Unmatched	0.61	0.55	2.8		0.33	0.74
	Matched	0.59	0.65	−2.6	5.0	−0.25	0.81
COVG5BANK	Unmatched	117.11	115.88	2.7		0.52	0.61
	Matched	116.72	121.04	−9.5	−251.2	−0.83	0.41
PCTBOND	Unmatched	23.69	22.49	4.2		0.52	0.61
	Matched	23.90	25.44	−5.5	−29.0	−0.50	0.62
PCTPNG	Unmatched	19.97	24.24	−17.6		−2.06	0.04
	Matched	20.20	23.14	−12.2	30.9	−1.17	0.24
USSHARE	Unmatched	0.29	0.28	6.8		0.82	0.42
	Matched	0.30	0.28	5.6	16.9	0.51	0.61
UKSHARE	Unmatched	0.08	0.12	−29.3		−3.01	0.00
	Matched	0.09	0.08	7.6	73.9	1.23	0.22
JPSHARE	Unmatched	0.12	0.14	−10.7		−1.22	0.22
	Matched	0.12	0.13	−5.5	48.4	−0.56	0.58
GRSHARE	Unmatched	0.28	0.22	25.1		3.17	0.00
	Matched	0.28	0.29	−4.2	83.2	−0.35	0.58

Table A3.1 *(cont.)*

Variable	*Sample*	*Mean*		*Pre-matching bias (%)*	*Reduction in bias (%)*	*t*	*P* > |*t*|
		Treated	*Control*				
FRSHARE	Unmatched	0.16	0.19	–18.5		–2.13	0.03
	Matched	0.16	0.16	–0.5	97.2	–0.05	0.96
LASTLOAN	Unmatched	2.33	5.09	–62.1		–6.60	0.00
	Matched	2.34	1.82	11.7	81.2	1.67	0.10
Spline 1	Unmatched	–32.54	–113.17	56.2		5.81	0.00
	Matched	–32.86	–20.81	–8.4	85.1	–1.44	0.15
Spline 2	Unmatched	–71.10	–265.66	54.4		5.61	0.00
	Matched	–71.85	–42.98	–8.1	85.2	–1.42	0.16
Spline 3	Unmatched	–87.82	–362.18	50.3		5.15	0.00
	Matched	–88.77	–49.28	–7.2	85.6	–1.37	0.17
GDP	Unmatched	10.16	10.02	8.7		1.00	0.32
	Matched	10.15	10.12	2.2	75.3	0.21	0.83
GDPPC	Unmatched	8.60	8.61	–1.2		–0.15	0.88
	Matched	8.60	8.64	–8.3	–566.9	–0.84	0.40
GROWTH	Unmatched	1.00	3.65	–46.7		–5.83	0.00
	Matched	1.09	0.58	9.0	80.7	0.78	0.44
CURRGDP	Unmatched	–3.01	–2.00	–17.1		–1.82	0.07
	Matched	–3.02	–2.48	–9.1	46.5	–1.06	0.29

EDTGDP	Unmatched	59.17	48.88	32.0		4.20	0.00
	Matched	58.99	62.95	–12.3	61.5	–1.08	0.28
STDRES	Unmatched	–0.28	–0.78	38.6		4.65	0.00
	Matched	–0.28	–0.16	–9.0	76.6	–0.83	0.41
CRASH	Unmatched	0.17	0.10	18.1		2.32	0.02
	Matched	0.17	0.15	4.9	72.8	0.43	0.67
CHECKS	Unmatched	0.99	0.86	20.5		2.44	0.02
	Matched	0.99	1.05	–9.7	52.7	–0.99	0.33
G5S	Unmatched	1.36	1.31	21.2		2.63	0.01
	Matched	1.35	1.36	–3.7	82.4	–0.31	0.76
SDS	Unmatched	0.31	0.32	–9.0		–1.05	0.29
	Matched	0.31	0.31	8.0	10.5	0.71	0.48
LIQRATIO	Unmatched	0.30	0.31	–6.4		–0.77	0.44
	Matched	0.30	0.30	7.3	–14.1	0.70	0.49
REVIEW	Unmatched	0.63	0.60	7.1		0.86	0.39
	Matched	0.63	0.64	–3.4	51.9	–0.33	0.74
CRISES	Unmatched	6.61	6.04	20.3		2.41	0.02
	Matched	6.61	6.43	6.4	68.5	0.62	0.54

Table A3.1 *(cont.)*

Variable	*Sample*	*Mean*		*Pre-matching bias (%)*	*Reduction in bias (%)*	*t*	*P > |t|*
		Treated	*Control*				
LIBOR	Unmatched	6.12	5.91	9.7		1.17	0.24
	Matched	6.15	5.77	17.4	–79.6	1.61	0.11
MEAST	Unmatched	0.12	0.17	–14.1		–1.63	0.10
	Matched	0.12	0.09	8.0	43.0	0.87	0.39
AFRICA	Unmatched	0.04	0.11	27.7		–2.96	0.00
	Matched	0.04	0.06	–8.6	69.1	–0.97	0.34
EURASIA	Unmatched	0.33	0.19	32.5		4.14	0.00
	Matched	0.32	0.31	2.6	92.0	0.23	0.82
AMERICAS	Unmatched	0.45	0.38	14.6		1.77	0.08
	Matched	0.45	0.49	–6.8	53.2	–0.63	0.53
EASIA	Unmatched	0.07	0.16	–28.4		–3.11	0.00
	Matched	0.07	0.06	5.3	81.5	0.65	0.52

Notes: The propensity score is the predicted probability that a country receives an IMF loan in a given year, based on observed values of each variable. Standardized bias is the difference of the sample means in the treated and control (non-treated) subsamples (treatment = IMF loan in a given country-year), as a percentage of the square root of the average of the sample variances in the treated and control groups.

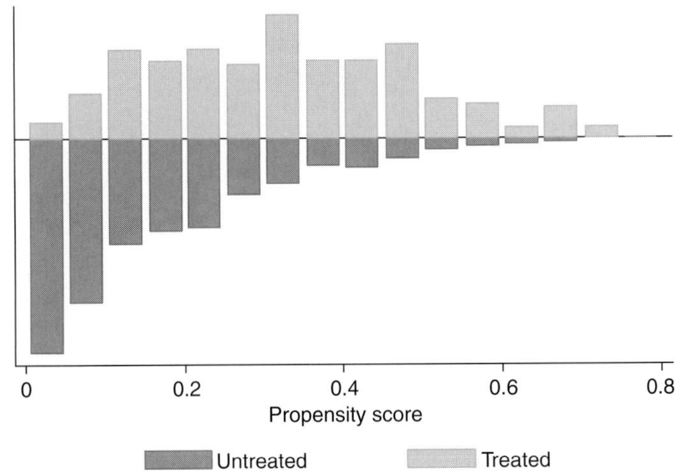

Figure A3.1 Propensity score histogram by treatment status (treatment = IMF loan)

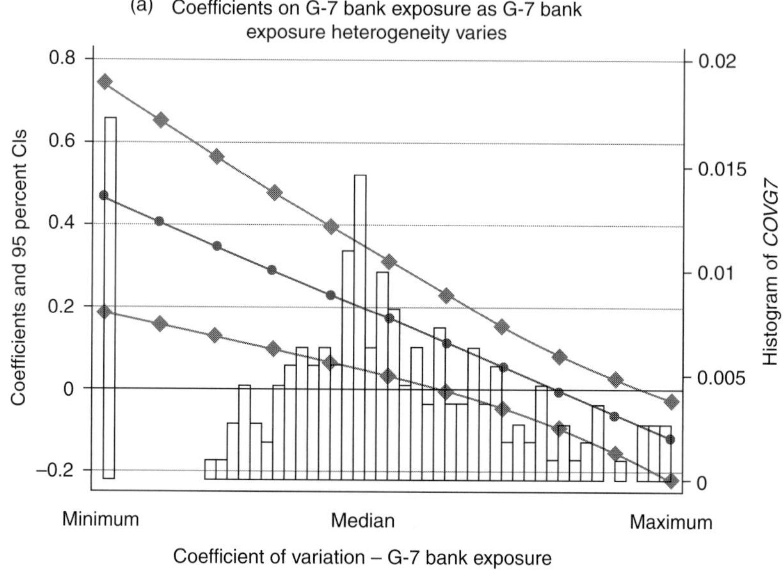

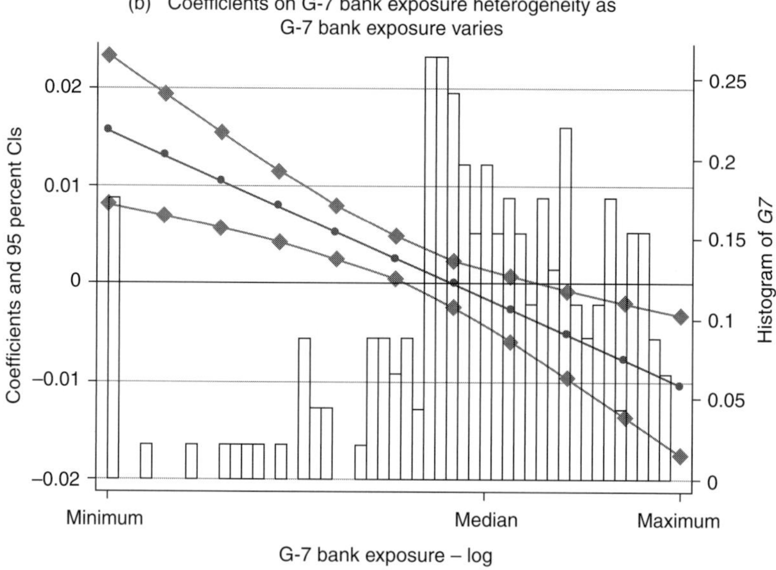

Figure A3.2 Interactive effects: G-7 and G-10 model specifications, amount/quota (G-7)

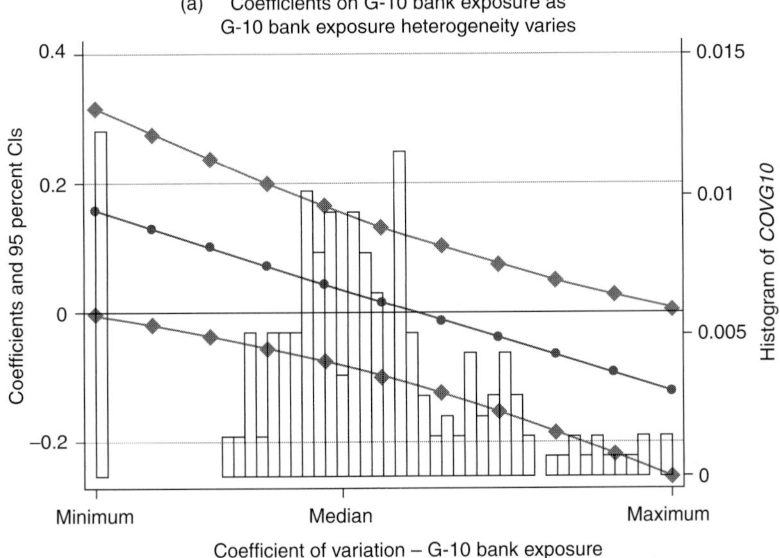

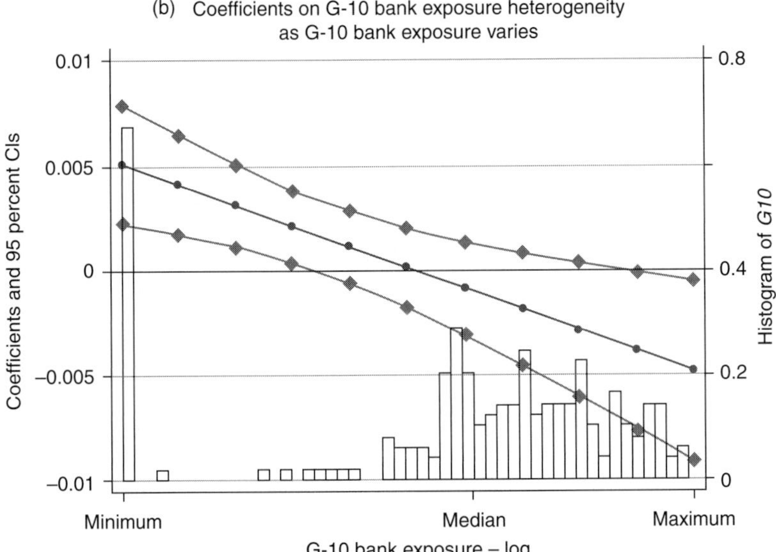

Figure A3.3 Interactive effects: G-7 and G-10 model specifications, amount/quota (G-10)

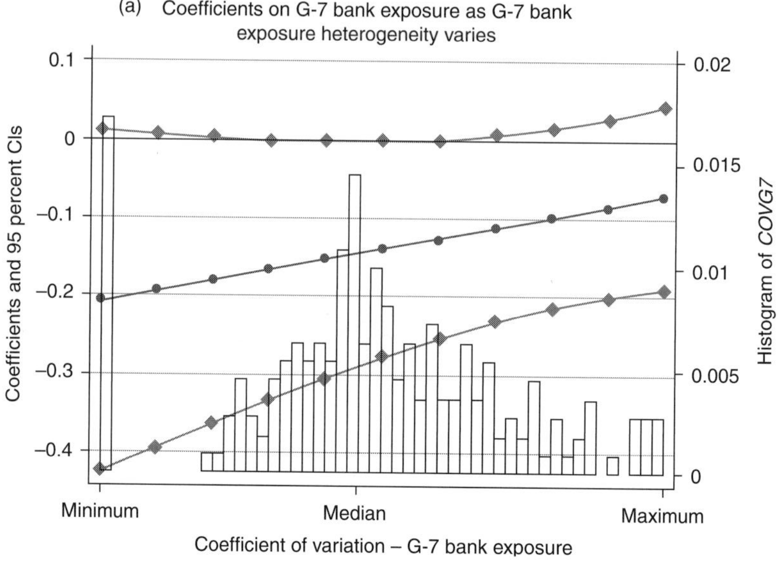

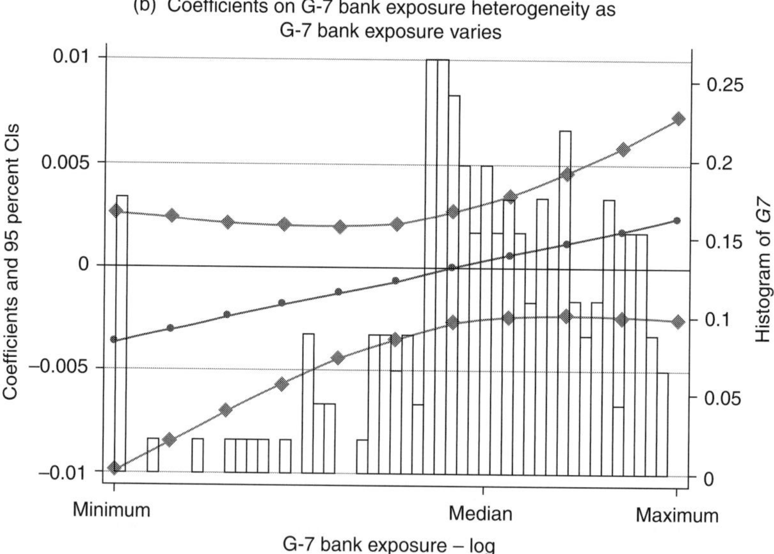

Figure A3.4 Interactive effects: G-7 and G-10 model specifications, total conditions (G-7)

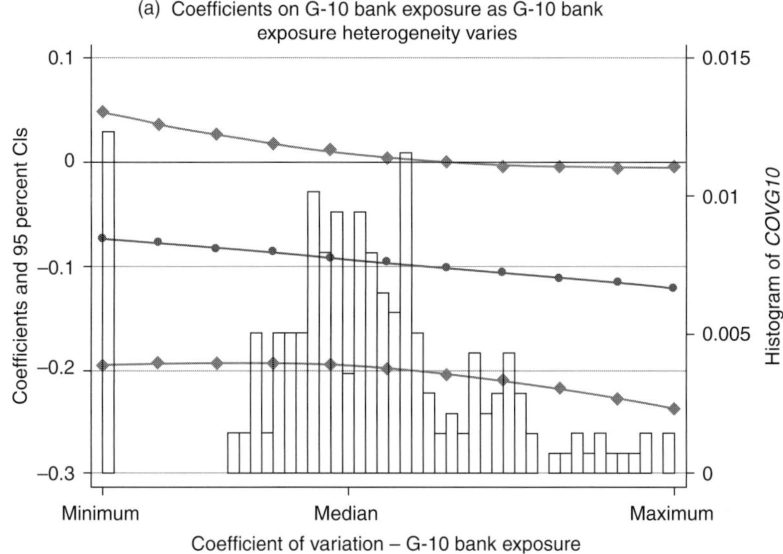

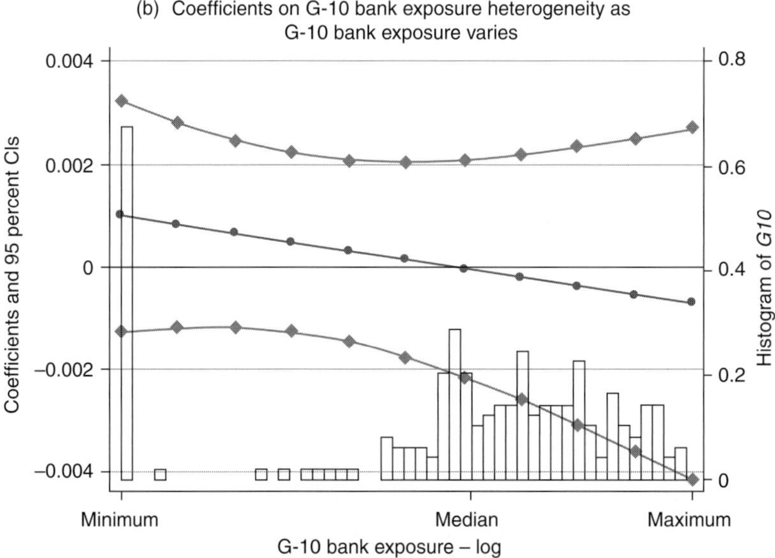

Figure A3.5 Interactive effects: G-7 and G-10 model specifications, total conditions (G-10)

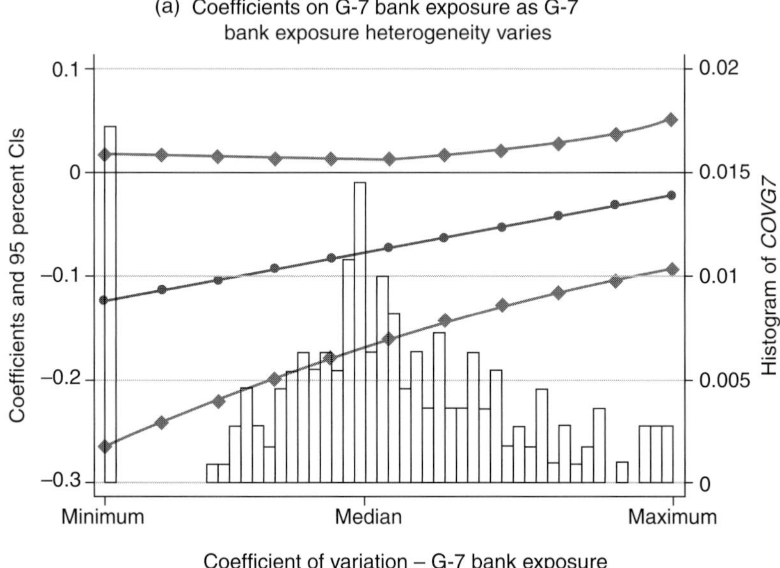

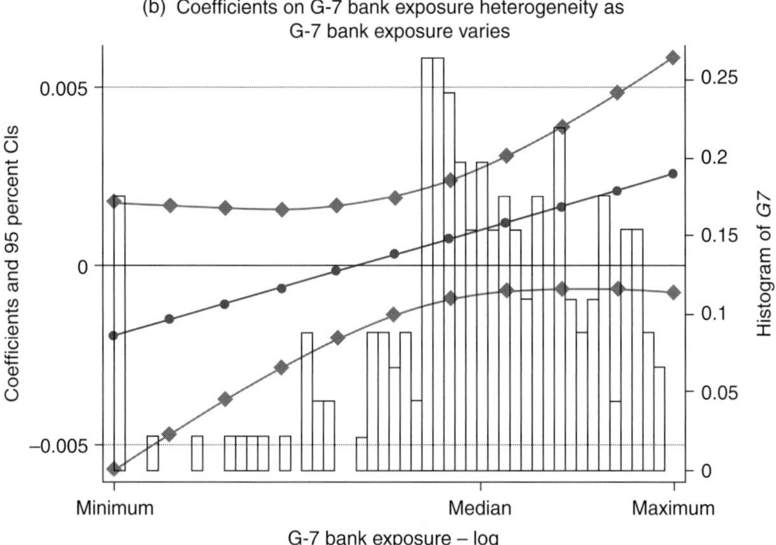

Figure A3.6 Interactive effects: G-7 and G-10 model specifications, performance criteria (G-7)

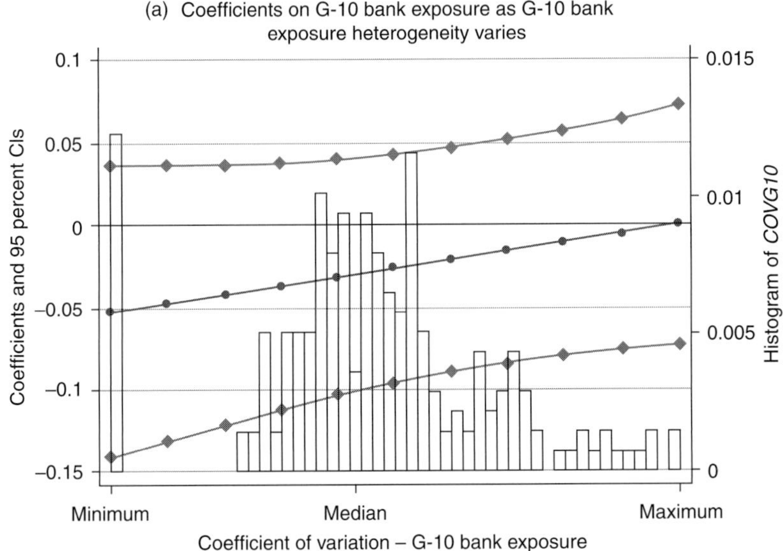

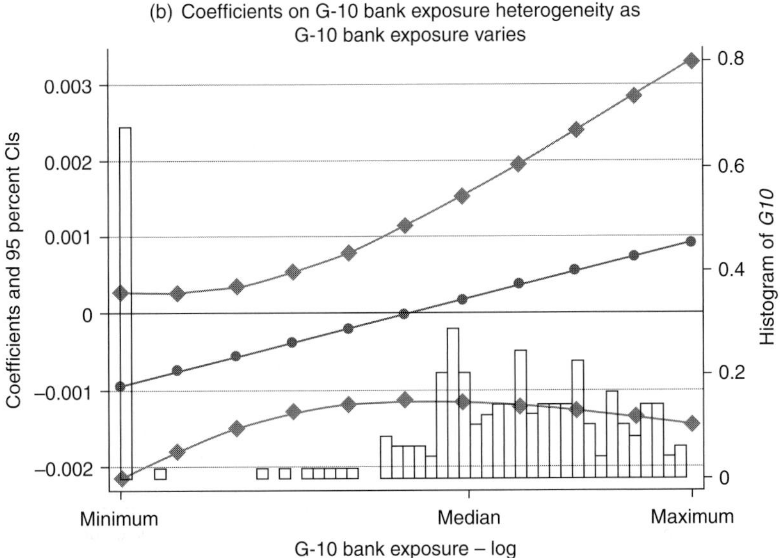

Figure A3.7 Interactive effects: G-7 and G-10 model specifications, performance criteria (G-10)

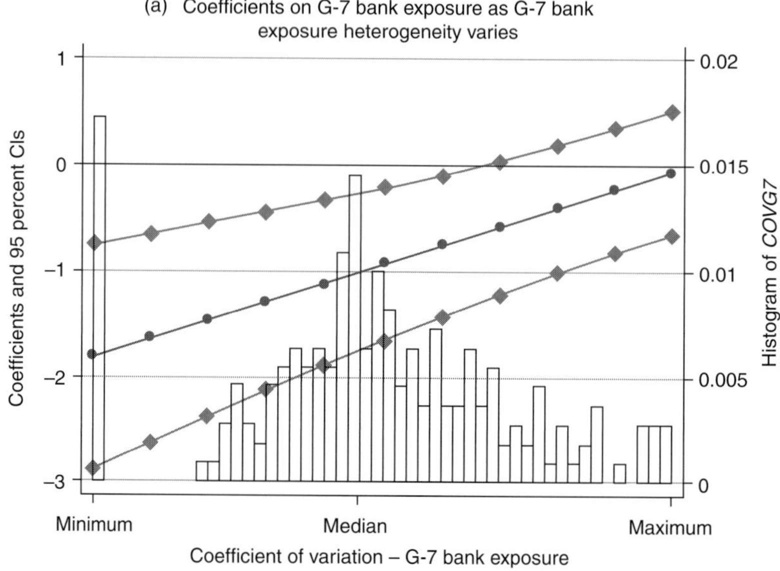

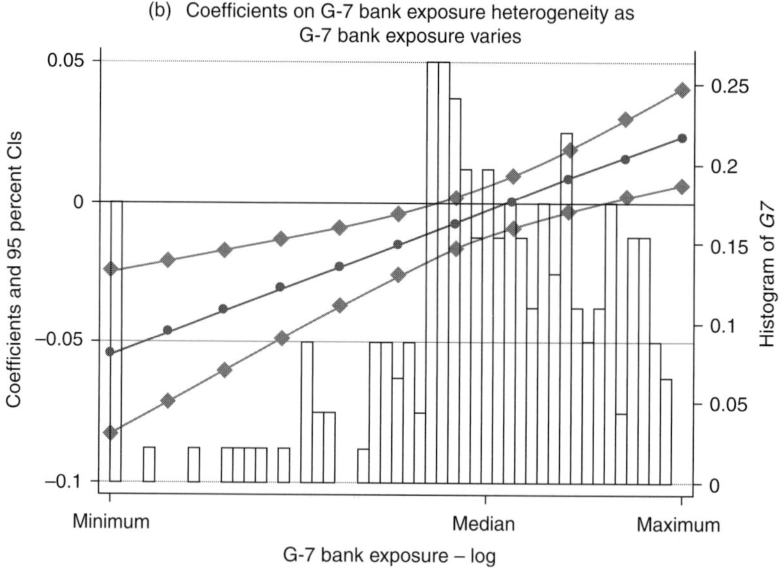

Figure A3.8 Interactive effects: G-7 and G-10 model specifications, prior actions (G-7)

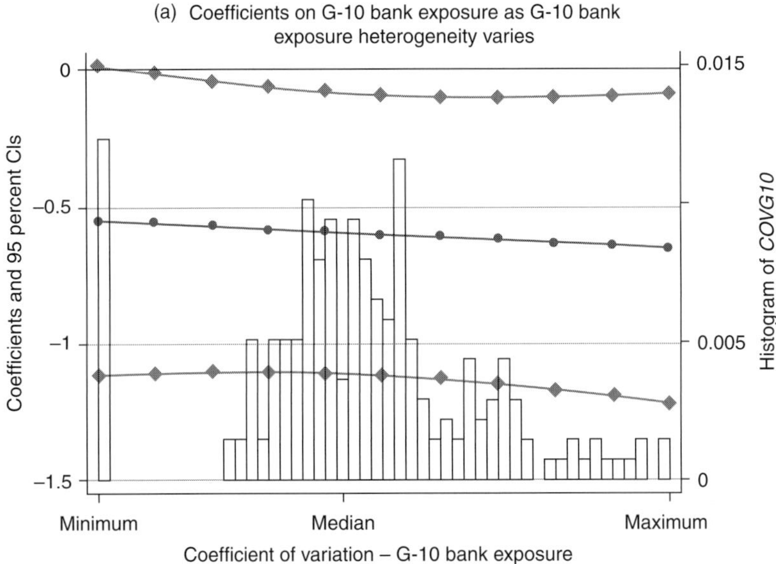

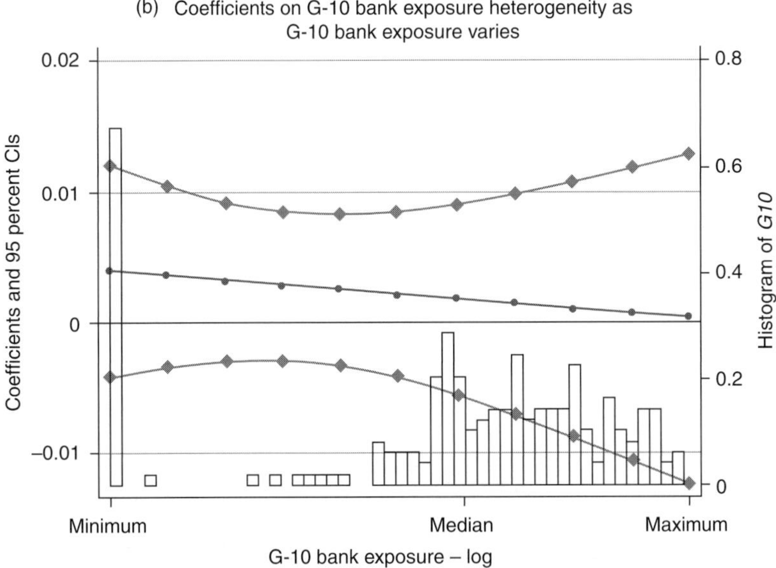

Figure A3.9 Interactive effects: G-7 and G-10 model specifications, prior actions (G-10)

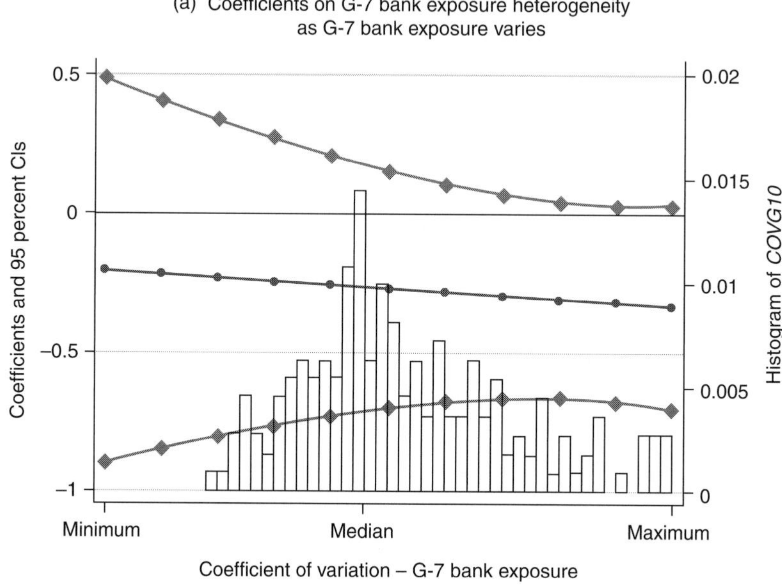

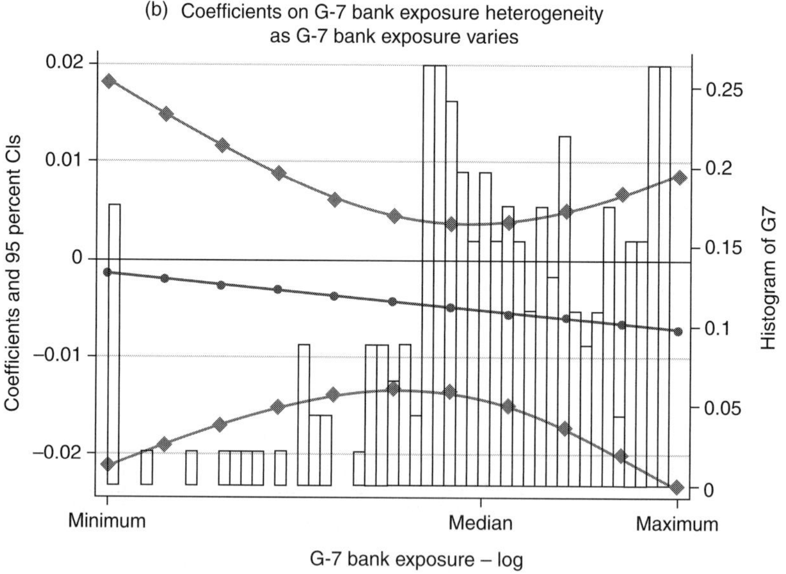

Figure A3.10 Interactive effects: G-7 and G-10 model specifications, benchmarks/targets (G-7)

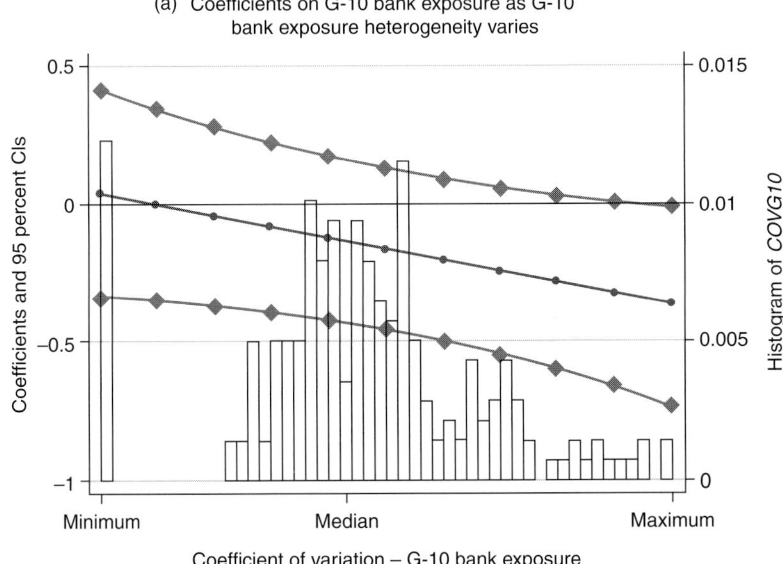

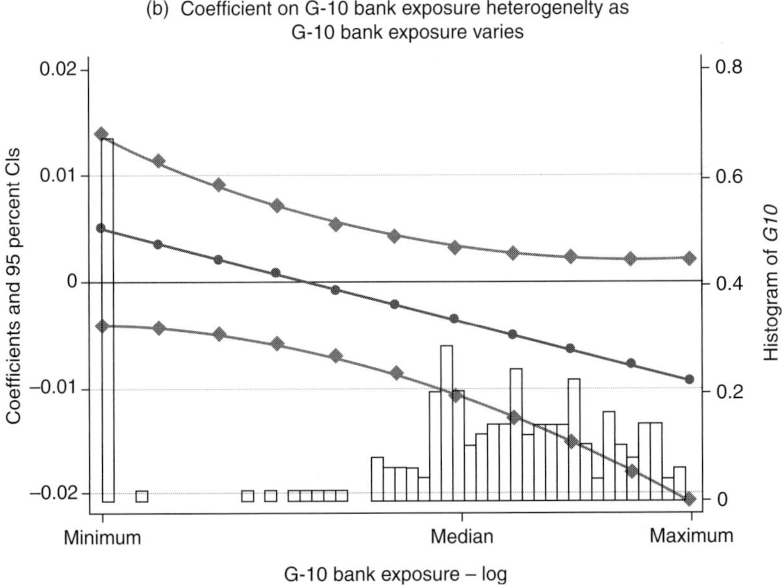

Figure A3.11 Interactive effects: G-7 and G-10 model specifications, benchmarks/targets (G-10)

References

Abadie, Alberto, David Drukker, Jane Leber Herr, and Guido Imbens. 2004. "Implementing matching estimators for average treatment effects in Stata." *Stata Journal* 4(3): 290–311.

Abbott, Kenneth, and Duncan Snidal. 2000. "Hard and soft law in international governance." *International Organization* 54(3): 421–56.

Achen, Christopher H. 1986. *The Statistical Analysis of Quasi-experiments.* Berkeley: University of California Press.

Andrews, David (ed.). 2006. *International Monetary Power.* Ithaca, NY: Cornell University Press.

Bagehot, Walter. 2006 [1873]. *Lombard Street: A Description of the Money Market.* New York: Cosimo Classics.

Banco de México. 1996. *The Mexican Economy 1996.* Mexico City: Banco de México.

1997. *The Mexican Economy 1997.* Mexico City: Banco de México.

BIS 1983. *Annual Report.* Basel: Bank for International Settlements.

2007a. *Annual Report.* Basel: Bank for International Settlements.

2007b. *Quarterly Review.* Basel: Bank for International Settlements.

Barnett, Michael, and Martha Finnemore. 2004. *Rules for the World: International Organization in Global Politics.* Ithaca, NY: Cornell University Press.

Barro, Robert, and Jong-Wha Lee. 2002. *IMF Programs: Who Is Chosen and What Are the Effects?* Working Paper no. 8951. Cambridge, MA: National Bureau of Economic Research.

Barth, James R., Gerard Caprio, and Ross Levine. 2005. *Rethinking Bank Regulation: Till Angels Govern.* New York: Cambridge University Press.

Beck, Nathaniel. 2001. "Time-series–cross-section data: what have we learned in the past few years?" *Annual Review of Political Science* 4: 271–93.

2004. "Longitudinal (panel and time series cross-section) data" (www.nyu.edu/gsas/dept/politics/faculty/beck/beck_home.html).

Beck, Thorsten, George Clark, Alberto Groff, Philip Keefer, and Patrick Walsh. 2001. "New tools in comparative political economy: the database of political institutions." *World Bank Economic Review* **15**(1): 165–76.

Beck, Nathaniel, and Jonathan N. Katz. 1995. "What to do (and not to do) with time-series cross-section data." *American Political Science Review* **89**(3): 634–47.

2004. *Time-series–Cross-section Issues: Dynamics, 2004.* Working paper. Society for Political Methodology, American Political Science Association, Washington, DC (http://polmeth.wustl.edu/retrieve.php?id=36).

Beck, Nathaniel, Jonathan N. Katz, and Richard Tucker. 1998. "Taking time seriously: time-series–cross-section analysis with a binary dependent variable." *American Journal of Political Science* **42**(4): 1260–88.

Berinsky, Adam. 1999. "The two faces of public opinion." *American Journal of Political Science* **43**(4): 1209–30.

Bird, Graham. 1996. "The International Monetary Fund and developing countries: a review of the evidence and policy options." *International Organization* **50**(3): 477–511.

Bird, Graham, and Dane Rowlands. 2003. "Political economy influences within the life-cycle of IMF programmes." *World Economy* **26**(9): 1255–78.

Bird, Graham, and Thomas Willett. 2004. "IMF conditionality, implementation and the new political economy of ownership." *Comparative Economic Studies* **46**(3): 423–50.

Blustein, Paul. 2001. *The Chastening: Inside the Crisis that Rocked the Global Financial System and Humbled the IMF.* New York: PublicAffairs.

Bordo, Michael, Barry Eichengreen, Daniela Klingebiel, and Maria Soledad Martinez-Peria. 2001. "Is the crisis problem growing more severe?" *Economic Policy* **16** (April): 51–82.

Boughton, James. 2001. *Silent Revolution: The International Monetary Fund 1979–1989.* Washington, DC: International Monetary Fund.

Brambor, Thomas, William Roberts Clark, and Matthew Golder. 2006. "Understanding multiplicative interaction models: improving empirical analyses." *Political Analysis* **14**(**1**): 63–82.

Braumoeller, Bear. 2004. "Hypothesis testing and multiplicative interaction terms." *International Organization* **58**(4): 807–20.

Broz, J. Lawrence. 2002. "The domestic politics of international financial rescues: Congressional voting on bailouts in the 1990s." Unpublished manuscript. University of California, San Diego (http://weber.ucsd.edu/~jlbroz).

2005. "Congressional politics of international financial rescues." *American Journal of Political Science* **49**(3): 479–96.

Broz, J. Lawrence, and Michael Brewster Hawes. 2006. "Congressional politics of financing the International Monetary Fund." *International Organization* **60**(1): 367–99.

Bryant, Ralph C. 2008. "Reform of IMF quota shares and voting shares: a missed opportunity." Washington, DC: Brookings Institution (www.brookings.edu/papers/2008/0408_imf_bryant.aspx?rssid=international+monetary+fund).

Buira, Ariel. 2004. "The governance of the International Monetary Fund." Washington, DC: G-24 Secretariat (www.g24.org/imfgover.pdf).

Buiter, Willem M. 2008. "Some suggestions for the G20 on November 15th." In Barry Eichergreen and Richard Baldwin (eds.). *What G20 Leaders Must Do to Stabilise Our Economy and Fix the Financial System*. London: Centre for Economic Policy Research, 17–20 (www.voxeu.org/reports/G20_Summit.pdf).

Calomiris, Charles. 1998. "The IMF's imprudent role as lender of last resort." *Cato Journal* **17**(3): 275–94.

Caprio, Gerard, and Daniela Klingebiel. 2003. "Episodes of systemic and borderline financial crises." World Bank electronic database.

Chang, Roberto. 1999. "Understanding recent crises in emerging markets." *Federal Reserve Bank of Atlanta Economic Review*, **84**(2): 6–16.

Chayes, Abram, and Antonia H. Chayes. 1993. "On compliance." *International Organization* **47**(2): 175–205.

Chwieroth, Jeffrey. 2008. "Cheerleading for liberalization: the International Monetary Fund and financial globalization in emerging markets." Paper presented at the first annual conference on the "Political economy of international organizations," Ascona, Switzerland, February 6.

Claessens, Stijn, and Kristin J. Forbes (eds.). 2001. *International Financial Contagion*. Boston: Kluwer Academic.

Cline, William R. 1983. *International Debt and the Stability of the World Economy*. Cambridge, MA: MIT Press.

1995. *International Debt Reexamined*. Washington, DC: Institute for International Economics.

2002. *Private Sector Involvement in Financial Crisis Resolution: Definition, Measurement, and Implementation*. Working Paper no. 18. Washington, DC: Center for Global Development.

Cohen, Benjamin J. 2002. "International finance." In Walter Carlsnaes, Thomas Risse, and Beth A. Simmons (eds.). *Handbook of International Relations*. London: Sage, 429–47.

Conway, Patrick. 2005. "The revolving door: duration and recidivism in IMF programs." Unpublished manuscript. University of North Carolina, Chapel Hill.

Copelovitch, Mark S. 2005. "Governing global markets: private debt and the politics of International Monetary Fund lending." Ph.D. dissertation. Harvard University, Cambridge, MA.

Crockett, Andrew. 1997. *The Theory and Practice of Financial Stability.* Essay in International Finance no. 203. Princeton, NJ: International Finance Section, Department of Economics, Princeton University.

Dobson, Wendy, and Gary Clyde Hufbauer. 2001. *World Capital Markets: Challenge to the G-10.* Washington, DC: Institute for International Economics.

Downs, George, David Rocke, and Peter Barsoom. 1996. "Is the good news about compliance good news about cooperation?" *International Organization* **50**(3): 379–406.

Dreher, Axel, and Nathan Jensen. 2007. "Independent actor or agent? An empirical analysis of the impact of US interests on IMF conditions." *Journal of Law and Economics* **50**(1): 105–24.

Dreher, Axel, and Jan-Egbert Sturm. 2006. *Do IMF and World Bank Influence Voting in the UN General Assembly?* Working Paper no. 06–137. Zurich: KOF Swiss Economic Institute, ETH Zurich (http://ideas.repec.org/p/kof/wpskof/06–137.html).

Dreher, Axel, and Roland Vaubel. 2004a. "Do IMF and IBRD cause moral hazard and political business cycles? Evidence from panel data." *Open Economies Review* **15**(1): 5–22.

2004b. "The causes and consequences of IMF conditionality." *Emerging Markets Finance and Trade* **40**(3): 26–54.

Eichengreen, Barry. 1991. "Historical research on international lending and debt." *Journal of Economic Perspectives* **5**(2): 149–69.

1999. *Toward a New International Financial Architecture: A Practical Post-Asia Agenda.* Washington, DC: Institute for International Economics.

Eichengreen, Barry, and Peter Kenen. 1994. "Managing the world economy under the Bretton Woods system: an overview." In Peter Kenen (ed.). *Managing the World Economy: Fifty Years after Bretton Woods.* Washington, DC: Institute for International Economics, 3–57.

Eichengreen, Barry, Kenneth Kletzer, and Ashoka Mody. 2005. *The IMF in a World of Private Capital Markets.* Working Paper no. 05/84. Washington, DC: International Monetary Fund.

Eichengreen, Barry, and Ashoka Mody. 2000. *Would Collective Action Clauses Raise Borrowing Costs?* Working Paper no. 7458. Cambridge, MA: National Bureau of Economic Research.

Eichengreen, Barry, and Richard Portes. 1995. *Crisis? What Crisis? Orderly Workouts for Sovereign Debtors.* London: Center for Economic Policy Research.

Eichengreen, Barry, Andrew K. Rose, and Charles Wyplosz. 1996. *Contagious Currency Crises.* Working Paper no. 5681. Cambridge, MA: National Bureau of Economic Research.

Elliott, Kimberly Ann, Debayani Kar, and J. David Richardson. 2002. *Assessing Globalization's Critics: "Talkers Are No Good Doers???"* Working Paper no. 02–5. Washington, DC: Institute for International Economics (www.iie.com/publications/wp/02–5.pdf).

Ferejohn, John. 1986. "Incumbent performance and electoral control." *Public Choice* **50**(1): 5–25.

Fischer, Stanley. 1999. "On the need for an international lender of last resort." Paper prepared for the joint luncheon of the American Economic Association and the American Finance Association. New York, January 3 (www.imf.org/external/np/1999/010399.htm).

Frankel, Jeffrey. 2000. "Globalization of the economy." In Joseph S. Nye and John D. Donahue (eds.). *Governance in a Globalizing World.* Washington, DC: Brookings Institution Press, 45–71.

Frankel, Jeffrey, and Andrew K. Rose. 1996. "Currency crashes in emerging markets: an empirical treatment." *Journal of International Economics* **41**(3/4): 351–66.

Frieden, Jeffry. 2005. *Global Capitalism: Its Fall and Rise in the Twentieth Century.* New York: W. W. Norton.

Gartzke, Erik. 2006. "The affinity of nations index, 1946–2002: version 4.0." University of California, San Diego (http://dss.ucsd.edu/datasets.htm).

Gawande, Kishore, and Pravin Krishna. 2003. "The political economy of trade policy: empirical approaches." In E. Kwan Choi and James Harrigan (eds.). *Handbook of International Trade.* Malden, MA: Basil Blackwell, 213–50.

Gelos, R. Gaston, Ratna Sahay, and Guido Sandleris. 2004. *Sovereign Borrowing by Developing Countries: What Determines Market Access?* Working Paper no. 04/221. Washington, DC: International Monetary Fund.

Gelpern, Anna. 2005. *After Argentina.* Policy Brief no. 05–2. Washington, DC: Peterson Institute of International Economics (www.iie.com/publications/interstitial.cfm?ResearchID=550).

General Accounting Office. 1996. *Mexico's Financial Crisis: Origins, Awareness, Assistance, and Initial Efforts to Recover.* Washington, DC: General Accounting Office.

George, Alexander L., and Andrew Bennett. 2005. "Process-tracing and historical explanation." In Alexander L. George and Andrew Bennett (eds.). *Case Studies and Theory Development in the Social Sciences.* Cambridge, MA: MIT Press, 205–32.

Giannini, Curzio. 1999. *"Enemy of None but a Common Friend of All?" An Internationalist Perspective on the Lender-of-Last-Resort Function.* Working Paper no. 99/10. Washington, DC: International Monetary Fund.

Gold, Joseph. 1979. *Conditionality.* Pamphlet no. 31. Washington, DC: International Monetary Fund.

Gould, Erica R. 2003. "Money talks: supplementary financiers and International Monetary Fund conditionality." *International Organization* 57(3): 551–86.

2006. *Money Talks: The International Monetary Fund, Conditionality, and Supplementary Financiers.* Palo Alto, CA: Stanford University Press.

Grossman, Gene M., and Elhanan Helpman. 1994. "Protection for sale." *American Economic Review* **84**(3): 833–50.

Hawkins, Darren, David A. Lake, Daniel L. Nielson, and Michael J. Tierney. 2006. "Delegation under anarchy: states, international organizations and principal agent theory." In Darren Hawkins, David A. Lake, Daniel Nelson, and Michael J. Tierney (eds.). *Delegation and Agency in International Organizations.* New York: Cambridge University Press, 337.

Heckman, James J. 1979. "Sample selection bias as a specification error." *Econometrica* **47**(1): 153–61.

Helleiner, Eric. 1994. *States and the Reemergence of Global Finance: From Bretton Woods to the 1990s.* Ithaca, NY: Cornell University Press.

Henning, C. Randall. 1999. *The Exchange Stabilization Fund: Slush Fund or War Chest?* Washington, DC: Institute for International Economics.

Hillman, Arye L. 1982. "Declining industries and political-support protectionist motives." *American Economic Review* **72**(5): 1180–7.

Ho, Daniel, Kosuke Imai, Gary King, and Elizabeth Stuart. 2007. "Matching as nonparametric preprocessing for reducing model dependence in parametric causal inference." *Political Analysis* **15**(3): 199–236.

Hoggarth, Glenn, Jack Reidhill, and Peter Sinclair. 2003. "Resolution of banking crises: a review." *Financial Stability Review* (December): 109–23.

IEO. 2003. *The IMF and Recent Capital Account Crises: Indonesia, Korea, Brazil.* Washington, DC: International Monetary Fund (www.imf.org/external/np/ieo/2003/cac/).

IMF. 1983. *Annual Report 1983.* Washington DC: International Monetary Fund.

2000. *International Capital Markets.* Washington, DC: International Monetary Fund.

2001. "Financial organization and operations of the IMF" (www.imf.org/external/pubs/ft/pam/pam45/contents.htm).

2004. "The Poverty Reduction and Growth Facility (PRGF)" (www.imf.org/external/np/exr/facts/prgf.htm).

2005. "IMF conditionality: a factsheet" (www.imf.org/external/pubs/ft/exr/facts/conditio.htm).

2008. *Global Financial Stability Report: Containing Systemic Risks and Restoring Financial Soundness*. Washington, DC: International Monetary Fund.

Institute for International Finance. 1998. *Capital Flows to Emerging Market Economies*. Washington, DC: Institute for International Finance.

James, Harold. 1996. *International Monetary Cooperation since Bretton Woods*. New York: Oxford University Press.

2001. *The End of Globalization: Lessons from the Great Depression*. Cambridge, MA: Harvard University Press.

Joyce, Joseph. 2004. "Adoption, implementation and impact of IMF programmes: a review of the issues and evidence," *Comparative Economic Studies*, **46**(3): 451–67.

Keohane, Robert. 1984. *After Hegemony: Cooperation and Discord in the World Political Economy*. Princeton, NJ: Princeton University Press.

Kenen, Peter B. 2001. *The International Financial Architecture: What's New? What's Missing?* Washington, DC: Institute for International Economics.

Kiewiet, Roderick, and Mathew McCubbins. 1991. *The Logic of Delegation: Congressional Parties and the Appropriations Process*. Chicago: University of Chicago Press.

Kim, Woochan, and Yangho Byeon. 2001. "Restructuring Korean banks' short-term debts in 1998: detailed accounts and their implications." Unpublished manuscript (http://papers.ssrn.com/sol3/papers.cfm?abstract_id=600223).

King, Gary, Michael Tomz, and Jason Wittenberg. 2000. "Making the most of statistical analyses: improving interpretation and presentation." *American Journal of Political Science* **44**(2): 347–61.

Kirshner, Jonathan. 1997. *Currency and Coercion: The Political Economy of International Monetary Power*. Princeton, NJ: Princeton University Press.

Knight, Malcolm, and Julio A. Santaella. 1997. "Economic determinants of IMF financial arrangements." *Journal of Development Economics* **54**(2): 405–36.

Koremenos, Barbara. 2005. "Contracting around international uncertainty." *American Political Science Review* **99**(4): 549–65.

Koremenos, Barbara, Charles Lipson, and Duncan Snidal. 2001. "The rational design of international institutions." *International Organization* **55**(4): 761–800.

Kraft, Joseph. 1984. *The Mexican Rescue*. New York: Group of Thirty.

Krueger, Anne. 2001. "A new approach to sovereign debt restructuring." Address given at the Indian Council for Research on International Economic Relations. Delhi, December 20 (www.imf.org).

Leuven, Edwin, and Barbara Sianesi. 2003. "PSMATCH2: Stata module to perform full Mahalanobis and propensity score matching, common support graphing, and covariate imbalance testing" (http://ideas.repec.org/c/boc/bocode/s432001.html).

Linn, Johannes F., Ralph C. Bryant, and Colin I. Bradford. 2008. "Experts critique proposal for International Monetary Fund quota reform." Washington, DC: Brookings Institution (www.brookings.edu/opinions/2008/0409_imf_linn.aspx?rssid=international+monetary+fund).

Lipson, Charles. 1985. "Bankers' dilemmas: private cooperation in rescheduling sovereign debts." *World Politics* 38(1): 200–25.

1986. "International debt and international institutions." In Miles Kahler (ed.). *Politics of International Debt*. Ithaca, NY: Cornell University Press, 219–43.

Lipworth, Gabrielle, and Jens Nystedt. 2001. "Crisis resolution and private sector adaptation." *Finance and Development* 38(2): 1–8.

Long, J. Scott, and Jeremy Freese, 2001. *Regression Models for Categorical Dependent Variables Using Stata*. College Station, TX: Stata Press.

Lustig, Nora. 1992. *Mexico: The Remaking of an Economy*. Washington, DC: Brookings Institution.

1996. *Mexico in Crisis, the U.S. to the Rescue. Did History Repeat Itself?* Brookings Discussion Paper (June). Washington, DC: Brookings Institution.

Lyne, Mona M., Daniel L. Nielson, and Michael J. Tierney. 2006. "Who delegates? Alternative models of principals in development aid." In Darren Hawkins, David A. Lake, Daniel L. Nielson, and Michael J. Tierney (eds.). *Delegation and Agency in International Organizations*. New York: Cambridge University Press, 41–76.

Lyne, Mona M., and Michael J. Tierney. 2002. "Variation in the structure of principals: conceptual clarification for research on delegation and agency control." Paper presented at the conference "Delegation to international organizations." Park City, UT, May 3, 2002.

Martin, Lisa L. 1992. "Interests, power, and multilateralism." *International Organization* 46(4): 765–92.

2006. "Distribution, information, and delegation to international organizations: the case of IMF conditionality." In Darren Hawkins, David A. Lake, Daniel L. Nielson, and Michael J. Tierney (eds.). *Delegation and Agency in International Organizations*. New York: Cambridge University Press, 140–64.

Martin, Lisa L., and Beth A. Simmons. 1998. "Theories and empirical studies of international institutions." *International Organization* **52**(3): 729–57.

Martin, Lisa L., and Ngaire Woods. 2005. "Multiple-state constituencies in the IMF: an agency approach." Paper presented at the sixth annual Jacques Polak Research Conference. Washington, DC, November 4 (www.imf.org/external/np/res/seminars/2005/arc/pdf/mart.pdf).

Meltzer, Allan. 2000. *Report of the International Financial Institutions Advisory Commission* ("Meltzer Report"). Washington, DC: Government Printing Office.

Mishkin, Frederic. 2006. *The Next Great Globalization: How Disadvantaged Nations Can Harness Their Financial Systems to Get Rich.* Princeton, NJ: Princeton University Press.

Modigliani, Franco, and Merton H. Miller. 1958. "The cost of capital, corporation finance, and the theory of investment." *American Economic Review* **48**(3): 261–97.

Mosley, Layna. 2003. *Global Markets and National Governments.* New York: Cambridge University Press.

2005. "Private governance for the public good? Exploring private sector participation in global financial regulation." Paper presented at the London School of Economics conference "Financial innovations: markets, cultures and politics." London, June 17 (www.unc.edu/~lmosley/MosleyFinRegulationMay2005.pdf).

Mosley, Layna, and David Andrew Singer. 2008. "Taking stock seriously: equity market performance, government policy, and financial globalization." *International Studies Quarterly* **52**(2): 405–25.

Mussa, Michael. 2002. "Reflections on moral hazard and private sector involvement in the resolution of emerging market financial crises." Paper presented at the Bank of England conference "The role of the official and private sectors in resolving international financial crises." London, July 23 (www.bankofengland.co.uk/conferences/conf0207/main.htm/mussa.pdf).

Mussa, Michael, and Miguel Savastano. 1999. *The IMF Approach to Economic Stabilization.* Working Paper no. 99/104. Washington, DC: International Monetary Fund.

Oatley, Thomas, and Jason Yackee. 2004. "American interests and IMF lending." *International Politics* **41**(3): 415–29.

Olson, Mancur. 1971. *The Logic of Collective Action: Public Goods and the Theory of Groups* (2nd edn.). Cambridge, MA: Harvard University Press.

Przeworski, Adam, and James Vreeland. 2000. "The effect of IMF programs on economic growth." *Journal of Development Economics* **62**(2): 385–421.

Rajan, Raghuram, and Luigi Zingales. 1995. "What do we know about capital structure? Some evidence from international data." *Journal of Finance* **50**(5): 1421–60.

Raustiala, Kal. 2006. "Form and substance in international agreements." *American Journal of International Law* **100**(3): 581–614.

Rieffel, Lex. 2003. *Restructuring Sovereign Debt: The Case for Ad Hoc Machinery.* Washington, DC: Brookings Institution Press.

Rodrik, Dani. 1997. *Has Globalization Gone Too Far?* Washington, DC: Peterson Institute for International Economics.

Rogoff, Kenneth, and Jeromin Zettelmeyer. 2002. "Bankruptcy procedures for sovereigns: a history of ideas, 1976–2001." *IMF Staff Papers* **49**(3): 470–507.

Roubini, Nouriel, and Brad Setser. 2004. *Bailouts or Bail-ins? Responding to Financial Crises in Emerging Economies.* Washington, DC: Institute for International Economics.

Rubin, Robert. 1998. "Strengthening the architecture of the international financial system." Remarks to the Brookings Institution. Washington, DC, April 14.

Rubin, Robert, and Jacob Weisberg. 2003. *In an Uncertain World: Tough Choices from Wall Street to Washington.* New York: Random House.

Sachs, Jeffrey, Aaron Tornell, and Andres Velasco. 1996. "The collapse of the Mexican peso: what have we learned?" *Economic Policy* **11**: 13–63.

Sartori, Anne E. 2003. "An estimator for some binary-outcome selection models without exclusion restrictions." *Political Analysis* **11**(2): 111–38.

Simmons, Beth A. 2000. "International law and state behavior: commitment and compliance in international monetary affairs." *American Political Science Review* **94**(4): 819–35.

2001. "The international politics of harmonization: the case of capital market regulation." *International Organization* **55**(3): 598–620.

Simmons, Beth A., and Daniel J. Hopkins. 2005. "The constraining power of international treaties: theory and methods." *American Political Science Review* **99**(4): 623–31.

Simmons, Beth A., and Lisa L. Martin. 2002. "International organizations and institutions." In Walter Carlsnaes, Thomas Risse, and Beth A. Simmons (eds.). *Handbook of International Relations.* London: Sage, 192–211.

Singer, David Andrew. 2007. *Regulating Capital: Setting Standards for the International Financial System.* Ithaca, NY: Cornell University Press.

Smith, Roy C., and Ingo Walter. 2003. *Global Banking*. New York: Oxford University Press.

Snidal, Duncan. 1985. "The limits of hegemonic stability theory." *International Organization* **39**(4): 579–615.

Southard, Frank A., Jr. 1979. *The Evolution of the International Monetary Fund*. Essays in International Finance no. 135. Princeton, NJ: Princeton University Press.

Spiegel, Mark M. 1996. *Collective Action Difficulties in Foreign Lending: Banks and Bonds*. Economic Letter no. 1996-24. San Francisco: Federal Reserve Bank of San Francisco.

Steil, Benn, and Robert Litan. 2006. *Financial Statecraft: The Role of Financial Markets in American Foreign Policy*. New Haven, CT: Yale University Press.

Stigler, George. 1971. "The theory of economic regulation." *Bell Journal of Economics* **2**(1): 3–21.

Stiglitz, Joseph. 2002. *Globalization and Its Discontents*. New York: W. W. Norton.

Stone, Randall. 2002. *Lending Credibility: The IMF and the Post-Communist Transition*. Princeton, NJ: Princeton University Press.

2004. "The political economy of IMF lending in Africa." *American Political Science Review* **98**(4): 577–91.

2008. "The scope of IMF conditionality." *International Organization* **62**(4): 589–620.

Stone, Randall, and Jonathan Steinwand. 2008. "The International Monetary Fund: a review of recent evidence." *Review of International Organizations* 3(2): 123–49.

Strand, Jonathan, and David Rapkin. 2005. "Voting power implications of a double majority voting procedure in the IMF's Executive Board." In Ariel Buira (ed.). *Reforming the Governance of the IMF and World Bank*. London: Anthem Press, 235–50.

Sturzenegger, Federico, and Jeromin Zettelmeyer. 2006. *Debt Defaults and Lessons from a Decade of Crisis*. Cambridge, MA: MIT Press.

Thacker, Strom. 1999. "The high politics of IMF lending." *World Politics* **52(1)**: 38–75.

Thomas, Alun, and Uma Ramakrishnan. 2006. *The Incidence and Effectiveness of Prior Actions in IMF-supported Programs*. Working Paper no. 06/213. Washington, DC: International Monetary Fund.

Tomz, Michael. 2001. "Sovereign debt and international cooperation: reputational reasons for lending and repayment." Ph.D. dissertation. Harvard University, Cambridge, MA.

Truman, Edwin M. (ed.). 2006. *Reforming the IMF for the 21st Century*. Special Report no. 19. Washington, DC: Peterson Institute for International Economics.

Uppal, Raman, and Cynthia van Hulle. 1997. "Sovereign debt and the London Club: a precommitment device for limiting punishment for default." *Journal of Banking and Finance* **21**(5): 741–56.

Van Houtven, Leo. 2002. *Governance of the IMF: Decision Making, Institutional Oversight, Transparency, and Accountability*. Pamphlet no. 53. Washington, DC: International Monetary Fund.

Vaubel, Roland. 1991. "The political economy of the International Monetary Fund: a public choice analysis." In Roland Vaubel and Thomas Willett (eds.). *The Political Economy of International Organizations*. Boulder, CO: Westview Press, 204–44.

1994. "The political economy of the International Monetary Fund: a public choice analysis." In Doug Bandow and Ian Vasquez (eds.). *Perpetuating Poverty: The World Bank, the IMF, and the Developing World*. Washington, DC: Cato Institute, 37–55.

Vines, David, and Christopher L. Gilbert. 2004. *The IMF and Its Critics: Reform of Global Financial Architecture*. Cambridge: Cambridge University Press.

Von Stein, Jana. 2005. "Do treaties constrain or screen? Selection bias and treaty compliance." *American Political Science Review* **99**(4): 611–22.

Vreeland, James. 2003. *The IMF and Economic Development*. New York: Cambridge University Press.

2005. "The international and domestic politics of IMF programs." Unpublished manuscript. Yale University, New Haven, CT.

White, William. 2000. *What Have We Learned from Recent Financial Crises and Policy Responses?* Working Paper no. 84. Basel: Bank for International Settlements.

Willett, Thomas. 2000. *A Soft-core Public Choice Analysis of the International Monetary Fund*. Claremont Colleges Working Paper no. 2000–56. Claremont, CA: Claremont Graduate University.

Wilson, Sven, and Daniel M. Butler, 2007. "A lot more to do: the sensitivity of time-series cross-sectional analyses to simple alternative specifications." *Political Analysis* **15**(2): 101–23.

Winship, Christopher, and Robert D. Mare. 1992. "Models for sample selection bias." *Annual Review of Sociology* **18**: 327–50.

Woods, Ngaire. 2006. *The Globalizers: The IMF, The World Bank, and Their Borrowers*. Ithaca, NY: Cornell University Press.

World Bank. 2003. *Global Development Finance*. Washington, DC: World Bank.

2005. *World Development Indicators*. Washington, DC: World Bank.
2006a. *Global Development Finance*. Washington, DC: World Bank.
2006b. *World Development Indicators*. Washington, DC: World Bank.

Wyplosz, Charles. 1999. "International financial instability." In Inge Kaul, Isabelle Grunberg, and Marc Stern (eds.). *Global Public Goods: International Cooperation in the 21st Century*. New York: Oxford University Press, 152–89.

Zhang, Zhaohui. 2001. "The impact of IMF term loans on US bank creditors' equity values: an event study of South Korea's case." *Journal of International Financial Markets, Institutions, and Money* **11**(3–4): 363–94.

Index